98

TECHNOLOGY UTILIZATION IDEAS FOR
THE 70'S AND BEYOND

PUBLICATIONS OF THE AMERICAN ASTRONAUTICAL SOCIETY

ADVANCES IN THE ASTRONAUTICAL SCIENCES

SCIENCE & TECHNOLOGY SERIES

OTHER PUBLICATIONS

Distributed by the AAS PUBLICATIONS OFFICE, P.O. Box 746, Tarzana, California 91356

AN AMERICAN **Astronautical** SOCIETY PUBLICATION

Volume 26

Technology Utilization Ideas for the 70's and Beyond

AAS SCIENCE AND TECHNOLOGY SERIES

A Supplement to Advances in the Astronautical Sciences

Edited by
F. W. FORBES
P. DERGARABEDIAN

Proceedings of a Special
AAS/AIAA Technical Event
Held October 30, 1970 at
Winrock, Arkansas at the
Invitation of
Governor Winthrop Rockefeller

DISTRIBUTED BY THE AAS PUBLICATIONS OFFICE, P.O. BOX 746, TARZANA, CALIFORNIA 91356

DEDICATED TO

Winthrop Rockefeller, Governor of Arkansas, 1967-1971

- - for his pioneering support of young people interested in aerospace, especially in stimulating their interest and in developing training materials

- - for his concern in applying aerospace technology to Earth-bound problems

- - for his sponsorship of the conference on "Technology Utilization Ideas for the 70's and Beyond" on which this book is based

Governor Winthrop Rockefeller

AAS PRESIDENT

Dr. Paul Dergarabedian   TRW Systems

DIRECTOR OF PUBLICATIONS

Dr. George K. Chacko   University of Southern California

SERIES EDITOR

Dr. Horace Jacobs   Lockheed-California Company

VOLUME EDITORS

Fred W. Forbes   AeroPropulsion Laboratory
                                  Wright-Patterson AF Base

Dr. Paul Dergarabedian   TRW Systems

ART STAFF

J. F. Johnson   Lockheed-California Company

J. C. Speas   Lockheed-California Company

Thanks are due Diana Will for final preparation
of the manuscript for the printer

OFFICE OF THE SECRETARY

MEMBERS OF THE AMERICAN ASTRONAUTICAL SOCIETY, GREETINGS!

I am most appreciative of the recent opportunity afforded me to participate in the Technology Utilization Awards Program held at Winrock Farms, Arkansas, to honor those who have made outstanding contributions to the interface between technology for national security and technology for civilian applications.

This interface is especially important today because we are faced with technology threats to both the military and civilian sectors. Dr. John S. Foster, Director of Defense Research and Engineering, has presented an alarming, but in my opinion, entirely true, analysis of the technological threat which the Soviet Union now poses. Dr. Foster estimates that we are still two to three years ahead of the Soviet Union in most areas of technology, but he projects that their defense Research, Development, Testing and Evaluation efforts, which are currently 40-50% greater than our own, will soon overtake us. If we lose our qualitative edge over a nation that is bigger than we are, which has more natural resources than we have, and which may be working harder than we are, then Western Democracy as it has developed over 200 years may well have to give way to something more acceptable to the Soviet Union.

In the face of this increasingly sophisticated threat, there can be no compromise in the assignment of resources to assure national security. Military engineers have a prime responsibility to develop hardware which does the job well at minimum cost. This assignment cannot be compromised to accommodate any secondary goal of technology fallout to the civil sector. A can-opener that is also designed to sharpen razor blades probably will do neither job very well. However, having done a job optimized to meet military objectives the military engineer also has an additional responsibility to look for other applications, military or civil. Since he developed the equipment in the first place, he is obviously well qualified to look for other applications.

The clear differences between the centers of gravity of technology for national security and the technology for civil applications must be recognized and maintained. However, we would be very foolish indeed if we fail to develop and capitalize upon the interface between the two. The challenge to your membership at this critical period of technological threat, with its ominous overtones to national security, is to bring about this interface between the two technologies. On a continuing basis, at the same time that technology is harnessed to meet and overcome sophisticated hostile threats to national security, advantage must be taken of that technology to improve the quality of life.

Grant L. Hansen
Assistant Secretary
Research and Development

PUBLICATIONS OF THE AMERICAN ASTRONAUTICAL SOCIETY IN MICROFORM

AAS MICROFICHE SERIES

Distributed by the AAS PUBLICATIONS OFFICE, P.O. Box 746, Tarzana, California 91356

The Honorable Grant Hansen has challenged members of the American
Astronautical Society to "bring about the interface between the two
technologies" - the aerospace and military on the one hand, and the
civilian applications on the other. The purpose of the interface is
"to improve the quality of life."

Research and development carried out by the aerospace industry over the
past two decades have led to the evolvement of military and civilian
systems designed to meet the nation's aerospace goals. Recently,
however, emphasis has shifted somewhat toward the need for systems
capable of combating the growing ecological and environmental problems
faced by the Nation. Fortunately, some of the technology developed by
the aerospace industry can be utilized to solve a number of our more
pressing environmental problems.

The Technology Utilization Committee of the American Astronautical
Society/American Institute for Aeronautics and Astronautics held a
symposium in November, 1970, at Winrock Farms, Arkansas to deal with
this issue. Approximately 78 abstracts of specific technology utilization ideas were received; of these, 45 were judged to have technical
merit sufficient to ask for preparation of a more detailed paper.
Finally, 35 papers were received and judged. They described how technology, which has been, or is being, developed for aerospace use, can
be applied to solving pollution, ecological, and conservation problems.
These papers are now incorporated in the present proceedings volume.

Two papers deal with applying aerospace power generation technology to
reduce air and thermal pollution from commercial electrical power
plants. "Pollution Control Using Advanced Energy Generation Systems"

describes a system consisting of a high-temperature gaseous core nuclear reactor coupled to a high-efficiency magnetohydrodynamic generator for electrical power production. Such a system could reduce the thermal pollution of power plants several-fold and completely eliminate particulate pollution of the atmosphere with little or no contamination of the Earth with nuclear by-products. The gaseous core nuclear reactor is being developed for space rocket systems while the magnetohydrodynamic generators are being studied for aircraft auxiliary power.

The second paper in this field, "Nonpolluting Central Power Stations," deals with the use of advanced-cycle electrical power systems based upon aerospace technology developed for use in aircraft gas turbines. Using a power plant consisting of a combined gas-turbine/steam-turbine system in which the hot exhaust of the gas turbine is used to raise steam to a higher temperature, the cost of base-load electrical utility power can be lowered while reducing the emissions of sulfur oxides by over 90% compared to conventional stations.

The need for physical methods of separating oil from the surface of sea water without the use of toxic chemical dispersants forms the basis for a paper entitled "Oil-Water Separation and Oil Harvesting System." The authors have devised a simultaneous oil-water separation and harvesting system utilizing techniques developed in the aerospace industry for the expulsion of liquid cryogens from propulsion and life-support system tanks containing liquid and gas in a low-g space environment.

A paper entitled "Organophosphorus Insecticide Decontaminant" discusses the development of an insecticide decontaminating solution which converts insecticides to products which can be disposed of by water washing without the extremely toxic effects to fish normally exhibited by unaltered insecticides. This decontaminant, developed by the Air Force because of its potential for use on and around aircraft, should prove useful in combating the growing insecticide pollution problem.

Another paper on the "Application of Aerospace Data Acquisition Technology to Atmospheric and Meteorological Investigations" presents a compact, lightweight airborne data acquisition system suitable for use in a single-engine aircraft. Built for aerospace use, its application to civilian atmospheric and meteorological investigations is discussed.

The following papers were selected for awards:

1. "Pollution Control Using Advanced Energy Generation Systems"
   Robert R. Barthelemy

2. "Organophosphorus Insecticide Decontaminant"
   B. C. Wolverton, Capt. R. Richter, Sandra M. Lefstad

3. "Oil-Water Separation and Oil Harvesting System"
   D. J. Graham, R. L. Johnson, P. G. Bhuta

4. "Application of Aerospace Data Acquisition Technology to Atmospheric and Meteorological Investigations"
   Richard A. Johnson, Michael R. Smith

5. "Nonpolluting Central Power Stations"
   F. L. Robson, A. J. Giramonti

In addition, two special awards were given for the following:

1. "Engineering for Ecological Systems with Specific Reference to Fisheries"
   Ernest B. Cohen, Edward R. Glaser, Edward Kaplan

2. "A Gradiometer System for Gravity Anomaly Surveying"
   Milton B. Trageser

Receiving honorable mention were:

1. "Applications of Systems Engineering for Solutions to Social and Economic Problems"
   Robert R. Smith, George Priftis

2. "Properties of Mature Severe Vortical Storms"
   F. Fendell, Paul Dergarabedian

The many other papers selected for presentation – and now included in this volume – cover a wide range of disciplines. These papers are indicative of the many aspects of aerospace technology that can be used to help solve our critical environmental problems.

The Editors

CONTENTS

POLLUTION CONTROL USING ADVANCED ENERGY GENERATION SYSTEMS

Robert R. Barthelemy
Air Force Aero Propulsion Laboratory
Wright-Patterson AFB, Ohio 45433

Abstract

One of the most critical problems facing the world today is the alarming increase in environmental pollution. The three most important forms of pollution are thermal heating of our water supplies, chemical pollution of the atmosphere and, to a lesser degree, the introduction of waste (nuclear and chemical) into the soil. This adverse situation arises primarily because it is impossible to convert all of the latent energy of chemical and nuclear fuels into desirable directed energy, either kinetic or electrical. Short of moving our conversion and manufacturing systems into space (which may eventually become necessary), our only technological recourse is to minimize the contaminating effects of our major conversion processes.

Recent Air Force developments in the fields of high temperature energy sources and advanced energy conversion processes could be utilized to significantly improve the processes used for generating electrical power. Although electrical power generation is not the sole contributor to environmental pollution, it plays a major part. The use of high temperature nuclear reactor thermal systems coupled to high efficiency generation systems could reduce the thermal pollution of generation plants several fold and completely eliminate particulate pollution of the atmosphere, with little or no contamination of the earth with nuclear by-products.

Two technical areas being pursued by the Air Force are applicable. Gaseous core nuclear reactors are being studied in basic and exploratory development for future space rocket uses. Such a system, however, could produce a power generation system working fluid at 4000°K. Exploratory development of magnetodydrodynamic (MHD) generators for airborne and space system power has shown high efficiency operation if high temperature gases are used. Coupled to 4000°K gases, these generators could convert 60-70% of the gas thermal energy into electrical power. This efficiency is 50% higher than the most modern advanced steam turbine plant and over 100% more efficient than conventional nuclear power plants. The amount of thermal pollution of cooling streams should be reduced by a factor of 3 to 5. In addition, the decreased cost of electrical power through improved efficiency operation would result in a savings of about one billion dollars/year at the present consumption rate.

Introduction

Over the past several years, the public has shown an increasing awareness and concern with environmental pollution caused by industry and the Government. The clamor over this problem and the people's demand for quick action has led to the consideration and implementation of remedial approaches to reduce the current and near-term rate of pollution. It is clear that these measures are needed, and indeed are long overdue. However, the current activity should not cloud our vision of the long-term aspects of the problem and the necessary solution to it.

In the United States the combustion of fossil fuels annually accounts for about 140 million tons of air pollutants, the major constituents being noxious sulfur oxides, nitrogen oxides, and fly ash. The combination of rapid population growth with an increasing rate of per capita energy consumption indicates that unless checked, the U.S. air pollution rate will double every decade. By the turn of the century, therefore, over one billion tons of these air pollutants might be deposited annually by the United States in the atmosphere.

In 1965 the total cooling water used by the electric utility industry alone amounted to 125 billion gallons per day. By the year 2000, without supplemental means of discharging heat to the environment, the cooling water requirements would be 1250 billion gallons of water per day. Since the average daily inland water runoff in the United States is only about 1200 billion gallons per day, the predicted requirement will result in the thermal pollution of the entire inland water supply of the United States.

If man is to survive on earth, dramatic long-term measures must be taken to change the pollution situation. There are only four alternatives: reduce the population growth, decrease the standard of living, make major improvements in the energy conversion processes, or transfer the major energy conversion and manufacturing activities into space.

The first two are socially oriented and may be difficult to achieve, while the last should be considered only in the very long term. The improvement of our energy conversion and utilization process is not only the most acceptable alternative, but also the most feasible. Significant technological improvements in the efficiency and pollution control of our processes can be accomplished if development of certain technologies is pursued. This paper will examine the possibility of significantly reducing the thermal and atmospheric pollution of electrical generating plants through utilization of technology being developed by the Air Force. Since the generation of electrical power is a, if not the, major contributor to environmental pollution, it is appropriate that we examine the potential of long-term developments in this area.

Air Force Developments

The most common approach to the generation of electrical power involves two basic processes: the creation of thermal energy through chemical or nuclear reactions and the conversion of the thermal energy to electricity. There are a number of devices which have been extensively developed in order to efficiently perform these processes. Fuel fired combustion burners provide thermal energy at temperatures of 2000-3000°K, while solid-core nuclear reactors operate well in the 1000-2000°K regime. Steam or gas driven turbo-generators have undergone years of development and operate quite

efficiently when coupled either with a solid-core nuclear reactor or a combustion fired gas burner. However, a fossil-fuel fired steam generating plant has a maximum efficiency of 35 - 40% and emits large amounts of pollutants. While a nuclear turbo-generation plant does not contaminate the air with chemical species, it poses some radiation problems and, because of its lower temperatures, operates at efficiencies of 25 - 35%. What is needed, therefore, is a generation scheme which (1) operates at the temperatures of coal fired plants, (2) can convert energy in an efficient manner at these temperatures, (3) eliminates chemical pollution of the atmosphere, and (4) negates (or minimizes) nuclear contamination of the surroundings.

Recent Air Force sponsored work in the field of high temperature gaseous (or colloidal) fueled nuclear reactor technology may make possible the development of nuclear systems which operate at peak temperatures around 4000°K and allow nuclear fuel recycling. Secondly, current developments in the Air Force magnetohydrodynamic (MHD) power generation program point to the practicality of efficient long-duration conversion of high temperature thermal energy to electricity.

Advanced Nuclear Reactors

Although only a minor amount of experimental work has been carried out on gaseous core nuclear reactors, some critical tests and a significant analytical effort have been accomplished. Using nuclear data obtained from more conventional reactor operation, detailed analytical design studies of gaseous fueled nuclear reactor systems have been undertaken. The more extensively studied concept has been one where the nuclear cavity is used to heat flowing gas for space propulsion systems, see Figure 1.

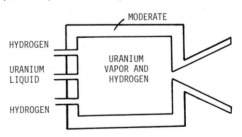

FIGURE 1 - GASEOUS CORE REACTOR

The results of these studies are quite pertinent to the application being considered since the only significant change involves the type of flow gas used (helium versus hydrogen). Simulated experiments to determine flow and criticality in the core have been carried out and have indicated that a practical flowing system is feasible. The second area of experimentation has been concerned with recovering the fuel which leaves the reactor. Cyclone-collector tests have shown that such a device should remove essentially all of the fuel after it has been precipitated through cooling.

The next phase of development of the advanced nuclear reactors would involve more subcomponent simulation, followed by pilot system non-nuclear tests. Although a significant amount of development is needed before a gaseous core nuclear system can be built, the critical work to establish feasibility has been accomplished and the utilization of the concept can be examined.

MHD Power Generation

The common method for converting thermal to electrical energy is to use a three-step process. First, the thermal energy released through combustion is used to heat a boiler in which steam is produced. The steam is then allowed to expand in a turbine and to rotate the drive shaft of an electrical generator. Third, the copper conductors of the generator are rotated through a magnetic field and electrical energy results. In an MHD device, an electrically conducting hot gas replaces the copper conductors and generates electricity by virtue of its motion through a transverse magnetic field (see Figure 2).

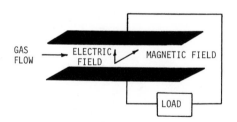

GAS FLOW → ELECTRIC FIELD ↕ ↗ MAGNETIC FIELD

LOAD

FIGURE 2 - MHD GENERATOR

MHD can, therefore, directly utilize thermal energy in the form of a hot gas by seeding the gas with an easily ionizable substance to make it conductive. In order to be electrically conductive, the gas temperature must be at least 2000°K, and higher temperatures will result in better conductivities. Ideally, an MHD generator should operate with gases at temperatures of 3000 - 4000°K, high level (> 40 kilogauss)

magnetic fields, little or no generator degradation with time, and at high efficiencies and high power levels. Developments in the MHD field over the last five years have shown that these operating conditions are feasible. A single MHD generator has produced over 30 megawatts of power for short periods and another has been run continuously at lower power levels for hundreds of hours. Several generators have used gases with temperatures above 3000°K and operation at higher temperatures has been demonstrated. Superconducting magnets have been built for MHD generators and have achieved field strengths in excess of 40 kilogauss. Generator operation corresponding to 60 - 70% thermal to electrical efficiency has been demonstrated and losses in generator electrodes and insulators have been minimized. Although continuous operation of very high power generators has not been carried out, the current developmental status of the various generator components indicates that the construction of a high power continuous system can now be undertaken and efficient operation should result.

Power Generation Application

A typical cycle which uses a gaseous core nuclear reactor and an MHD generator for commercial power production is shown in Figure 3.

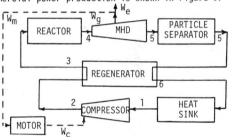

FIGURE 3 - GENERATION CYCLE

A temperature-entropy diagram for this cycle is depicted in Figure 4.

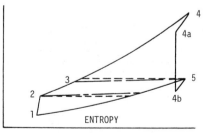

FIGURE 4 - CYCLE T-S DIAGRAM

The reactor produces a temperature of 4000°K in a working fluid consisting of helium plus 1% potassium (for electrical conductivity in the MHD generator). The gas leaves the reactor (4), is expanded (4a) to about Mach 1.2, produces electrical power in the MHD generator (4b), and is diffused to reduce velocity and to increase pressure (5). The temperature of the gas on leaving the MHD generator is 2000°K and the vapor pressure of uranium at this point is 10^{-6} atmospheres. Hence, any uranium vapor should have condensed out into droplets where it can be collected in the particle separator. Similarly, the ionizable seed material can be separated at this stage. Both the fuel and the seed can be reprocessed to remove radioactive material and burnt fuel and fed back into the reactor, with the appropriate make-up fuel and seed added. As it leaves the separator, the helium should contain no more than 10^{-6} mole fraction of uranium or seed. If a cleaner gas is needed, further separation can be accomplished.

The helium leaving the separator passes into a regenerator where its temperature is reduced (6). At this point, two options are available. One is to reject heat to a steam boiler-turbine system which would provide shaft horsepower to drive the compressor. The second approach is to regenerate to a lower temperature and reject heat to a cooling system prior to entering the compressor. An analysis of both cycles indicated that the second approach offers the highest overall efficiency, even though some of the power produced in the MHD generator must be used to drive the compressor. This is primarily due to the low efficiency of the steam cycle coupled to the high peak temperature available with the gaseous core reactor.

After leaving the cooling system (1), the gas passes through the compressor (2), is heated in the regenerator (3), and returns to the reactor for nuclear heating. The compressor in this cycle is driven by an electrical motor with power provided from the MHD generator.

Cycle Analysis

The work output of the cycle is in the form of electricity produced in the MHD generator. The equation governing the MHD output is

$$(1) \quad W_{MHD} = M_{He} \; n_g \; C_p \; (T_4 - T_5)$$
$$= M_{He} \; n_g \; C_p T_4 \; (1 - (\tfrac{p5}{p4})^{\frac{\gamma-1}{\gamma}})$$

where n_g is the generator efficiency, M_{He} is the flow rate of helium in moles/second, C_p is the molar heat capacity of the gas, and T and γ represent the temperature and ratio of specific heats, respectively. The heat input in the reactor is given by

$$(2) \quad Q_{in} = M_{He} \; C_p \; (T_4 - T_3)$$

and the compressor input is

$$(3) \quad W_c = M_{He} \; C_p \; (T_2 - T_1)/n_c$$
$$= M_{He} \; C_p \; T_1 \; [(\tfrac{p2}{p1})^{\frac{\gamma-1}{\gamma}} -1]/n_c$$

where n_c is the compressor efficiency. Since the motor driving the compressor must convert electrical power to shaft power, it has some inefficiency and

$$(4) \quad W_c = n_M \; W_M$$

where n_m is the efficiency of the motor and W_m is the electrical power required by the motor. The overall cycle efficiency is given by

$$(5) \quad n_{cy} = \frac{W_g - W_M}{Q_{in}} = \frac{W_g - \frac{W_c}{n_M}}{Q_{in}}$$

In order to maximize the cycle efficiency, the compressor requirement and heat input should be minimized. The pressure ratio across the MHD generator will be about 2, i.e., p4/p5 = 2 and, assuming pressure losses in the regenerator and reactor of .3, then p2/p1 = 2.3. If the outlet temperature of the heat sink is 350°K and the compressor efficiency is 0.85, then

$$(6) \quad W_c = M_{He} \frac{C_p \; (350°K)}{(.85)} \left[(2.3)^{\frac{\gamma-1}{\gamma}} -1 \right]$$

Minimizing Q_{in} can be done by maximizing T_3 through regeneration. If we assume that the temperature difference needed to drive heat from the low pressure to the high pressure gas stream is 100°C (which is reasonable for gas-to-gas heat exchangers) and that the exit temperature from the MHD generator is 2000°K, then

$$(7) \quad T_3 = T_5 - 100°K = 1900°K$$

Hence,

$$(8) \quad n_{cy} = \frac{n_g \; (T_4 - T_5) - \frac{T1}{n_M n_c} \left[(\tfrac{p2}{p1})^{\frac{\gamma-1}{\gamma}} -1 \right]}{(T_4 - T_3)}$$

which becomes, for T_4 = 4000°K and helium

$$(9) \quad n_{cy} = n_g (\tfrac{2000°K}{2100°K}) - \frac{140°K}{2100°K(n_M \; n_c)}$$

For n_c = .85 and n_m = .9

$$(10) \quad n_{cy} = .95 \; n_g - .085$$

Since MHD generator efficiencies of .7 - .8 are anticipated, cycle efficiencies of 58 - 67% are possible.

Nuclear Reactor

In order to provide a basis for sizing the system, a net power output of 2000 megawatts electrical was assumed, which should be typical of future power plants. Using equations (1) and (3) and a generator efficiency of .75 leads to a helium flow rate of 1100 pounds/second and a heat input of 3200 megawatts. This heat input could be provided by a graphite moderated reactor operating with a neutron flux density of 10^{15} neutron/cm^2/sec. The power density of the reactor would be 0.2 megawatts/cubic foot at a fuel density of approximately 0.02 pounds/cubic foot. A typical reactor cavity would be a cylinder with a radius of 15 feet and a length of 22 feet. The cavity would operate at a total pressure of 20 atmospheres and a uranium partial pressure of one atmosphere. The total amount of uranium in the reactor would be 320 pounds. Hence, the amount of uranium escaping capture in the particle separator would be no more than 0.1 pounds.

MHD Generator

In order to produce a net power output of 2000 megawatts, the MHD generator must deliver about 2300 megawatts. The equation governing power generation in an MHD generator is roughly

$$(11) \quad \frac{P}{V} = K (1-K) \sigma v^2 B^2$$

where P/V is the power density, K is the loading factor, T is the gas electrical conductivity, v is the gas velocity, and B is the magnetic field strength. At the inlet to the generator, the gas conductivity is about 30 mhos/foot and the velocity is 7000 feet/second. With proper loading K = 1/2 and a reasonable magnetic field strength is 40,000 gauss. Using these values, the power density is 65 megawatts/cubic feet. With a typical aspect ratio of 5, the generator channel would be about 2 feet in diameter and 10 feet long. The overall generator dimensions, including magnet, would be approximately 10 feet in diameter and 20 feet long.

Application Benefits

The utilization of the proposed advanced technology for power generation has two primary benefits: the negation of atmospheric pollution and a significant reduction in thermal pollution. The cycle involves no combustion products and operates at efficiencies which are about twice those of existing plants. Since the amount of heat rejected by a plant per kilowatt of electrical output is proportional to $(1-\eta_{cy})/\eta_{cy}$, an efficiency of 60% reduces thermal pollution by over 300% compared to present-day plants. Although radioactive pollution is still possible, continuous in-plant reprocessing of the fuel should reduce the risk of pollution associated with fuel shipments. In addition, the low heat rejection demands should allow the selection of plant sites which minimizes the dangers associated

with plant accidents. One disadvantage of the system is that the entire plant may be radioactive because of fission products and fuel entrainment after the separator. This could be eliminated, however, by ensuring complete removal of the uranium and fission products from the gas by sophisticated separation processes. Use of this technique would confine the radioactivity to the nuclear cavity and MHD generator which could be shielded for safety.

Conclusions

The exponential increase in environmental pollution caused by our major energy conversion processes cannot be checked by minor improvements in our operating procedures. If we are to maintain the standard of living enjoyed by our population while simultaneously decreasing the pollution problem, substantial improvements are necessary. Fortunately, technology developed for other purposes can be utilized to provide such improvements. With continued development and application, gaseous core nuclear reactors and MHD generators can provide significant reductions in the pollution caused by commercial electrical power generation. Such application also provides a basis for long-term improvements through employment of fusion nuclear power systems.

References

Gritton, E. C. and Pinkel, B., "The Feasibility of the Gaseous Core Nuclear Reactor for Electric Power Generation", Rand Memorandum RM-5721-PR, June 1969.

Barthelemy, R. R. and Mac Ewen, Capt, H. H., "Advanced Space Power Systems", Seventh Space Congress, Cocoa Beach, Florida, April 1970.

Rosa, R. J., "Magnetohydrodynamic Generators and Nuclear Propulsion", ARS Journal, August 1962, 1221-1230 (1962).

Ragsdale, R. G., "Outlook for Gas-Core Nuclear Rockets", Astronautics and Aerospace Engineering, August 1963.

Millionshchikov, M. D., et al, "The Potential Use of Gas-Turbine Plants and MHD Generators in Atomic Power Stations", IAEA Liaison Group on MHD Electric Power Generation, Moscow, USSR, November 1969.

Wright, J. H., "Electric Power Generation and the Environment", Westinghouse Engineer, Vol. 30, Nr. 3, May 1970.

ORGANOPHOSPHORUS INSECTICIDE DECONTAMINANT

B. C. Wolverton,* R. Richter,** Sandra M. Lefstad†
Air Force Armament Laboratory (AFSC)
Eglin AFB, Florida 32542

Abstract

An organophosphorus insecticide decontaminating solution has been developed that can be used on and around aircraft and spray equipment. This solution converts the insecticides to products which can be disposed of by water washing without the extremely toxic effects to fish normally exhibited by the unaltered insecticides. The solvent component of this decontaminant is dipropylene glycol monomethyl ether (DPGME), a water-soluble, nonhazardous substance used in numerous commercial products. The active ingredient is monoethanolamine (MEA), which is also a common industrial chemical. Twenty-five percent by volume of MEA is the optimum concentration to neutralize O,O-dimethyl S-bis(carbethoxy) ethyl phosphorodithioate (malathion), while half this concentration is used to neutralize the nonsulfur-containing insecticide 1,2-dibromo-2,2-dichloroethyl dimethyl phosphate (naled), to prevent an excessive temperature increase caused by the exothermic reaction.

Introduction

The organophosphorus insecticides have rapidly gained public acceptance because of their wide spectrum of insecticidal effectiveness and the ease at which they can be degraded by environmental factors such as soil, water and vegetation. These insecticides normally do not persist in the environment more than several weeks, whereas chlorinated insecticides such as DDT persist for years, even under adverse environmental conditions.

The effective, nonpersistent nature of organophosphorus insecticides makes them ideal for both civilian and military insecticide programs; however, formulations of the highly active concentrates of these insecticides for ultra-low-volume aerial applications and other applications require special precautions during filling and handling operations. To reduce the risk of accidental exposure of workers and avoid environmental pollution, a rapid-acting, noncorrosive decontaminating solution is highly desirable when working with insecticide concentrates.

For the toxicity studies in this investigation, malathion was used as a representative for the sulfur-containing insecticides, while naled was chosen to represent the nonsulfur-containing, highly reactive insecticides. In both insecticides, the parent compounds are highly toxic to fish and related aquatic life.

Materials and Methods

Insecticides used in this study were malathion, technical (95%), American Cyanamid Co.; naled, technical (85%), Chevron Chemical Co.; dichlorvos, technical grade, Shell Chemical Co.; fenthion, technical (93%), Chemagro Corp.; and TEPP, technical (100% active ingredients), Miller Chemical and Fertilizer Corp. Chemicals used in the decontaminating solution were dipropylene glycol monomethyl ether, reagent grade, Dow Chemical Co., and purified monoethanolamine from Fisher Scientific Co. Chemicals for the extraction procedure included hexanes (Fisher Scientific Co.), certified for pesticide residue analysis, a saturated U.S.P. grade sodium chloride solution, and anhydrous sodium sulfate, certified ACS grade. Thin-layer chromatograms were developed with chloroform, N.F. grade, Fisher Scientific Co. Silica gel G for thin-layer chromatography was obtained from American Optical Co.

Decontamination Procedure

Insecticides were exposed to the decontaminating solution in a volume-to-volume ratio of 10 parts decontaminant to one part insecticide. For the decontamination of naled, solutions containing 12.5% MEA were used. Solutions formulated with 25% MEA were used to decontaminate malathion, dichlorvos, and fenthion. The reactions were allowed to proceed at room temperature for 30, 60, 120, and 240 minutes. At the end of each time period, the unaltered insecticides were extracted and assayed by gas chromatography and thin-layer chromatography. All experiments were performed in triplicate.

Extraction Procedure

The decontamination mixture was added to 50 ml distilled water in a 250-ml separatory funnel. The unaltered insecticides were

*Chief, Assessments Branch, AFATL (AFSC)
**Project Scientist
†Research Assistant

extracted from the aqueous mixture with 30 ml hexanes which were added in 10-ml aliquots. To aid in the separation of the hexanes and aqueous layers, 15 ml of a saturated sodium chloride solution were added. The hexanes layer was placed over 10 grams anhydrous sodium sulfate. The extract was filtered and stored at 5°C if the sample could not be readily analyzed on the gas chromatograph. To test the efficiency of the extraction scheme, insecticides were exposed to dipropylene glycol monomethyl ether in the absence of MEA. This mixture was subjected to the same extraction procedure as the decontaminated mixture.

Gas Chromatography

Gas-liquid chromatography was used for the detection of unaltered insecticides. A Tracor MT-220 gas chromatograph equipped with a flame photometric detector was employed. A 6 foot by 1/4 inch glass column containing Chromosorb "W", 80/100 mesh, coated with 10% Dow 200 was conditioned for 48 hours at 200°C before use. This column was used for the analysis of malathion. The inlet temperature was held at 175°C, the column-oven temperature at 170°C, and the detector temperature at 190°C. For the analysis of naled, TEPP, dichlorvos and fenthion, a 6 foot by 1/4 inch glass column containing Chromosorb "G", 100/120 mesh, coated with 2% SF-96 was used. This column was conditioned at 225°C for 36 hours prior to use. The injector temperature was maintained at 185°C, the column-oven temperature at 175°C, and the detector temperature at 190°C. Gas flow rates for all gas chromatographic analyses were helium 65 cc/minute, hydrogen 180 cc/minute, oxygen 25 cc/minute, and air 90 cc/minute. Peaks obtained from the decontamination mixture extracts were compared with calibrated peaks obtained from a known concentration of insecticides in hexanes.

Thin-layer Chromatography

Glass 20 inch by 20 inch plates were coated with a 250 μ thick layer of silica gel G after the procedure of Stahl.[1] The plates were dried at room temperature, activated at 110°C for one hour and stored in a drying cabinet until needed. Chromatograms were developed in a closed tank to maintain a solvent-saturated atmosphere. The solvent front was allowed to run 18 cm from the bottom edge of the plate (16.5 cm from the starting line); this required approximately 45 minutes. After evaporation of the solvent, the plates were exposed to iodine vapors for five minutes, and all visible spots were marked. The plates were then sprayed with Hane's reagent,[2] heated at 110°C for five minutes, and exposed to

ultraviolet light (3660 A). Phosphate derivatives gave yellow spots at low concentrations and blue spots at high concentrations; both increased in intensity over a three-day period.

Fish Toxicity Studies

Acute median tolerance limit (TLm) evaluations were performed in accordance with the Routine Bioassay Method.[3] The test species, mosquitofish (Gambusia affinis, Baird and Girard), was seined from ponds on Eglin AFB Reservation, Florida. The mosquitofish, total length 20-30 mm, were acclimatized in the laboratory in rectangular 10-gallon holding tanks for a minimum of 10 days before they were used. Water temperature in holding tanks and test containers was maintained at 22°C. Test animals were fed Longlife Pool Fish Food* daily. None were fasted prior to testing. Test containers were cylindrical 4.5-gallon laboratory glass jars, each housing 10 fish. Water temperature was maintained at 22°C and water depth at 250 mm. Between tests, containers were washed with detergent and rinsed with acetone. Test animals were observed hourly for the first eight hours, and at 24-hour intervals thereafter throughout the 96 hours of observation. TLm values were determined by the Reed-Muench Method.[4]

Corrosion Tests

Aluminum 7075 and 2024 strips measuring 1.0 inch by 6.0 inches by .070 inch were sanded with fine flint paper, washed with soap and water, and rinsed first with distilled water and then with acetone. The strips were oven dried for 15 minutes and weighed on an Ainsworth semi-micro balance. They were then placed in 40 ml of various solutions using 100-ml glass graduated cylinders for 96 hours for Aluminum 7075 and 144 hours for Aluminum 2024. After 96 and 144 hours, the malathion and naled samples were decontaminated using 25% MEA and 75% dipropylene glycol monomethyl ether. All samples were rewashed with soapy water, rinsed with distilled water and then with acetone, dried at 150°C for 15 minutes, and reweighed.

Samples of Aluminum 2024, 1 inch by 2 inches by 0.032 inch, and Aluminum 7075, 1 inch by 2 inches by 0.1 inch, were prepared according to the procedure previously described. The samples were placed in a solution containing 42% methanol, 53% water and 5% sodium hydroxide. Samples immersed in methanol and water served as controls. After 48 hours the samples were cleaned, dried, and reweighed.

---

*Longlife Fish Food Products, Division of Sternco Industries, Inc., Harrison, New Jersey.

Results and Discussion

Gas Chromatography

Gas chromatography data demonstrate that the decontaminating solution is effective in neutralizing the insecticides studied. Although neutralization rates differ widely, naled is destroyed completely after 30 minutes and most of the malathion in 60 minutes. Fenthion, one of the more stable organophosphorus insecticides, requires a higher concentration of MEA or a longer reaction period. After 240 minutes exposure to a 25% MEA solution, approximately 50% fenthion remains unaltered (Table 1).

The qualitative and quantitative determination of insecticide in each spot was made by comparison of the R_F-value and the area of the spot with those of simultaneously developed references of known concentrations. Lowest detection limits and R_F-values for the insecticides investigated are given in Table 2. In the case of malathion, the gradual time dependent disappearance of the spot was accompanied by a corresponding appearance of others, belonging to impurities in the original malathion sample and to unidentified reaction products. These spots were visualized by iodine vapors as well as Hane's reagent and had R_F-values of 64, 56, 51.5, 22.5, 16.5, 12 (streaking), and 0.

Compound	0 min	30 min	60 min	120 min	240 min
Malathion:15% MEA in DPGME	100.00	35.0	16.9	1.3	0.3
Malathion:25% MEA in DPGME	100.00	19.6	2.4	<0.1	<0.1
Naled:12.5% MEA in DPGME	100.00	<0.1	<0.1	<0.1	<0.1
Dichlorvos:12.5% MEA in DPGME	100.00	5.3	-	-	-
Dichlorvos:25% MEA in DPGME	100.00	<0.1	<0.1	<0.1	<0.1
Fenthion:25% MEA in DPGME	100.00	77.8	63.3	57.1	48.9
TEPP:12.5% MEA in DPGME	100.00	0	0	0	0

TABLE 1. Percent insecticide remaining after exposure to decontaminating solutions.

Thin-layer Chromatography

The residual insecticide amounts determined by gas chromatography were substantiated by thin-layer chromatography. Based on the detection limits determined with standards of known concentrations, a sufficient volume of each hexane extract was applied to a single spot to allow the detection of insecticide concentrations with a lower limit of 80 ppm, corresponding to the destruction of up to 99.8% of the original amount of insecticide.

For the reaction of dichlorvos and the 25% MEA solution, the spot corresponding to dichlorvos disappeared, while another spot with an R_F-value of 16.5 became visible after a reaction time of 30 minutes.

Fish Studies

Data obtained from fish studies indicate that the MEA decontaminating solution is highly effective in neutralizing the toxic effects of naled and malathion when 10 parts of the decontaminating solution are allowed to react with one part of the insecticide for approximately one hour. The data shown in Table 3 suggest that the mixture containing both insecticides and decontaminating solutions is less toxic to fish than the decontaminating solution alone, which already is relatively nontoxic.

Corrosion Data

Studies conducted with aircraft type Aluminum 7075 and 2024 indicate the MEA decontaminating formulations are noncorrosive to these metals relative to a dilute sodium

Insecticide	Detection Limit (μg)		R_F
	Iodine Vapor	Hane's reagent	
Fenthion	1.0	0.5 (blue)	85.0
Malathion	2.0	2.0 (blue)	42.5
Naled	30	3.0 (yellow)	32.0
		30 (blue)	
Dichlorvos	30	3.0 (yellow)	24.0
		10 (blue)	

TABLE 2. Thin-layer chromatography data on selected insecticides.

Compound	24 hr	48 hr	72 hr	96 hr
Malathion	4.75	4.55	4.40	3.57
Naled	1.364	1.364	1.313	1.182
25% MEA in DPGME	1840	1800	1791	1718
10:1 25% MEA in DPGME:95% malathion	2282	2182	2150	2073
10:1 12.5% MEA in DPGME:85% naled	2308	2109	2009	1945
MEA	375.00	365.90	345.31	329.16
DPGME	>8000	>8000	>8000	>8000

TABLE 3. TLm values in ppm for mosquitofish (Gambusia affinis).

hydroxide solution, which is also capable of neutralizing organophosphorus insecticides. Samples of Aluminum 2024 and 7075 exposed to a sodium hydroxide solution had an average weight loss of 0.91725 g and 1.5453 g, respectively. The only other aluminum samples showing significant weight changes from corrosion were the ones exposed to technical grade naled (Tables 4, 5 and 6).

Kinetics of Malathion Neutralization

The decontamination of malathion appears to follow the kinetics of a second order reaction. The order of a reaction may generally be determined by substituting the observed reactant concentrations at various time intervals into a theoretical rate equation of an assumed order. If the rate constant k is found to be independent of reaction times and initial concentrations, it can be concluded that the reaction is of the same order as the one assumed. Thus, with a second order rate equation for the decontamination of malathion,

Solution	Initial Weight of Metal (g)	Final Weight of Metal (g)	Weight Difference
Malathion	24.67000	24.66867	-.00133
Malathion	24.48288	24.47959	-.00329
25% MEA in DPGME	23.71367	23.71300	-.00067
25% MEA in DPGME	24.12204	24.12133	-.00071
15% MEA in DPGME	24.74874	24.74800	-.00074
15% MEA in DPGME	24.91125	24.91051	-.00079
Malathion:25% MEA in DPGME	24.30125	24.30061	-.00064
Malathion:25% MEA in DPGME	25.26655	25.26570	-.00085
Malathion:15% MEA in DPGME	23.50300	23.50235	-.00065
Malathion:15% MEA in DPGME	24.43257	24.43194	-.00063
Naled	25.11040	25.13540	+.02500
Naled	24.78122	24.79827	+.01705
Naled:15% MEA in DPGME	25.58035	25.57984	-.00051

TABLE 4. Half immersion of Aluminum 2024 strips for 144 hours.

Solution	Initial Weight of Metal (g)	Final Weight of Metal (g)	Weight Difference
Malathion	18.82421	18.82200	-.00221
Malathion	18.75295	18.75078	-.00217
25% MEA in DPGME	18.84717	18.84593	-.00124
25% MEA in DPGME	18.81636	18.81526	-.00110
15% MEA in DPGME	18.83721	18.83665	-.00056
15% MEA in DPGME	18.76669	18.76623	-.00046
Malathion:25% MEA in DPGME	18.80413	18.80296	-.00117
Malathion:25% MEA in DPGME	18.76313	18.76282	-.00031
Malathion:15% MEA in DPGME	18.75822	18.75749	-.00073
Malathion:15% MEA in DPGME	18.62396	18.62314	-.00082
Naled	18.61326	18.62196	+.00870
Naled	18.79009	18.79500	+.00491
Naled:15% MEA in DPGME	18.74045	18.74006	-.00039
Naled:15% MEA in DPGME	18.68931	18.68947	+.00016

TABLE 5. Half immersion of Aluminum 7075 strips for 96 hours.

	Initial Weight (g)	Final Weight (g)	Weight Change
Four samples Aluminum 7075 in 42% methanol, 53% water, 5% NaOH	9.1187	7.6468	-1.4719
	9.2435	7.6700	-1.5735
	9.2331	7.7580	-1.5711
	9.3228	9.0433	-1.5648
Four samples Aluminum 2024 in 42% methanol, 53% water, 5% NaOH	2.9009	1.9304	0.9705
	2.8900	1.9273	0.9627
	2.9049	1.9426	0.9623
	2.9125	2.1390	0.7735

TABLE 6. Complete immersion of Aluminum 7075 and 2024 strips for 48 hours.

$$r = \frac{dc_{malathion}}{dt} = -kc_{malathion}\,c_{MEA} \tag{1}$$

the corresponding integrated rate equation is

$$kt = \frac{1}{c_{0MEA} - c_{0malathion}} \ln \frac{(c_{0MEA} - c_{0malathion} + c_{malathion})\,c_{0malathion}}{c_{0MEA}\,c_{malathion}} \tag{2}$$

where $c_{0malathion}$ is the initial concentration of malathion (t = 0)
c_{0MEA} is the initial concentration of MEA
$c_{malathion}$ is the concentration of malathion at time t
c_{MEA} is the concentration of MEA at time t

Upon substituting the observed malathion concentrations, the corresponding reaction times and the initial concentrations of MEA and malathion into equation (2), k is found to be constant within the limits of experimental error (Table 7). The neutralization of malathion is a second order reaction, with a rate constant, k, of 0.0160 1 mol^{-1} min^{-1}.

Having determined the appropriate rate equation and the value of the rate constant, the results of the kinetic study can be extended to other than the actual test conditions. In Figure 1, a series of curves derived from equation (2) have been plotted to predict the time required for the neutralization of 99% of a given quantity of technical grade (95%) malathion ($t_{0.99}$) as a function of the concentration of MEA in the decontaminant and the ratio of decontaminant solution to malathion. As can be seen from Figure 1, the decrease in $t_{0.99}$ becomes continuously smaller as the concentration of MEA is increased. Also, as the ratio of decontaminant to malathion goes beyond 10.1, the decrease of $t_{0.99}$ becomes negligible.

Theoretical Mechanisms

With the large variety of organophosphorus insecticides available today and more likely to be developed in the future, this study was restricted by necessity to a small number which may be considered characteristic examples of the entire class. It would be of interest if the results could be generalized to all organophosphorus insecticides, both to predict decontamination rates and to determine the toxicity of breakdown products. For this purpose, the reaction mechanism must be considered in more detail.

Most organophosphorus insecticides are esters or anhydrides of phosphoric, phosphorothioic, or phosphorodithioic acids. In these compounds, the higher electronegativity of oxygen (3.5) and sulfur (2.5) in comparison to that of phosphorus (2.1) places a positive charge on the phosphorus atom, making it the electrophilic center of the molecule. As a consequence, organophosphorus insecticides can react with nucleophilic agents by direct displacement at the phosphorus atom.

I   II   III

Kinetic analysis of a large number of solvolyses of organophosphorus insecticides and their reactions with various nucleophiles has led to the conclusion that they proceed by a one-step mechanism similar to the S_N2 reaction at saturated carbon. In this type of reaction, the new bond is formed simultaneously with the breaking or, in some instances, shortly after the weakening ("S_N1" character) of the old bond. However, for the sake of clarity, the designations "S_N1" and "S_N2" should be used only for displacement reactions at saturated carbon.

MEA can be considered to be a typical nucleophile which will react with organophosphorus insecticides by the mechanism above. This has been found to be the case in the reaction of MEA and several phosphorus compounds analogous to organophosphorus insecticides.[5] It was found at the same time that for the two

t (min)	c_{0MEA} (mol 1^{-1})	$c_{0malathion}$ (mol 1^{-1})	$c_{malathion}$ (mol 1^{-1})	k (1 mol^{-1} min^{-1})
30.0	3.73	0.320	0.0628	0.0152
60.0	3.73	0.320	0.0078	0.0178
30.0	2.24	0.320	0.112	0.0164
60.0	2.24	0.320	0.0540	0.0144

TABLE 7. Calculated values for reaction constant k in decontamination of malathion.

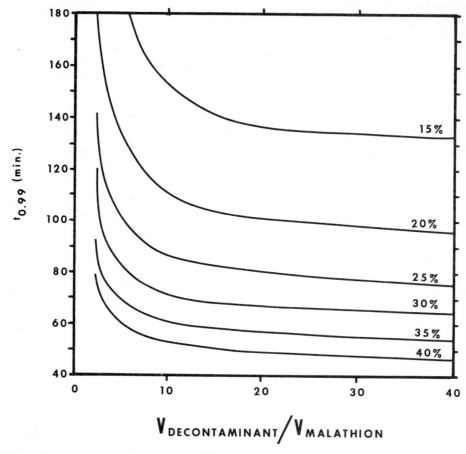

FIGURE 1. Time required to decontaminate 99% of a malathion sample as a function of ratio of decontaminant to malathion and concentration of monoethanolamine.

nucleophilic functions of MEA, the hydroxyl and the amino group, the reaction of the amino group predominates.

As to the factors which determine the reaction rate, the most important ones are steric effects and the influence of the substituents on the magnitude of the positive charge on phosphorus.[6,7] Increasing size of the substituents on the phosphorus atom will cause increasing steric hindrance in the transition state and, therefore, reduce the reaction rate. The reaction rate will also be reduced by substituents with a decreased electron-withdrawing effect. This would reduce the positive charge on phosphorus, rendering it less susceptible to nucleophilic attack. Thus, because of the difference in electro-negativity between oxygen and sulfur, the reaction rate of a phosphate ester will be slower than that of the corresponding phosphorodithioate ester. The same

factors appear to control the hydrolysis rates of organophosphorus insecticides, and it would therefore be expected that the relative rates of decontamination with MEA would be similar to those observed during hydrolysis.[8] However, it should be kept in mind that although the relative hydrolysis rates may be similar, the rates of neutralization with MEA are much faster than the corresponding hydrolysis rates in river or lake water. Thus, for the hydrolysis of malathion, a typical half-life (pH 6) is 26 days,[9] while for neutralization with a tenfold volume of 25% MEA, the half-life is only 12 minutes.

The major alternative to a displacement reaction at phosphorus is a chemical reaction on the substituent X which, for organophosphorus insecticides, usually is a reactive carbon-containing compound. Although oxidation reactions are unlikely under the conditions of the decontamination, chemical reactions involving nucleophilic substitution reactions at saturated and unsaturated carbons and elimination reactions are possible. The nature and extent of the reactions depend strongly on the chemical structure of the substituent X. Since X is different for almost every organophosphorus insecticide, these reactions must be investigated in each particular case and cannot be discussed in general. Thus, for organophosphorus insecticides with substituents particularly sensitive to interactions with amino and hydroxyl functions, the decontamination rates may not correspond to predicted values.

In summary, MEA solutions can react with organophosphorus insecticides by a nucleophilic displacement reaction at phosphorus. The relative decontamination rates will be similar to the known relative hydrolysis rates. Depending on the nature of the substituent, certain exceptions may be found which will not be decontaminated by the theoretical mechanism.

Acknowledgments

The authors thank Capt C. J. Madura for the corrosion tests and SSgt R. C. Voigt for the fish toxicity studies included in this report.

References

1. E. Stahl (Ed.), Thin-layer Chromatography--A Laboratory Handbook. Academic Press, New York, 1965.
2. C. S. Hanes, F. P. Isherwood, Nature 164, 1107 (1949).
3. Standard Methods for the Examination of Water and Wastewater. Part IV. Bioassay methods for the evaluation of acute toxicity of industrial wastewater and substances to fish. American Public Health Association, Inc. Boyd Printing Co., Inc., New York, 1965. pp. 457-475.
4. D. J. Finney, Statistical Method in Biological Assay. 2nd ed. Hafner Publishing Co., New York, 1965. pp. 533-535.
5. R. Greenhalgh, M. A. Weinberger, Can. J. Chem. 45, 495 (1967).
6. R. D. O'Brien, Insecticides--Action and Metabolism, Academic Press, New York, 1967.
7. R. F. Hudson, Structure and Mechanism in Organophosphorus Chemistry, Academic Press, New York, 1965.
8. J. H. Ruzicka, J. Thomson, B. B. Wheals, J. Chromatog. 31, 37 (1967).
9. G. O. Guerrant, L. E. Fetzer, Jr., J. W. Miles, Pesticides Monitoring Journal 4, 14 (1970).

OIL-WATER SEPARATION AND OIL HARVESTING SYSTEM

D. J. Graham*, R. L. Johnson[†] and P. G. Bhuta[†]
TRW Systems Group
Redondo Beach, California

The interfacial surface tension between two immiscible liquids, in this case oil and water, is utilized to selectively withdraw oil from a mixture of oil and water. Laboratory tests with a variety of petroleum products have verified the concept and data concerning operating parameters have been collected. The technique is an adaption of aerospace technology in which a liquid is separated from a liquid-gas mixture in low-g by the use of surface tension screens. A laboratory model of an oil-water separator using the concept has been assembled and successfully tested. This separation concept, deployed in a number of different configurations, has direct application to many diverse water pollution problems such as open sea spills, harbor spills and industrial waste water processing.

INTRODUCTION

Recent accidents in the Santa Barbara Channel off the California coast and in the Gulf of Mexico off the Louisiana coast have clearly indicated the need for physical methods of separation of oil from the surface of sea water without the use of toxic chemical dispersants. The authors have devised a simultaneous oil-water separation and harvesting system[°] utilizing techniques developed in the aerospace industry for the expulsion of liquid cryogens from propulsion and life support system tanks containing liquid and gas in a low-g space environment (Reference 1). The oil separation system physically removes the oil selectively from the water surface without the addition of toxic chemicals.

RELATED AEROSPACE TECHNOLOGY

In certain spaceflight situations it is necessary to extract liquid from a tank containing liquid and gas (e.g. subcritical storage of life support and propulsion fluids) while in a low gravity environment (see Figure 1). In these space applications the liquid is preferentially removed from the liquid and gas mixture inside the tank as it comes into contact with a fine micronic screen located

near the tank wall. The region behind the screen is filled with liquid and is connected to the tank liquid outlet. A slight reduction in pressure is maintained in the liquid region behind the screen so that a pressure difference exists across the screen which satisfies the inequality

$$p_1 - p_2 < \frac{K\sigma}{r} \qquad (1)$$

where (see Figure 1)

p_1 is the pressure in the tank interior

p_2 is the pressure in the liquid region behind the screen

σ is the liquid-vapor surface tension

r is the screen pore radius

K is a constant of proportionality depending on the type of screen mesh

If the pressure difference ($p_1 - p_2$) exceeds the right hand side of inequality (1) then the surface tension forces are unable to maintain the liquid-gas interface across the screen pores and gas passes through the screen into the liquid region behind the screen. However, with inequality (1) satisfied the gas cannot pass through the screen whereas any liquid in contact with the screen (see Figure 1) is drawn through the screen, its flow through the screen not being impeded by the existence of liquid-vapor interfaces. If, in addition, the viscous pressure losses due to liquid flow through the screen do not exceed the right hand side of inequality (1) then liquid, exclusive of gas, will be separated from the liquid-gas region inside the tank.

[†] Manager, Applied Mechanics Laboratory
[+] Manager, Advanced Technology Department
[*] Member of the Technical Staff

[°] A U.S. patent is currently pending.
[!]

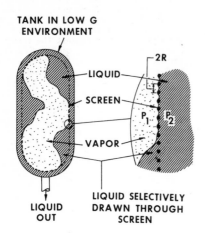

FIGURE 1.   LOW-G GAS LIQUID SEPARATION.

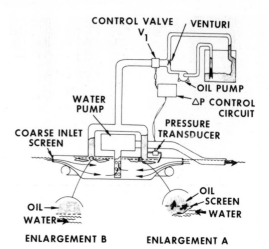

FIGURE 2.   OIL-WATER SEPARATOR.

PRINCIPLE OF OPERATION

The principle of operation of the oil-water separation and oil harvesting system is based on the mechanism described in the paragraphs above, that is, the interfacial surface tension between oil and water is used to selectively separate oil from an oil-water mixture. Figure 2 is a schematic of one configuration of the separation system. This configuration could be quite effectively used in a relatively calm environment such as a harbor. The region behind the screen is filled with an oil in which the oils to be collected are miscible and a slight reduction in pressure behind the screen is imposed by the pump and venturi circuit. A differential pressure transducer monitors the pressure difference across the screen and maintains this difference in a narrow band about its initial value by the adjustment of a proportional control valve and servo control circuit. An oil-water mixture is brought into contact with the screen by a second pump located at the top of the separator. The purpose of the basin beneath the screen is to ingest into the separator a relatively oil rich sample of water near the surface. Local velocities of the oil-water mixture are reduced due to the large area inside the basin and oil is bouyed by gravity to the top of the unit and into contact with the screen. Water is exhausted from the unit while the oil is selectively drawn through the screen as shown in enlargement A of Figure 2. As oil wets the screen the pressure difference across the screen drops. This is sensed by the pressure transducer and the control valve is opened accordingly to return the screen pressure difference to its set initial value and thus maintain a maximum oil flow through the screen. In areas where no oil is in contact with the outside of the screen, (enlargement B of Figure 2), the interfacial surface tension between oil and water forms a passive barrier for the passage of water. Oil is thus selectively separated from the water surface and can be easily stored for disposal or reuse.

LABORATORY TEST PERFORMED

Laboratory tests have been performed to confirm the principle of operation and to obtain breakthrough pressure difference and collection rate data. Laboratory collection tests were performed with crude oil, kerosene and Bunker C and a cylindrical screen element in the configuration shown in Figure 3. Photographs of an actual screen element and the hardware used in the test are shown in Figures 4 and 5.

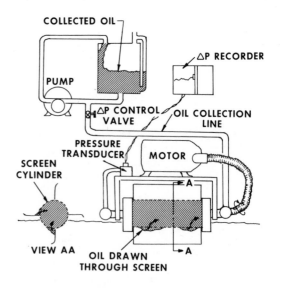

FIGURE 3.   LABORATORY TEST CONFIGURATION.

FIGURE 4.   LABORATORY SCREEN ELEMENT.

FIGURE 5.   LABORATORY TEST APPARATUS.

The screen elements were of a cylindrical design for ease of fabrication and had a screen area of 0.1 ft^2. In operation the screen cylinder was rotated to cause oil floating on the surface of the water to be drawn under the surface by the four metal fins and then bouyed up against the screen where it was drawn through by the pressure difference maintained by the pump. Limited measurements taken during these tests indicated that for a 50 x 250 mesh screen collection rates as high as 5 GPM/ft^2 screen can be obtained when collecting Santa Barbara crude oil (which has a viscosity about that of Navy Special Fuel Oil). During the oil collection tests it was noted that the screen difference variations which occurred as more or less oil came in contact with the screen was quite easily compensated for by manually adjusting valve V1. In all tests the screen pressure difference was kept at a level of 1.5" of water, although the breakthrough pressure for crude oil and the 50 x 250 mesh was found to be about 3" of water. High response servo-control circuits are commercially available which can automatically maintain operational screen pressure differences below 1.0" of water.

APPLICATIONS

The applications of a surface tension selective separation device as described above are myriad. Not only can it be used to recover spills of crude or other oils on the open sea and in the harbors but also for the reclamation of immiscible liquids from industrial process waste water. Specifically, the deployment of an oil-water separator such as shown in Figure 2 would result in a cleaner effluent discharged into municipal sewage systems from industrial and military waste water settling ponds.

REFERENCES

(1) U. S. Patent No. 3,492,793, "Liquid-Vapor Separator and Cryogenic Liquid Converter," awarded to P. G. Bhuta and R. L. Johnson on 3 February 1970.

APPLICATION OF AEROSPACE DATA ACQUISITION TECHNOLOGY
TO ATMOSPHERIC AND METEOROLOGICAL INVESTIGATIONS

Michael R. Smith
Assistant Research Engineer
Mississippi State University
State College, Mississippi

and

Richard A. Johnson
Specialist, Program Operations
Management & Technical Services Department
General Electric Company
Bay St. Louis, Mississippi

ABSTRACT

This paper presents the efforts of researchers at Mississippi State University to utilize space-age technology in the development of
a self-contained, airborne data acquisition system for use in atmospheric and meteorological
studies. The system was developed at the NASA
Mississippi Test Facility with the aid of engineers and personnel provided by the site contractor, the General Electric Company. The compact,
light weight airborne data acquisition system
(ADAS) is capable of recording fourteen variables
in its present configuration and is suitable for
use in a single-engine aircraft. The ADAS has
been utilized in several environmental science
investigations associated with atmospheric diffusion processes and weather modification.

INTRODUCTION

The recent emphasis on environmental science
research in the United States has provided substantial impetus to research programs in the general area of atmospheric and meteorological
sciences. Researchers are developing numerous
prediction methods for use in the control of air
pollution, weather modification, sound propagation
and related phenomena; however, one of the most
pressing problems facing these scientist is the
acquisition of reliable data on the structure of
the atmosphere and the effect of atmospheric properties and anomolies on the observed phenomena.
For a large scale investigation several airborne
data acquisition systems have been developed by
the National Aeronautical and Space Administration, the Atomic Energy Commission, and other
government agencies. Some of these systems are
extremely sophisticated; providing for on-board
monitoring of numerous individual parameters and
in some cases, on-board processing of the data.
For small scale investigations such as those that
might be conducted by a university research group
there is a serious lack of airborne data acquisition systems which will provide accurate and reliable data acquisition at an economical price.

This paper presents the results of efforts
by researchers at Mississippi State University to
utilize space-age technology in the development

of a self-contained airborne data acquisition
system for use in the atmospheric and meteorological studies. The system was developed at the
NASA Mississippi Test Facility with the aid of
engineers and personnel provided by the MTF contractor, the General Electric Company. The basic
system was developed with off-shelf components
and excess aerospace assemblies and is designed
to be mounted in a light, single-engine aircraft
which will provide economical operation for small
scale investigations. In addition, the data acquisition and data processing facilities of the
NASA Mississippi Test Facility have been utilized
to the maximum in providing real time data processing and graphical and tabular presentations
of the experimental data.

The airborne data acquisition system is capable of handling 18 independent measurements in
its present configuration and the experimental
data may be telemetered directly to the data handling center at the NASA Mississippi Test Facility
or may be recorded on-board as the individual
situation requires. Most of the equipment utilized in the development of the data acquisition
system was performing service in another capacity
prior to its utilization in the data acquisition
system. The airborne data acquisition system
has been utilized in several experimental investigations involving the probing of rocket exhaust
plumes which are generated during the static firing of rocket engines, the probing of natural
cumulus clouds, and weather modification studies.
The ability of this system to accurately measure
the selected parameters has steadily improved to
a level found only in the most sophisticated of
airborne data acquisition systems currently available.

SYSTEM DEVELOPMENT

In developing the Airborne Data Acquisition
System (ADAS) it was desired to maximize the utilization of the data acquisition and data processing facilities at the NASA Mississippi Test Facility and also provide a system which could
operate independently of these facilities in the
data acquisition phase of an investigation.
These considerations lead to the development of
a ADAS with both on-board recording and telemetry

capabilities. In addition it was desired to develop a self-contained system which did not depend upon the aircraft power and flight systems. This feature provides for a more flexible system in that it can be installed in an aircraft with either 12 volt or 24 volt electrical systems and also it is easier to satisfy Federal Aviation Regulations (FAR's) governing the installation of the ADAS in an aircraft.

Design Criteria and Assumptions

In performing various atmospheric investigations, the researcher is presented with some basic requirements which must be satisfied. In reviewing these requirements the authors have employed the analogy of a "typical atmospheric research project" to delineate the class of experiments for which the use of the ADAS is intended and to present the major design criteria and assumptions. In addition it was necessary to develop the ADAS in a minimum time in order to support an active research program. The major specifications are listed below:

1. Adapt existing space technology and excess hardware for use in an Airborne Data Acquisition System.

2. Develop a working data acquisition system in a minimum time phase to take advantage of current atmospheric phenomenon.

3. Develop a system to collect a minimum of ten (10) parameters of data and be compact enough to be installed in a light, single-engine aircraft to allow:

   (a) Minimum disruption of natural cloud formations during penetrations.

   (b) Minimize overall cost by using small aircraft during sustained data collection.

4. Data to be collected must be compatible with National Data Center Standards for diversified processing capabilities and universal application of the resultant data.

5. Utilize both on-board recording and telemetry to minimize Loss of Signal (LOS) and provide "real time" digital data processing for rapid post-mission analysis.

6. Maximize utilization of existing facilities and capabilities at the Mississippi Test Facility with regard to support of Environmental Science Research Projects.

The initial measurement requirements were for ambient wet and dry bulb temperatures, liquid water content, aircraft airspeed, pressure altitude, relative humidity, event markers, and voice annotation during data collection. It was assumed that this airborne package would utilize data acquisition and data processing facilities at the Mississippi Test Facility for recording

and real time processing whenever possible and that normally the on-board recorder would provide back up capability. In some instances, however, the on-board analog recorder would provide the prime acquisition function and the recorded data would be processed later through available processing facilities.

HARDWARE DESCRIPTION

Much of the equipment utilized in the ADAS was performing prior service in another capacity before being selected for this application. The telemetry equipment obtained was an excess S-IV B, Saturn V, third stage rocket unit. The seven channel analog recorder, power supplies, signal conditioners, resistance bridges, and the various sensing devices were obtained from the MTF equipment pool. Other special devices such as the liquid water content unit and the cascade impactor were procured separately. All interface equipment, antennae hardware, sensor and transducer mounts, remote control and monitor panel, and the overall system configuration was designed especially for this application and fabricated at the Mississippi Test Facility.

Hardware Configuration

A detailed block diagram of the Airborne Data Acquisition System (ADAS) is shown in Figure 1. As denoted within the area marked, EXTERIOR MOUNTING, the liquid water content (LWC) pickup head, the wet and dry bulb thermistors, and the static and total pressure probes are mounted outside the aircraft. The static pressure drives the two 0-15 PSIA pressure transducers for the altitude measurement, and in addition, combine with the total pressure across the 0-5 PSID differential pressure transducers to provide aircraft airspeed. The output of the altitude transducers is 0-5VDC and is sent directly to the sub-carrier oscillators (SCO) of the T/M unit. Two dry bulb thermistors and two wet bulb thermistors with associated water reservoirs are mounted in the same aircraft location as the pressure devices. The thermistors are connected to the resistance bridge completion and calibration panel inside the aircraft. The signal output of the four bridge networks is 0-300 mv and requires signal conditioning, which is provided by the DC medium gain amplifier and the analog voltage output of 0-5 VDC is sent to the SCO's.

The liquid water content (LWC) pickup head, also located outside the aircraft, collects water droplets and deposits them on the heated surface of a temperature variable resistive wire. The greater the concentration of liquid water, the greater the cooling effect on the wire element, and this change in the wire resistance is measured as the difference in water content from a calibrated reference. The output voltage of 0-65 mv sent from the LWC control box to the DC medium gain amplifier for conditioning and from there to the SCO. The telemetry unit contains eighteen (18) sub-carrier oscillator units (SCO). Each FM channel is sufficiently separated from

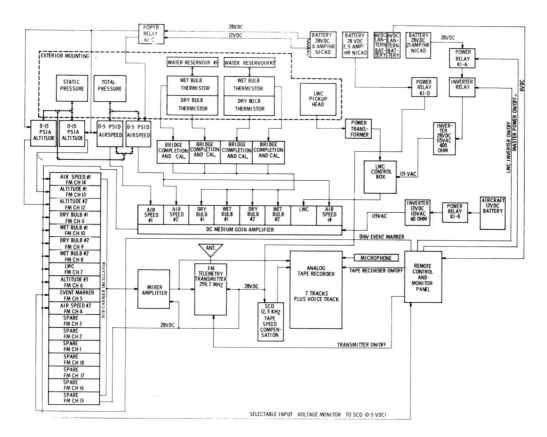

Figure 1.   Block Diagram of the Airborne Data Acquisition System

TABLE I

IRIG CONSTANT PERCENTAGE DEVIATION FREQUENCY SYSTEM

FM Channel No.	Center Frequency (Hz)	Deviation (Hz)	Lower Limit (Hz)	Upper Limit (Hz)	Maximum Deviation (percent)	Maximum Intelligence Frequency (Modulation Index 5) (Hz)
1	400	+30	370	430	+7.5	6.0
2	560	42	518	602	+7.5	8
3	730	55	675	785	+7.5	11
4	960	72	888	1,032	+7.5	14
5	1,300	98	1,202	1,399	+7.5	20
6	1,700	128	1,572	1,828	+7.5	25
7	2,300	173	2,127	2,473	+7.5	35
8	3,000	225	2,775	3,225	+7.5	45
9	3,900	293	3,607	4,193	+7.5	59
10	5,400	405	4,995	5,805	+7.5	81
11	7,350	551	6,799	7,901	+7.5	110
12	10,500	788	9,712	11,288	+7.5	160
13	14,500	1,088	13,412	15,588	+7.5	220
14	22,000	1,650	20,350	23,650	+7.5	330
15	30,000	2,250	27,750	32,250	+7.5	450
16	40,000	3,000	37,000	43,000	+7.5	600
17	52,500	3,940	48,562	56,438	+7.5	790
18	70,000	5,250	64,750	75,250	+7.5	1,050

the adjacent channels to eliminate cross modulation. The SCO performance data are shown in Table 1.

The output of the SCO's is sent to the mixer or summing amplifier, the output of which is a summation of the total inputs. The outputs of the mixer amplifier is then sent to both the FM telemetry transmitter and the analog seven track tape recorder. The transmitter sub-assembly which operates in this case at 259.7 MHz and is remotely controlled from the remote control and monitor panel, by the pilot, is connected to an antenna ($\frac{1}{4}$ wave length ground plane probe) mounted underneath the fuselage of the aircraft. This antenna provides E-plane coverage of 170 degrees and H-plane coverage of 360 degrees about a point 0.5 inches below the center of the underside of the fuselage. The telemetry transmitter as presently configured provides one (1) watt output into a fifty (50) ohm load. All measurement data available to the T/M unit is also provided to the on-board analog recorder. The analog seven track recorder operated in the direct mode has a frequency response of 100 Hz - 25 KHz with a 1 volt peak to peak input. With the present instrumentation recorder, the frequency response of the recorder limits the acquisition of reliable data to the first fourteen (14) channels. In addition to the seven (7) direct tracks, a side track is also provided for voice annotation of recorded data. Tape speed conpensation is provided through the use of a 12.5 KHz SCO signal directly recorded on a second recorder track and is used for synchronization when playing back the tape through a ground based recorder for data analysis.

The Remote Control and Monitor Panel mounted below the aircraft instrument panel provides pilot capability to control power application to the various subsystems through master power relay K-1. In addition to individual on/off control of the T/M transmitter output, LWC control box and analog recorder, this remote panel enables the pilot to insert event markers into the data stream for sequencing and timing and to monitor the input voltage signals into the SCO for the various measurements in operation. The Remote Control and Monitor Panel may be quickly installed or removed from the aircraft.

Since all of the equipment in this application was originally designed for other purposes, the power sources are also varied. The 115V 400 Hz power required by the LWC is provided by a 28VDC to 115V 400 Hz inverter and a 28 VDC NICAD battery. Individual 28 VDC NICAD batteries provide power for the entire telemetry unit, tape speed compensation and the static pressure and total pressure transducers; the latter obtaining 12 VDC through a voltage divider arrangement. The DC medium gain amplifier uses 115V, 60 Hz from a 115V/12V inverter and the aircraft 12 VDC battery. Obviously, additional design effort here have resulted in a much simpler and far lighter power package; however, since they still fell within the original weight considerations,

it was felt the redesign was not worth the increased cost and additional time required to do the job.

Modification of Equipment

Modifications to the aircraft to mount the ADAS unit and the sensors were only of a temporary nature and no structural modifications were required. The following temporary modifications were performed:

(a) Remote Control and Monitor Panel installed under instrument panel with cable connecting to ADAS behind pilot.

(b) Cascade Impactor pickup head installed in the existing storm window by the pilot's left side. Two hoses are connected to this head and provide passage for air samples.

(c) Under the left wing immediately aft of the landing gear a Liquid Water Pickup Head is installed using existing holes in the inspection plate. This unit is extended vertically downward for 10 inches and is connected by three #8 cables which run up and through the pilot left vent. These cables are taped to the exterior of the aircraft with a special metallic tape and carry approximately 1.75 volts.

(d) Under the right wing of the aircraft two WET/DRY Temperature Heads are enclosed in a special mount. This unit is mounted using existing inspection plate holes and extends vertically downward for 8 inches. These heads are electrically connected to carry resistance signals through #22 wire which is taped to the aircraft exterior and enters through the rear air vent on the right side on the aircraft.

All electronic equipment utilized in this application retains its original configuration and in some cases was only recalibrated to conform to different requirements. All interface equipment cabling, antenna hardware, sensor and transducer mounts and overall system configuration was designed and fabricated specifically for this application.

GENERAL DESCRIPTION OF THE ADAS

The assembled Airborne Data Acquisition System (ADAS) set up for a preflight bench checkout is shown in Figure 2. The ADAS consists of four primary equipment grouping: the signal source and signal conditioning equipment, on-board analog recording unit, RF telemetry package, and special power sources. The system is designed to operate as an integrated data acquisition system and will perform in the following configurations:

1. Telemetry configuration - acquired data telemetered to ground receiving station for recording on wideband tape and real time digital processing.

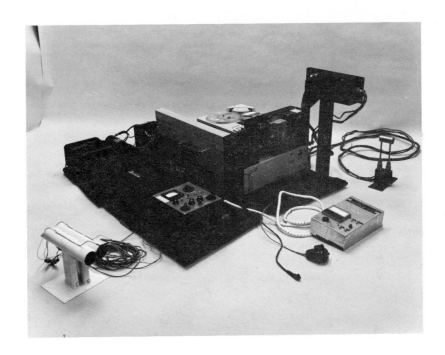

Figure 2. The Complete ADAS Unit and Related Sensors

Figure 3. Installation of the ADAS Unit in a Single Engine Aircraft

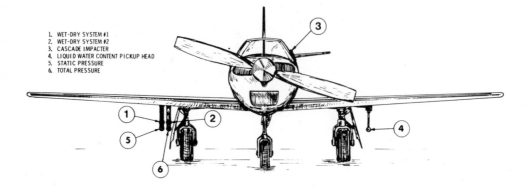

1. WET-DRY SYSTEM #1
2. WET-DRY SYSTEM #2
3. CASCADE IMPACTER
4. LIQUID WATER CONTENT PICKUP HEAD
5. STATIC PRESSURE
6. TOTAL PRESSURE

Figure 4. Schematic of Sensor Mounting Locations on the Aircraft

Figure 5. Photograph of Piper PA-24 Aircraft with ADAS Unit and Sensors Installed

2. On-board recorder configuration - acquired data is recorded direct on analog tape from output of mixer amplifier. Data tapes are later removed from the aircraft and processed through a ground data handling center.

3. Standard configuration - using both telemetry and on-board analog recorder simultaneously when measuring atmospheric phenomena.

The compactness of this ADAS is exemplified by Figure 3 showing the unit installed in a Piper Commanche (PA-24-250). In the upper foreground (1) is the FM telemetry transmitter unit with SCO's and mixer amplifier: In the lower foreground (2) is the DC medium gain signal conditioner amplifiers; and in the rear (3), the analog seven track recorder the left panel (4) mounts resistance bridges and calibration, control and interface patching. The special power supplies are floor mounted to the rear of this assembly. Not shown on this photograph is the remote power and control switches and the signal monitor display mounted under the aircraft control panel, enabling the entire unit to be controlled by the pilot. The installation locations of the various externally mounted sensing devices are shown in Figures 4 and 5. The complete ADAS is capable of being installed by two men in a single engine aircraft with sensors mounted outside the aircraft and calibration and ground checks completed, within five hours. The entire electronics package, including power sources, is securely mounted on a 3/4 inch thick plywood floor measuring 45 x 48 inches. The overall dimensions of the electronics package is 25 x 27 inches and is 14 inches high. The total weight of the ADAS including all equipment and sensors is slightly less than two hundred fifty (250) pounds. The DC batteries are mounted in spill-proof canisters.

The floor is installed in the aircraft with four (4) number 12 bolts which attach to the seat mounting brackets and one (1) number 12 bolt which attaches into the rear cargo hold-down bracket. The floor installation conforms to Federal Aviation Administration recommended procedures.

The complete ADAS installation has been approved by the FAA and the aircraft is certificated in the RESTRICTED category and operated according to FAR 91.39 (operating limitations for restricted category civil aircraft). When the ADAS system is removed from the aircraft, it may be operated in the NORMAL category. This feature is extremely attractive to researchers who can not afford to support an instrumented aircraft in that it permits installation of the ADAS in a leased aircraft which can be used for short-term investigations.

AIRBORNE OPERATIONS

Initial Flight Tests

Flight tests were conducted during the spring of 1970 at the NASA Mississippi Test Fa-

cility to test the operation of the ADAS and the quality of telemetry data received and processed by the MTF Data Handling Center. Numerous data runs were made at various times to flight check, calibrate and establish operating characteristics of the individual measurements. Extensive data collection was performed on rocket exhaust plumes during the static firings of the Saturn V, first and second stage booster rockets at MTF. Pre- and post- test calibrations were run between the aircraft and the Data Handling Center to establish reliability and accuracy of data acquired during static firing measurements.

As with any new system, minor problems developed in the early phases of operation but all were systematically eliminated. That they were minor in nature and short lived was due in no small part to the quality of equipment utilized and the ability of the technical personnel involved.

General Mission

Prior to an airborne mission, the ADAS is bench checked and calibrated in the laboratory, and the calibrations and operational characteristics are checked after installation of the ADAS in the aircraft. In most cases, it takes approximately one hour to warm-up and ground check the unit.

On a particular mission the pilot may elect 1) to transmit the data by telemetry to the MTF Data Handling Center or another ground station; 2) to use only the on-board analog recorder; or 3) to use both concurrently during the sampling operations.

Since the altitude and airspeed of the aircraft usually varies during the mission, it is customary to conduct both pre- and post-test airborne calibrations. The aircraft is usually flown at a minimum of three altitudes and three airspeeds which assures a typical range of the variables being monitored. These calibration data are used in conjunction with the laboratory calibration data for the various transducers to obtain the corrected data.

PROCESSING OF AIRBORNE DATA

Utilization of the MTF Data Handling Center (DHC) for processing of the airborne data has proved to be significantly advantageous both from the standpoint of accuracy of the results and the speed of data reduction. For missions conducted within about 100 statute miles of the NASA Mississippi Test Facility, the acquired data are usually telemetered to the MTF/DHC for real time processing and the analog recorder is used as a back up system. When missions are conducted which require the use of the analog recorder as the prime means of data acquisition, the analog tapes can be processed at either the MTF/DHC or other equivalent facilities. The methods of processing data from both types of missions are discussed in the following paragraphs.

The MTF/DHC has the capability to receive, condition, and record the data from a FM system using an analog receiving station and a Scientific Data System SDS-930 digital computer system. The FM signal is received via an antenna mounted on the roof of the DHC and the signal is patched to a FM receiver. The output of the receiver is fed into a patching matrix where the data can be simultaneously or independently presented to an analog recorder and/or to the digital acquisition system. The digital acquisition system performs the same function whether or not the signal is presented real time or from an analog tape playback. When the analog recorder is used as the means of data acquisition, the analog tapes are fed directly into the digital acquisition system at the time of processing. The remainder of the data reduction process is identical to that used for the telemetered data.

The digital acquisition system, under software control, selects the desired signal and routes it through a switching matrix to a bank of IRIG discriminators. Each discriminator has a set of IRIG filters specifically matching the center frequency of the IRIG SCO's in the FM transmitter. The discriminator, therefore, converts a given IRIG frequency to a corresponding DC voltage output. The output of each discriminator is patched to one of the inputs of a 15 channel multiplexer. The multiplexer may be selected to scan the inputs such that all inputs are sampled at 10, 100, or 1000 samples-per-second each.

The output of the 15 channel multiplexer is routed to an analog-to-digital converter where a conversion takes the form of:

0% input =	-10,000 counts
25% input =	- 5,000 counts
50% input =	0 counts
75% input =	+ 5,000 counts
100% input =	+10,000 counts

The output of the A/D converter together with time-of-day, test serial number, day-month-year, and other fixed data are buffered into the computer. The computer writes the data onto tape in a raw digital format. Simultaneously, if requested, the computer will apply the conversion coefficients contained on the calibration tape to ten or less measurements and output them in engineering units to the line printer. The real time tabs permit immediate results to be made available to the user. They can also be used as a method of signal conditioning and SCO calibration when performed end-to-end using real time tabs and voice communication between the Data Handling Center and airborne FM transmitter.

The data acquisition software consists of several programs that are called in and executed sequentially. Each program performs a unique function in the run stream which results in a raw digital tape containing header records describing the measurements and their relative locations inside each digital record on tape. Also contained

in the header records are the correction coefficients derived from the pre-acquisition discriminator calibrations, post-acquisition discriminator calibrations and an average of the two.

The data acquisition may be from wideband tape or real time. For wideband tape playback, the computer sends the desired start/stop time to the tape search equipment and waits for the interrupts from the tape search equipment. The tape search equipment starts the tape in motion and searches the tape (either forward or reverse) for the requested start time. Upon reaching this point the search equipment starts the tape forward in a search slow mode and upon reaching the exact start time requested issues a reproduce interrupt to the computer. The computer will continue to acquire data until the exact stop time requested is reached and the tape search equipment issues a stop interrupt to the computer.

The real time acquisition mode is identical to the tape search mode except the start/stop interrupts are generated by an operator via switches located on the master control console. Should the computer be performing real time tabs and recording tape simultaneously, the tabs may be stopped and started at an operator's discretion using the ready switch on the line printer and without interfering with the digital tape recording.

Following data acquisition, the first step toward achieving meaningful data reduction is the generation of an engineering units (EU) tape which is as free as possible of system errors introduced by SCO or ground station errors. The Data Handling Center performs this function using a program which accepts control cards describing the type of corrections to be applied to the data while converting to engineering units using the transducer calibration coefficients contained on the cal tape generated from the information supplied by the user. The options for FM are inflight corrections, pre discriminator calibration correction, post discriminator calibration corrections or an average of the pre and post cals.

The program then reads the raw digital tape, applies the requested correction coefficients, applies the transducer conversion and writes out a new tape called an engineering units (EU) tape. The engineering units tape contains header records describing the measurement number, relative location within each record, T/M assignment, high and low range and EU code identifier (i.e., DEGS FAH, PSIA, etc.). Following the header records are the data records. Engineering units are represented as a percent of data range for each measurement.

The two basic modes for displaying final data are tabulations (either lineprinter or 4020 plotter) and X-Y plots (either direct develop output or 35mm film and Xerox hardcopies). The tabulation program has many options such as tab all points, averages, floating limits, fixed limits, etc., and the X-Y plot program has varied uses that can be designated to meet particular requirements.

APPLICATION OF THE ADAS TO ENVIRONMENTAL SCIENCE INVESTIGATIONS

The ADAS has been used to obtain data in several environmental science investigations. Included in these investigations have been probings of the exhaust plume generated during the static firing of rocket engines, mapping of micro-meteorological conditions in the vicinity of a weather station, and delineation of the structure of natural clouds under various meteorological conditions.

The ADAS was designed primarily to acquire data related to the growth and dissipation of rocket exhaust plumes which are generated during the static firing of the S-IC and S-II rocket engines. These rocket engines, which comprise the first and second stage boosters on the Apollo V system, are captive fired at the NASA Mississippi Test Facility prior to being employed in a manned space flight.

The exhaust cloud or plume generated during the static firing has many characteristics which resemble a natural cloud and considerable interest has been exhibited toward the possibility of using this isolated cloud as a well defined model for weather modification research. These interests are directed at both the modification of precipitation and electro-static discharge in natural clouds and thunderstorms. In addition, the exhaust cloud could cause an air pollution problem in the event toxic additives are used in the propellants and it was desired to determine the diffusion characteristics of the exhaust plume of various rocket engines under various meteorological conditions. In each case it was necessary to have information on the physical characteristics of the exhaust plume.

The ADAS has been installed in a Piper PA-24-250 aircraft and has been flown through both the S-IC and S-II exhaust clouds. Penetrations have been made at altitudes ranging from 3,000 feet to 8,000 feet on the S-II cloud (maximum height 10-12,000 feet) and 8,000 to 14,000 feet on the S-IC cloud (maximum height 12-20,000 feet). On a typical mission six to ten passes are made through the cloud to determine the wet and dry bulb temperature profiles, the liquid water content, the relative humidity distribution, and the distribution of particulate matter and tracer materials.

During the exhaust cloud penetrations, large vertical velocities are encountered which cause

the aircraft to ascend and descend when flown at near constant airspeed. The temperature changes associated with the altitude changes tend to mask the trend of the temperature distribution within the cloud. However, since the pre and post calibration data are available to the computer it is possible to establish a temperature-altitude correlation and non-dimensionalize the local temperature with respect to the ambient temperature at the respective altitude. In this manner it is possible to obtain a more realistic representation of the temperature variation through the exhaust cloud. If the calibration data was not stored on the acquisition tape, the preceding operation would require a separate computer run. In a similar manner other corrections and special data operations may be performed at the time the raw data are originally processed.

The investigations on the effect of various meteorological conditions on the structure of natural clouds was conducted in approximately the same manner as for the rocket exhaust clouds. The primary difference in the nature of the operations was that the natural cloud missions often extended over 3-5 hour periods and over geographical locations up to 100-150 miles apart. In these cases it was desirable to recalibrate for each particular cloud probe, which would typically require 5-10 penetrations. The handling of such voluminous calibrations would be very difficult if manually recovered, but are expeditiously processed by computed and significantly increase the reliability of the output.

CONCLUDING REMARKS

The Airborne Data Acquisition System discussed herein, represents a unique application of aerospace technology and excess hardware to problems in the environmental sciences. The development of the ADAS has provided an economical means of obtaining atmospheric and meteorological data using a light single engine aircraft. The system can be installed in the aircraft and ground calibrated with less than ten man-hours of effort. The maximum telemetry range of the ADAS is unknown; however, missions have been conducted as far as 100 miles from the ground receiver station and at altitudes of about 1,000 feet MSL.

The utilization of the data processing facilities at the NASA Mississippi Test Facility in conjunction with the airborne data acquisition missions has provided a real-time data processing capability which is extremely valuable for basic research investigations and programs which involve the evaluation and development of sensors and sampling techniques.

NONPOLLUTING CENTRAL POWER STATIONS*

F. L. Robson and A. J. Giramonti
United Aircraft Research Laboratories
East Hartford, Connecticut 06108

Abstract

Advanced-cycle power systems based upon aero-space technology developed for use in aircraft gas turbines have the potential of lowering the cost of base-load electric utility power while reducing the emissions of sulfur oxides from fossil-fueled power stations by over 90% compared to conventional stations. An additional benefit of reducing thermal pollution of water by 50% would also be achieved.

Currently, electric utilities emit nearly half of the total sulfur oxides in our atmosphere. At present, effort to control these emissions has been concentrated on methods of treating the stack gas after combustion. These methods have proven to be both costly and unreliable. An alternate method of reducing sulfur oxide emissions would be to remove the sulfur from the fossil fuels before combustion. The processes which would convert the fuel and desulfurize it to levels which would comply with increasingly more stringent air pollution regulations are expensive. However the desulfurized fuels would be suitable for use in advanced-cycle power systems which could operate at efficiencies significantly higher than projected for conventional steam power systems; thus the cost of producing electric power could continue its historical pattern of decrease.

One of the most promising advanced-cycle power systems consists of a combined gas turbine-steam turbine (COGAS) system in which the hot exhaust of the gas turbine is used to raise steam in an unfired waste-heat recovery boiler. The gas turbine used in this system would be an evolution of current turbomachinery and would utilize aero-dynamic and blade cooling concepts and blade materials which are now used or proposed for use in advanced aircraft gas turbines. Approximately two-thirds of the power output would come from the gas turbine and one-third from the steam turbine.

Using technology judged to be available by 1980, the COGAS system could achieve overall station efficiencies of approximately 55%, with the potential of even higher efficiencies with more advanced technology. Conventional fossil-fuel steam stations currently have station efficiencies of approximately 38%, and projections for future steam stations indicate only minor increases.

In order to establish the commercial viability of the COGAS system operating in conjunction with the fuel desulfurization system, the cost of producing electric power must be determined. Thus, this paper describes an economic analysis of the entire advanced-cycle power system, including fuel processing plant. The results indicate that the cost of power at the station busbar can be reduced by as much as 15% in comparison with the cost of power from projected conventional steam power stations. At the same time, stack emissions of sulfur oxides can be substantially eliminated.

Introduction

The combustion of coal and residual oil by the electric power generation industry in the United States contributes nearly 50% of the more than 30 million tons of sulfur oxides annually emitted.[1] Currently, extensive effort is being expended to devise methods of removing these sulfur oxides from the power station effluent. While some of these stack gas cleaning methods show promise in reducing the emissions of pollutants, the performance and economy of the power station are usually compromised. An alternative method of reducing the emission of sulfur oxides involves the removal of sulfur from the coal or residual oil before combustion. To do this would require relatively complex and expensive fuel conversion and desulfurization equipment which would result in a significant increase in the cost of fuel delivered to the power generating system. In order to offset this increased fuel cost, the thermal efficiency of electric power generation should be increased by using advanced-cycle power systems based upon the adaptation of aerospace technology to industrial use.

Under the auspices of the National Air Pollution Control Administration and with subcontracting assistance of Burns and Roe, Inc. and FMC Corp., a study was carried out by the United Aircraft Research Laboratories on the technical and economic feasibility of desulfurizing coal and residual fuel oil for use in advanced-cycle power systems suitable for use by the electric power industry. The results of this study indicate that power systems incorporating advanced-design industrial gas turbines used in combination with steam turbines

---

* The following abstract describes a portion of a study carried out under Department of Health, Education, and Welfare Contract CPA-22-69-114.

(COGAS systems) offer the potential of generating power at costs significantly less than those presently encountered or projected for future steam stations even though COGAS systems must burn costly, desulfurized fuels.

Aerospace Gas Turbine Technology

The majority of industrial gas turbines now being manufactured are based upon technology initially developed for industrial compressors and steam turbines. These machines are rugged and very heavy. On the other hand, aircraft-type gas turbines are generally designed for high power density, light weight, quick startup capability, and short installation time. However, the existing differences between design philosophies for these two classes of gas turbines will diminish as a result of continuing efforts to improve thermal efficiency of industrial gas turbines.

By adapting recent, and continuing, advances in aerospace technology to industrial turbomachinery, substantially improved large capacity, simple-cycle gas turbine power systems with appreciably higher thermal efficiencies could result, leading to their widespread use in base-load power generation applications. These advances in aerospace technology were achieved during extensive research and development efforts on military and commercial aircraft gas turbines and include improvements in materials technology, blade cooling techniques, aerodynamic flow path design, high-heat-release burners, and modular fabrication techniques.

While meaningful improvements in aerodynamic performance are projected for future gas turbines (from 88% to 93% compressor polytropic efficiency and from 87% to 92% turbine adiabatic efficiency), the most significant increases in gas turbine performance will result from increases in turbine inlet temperature. These increased temperatures will be a direct result of improvements in materials and blade cooling techniques.

Advanced Materials

In current aircraft gas turbines extensive use is made of nickel-base alloys in the hot turbine sections. Casting alloys such as B-1900 and Inco IN-100 have superior thermal fatigue characteristics when used for turbine blades. By proper heat treatment it appears that formation of the troublesome sigma phase can be avoided[2,3] so that these alloys will be suitable for long lifetime service that would be expected of base-load machinery, i.e., approximately 100,000-hr lifetime.

Turbine blade materials for the second-generation gas turbines (available during the 1980's) will include nickel-base alloys and modified B-1900 A and unidirectionally solidified eutectic alloys such as Ni_3Al-Ni_3Cb[4] currently

under development for advanced high-temperature aircraft turbines. Although an accurate prediction of third-generation (1990's) materials properties is difficult, it is reasonable to assume that chromium- and columbium-type materials currently being investigated will be used. The predicted long-term creep-strength characteristics for the three generations of advanced turbine-blade materials are shown in Fig. 1.

FIGURE 1

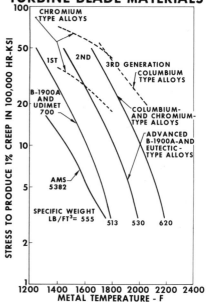

CREEP STRENGTH FOR ADVANCED TURBINE BLADE MATERIALS

Coatings for blades and vanes such as the aluminum-base Type UC (developed by the Chromalloy Corp.) and Jo-Coat, while having lifetimes of only several thousand hours in aircraft applications, could be modified for use on advanced industrial turbines to meet the much longer lifetime requirements.[5] Also, recent progress in the ability to coat columbium-base alloys may allow their usage by the third-generation time period.

Advanced Turbine Cooling Techniques

Currently, only the first-stage vanes and disks of industrial gas turbines are cooled. This cooling is presently accomplished by means of air extracted from the compressor and injected directly into the turbine sections to be cooled. It will be necessary to cool successive stages of blades and vanes if long-life operation at high turbine inlet temperature is to be realized.

Aircraft turbine cooling systems have progressed from simple convective cooling configurations to advanced convective designs utilizing impingement cooling of the inside of the leading edge as typified in Fig. 2. The cooling air enters the central cavity of the impingement-convection-cooled blade. The blade tip is capped so that the cooling air must flow from the cavity through a series of orifices that cause the air to impinge upon the inside surface of the leading edge. After cooling the leading edge, the air then enters small finned passages extending chordwise through the mid-chord region of the blade. The cooling air is finally ejected from the extreme trailing edge into the gas stream.

FIGURE 2

ADVANCED BLADE COOLING CONFIGURATIONS FOR AIRCRAFT POWERPLANTS

IMPINGEMENT–CONVECTION   TRANSPIRATION COOLED

The use of advanced impingement-convection cooling techniques should allow second-generation base-load turbine operation at turbine inlet temperatures as high as 2400 F. Another cooling technique that could be used is film cooling, in

which air from the hollow core of the blade would be injected through slots in the blade wall to form a layer of coolant which acts like an insulating blanket over the surfaces to be protected. Transpiration cooling, another advanced cooling technique in which cooling air passes through porous blade material, could be used to achieve third-generation turbine inlet temperatures approaching 3000 F.

Adaptation of Aerospace Technology to Industrial Gas Turbines

The combination of advanced materials and cooling techniques will allow significant increases in turbine inlet temperatures. These increases are depicted in Fig. 3, in which turbine inlet temperature is shown as a function of time. These high operating temperatures will lead to gas turbines with high performance and increased output per engine.

FIGURE 3

TURBINE INLET TEMPERATURE PROGRESSION FOR BASE-LOAD OPERATION

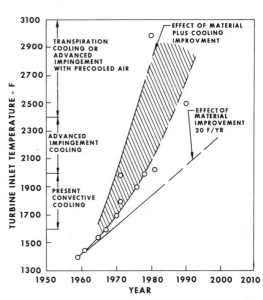

Performance

A parametric performance map for industrial gas turbines based on projected second-generation aerospace technology is presented in Fig. 4. The performance estimates presented in this figure are based on usage of a low-Btu fuel derived by gasification of coal or residual fuel oil. Such a low-Btu fuel would consist mainly of CO, H_2, and N_2 and

31

FIGURE 4

SECOND-GENERATION BASE-LOAD
SIMPLE-CYCLE GAS TURBINE PERFORMANCE

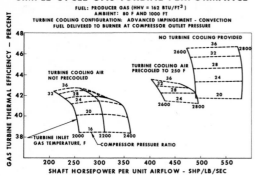

FUEL: PRODUCER GAS (HHV = 162 BTU/FT³)
AMBIENT: 80 F AND 1000 FT
TURBINE COOLING CONFIGURATION: ADVANCED IMPINGEMENT - CONVECTION
FUEL DELIVERED TO BURNER AT COMPRESSOR OUTLET PRESSURE

have a higher heating value of approximately 162 Btu/ft³, compared to 1000 Btu/ft³ for natural gas. The sulfur content of the gasified fuel would be approximately one-hundredth of that of the raw fuel. This gaseous, desulfurized fuel would be quite suitable for use as fuel in high-temperature gas turbines. Since gasification processes operate most economically at elevated pressure, the low-Btu fuel gas would be supplied to the gas turbine burners at the pressure corresponding to the gas turbine compressor pressure ratio. The nitrogen contained in the fuel gas would essentially displace excess air normally compressed by the compressor resulting in reduced compressor work, increased net gas turbine power, and a 2 to 3 point efficiency advantage compared to gas turbines burning a high-Btu fuel.

The performance estimates presented in the left portion of Fig. 4 incorporate the same cooling techniques that would be employed in aircraft engines, i.e., air bled from the main compressor would be used directly for cooling the hot turbine parts. Stationary industrial engines have an advantage over aircraft engines in that the cooling air bled from the compressor, which is typically at 700 to 1000 F, could be taken external to the engine and precooled to the 150 to 250 F range. Two advantages of precooling become apparent: (1) for a given bleed flow rate, a higher turbine inlet temperature could be attained, and (2) for a given turbine inlet temperature, less bleed flow would be required. In either case, the amount of useful work output by the gas turbine per lb of inlet air would be increased.

The improved performance made possible by precooling the bleed air is also shown in Fig. 4. With no precooling, the maximum temperature attainable, commensurate with reasonable lifetimes, would be approximately 2400 F. This would allow a maximum efficiency of about 42% and a corres-

ponding specific work of about 300 hp/lb air/sec. Specific work indicates the physical size of the turbomachinery and, thus, is a guide to machine costs. By precooling the bleed air to 250 F, 2800 F could be attained with an efficiency of nearly 44%. More importantly, the specific work would be increased by over 50% to about 460 hp/lb/sec.

If materials could be developed to withstand high turbine inlet temperatures without cooling, the performance map at the far right of Fig. 4 would result. These estimates represent the theoretical limit of performance.

Unit Size

The increase in specific work allows very high power outputs from turbomachinery of relatively modest dimensions. Thus, unit outputs of 200 Mw and above could be realized from machines handling approximately 1000 lb/sec of air and having maximum diameters of the order of 10 ft. The general size of a projected 250-Mw gas turbine is given in Fig. 5.

FIGURE 5

250-MW BASE-LOAD GAS TURBINE

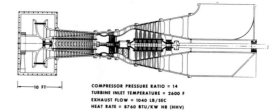

COMPRESSOR PRESSURE RATIO = 14
TURBINE INLET TEMPERATURE = 2600 F
EXHAUST FLOW = 1040 LB/SEC
HEAT RATE = 8760 BTU/KW HR (HHV)

COGAS Power Systems

While the performance of industrial gas turbines incorporating aerospace technology could be significantly better than presently attainable, power system efficiencies could be further improved if the large amount of high grade heat in the gas turbine exhaust could be recovered. A schematic diagram of a COGAS power system that recovers the exhaust heat by raising steam is shown in Fig. 6. If high-temperature gas turbines were used in such a system, gas turbine exit temperature would be over 1100 F so that 1000-F, 2400-psi steam could be raised for use in a steam turbine without firing the boiler. The gas turbine would supply approximately 60% of the total system power.

Presently, the only large-capacity, base-load COGAS power systems operating in the United States are of the exhaust-fired type, i.e., the gas turbine serves as an air preheater with additional fuel being burned in the boiler[7,8] While the

COMBINED GAS-STEAM TURBINE SYSTEM

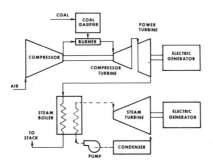

PERFORMANCE OF EXHAUST-FIRED COMBINED SYSTEM

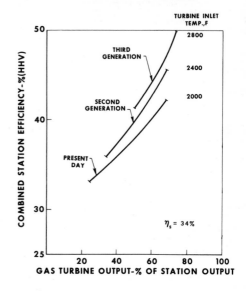

efficiencies of these systems are higher than for conventional steam systems, their size is limited by the air handling capacity of current industrial gas turbines. Thus, very large (over 500-Mw) COGAS units would be impractical because of the number of gas turbines required. Since the gas turbine exit temperature for these systems is relatively low (750 F to 900 F), exhaust firing in the boiler is required in order to obtain good steam conditions.

The performance of such existing systems is limited, however, since the heat added to raise steam is utilized only at the steam cycle efficiency, whereas the heat added in the gas turbine is utilized at the combined cycle efficiency. Thus, maximum cycle efficiency would be expected when all the heat added to the cycle is added in the gas turbine. This is shown in Fig. 7 where power system efficiency, including all auxiliary loads and generator losses, is shown as a function of gas turbine participation. At the left or lower end of the curves, the gas turbine participation is small, i.e., the system is exhaust fired to the limit set by the available oxygen in the turbine exhaust. As turbine participation increases (firing decreases) the system efficiency increases until a maximum is reached at the point where there is no exhaust firing. This occurs at approximately 60% to 70% gas turbine participation. The performance shown in Fig. 7 is based upon the use of non-precooled bled air in the gas turbine and a 34% efficient steam cycle.

Gas Turbine Characteristics

In order to raise high grade steam from the turbine exhaust alone, high exhaust temperatures are required. The pressure ratio of gas turbines for COGAS use would be appreciably less than for straight gas turbines at the same turbine inlet temperature. Some of the more important characteristics of the gas turbine portion of a nominal 1000-Mw COGAS power system are given in Table 1 for three generations of technology.

Steam System Characteristics

It is current practice in conventional steam plants to operate at steam conditions of 2400 to 3500 psi with 1000 F throttle and 1000 F reheat. By using several stages of regenerative feedwater heating, steam cycle efficiencies (exclusive of boiler losses) of nearly 45% can be obtained. A steam system recovering heat from a turbine exhaust would not have regenerative feedwater heating since it would be more efficient to use low-grade heat in the stack gases to heat the feedwater. A 2400 psi/1000 F/1000 F steam system having a nominal cycle efficiency of 40% was selected for use in the COGAS system. Characteristics of this system are given in Table 2.

Trade-off studies relating system performance to boiler cost indicate that a 40 in. H_2O boiler pressure drop would result in the most cost effective system. Characteristics of the heat recovery boiler are also given in Table 2.

COGAS System Performance

The projected performance of the three generations of COGAS systems is shown in Fig. 8, in which the power system efficiency, including all losses except those in the fuel conversion system, and the system specific output are given. The choice of pressure ratio would be based upon a balance between efficiency and specific power, i.e., between operating costs and capital costs. As can

TABLE 1

SELECTED CHARACTERISTICS OF GAS TURBINE PORTIONS OF COGAS POWER SYSTEMS

	First Generation	Second Generation	Third Generation
Number of Gas Turbines	3	2	2
Nominal Output Per Gas Turbine, Mw	193	314	348
Number of Spools	1	1	2
Compressor Pressure Ratio	8	12	20
Turbine Inlet Temperature, F	2200	2800	3100
Turbine Cooling Air Temperature, F	200	200	200
Compressor Exit Temperature, F	582	691	861
Exhaust Gas Temperature, F	1297	1514	1485
Compressor Airflow, lb/sec	1110	999	810
Exhaust Gas Flow, lb/sec	1292	1268	1063
Bleed for Turbine Cooling, % of Airflow	4.71	8.54	9.0
Gas Generator Length, ft	20.9	15.3	15.1
Power Turbine Length, ft	12.4	11.4	10.7
Overall Engine Length*, ft	33.3	26.7	25.8
Inlet Diameter, ft	9.6	8.3	7.7
Combustor Diameter, ft	9.4	7.8	6.6
Power Turbine Exit Diameter, ft	11.3	11.0	10.4
Number of Exhaust Ends	1	1	1
Exit Axial Velocity, ft/sec	850	850	800
Power Turbine Rotational Speed, rpm	1800	1800	1800
Power Turbine Back Pressure, in. H_2O gauge	40	40	40

* From compressor inlet stage to power turbine exit stage

TABLE 2

SELECTED CHARACTERISTICS OF STEAM PORTIONS OF COGAS POWER SYSTEMS

	First Generation	Second Generation	Third Generation
Steam Turbine			
Number of Turbines	1	1	1
Nominal Output, Mw	431	381	312
Type	TC-DF	TC-DF	TC-DF
Throttle Temperature, F	1000	1000	1000
Throttle Pressure, psig	2400	2400	2400
Throttle Flow, thousand lb/hr	2413	2136	1750
Reheat Temperature, F	1000	1000	1000
Reheat Pressure, psig	569	569	569
Reheat Flow, thousand lb/hr	2382	2109	1728
Heat Recovery Boiler			
Boiler Inlet Gas Pressure, in. H_2O gauge	40	40	40
Feedwater Temperature to Boiler, F	132	145	159
Secondary Superheater Inlet Gas Temperature, F	1297	1514	1485
Secondary Superheater Duty, million Btu/hr	301.0	266.5	218.3
Secondary Superheater Surface Area, ft^2	43,361	23,810	20,596
Reheater Inlet Gas Temperature, F	1222	1416	1390
Reheater Duty, million Btu/hr	467.9	414.3	339.3
Reheater Surface Area, ft^2	79,399	44,598	38,423
Primary Superheater Inlet Gas Temperature, F	1104	1262	1240
Primary Superheater Duty, Million Btu/hr	652.2	577.4	472.9
Primary Superheater Surface Area, ft^2	121,122	71,312	61,718
Vaporizer Inlet Gas Temperature, F	937	1043	1027
Vaporizer Duty, Million Btu/hr	734.1	650.0	532.3
Vaporizer Surface Area, ft^2	261,314	148,033	127,907
Economizer Inlet Gas Temperature, F	745	788	780
Economizer Duty, Million Btu/hr	1577.9	1369.8	1096.5
Economizer Surface Area, ft^2	720,629	796,233	623,188
Final Stack Temperature, F	314	219	241

FIGURE 8

PERFORMANCE OF UNFIRED WASTE-HEAT COMBINED CYCLE

FUEL - 162 BTU/FT³ GAS SUPPLIED AT BURNER PRESSURE AND 150 F
STEAM CYCLE - 2400 PSIG/1000 F/1000 F, EFFICIENCY = 38.8%

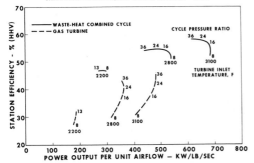

be seen in Fig. 8, the efficiency remains nearly constant over a range of pressure ratios so that the pressure ratio giving maximum specific output on the essentially flat portion of the curve would be selected. As indicated in Table 1, pressure ratios of 8, 12, and 20 were selected for turbine inlet temperatures of 2200 F, 2800 F, and 3100 F, respectively. The corresponding COGAS system efficiencies at these temperatures are about 47%, 55%, and 58%, respectively. Also shown in Fig. 8 are the efficiencies of straight gas turbines operating at similar conditions. The advantages in efficiency due to the heat recovery system are readily apparent.

Power System Economics

Historically, the electric power industry has striven to reduce the cost of producing power. This is evidenced by the fact that the busbar cost of power has been reduced significantly over the decades. It is projected[6] that a conventional coal-fired 1000-Mw station could have busbar power costs (with 20¢/million Btu fuel) of 6.23 mills/kwhr, 5.76 mills/kwhr, and 5.71 mills/kwhr for the first-, second-, and third-generation time periods, respectively, thus continuing the historical trend. However, the addition of stack gas cleanup methods to abate sulfur oxide emissions and recent increases in the price of coal would add to this cost.

The busbar cost of power is the annual owning and operating expenses divided by the annual kwhr generated. The annual owning costs include the capital charges due to interest, taxes, insurance, and depreciation (equal to approximately 14% of the plant capital cost), and the operating costs include maintenance, supplies, and fuel. The fuel cost for a conventional coal-fired station operating at 70% load factor is in the range of 1.7 to 1.9 mills/kwhr for fuel at 20¢/million, a reasonable 1968-69 cost of coal at a mine-mouth location. However, the fuel cost for the COGAS power station

---

must include the cost of converting the fuel to a gas, desulfurizing the gas to levels that could meet sulfur oxide abatement regulations, compression of air required for the gasifier, and supplying steam and other utilities for the fuel conversion process.

Fuel Cost

The fuel processing system consists of coal handling equipment, gasification vessels, heat recovery equipment, desulfurization and sulfur recovery equipment along with their associated piping and controls, air compression, and other miscellaneous equipment. The cost of fuels delivered to the COGAS power system must include capital charges for this equipment as well as the cost of the raw fuel and other operating and maintenance expenses.

It has been estimated[6] that the capital cost of the fuel conversion system for a second-generation (1980's) 1000-Mw power station would be about $28/kw, equivalent to approximately 0.64 mills/kwhr at a 14% per year capital charge. Maintenance and other operating costs would be the equivalent of 0.27 mills/kwhr*, while the cost of the raw fuel would be 1.44 mills/kwhr giving a total fuel cost of 2.35 mills/kwhr, or approximately one-third more than the projected cost of fuel for a conventional 1980 steam station[6].

Power System Cost

The capital cost of the power system can be broken down into two main parts, the direct costs for equipment which are based on Federal Power Commission Account Numbers, and the indirect costs such as engineering, construction supervision, interest during construction, and escalation. The indirect costs are a function of the plant construction time which is nominally four years for conventional steam stations and as much as eight years for nuclear stations. Because the gas turbines described herein would be shop assembled and modular construction would be used for the waste-heat recovery boiler, construction time for a COGAS system could be reduced to three years or less, thus substantially reducing the station cost.

The estimated capital costs for a 1000-Mw second-generation conventional steam station and a COGAS power system are given in Table 3. The total direct COGAS station cost of $66.8 million is approximately half of that projected for a conventional coal-fired station ($111.4 million), and the total installed cost of $99/kw is nearly $64/kw less than estimated for the conventional steam plant.

The major reason for the significant reduction in costs is that about 60% of the power output would be by gas turbines which are less expensive than steam systems. Also, because of the compactness of the gas turbine, appreciable savings

---

* A sulfur recovery credit of $25 per long ton is
  included in this figure.

TABLE 3

CAPITAL AND OPERATING COSTS FOR 1980-DESIGN POWER STATIONS

1000-Mw Nominal Output

Federal Power Commission Acct. No.	Description	Conventional Steam	COGAS
		(Capital Costs, Thousand Dollars)	
310 or 340	Land and Land Rights	225	225
311 or 341	Structures and Improvements	9,108	7,743
343	Prime Movers (gas turbine)	--	15,329
344	Electric Generators (for gas turbine)	--	5,960
312	Steam Generator Equipment	55,492	14,200
314	Steam Turbine-Generator Equipment	34,612	14,568
315 or 345	Accessory Electrical Equipment	10,138	5,626
316 or 346	Miscellaneous Powerplant Equipment	463	293
353	Station Equipment	1,572	1,609
	Other Expenses	1,250	1,250
Total Direct Cost		111,415	66,803
	Engineering, Design, Construction Supervision	13,236	10,590
	Escalation During Construction	18,570	7,449
	Interest During Construction	18,203	9,163
Total Installed Powerplant Cost		162,674	94,005
Installed Cost Per Net Kilowatt*		163	99
		Annual Operating Costs, mills/kwhr	
Fixed Costs @ 14% per annum, 70% load factor		3.67	2.26
Operation, Maintenance, and Supplies		0.31	0.626
Fuel		1.77	2.350
Total Cost of Power at Busbar		5.76	5.24

* The net station output accounts for auxiliary losses and, for the COGAS station, the power
   requirements of the fuel processing system

in building size and foundation requirements could
be realized resulting in further cost reductions.

Busbar Power Cost

The cost of generating power at the busbar is
the true measure of a power system attractiveness.
If the gasified-coal-fired COGAS system is to be an
acceptable alternative to stack gas cleaning
methods to reduce sulfur oxide emissions, the
overall cost of generating power must be competitive.
The estimated busbar costs for the three generations
of power systems are shown in Fig. 9. First-
generation advanced-cycle COGAS systems do not
demonstrate any cost advantage although there
could be less sulfur oxide emissions from this type
of station than from a conventional station with
stack gas cleanup. It is not until the second
generation that aerospace technology could be fully
utilized to give the performance increase required
to offset the increased fuel costs. Additional
breakdown of the busbar cost for a second-generation
COGAS system is also given in Table 3. The value
of 5.24 mills/kwhr for the COGAS station is about
0.5 mills/kwhr or 10% less than projected for con-

ventional stations with no pollution control. This
trend is continued as shown in Fig. 9, into the
third-generation power station where the COGAS
system is projected to have about a 12% lower busbar
power cost.

FIGURE 9

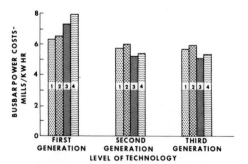

BUSBAR POWER COSTS FOR COAL BASED POWER STATIONS

1   CONVENTIONAL STEAM-ELECTRIC STATION BURNING UNTREATED COAL
2   CONVENTIONAL STEAM-ELECTRIC STATION BURNING UNTREATED COAL
    WITH 85% EFFECTIVE SULFUR OXIDE STACK GAS CLEANING
3   COGAS STATION BURNING DESULFURIZED FUEL
4   BASE-LOAD GAS TURBINE STATION BURNING DESULFURIZED FUEL

Concluding Remarks

The adaptation of current and prospective, future aerospace technology to industrial gas turbines could allow significant improvement in the performance of these machines. If these gas turbines were used in COGAS systems, their increased performance could offset the additional cost of using a desulfurized fuel. In fact, these systems could result in decreased power costs while improving the environment. The gasification of coal and oil allows sulfur to be easily removed. It has been projected[6] that the emissions from a gas-turbine based power system burning a desulfurized fuel could be of the order of 30 ppm or less compared with typical emissions from current coal-fired power stations of 3000 ppm, both corrected to the same excess air.

An additional benefit arising from the use of gas-turbine based power systems would be the reduction in thermal pollution of rivers and streams. While the cost estimates presented herein for COGAS systems include the use of cooling towers so that these stations would not be thermal polluters, these cooling towers could be eliminated and the COGAS system would reject to cooling water only about 50% of the heat that would be rejected by a conventional steam system.

References

1. Rohrman, F. A., S. H. Ludwig, and B. S. Steigerwald: The Sources of Air Pollution and Their Control. U.S. Public Health Services Publication 1598, Revised October 1967.

2. Starkey, N. E.: Long-Life Base-Load Service at 1600 F Turbine Inlet Temperature. ASME Paper 66-GT-98, March 1966.

3. Selected Technology for the Electric Power Industry. Proceedings of NASA Conference, September 1968.

4. Thomson, E. R., and F. D. George: Investigation of the Structure and Properties of Ni_3Al-Ni_3Cb Eutectic Alloy. United Aircraft Research Laboratories Report H-910681-4, July 1969.

5. Biancardi, F. R., and G. T. Peters: Status Report on the Utilization of Low-Cost Fuels in Gas Turbines. United Aircraft Research Laboratories Report F-110278-23, October 1967.

6. Robson, F. L., and A. J. Giramonti: Final Report on the Technological and Economic Feasibility of Advanced Power Cycles and Methods of Producing Nonpolluting Fuels for Utility Power Stations. United Aircraft Research Laboratories Report J-970855-13, November 1970.

7. Sheldon, R. C. and T. D. McKone: Performance Characteristics of Combined Steam-Gas Turbine Cycles. American Power Conference, March 1962.

8. Zysin, V. A., I. I. Kirillov, et al: Development of Combined Steam and Gas Turbine Plants. Thermal Energy, October 1968.

ENGINEERING FOR ECOLOGICAL SYSTEMS

WITH SPECIFIC REFERENCE TO FISHERIES

Dr. Ernest B. Cohen
Management Scientist
Atlantic Richfield Co.
Philadelphia,
Pennsylvania 19101

Dr. Edward R. Glaser
Assistant Professor of E. E. &
Environmental Engineering
Drexel University
Philadelphia, Pennsylvania 19104

Mr. Edward Kaplan
Graduate Student
University of Penn
Philadelphia,
Pennsylvania 19104

ABSTRACT

One of the most promising long term applications of advanced aerospace technology is the control of natural ecological systems. Since civilization is having a constantly increasing impact on nature, systems engineering should be used to insure that the impact is beneficial. A number of possible goals can be considered for controlling ecological systems. In increasing order of sophistication these are: maximizing the production of natural products, maximizing the efficiency of harvesting natural products, and stabilizing related socioeconomic activities.

Spin-offs from the aerospace program will be utilized for this work. In fisheries, sensing and communication technology based on satellite platforms can be directly applied to ecological control. Experience in constructing world-wide information nets should be used to monitor and control the exploitation of ocean biological resources. However, the greatest spin-off from the aerospace industry to ecological control is the competence to manage large projects involving considerable research and development.

The technology of managing system development first evolved for physical hardware systems such as aircraft. Later, the operational control problem was recognized, and software aspects of aerospace projects have been included with the system management.

Aerospace systems management has developed techniques to cope with unknowns and uncertainty. Parallel development program on components and directed research to obtain required hardware technology are common in large system projects. Management control techniques are used to cope with both program and technical uncertainty. The most important management spin-off from aerospace is the systems engineering cycle, which proceeds in well defined stages from problem definition (mission) to implementation of the solution. The capability of integrating a large complex development program is the technology of creating and utilizing technology.

When a systems engineer considers the problems of controlling ocean fisheries, he is presented with an exceedingly complex system of population dynamics with many feedback loops linking the growth rates and population levels of most species. These natural systems are inherently stable, at least in the classical sense that population level oscillations are bounded. However, man has often changed the environment so that formerly stable systems become unstable. Therefore, human activities are also part of the ocean ecology to be optimally controlled. Where the population levels are still inherently stable, then ecological control can be practiced as a long time-constant feedback loop which modifies the parameters of the system. In this mode, observation of natural perturbations on the ecological system can help to determine optimum levels of fishing intensity.

Where present human intervention has adversely affected the ecosystem, a new socio-economic feedback path must be constructed. Sophisticated use of legal restrictions, economic incentives (taxes/subsidies) and techniques to control motivation can restabilize the natural system. In this manner we can attain goals such as the sustained maximum production of useful products.

In order to implement control of ecological systems, it is first necessary to determine the natural system dynamics. The system can then be simulated. Optimum monitoring outputs and control inputs can be derived from the simulation. Optimum control implies maximum effect with minimum human intervention. In addition, the "managed" ecosystem must have high inherent stability, so that extinction of natural species is not inadvertently initiated due to inadequate knowledge of system dynamics.

The theoretical points are illustrated with natural examples drawn from the fishing industry and the marine ecology it exploits. In the ocean ecology, the food web concept can be used to illustrate the dynamic relations, and man can be considered primarily as a predator. Social control of the fishing industry, via regulations on the market economy, then becomes part of the total ecological system dynamics.

Introductory Concepts

While aerospace engineers have been striving to perfect life support systems for space travel, they have been supported by a more sophisticated system than they could ever design. "Spaceship Earth" has been circling our sun with billions of human passengers and uncountable numbers of other life forms long before there were aerospace engineers. The various life forms exchange essential constituents in a complex web in which the whole planet is involved. This whole ongoing process is powered by the radiant energy emitted by the sun.

The web of life is relatively stable because it contains many feedback loops, with different time constants. This natural control structure can be analyzed in the marine subsector because the overall interactions between life forms can be approximated with relatively simple equations. The present paper examines the ecology of oceanic fisheries and evaluates the application of control engineering techniques to optimize this subsector for human benefit. In what follows we will outline the application of control engineering to ecological problems, using fisheries as a specific example. We will first discuss the needs for and goals of ecological control, especially as seen in terms of potential food resources from oceans. Next will follow a discussion on aerospace management concepts of complex projects as well as other spin-offs from our space programs which are applicable to the ecological management problem. The development of some sophisticated management techniques will be outlined. Conclusions will relate directly to both present and future projects for ecological control and fishery management.

Need for Ecological Control

It is only recently that the need for active ecological control became obvious to a significant proportion of the population. In previous ages, the number of human beings was much smaller and they had too few tools to make a deep impact on the earth's mineral resources, although stone age man was already capable of making many species of large mammals extinct(7).

That non-renewable resources, minerals and fossil fuels, are limited has long been obvious. Now it has also become obvious that the maximum utilization rate of renewable resources is limited and these must be used efficiently because the prospect of destructive overuse is in sight. At present about 10% of the earth's total land area is already used for agriculture(2). Food from the sea is a valuable supplement to land sources, particularly for proteins. It is essential to optimize use of this resource.

Unfortunately, not only is this resource limited, but attempts to harvest too much will lead to long term lower total yield. It is no longer true that fishery production is limited by available equipment and manpower, with occasional local over-fishing of a few species. Over-fishing is now widespread. As soon as the habits of a species are known, the stock is exploited. Repeatedly, the initial high yields in a new fishery have encouraged over-fishing and drastically reduced the catch within a decade. We can no longer afford such abuse of an essential renewable natural resource.

Goals of Ecological Control

The normal procedure in an aerospace system project is to start with a mission definition. In applying systems engineering to ecological control, the mission analysis is even more important since not even a preliminary mission definition is available. Most fishery research today is concerned with sub-goals, such as improving the technical capability to locate schools of fish.

The first overall goal we can consider would be to maximize the total harvest since the ocean is a major source of human food. This implies that we should minimize "trash" species that compete for food and other resources with desirable species. We might also consider minimizing predators that compete with man for harvesting the food fish. The most important part of maintaining maximum total productivity is not exceeding the optimum harvest rate for each species, the rate for maximum sustained yield.

However, maximum total productivity implies harvesting species which are near the base of the food web. These species are usually small and hard to catch, and not always desirable as human food. A trade-off is required between the low manpower required to harvest a fish like tuna, and the fantastic costs anticipated in trying to harvest directly the vast production of plankton. This more sophisticated goal could be formulated as "maximum productive return on resources used." Even this goal may not be sufficiently general and really relate to fundamental overall requirements. Any treatment of the ocean as a source of food would not be complete without considering the impact on human society. The ocean resources will never be available in fixed quantities. Weather and climate, through their impact on the biological cycles of different species, can make drastic changes in the standing crop and the allowable harvest.

From the human point of view it is desirable that the total availability of ocean-derived food be fairly constant from year to year. It is also desirable to stabilize employment and income from the fishing industry. The impact of weather, unusual growth of predator or prey populations, or similar ecological events on the fishery itself, should be minimized. Moreover, the system should be fairly stable in spite of moderate errors in setting catch quotas or other control measures. A stable ecosystem means that periods of high productivity will not come from overfishing and result in prolonged periods of low production.

Assuring long-term stability implies a much more sophisticated approach to control than that required for merely maximizing output. It is obvious that there already is some degree of stability in the marine ecology, since species naturally subject to unbounded population oscillations would have already become extinct. However, many species should be deliberately preserved from extinction just for their stabilizing control properties. As a recent ecology test (15, p. 157) notes: ".....it seems to be a general principle that complicated natural systems are stabler than simpler ones."

Spin-Offs from Space Programs

The establishment of human control over oceanic ecosystems poses many requirements. We must develop an understanding of the underlying relationships which control the growth rates of the species in the oceanic food web. We must be able to measure the physical characteristics of the environment as well as the population densities of the species. These measurements must be transmitted and analyzed in a short time period to monitor the impact of fishing fleets and of possible nutrient fertilization efforts.

Many of these requirements can be met by existing space programs, or by the extension of concepts developed in space programs. These programs and concepts can be considered in terms of: hardware (both monitoring and communications satellites), software and the management of complex research and development projects.

Satellite Applications

Perhaps the most immediate contribution of aerospace hardware technology to ecology is in the use of monitoring and surveillance techniques. We may use sensors carried aboard high altitude aircraft or by satellite.

Sensing can be done using a wide region of the spectrum. At long wave lengths (passive) microwave radiometry can be used for surface and possible near-subsurface temperature measurement. Active microwave sensors (radar clutter analysis) may be useful in determining wave heights and wave patterns. Multi-spectral photography in the visible and near infrared should be useful in determining the presence of phyto-plankton (and possibly the presence of oil on the water). In fact, sensing of these bands is done routinely by numerous meteorological satellites, and it may be that relatively little effort and expenditure is required to utilize such sensors for ecological monitoring. If this is so, then we could greatly increase the utilization of satellite data. For instance, surface isotherm data could provide information about surface currents, and therefore be used in predicting phytoplankton development. Beverton and Holt (1) suggest national and eventual international regulation of fishing as the only optimum way to maximize yield while minimizing effort. Some of the information input required by their models, such as phytoplankton growth, water current and temperature data, could probably be obtained using existing aerospace technology.

Global communication is one of the most highly developed spin-offs of the space program. We are now able to relay data from satellite to satellite as well as from ground stations to ground station via satellite. A significant data communications capacity has been built into weather satellites (The Nimbus APT System) as well as many civilian communication systems. These satellites could readily provide increased communications with fishing fleets or other oceanic work stations and shore facilities.

Software

An important spin-off from the meteorological and other surveillance satellite systems is the software which enables the rapid (nearly real-time) handling of millions of bits of information and the assembly of maps which are literally global in extent. This ability is definitely needed for fishing-fleet direction and may be important for oceanic fertilization procedures.

Management of Complex Development Projects

The most important technical spin-offs from the space program to be applied to operating "Spaceship Earth" are neither hardware nor software. The essential spin-off will be the technique of managing a complex development project with an (initially) inadequate knowledge of the basic science involved. A major contribution of the aerospace industry has been the creation of a technology for handling large systems projects. These projects involve: research, state-of-the-art development, the interaction of several disciplines and the efforts of thousands of scientists. The project itself is directed towards an end product of extreme complexity, both in mission and equipment.

In ecological control, we must simultaneously develop a new technology, apply it, and live as part of the system with the effects of applying the technology. Development of new technologies has been accomplished in past aerospace programs. The last problem, however, is a qualitative advance over even the largest space projects, but one that would have been impossible without learning on smaller projects, like Apollo. Man's involvement in the ecosystem and his simultaneous control of that system brings the concept of adaptive control to a higher level of sophistication.

Relative State of the Art

Probably the greatest invention of this century is the technique of directed, efficient technical development, as exemplified in Systems Engineering. Systems engineering techniques were originally developed for space and military programs. To apply these techniques to new fields it is necessary to explicitly define systems engineering and understand how it developed and its role in aerospace projects.

Hardware System Development

Over the millenia of history, individuals have always been developing new tools and devices. Many of these devices worked but were "failures", i.e., they performed only part of the intended job or had serious unintended side effects. As new developments became increasingly complex and costly, especially in military and space programs, systems engineering was incorporated into these projects to prevent the occurrence of "successful failures".

As a first step, a mission analysis is required to specify exactly what the total system is intended to do. The design of each component can then be evaluated in relation to the system goal or mission. What was probably the first project organized on a system basis antedates the space age by almost 100 years and surprisingly, was a civilian project. It was Edison's development of the incandescent lamp to replace gas lighting (8). The system, including the light source, the power generator and the means for power distribution, was considered as a whole. The design goal was in the 19th century tradition: sufficient efficiency in distributing energy so that the system operation would return a high interest rate on the capital investment required.

Most modern systems projects have been military. Within the narrow bounds of military thinking, defining technical goals has been relatively straightforward. Subject to economic constraints, the weapons systems should have superior technical performance to those of any potential opponent. This approach leads to continually increasing performance requirements on all weapons systems. In general, these hardware goals have usually been met, through the means of extensive research and development programs, guided by systems engineering. However, as shown by the experience in Viet Nam, systems engineering is not completed without consideration of the use of the hardware.

The bulk of modern civilian systems projects have been in the fields of air transportation and communications. The work has been largely hardware oriented, with attention centered on the economics of the system itself, and not the context of use. For example, the development of larger and faster aircraft has outpaced airport development and connecting ground transportation to cities. For shorter trips, the overall speed and economy is now limited by the ground facilities. The finest work in systems engineering to date has been the space program, and project Apollo in particular. The technical difficulties were such that an integrated systems approach to design and operation was essential for success.

Combined Hardware/Softwave Projects

In the course of developing major space projects, it became clear that optimizing the hardware alone was not sufficient. The procedures for operating the hardware system, for maintaining hardware, for training personnel and similar support tasks had to be optimized as well. While some of this work involved the development of computer programs (computer software) the largest portion involved the interaction of people with the hardware (human factors).

This widened scope of systems engineering considerations is still in the process of gaining acceptance. Since systems engineers have not usually been trained in human physiology and psychology, they are often not aware of the human factors involved. Of course, when it is an obvious matter of life support in an alien environment, as is true of all manned space projects, consulting specialists are brought in as needed. However, social factors (group human factors) are rarely considered, even when the project may have a severe impact upon the environment and be a matter of life or death for many people. Operating "Spaceship Earth" has not been given the same attention as operating spaceship Apollo.

Coping with Unknowns

The space program has been a proving ground for the concept of directed research as part of major systems projects. The development of manned space flight would have taken many decades if basic research and hardware development were not undertaken in parallel. The research is scheduled during the initial phases of a project in order to provide basic data for the hardware design at the time this data will be required. For example, the design of landing gear for the Apollo lunar module proceeded while the required data on lunar surface conditions were being obtained from the Ranger, Orbiter, and Surveyor projects.

Coping with Uncertainty

Space-systems engineering includes control of design margins to minimize failures. The Contingency Accommodation Planning (CAP) technique developed by one of the authors (3) extends the concept of design margin to include protection against complex contingencies, as well as simple failures. By including extra resources (men, money, material, time) in the systems plans, it is possible to revise the project to cope with schedule slippages, design changes, component failures, mission redefinition, or other contingencies which could not have been predicted in advance. The technique is based on statistical estimates at each stage of a project of the degree of uncertainty and the possible interconversion of spare resources to correct for errors and out-of-tolerance situations.

Systems Cycle (Problem Definition to Solution

The successes of systems engineering are largely due to providing feedback in the system-design cycle. A mission (goal or value function) is tentatively accepted. Based on these mission requirements, a series of trade-offs are performed leading to a first-cut design. The design performance is then compared back to the tentative mission definition, and the mission is refined to conform more closely to reality. A new design is then developed for the refined mission. Meanwhile, similar design iterations take place at the subsystem and component levels. After a number of iteration cycles, the design matches the requirements at all levels. When this paradigm for system engineering is compared with the ecological control problem, it becomes obvious that the goal (mission) is poorly defined. At the same time, we realize that the poorly defined goals must be implemented with interim systems, since "Spaceship Earth" is already in existence and operating. Furthermore, major portions of the dynamic relations in an ecosystem are beyond our capability to modify. It will require a major extension of present systems engineering techniques to consciously iterate modifications to an existing macro-system. The inadvertent misapplication of technology has already caused the extinction of many species and permanently modified the environment for others.

Integrated Control of Program

As a natural corollary to handling the complete system-design cycle, it is obvious that a single agency must have administrative cognizance of each major systems project. This prevents local sub-optimization, i.e., optimizing the design and operation of each component subsystem on its own independent criteria, rather than on its impact on total system performance. This is an important concept, since the components of most present macro-systems are not operated by the same authority. Marine ecological control involves the cooperation of operating agencies from different countries. It can only succeed if some coordinating body integrates control of the program. The overall task is probably several orders of magnitude more complex than Project Apollo.

Basic Ecological Theory

Prior to the discussion of any development program it is important to note the real-world (i.e. natural) context in which the program is to operate. For instance, discussions twenty years ago about communications satellite systems usually began with a statement of orbital equations and the propagation range equation. Similarly, a discussion of a program to develop ecological control capability should start with a discussion of the food web of the ecosystem and the growth equations for the species in the food web.

The food web is a model used to provide a context for the understanding of ecological interactions. In its most common form the food web shows the flow of energy in an ecosystem. Figure 1 shows a simple food chain, a portion of a food web. Energy enters at the bottom as incident radiation (sunlight).

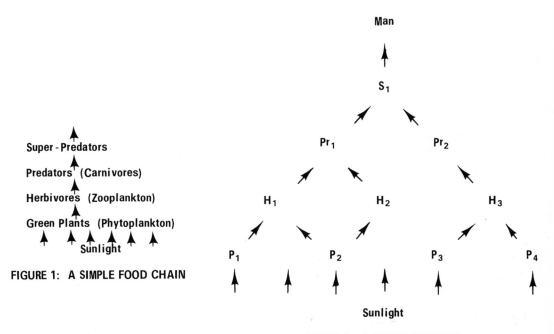

FIGURE 1: A SIMPLE FOOD CHAIN

FIGURE 2: A SIMPLE FOOD WEB

The energy is absorbed by the floating green plants, (the phytoplankton), and converted to carbohydrates, fats, etc. Floating or swimming herbivores, the zooplankton, eat the plants. The zooplankton are, in turn, eaten by their predators, who are eaten by super-predators, etc. Man can be considered as a predator in the food web.

A simple food web is shown in Figure 2. Here the individual species of plants, herbivores, etc. are shown. The arrows indicate that certain herbivore species may restrict their diets only to certain phytoplankton species.

Figure 3 shows some of the complications which are found in actual food webs. In figure 3 the species at a given level may be eating species from other levels beside that immediately below it. A further complication is that predators eating the plankton may be also consuming eggs or young of their own species. This is shown in Fig. 3 by the looped arrow around Pr. 2.

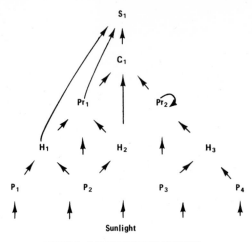

FIGURE 3: A MORE REALISTIC FOOD WEB

The ratio of energy flow from a species (to its predators) divided by energy flow to a species (from its prey) is referred to as the ecological efficiency. For aquatic food webs ecological efficiency usually lies in the range from .05 to .15 (14). The value .10 is often used, but it should be regarded as a "rule-of-thumb" and not as the average value of ecological efficiency in an aquatic food web.

From the preceding, it appears that harvesting closer to the energy source, (plants if possible), would result in larger yields. Since marine plants, and even some marine herbivores, are one-celled organisms, it is difficult to harvest them efficiently. At present, the optimum technique appears to be harvesting mainly first-level carnivores. In any case, we have to guard against overfishing of each species. Since the setting of optimum catches is an important aspect of marine ecological control, the theoretical basis for the concept is discussed in some detail below.

A complex food web, such as that shown in Figure 3, is a geometric model for the ecosystem. Representing this model as a set of simultaneous, non-linear differential equations is the next step in defining the context of our ecological problem. These are the growth equations of the various species. The equations are often written in terms of the biomass of the species, as opposed to just counting individuals.

$$\dot{N}_j = a_{jo} N_j + \sum_{i=1}^{n} a_{ij} N_i N_j - a_{jj} N_j^2 - \sum_{k=1}^{m} a_{kj} N_j N_k \tag{1}$$

where $\dot{N}_j$ = rate of change of biomass of the jth species

a_{jo} = exponential growth constant for N_j in the absence of other

species and when N_j is "small"; a_{jo} may be + or -.

$a_{ij} N_i N_j$ = terms due to species on which N_j is preying

$a_{kj} N_j N_k$ = terms due to species preying on N_j.

$a_{jj} N_j^2$ = possible term describing the effect of a "large" N_j population on the

N_j growth rate.

There will be at least one equation for each species in the food web. For many of the species in a marine food web we would have a more realistic model if we considered separately the individuals of a given age class (cohort) of the particular species. This would lead to a separate equation for each cohort. This approach will greatly multiply the number of equations, but it enables us to allow for adults of one species preying upon juveniles of another species and vice versa, simultaneously. This situation is found in the interactions between trout and shiners in fresh-water aquatic systems (15). It also enables us to account for adults of one species consuming juveniles of the same species. Therefore a differential equation model of a food web would require one equation (similar to equ-1) for each cohort of every species present. It should be noted that equations such as (equ-1) assume a homogeneous environment. In fact the marine environment is non-homogeneous, since there is a gradient of illumination, temperature, and phytoplankton population density, which are functions of depth. Some work on non-homogeneous environments for exceedingly simple food webs has been initiated (5) (13). The non-linear character of even the simplest ecological equations means that we must use computer simulation to gain an understanding of the behavior of the mathematical model. Simulation has been done only on rather simple food webs; and mostly with assumed values of the coefficients, not measured values (4). The reason for this lack of progress is that few coefficients have been measured in natural ecosystems for equations such as (equ-1).

Therefore, the context in which the discussion of ecological control is to take place is a context where the basic behavior of the equations of the mathematical model is not well known and where the coefficients are still to be measured. Obviously this is an area in which a great deal of work is yet to be done.

State Space Concepts

Let us consider the factor a_{jo} in equation (equ-1). It was defined as the exponential growth constant for N_j in the absence of other species. If N_j is a phytoplankton species, then a_{jo} will be positive. For small values of N_j the populations will grow exponentially, i.e.

$$N_j(t) = N_j(0) e^{a_{jo} t} \qquad (2)$$

Even for such a simple case, a_{jo} is not a simple constant. For the phytoplankton species in question it depends on the incident radiation, the con-centration of dissolved nutrients in the seawater and many other physical-chemical factors. We will consider all the relevant physical-chemical factors to define a state space. The value of a_{jo} is therefore dependent on the position of the phytoplankton in this state space. We expand this concept to include the popula-tions of other species as biotic state variables. Then the value of $\dot{N}_j$ depends on the position in a state space consisting of both physical-chemical variables and biotic variables.

Some sort of diagram would be useful in keeping track of the importance of the large number of state variables on the growth rate of a particular species. This should prove useful as a step in the eventual computer programming required for the differential equation model.

The block diagram(s) to be used will show the state variables as dots (or nodes, where appropriate). An interaction between two state variables will be shown by a line connecting the two state variables. On the line will be a divided square or a rectangle (half-square) denoting the transfer function, (or the term in a non-linear differential equation) which describes the interaction. If each of the two state variables affects the other, then a divided square will be used, with arrows going in both directions. If one state variable affects the other, but there is no complimentary interaction, then a rectangle (half-square) will be used with only one arrow.

Figure 4 shows the effect of some physical state variables on a biotic state variable. Note the use of arrows, divided squares, and half-squares.

It is suggested that a separate block diagram be made for each important biotic state variable similar to figure 4. Each of these diagrams could then be used to write the equation for the rate of change of the biomass density of the species described.

Similarly, a separate block diagram can be made for each physical state variable. These block diagrams can be used to aid in writing the equations for the rates of change of the physical state variables.

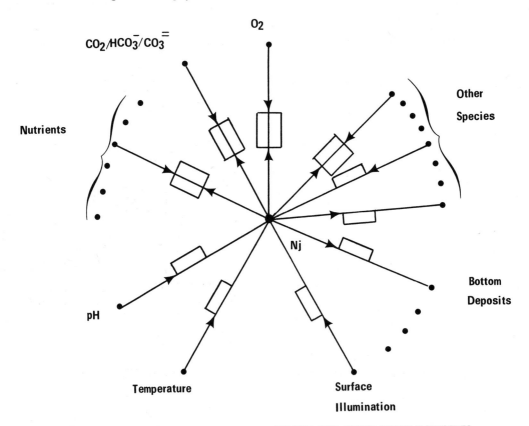

FIGURE 4: INTERACTION BETWEEN THE N_j SPECIES AND OTHER STATE VARIABLES, (SEE TEXT).

Maximum Sustained Harvest

The concept of maximum sustained yield can be illustrated by plotting productivity vs. standing crop and harvest rate vs. standing crop on the same set of axes, as done in Figure 5. (Productivity is the rate at which new biomass is generated in a population. Harvest rate is the rate at which biomass is removed from the population). Let us assume that harvest rate is proportional to the product of fishing intensity, I, and standing crop of a particular species N_j. This relation is shown in Figure 5 as a series of straight lines with different slopes, all passing through the origin. A typical curve of productivity vs. standing crop, in the absence of harvest, is also shown in Figure 5. Note that at low values of N_j the species will increase exponentially, as predicted from equation 2. The exponential increase is shown as a straight line on the curve of productivity vs. standing crop, (as seen by differentiating equation 2). At "moderate" values of standing crop the competition between the individuals in the species will limit growth below exponential rates. Finally, at high values of N_j, intra-specific competition will bring the productivity to zero*. This is shown as Point P.

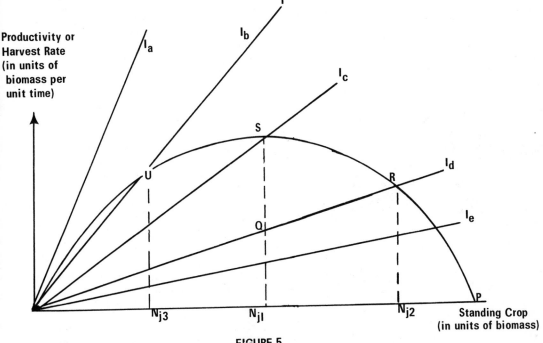

FIGURE 5.
SIMPLIFIED FISHERY STATE SPACE

---

*See MacArthur and Connell (10, p. 152 ff) for a somewhat similar argument in which the interactions of a predator species and a prey species are discussed.

Now consider the effect of various harvesting intensities on the N_i population. Assume that harvesting occurs at intensity I_d, and that the value of the standing crop is N_{i1}. This corresponds to point Q on Figure 5. The rate of change of N_i will be the difference between the productivity and the harvest. Since this difference is positive, N_i will increase and the system will come to rest at point R, where the productivity and the harvest rate are equal, so that $\dot{N}_i = 0$ and the standing crop is N_{i2}. Now consider the situation when the standing crop is N_{i1} and harvesting proceeds at intensity I_c. This is point S and represents a maximum sustainable harvest. The harvest may be continued indefinitely since the harvest rate is equal to the productivity and therefore the standing crop remains at the value N_{i1}. If we were to increase the harvest intensity to I_b (point T) we would obtain a higher harvest, temporarily. But the difference between productivity and harvest rate is now negative, and so the standing crop will decrease from N_{i1} to N_{i3}, with the system coming to rest at point U. Therefore, beginning with a standing crop, N_{i1}, we can sustain a large harvest if harvesting intensity I_c is used. But increasing the harvesting intensity to I_b will only temporarily increase the harvest. It leads to reducing the standing crop to N_{i3}; and the corresponding harvest at point U is less than that at point S, even though a greater harvest intensity is employed. Note that this implies a greater expenditure to obtain a smaller harvest. Finally, if harvesting intensity I_a is employed with any value of standing crop, then the harvest rate will exceed the productivity, causing the standing crop to decrease, until the species goes extinct or harvesting is suspended. Historical experience indicates that a situation analogous to harvest intensity I_a was followed during the 19th century for the American buffalo, sperm whales and fur-bearing seals (11), and during the 20th century for blue whales (12).

The discussion centering on Figure 5 is only meant to be illustrative. Many factors have been omitted, such as the age structure of the populations and the random fluctuations in the marine environment. Also, man is not the only predator and the total food web has many stabilizing predator-prey-habitat inter-actions. However, many species are drastically overfished today, even if not in immediate danger of extinction. Under competitive economic conditions, high prices tend to encourage over-optimum fishing intensity. Wherever this is the case, additional system controls, such as taxes to modify the economic relations, should be considered to restore the optimum balance. These economic considerations are discussed below.

Possible Simplifications in Food-Web Modeling

It may be possible to assume that many of the physical state variables have a negligible effect on biotic state variables if the physical state variables are within certain limits. For instance, the growth rate of phyto-plankton species may be almost independent of copper ion concentration if the concentration is above a minimal (deficiency) level and below a toxic level. Therefore, an initial, highly simplified model may assume that most of the ionic concentrations are be-tween the limits of deficiency and toxicity and ignore the effect of these ions on the growth rates of the various species. Later, more sophisticated models could include the effects of various ions when present at very low concentrations (deficiency) and also at high concentrations (toxicity).

For an initial model it may be adequate to consider only those species which make up a given percentage, (say 80%), of the total biomass. This would greatly simplify the modeling by reducing the number of biotic state variables. The

reduction would be significant since the usual distribution of species is to have
a few with a large portion of the total biomass in the ecosystem and many species
with a small portion of the total biomass.

Perturbation of Marine Ecology by Man

What is man's effect on a marine ecosystem? Man can appear as merely another
species in the food web through the effects of commercial fishing, which may be
regarded as predation on particular species. In addition, man presently adds
both organic matter and nutrients to the marine environment. This is accomplished
by the dumping of organic refuse and sewage sludge at sea. However, the standing
crop of the marine food web is not necessarily enhanced by these practices since
harmful pollutants are also introduced which may decrease the populations of
particular species. A better understanding of the marine food web may lead us to
undertake the addition of phosphates and nitrates as a cost-effective method of
increasing marine food production. The artificial pumping of nutrient-rich water
from the ocean bottom to the surface should be evaluated. Upwelling occurs
naturally off the Peruvian coast and creates a region of high productivity.

As mentioned in the above, there are two basically conflicting goals of
marine ecosystem management. We can seek to maximize the harvested crop of
particular species on a steady-state basis, and/or we can also seek to preserve
the stability of the ecosystem.

The term "stability" used in this discussion is derived from the observation
that an ecosystem in a given region is usually at or near a state of equilibrium;
that destroying particular species (or severely reducing the numbers of
particular species) will move the ecosystem from the previous equilibrium; and
that recolonization of the destroyed species (or reproductive growth of the
diminished species) will re-establish the previous equilibrium. However, if the
equilibrium is perturbed sufficiently, the ecosystem may seek a different
equilibrium point which makes recolonization and the re-establishment of the
previous equilibrium unlikely. A reduction in the number of species in a food
web may seriously decrease the stability of the ecosystem, and reduce the
probability of recovery from subsequent perturbations in the environment, both
natural and man-made.

Developing Ecological Control Capability

Developing human control over a large-scale natural system is qualitatively
different from the development of a large hardware system. The natural system
already exists. We must proceed in an evolutionary manner from the present hap-
hazard human interference to the future optimized control. In addition, we, as part
of the human social organization, are also part of the control dynamics. While
working towards optimum yields, we must first be sure to maintain stability
throughout the development period. Until the dynamic response of the system is
fully known, we must limit the magnitude of human interference. This implies
rigid fishing quotas, tightly enforced, as interim measures.

Theory and Implementation

Present control techniques are probably non-optimal because they are not
based on a sufficient understanding of the dynamic relations involved. Feedback

control involves some means of affecting a process, and some means of measuring the output of a process. Optimum control in an ecological framework also involves measurement of uncontrollable environmental parameters (i.e., weather) which affect the system and accurate estimates of the transfer functions, or non-linear relationships, relating all significant portions of the system to each other. The final control can only be as good as the theoretical structure. Development of the theory involves extensive use of computer modeling and simulation, as discussed below.

Determining System Dynamics

One of the first steps in a Research and Development program to develop an ecological control capability will be the simulation of equations such as discussed above to determine the system dynamics. The equations should initially be simulated with the best values of coefficients, (measured or estimated), available at that time. The simulation effort should not be delayed to wait for measurements of the coefficients. The simulation can then be used to determine which coefficients have the greatest effect on the dynamics of the ecosystem. Thus, even early simulation efforts enable us to direct the measurement effort toward ecologically important parameters.

The determination of system dynamics is an iterative process involving simulation, measurement, and refining the simulation. Since some of the system processes have long time constants, of the order of years, the accurate determination of system dynamics will not be completed quickly. These time constants are basically derived from the life cycle of the various species involved. If one species has a poor spawning in a particular year, due to temporary pollution or bad weather, there will be a deficiency in that particular year-class (or cohort). If competition between cohorts is present, then the next year-class should have a reduced mortality. On the other hand, later spawnings may also be smaller than usual due to reduced numbers of adults. The effects of one extremely deviant year-class may be measurable for a decade in some species.

The basic equations described above contain coefficients to represent each significant interaction between species. The equations must also contain any significant interactions that exist between age classes within a given species. The developing of the computer simulation models will be a joint effort between marine biologists and simulation engineers.

Determining "Optimum Control Inputs"

As the computer models are developed, they would be run to determine "optimum control inputs". The term "optimum control inputs" is used to describe those variables which can be changed at low expense and/or have a large effect on the system state. Human intervention in the ecosystem via these inputs would have a low cost/effectiveness ratio. The significant optimum control inputs would exist in regions of the system state space which have a high potential harvest rate and great stability. Note that the existence of great stability (against natural and man-made perturbations in the environment) and the existence of optimum control inputs may be contradictory requirements. However, if several regions of the system state space are found which have a high potential harvest rate and great stability, then we would choose to operate at those regions in state space where optimum control inputs also exist.

The simulation programs will show, for instance, that the destruction of a competing predator may increase the harvested crop for man of a particular fish species. However, removing one species (man's competition) reduces the complexity of the food web and may reduce the stability. Also the simulation, if sufficiently accurate, will show the changes elsewhere in the ecosystem caused by the removal of the particular predator species. These changes may include an increase in population for other species preyed upon by that predator, and also a decrease in population for species which used that predator as a food supply, or complete with other species controlled by the predator.

In a like manner, we will determine optimum monitoring outputs. These are system phenomona which can be economically measured with adequate precision, and provide maximum information about the location of the ecosystem in state space.

We have to search for variables with a low cost/effectiveness ratio since it is not possible to freely redesign a natural system as we might wish. However, if there is a desirable species which can be artificially hatched in quantity and the increase in numbers will not be minimized by an increase in predator population or by competition with other species, then rearing this species would be an optimum control input. At present, almost no attempts are made to influence the ecological balance of the open seas. However lakes, rivers, bays, and shallow off-shore waters have been the sites of experiments in fish stocking, habitat modification, fertilization, predator removal, etc.

Simulation and Experimentation for Stability

The first set of simulations would be run until a basic feature of the marine environment is achieved in the simulation -- the relative stability of the ecosystem. A second set of simulations would later be run in parallel with measurements of the populations and coefficients of various species. These simulations would seek to match the effects of minor perturbations caused by changes in man's activities, such as altered fishing patterns (caused by normal variation in weather conditions, etc.). When we are fairly confident that the model and computer simulation are reasonably accurate, then a third set of simulations would commence. These simulations would seek to determine the optimum control inputs described above.

The results of the previous simulations would be tested by experiments in the marine environment. These experiments would probably not go so far as to attempt to remove a particular species from the food web, but might institute a program of harvesting to reduce their numbers. Other experiments might involve the attempted enrichment of the food web, or the artificial stocking of species. If these experiments matched the predictions of the simulations in their effects on various population levels of the species in the food web, then we would have a degree of confidence in the stability predictions made by the simulations.

Closing the Social Control Loop

Ecological control in the future will be conducted by humans on the basis of decisions and value judgements made by other humans. Many of the activities, e.g., fishing, will be essentially the same as at present. The difference is that these activities will be controlled in intensity and modified in detail in order to maximize the benefits derived from the marine ecological system.

It is conceivable that large harvest rates and a high level of ecosystem stability could be achieved by close monitoring of the physical and biological components of the marine ecosystem, coupled with rapid analysis, simulation and short-term changes in harvesting and fertilization activities. This pre-supposes a strong central authority and essentially immediate response to its commands.

However, since the decisions and operations will be conducted by human beings, they will have a tendency to optimize the effect of these operations and decisions to their own immediate benefit. These attempts at very local, very temporary optimization are often catastrophic when viewed from a larger perspective. This situation is often unstable and has resulted in overfishing (12) or similar drastic sub-optimal results (6). Therefore, a preferable approach would be the establishment of a situation in which a combination of economics and the legal structure would lead to action on the part of individual fishing corporations or nations, which would bring about large harvest consistent with ecosystem stability. This arrangement would be preferable from the point of view that the economic conditions and the legal structure provide an extra loop around the direct inter-actions of man and the ecosystem.

Considering the latent instability of large centralized organizations, part of any meta-optimum system is a meta-control loop arranged so that local optima are (nearly) consonant with the global optimum. To the extent that this is so, it will not be necessary to use strong legal measures to insure that operating decisions are effective. Thus, instead of directives controlling innumerable actions on the micro-scale, we would need relatively few changes in the economic-legal structure (i.e., on the macro scale) to bring about significant changes in the direct effect of man on the ecosystem. This eventual mode of control would obviate the need for nearly real-time surveillance and data analysis. However, some sampling of the ecosystem on a global scale would still be needed to check on the proper working of this somewhat more subtle method of ecological control.

The authors admit that the criteria and the justification for social control loops are beyond the scope of this paper. However, it is necessary that an effective but non-coercive social control policy be part of the implementation of an ecological control system. This policy would have to stabilize the total system by providing negative feedback on the human side. For example, readily available alternative employment will discourage the harvesting of declining fish species, while the lack of alternatives would force fishing communities to over-harvest in a desperate attempt to provide sufficient income. In this regard, the present market response (price as a function of supply and demand) tends to have a de-stabilizing effect through positive feedback. The understanding of social dynamics and incorporation of appropriate meta-control loops will be essential to the successful implementation of marine ecological control.

It should be noted that the simulations needed to pre-test such an adaptive control system are not yet in existence since they involve the effects of economic and legal changes.

Operating Marine Ecological Control

The operation of an ecological control system should be considered at two levels. There will be the day-to-day activities of harvesting, fish stocking and fertilizing. These activities will have their own inner control loop which consists of such elements as fishing quotas and monitoring subsystems to determine actual fish catch and compare this to the quotas. The activities of the operating agencies are expected to be similar to existing practices, although improved in detail. For example, improved environmental sensing can minimize lost fishing time in locating schools of fish. Improved communication can also decrease delays in reporting catches and thereby help keep harvesting operations closer to the optimum.

Consider Figure 6 which shows the present dynamics of fishery operations. Each box in the figure contains a whole complex dynamic process in itself. For example, the "harvesting" operation interacts with the various species as discussed above. Conceptually, we can consider the harvesting as a single process. The marine ecology has a dynamic response to various rates of harvesting.

The market is governed by another dynamic system, generally called "supply and demand". Changes in the catch landed from fisheries will affect the market price and thereby the profitability of fishery operation. The anticipated profitability of fishing governs the availability of capital to be invested in the industry. The investment of capital and the availability of manpower governs the fishing intensity, which in turn affects the harvest. The present interaction between marine ecology and human activity can be considered as a natural system with its own control dynamics. The system does not always operate optimally for human purposes.

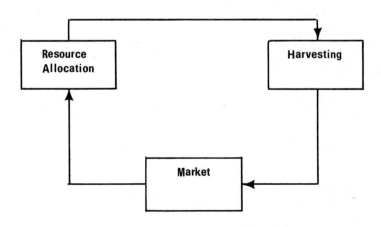

FIGURE 6: PRESENT FISHERY OPERATION

The system can be extended to that shown in Figure 7. The harvesting operation is guided by a local fishery operating agency. This agency has a number of
functions, including any fish stocking and fertilizing operations desired, and the
supply of local environmental and system state data to the harvesting activity.
It also monitors the effect of all activities on the local marine ecology, and
regulates fishing activity. This is the "inner loop" of fishery control.

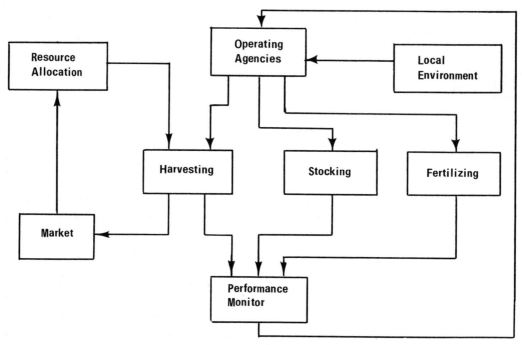

FIGURE 7: SINGLE LOOP FISHERY CONTROL

Addition of the "outer loop" is shown in Figure 8. The major change would
be the creation of an international technical fishery control agency. This agency,
the outer loop, monitors and controls the performance of the inner loop. It can
also provide a number of auxiliary functions, such as co-ordinating research on
marine ecology. The major functions of this body would be to:

1) Determine the system state of the marine ecology and associated human
    activities.

2) Simulate the effect of various human control policies and
    environmental influences.

3) Provide guidance and technical direction to the local operating agencies.

4) Influence the allocation of resources (through taxes and/or subsidies) to
    harvesting operations.

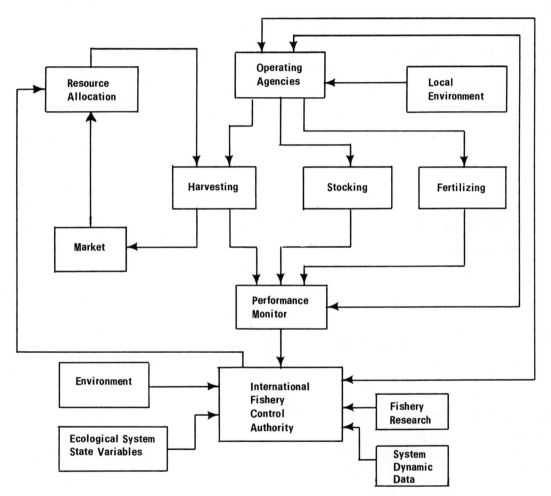

FIGURE 8: ADDITION OF OUTER CONTROL LOOP

59

We have already mentioned models of food webs, population growth, predator-prey interaction and other processes in ecological systems. A marine resource system involving such dynamics would contain many non-linear elements, not to mention numerous multiloop structures. Once a mathematical or computer model for the dynamics of this living system is developed, the operation of such a system is performed via adaptive control. That is, we add components to the model which simulate the regulatory system. These additional components are modified until the overall system shows stable output in spite of deviations in input or system processes, and shows near-optimum harvest potential.

We can expect that the marine ecology is basically quite stable and tolerant of moderate mismanagement. This permits us to have a fairly long response-time for the outer loop. When the simulation shows the need for changed dynamics in the regulatory (inner loop) sub-system, these can be implemented over a matter of years. On the other hand, the simulation models also provide direct input to the regulatory sub-system. When the simulations predict a higher allowable catch, the local "set points" (quotas, prices, etc.) can be adjusted to correspond.

This outer loop would have relatively long time constants (years to decades) because its role is to adjust the system relations between man and the marine ecosystem to achieve long-term optimization. Problems requiring faster response would have to be handled by the inner control loop agencies directly.

The inner loop should not merely be an administrative device to transmit detailed orders from a higher authority to the operating agencies. For example, a tax (and/or subsidy) inversely related to the estimated stock can be imposed on the catch of each ton of fish of a particular desirable species. This would minimize user demand for that particular species via high prices, without increasing the incentive to catch more of that fish. Otherwise, the decreasing supply/demand ratio as a desirable species becomes scarce could possibly more than compensate for the increasing costs of harvesting more intensively. This effect could drive marine species to extinction, just as it has severely threatened certain rare mammals on land. To be a useful motivating device, these taxes must be imposed before the commitment is made to allocate men and equipment to that particular fishery. This implies that the labor and capital can be alternatively deployed either in other fisheries or in other non-fishing activities. An understanding of these social dynamics are just as germane to the total ecological control problem as food webs and predator-prey interactions.

Conclusion

The prospect of controlling the natural ecology for human benefit has the greatest challenge in marine fisheries. The oceans are vast, and the average productivity per acre low. It does not appear economically feasible to ever replace the natural ecological cycle in the open oceans with the marine equivalent of farms and ranches. The effect of human intervention must be to perturb an exceedingly complex dynamic system, rather than replace it with a simpler one more amenable to direct control.

The overall project, to rationally control oceanic life, has many sub-projects, in some of which aerospace technology can be directly applied. The greatest contributions to this project from the aerospace industry are the techniques of organizing and controlling large-scale research and development projects. This is generally called "Systems Engineering". Systems Engineering also encompasses the discipline of control engineering.

To improve the utilization of oceanic food sources involves both increasing the quantities available and stabilizing the system to prevent large-scale fluctuations. To increase the quantity available for human use we can both increase the primary production of biomass and also redirect more of this biomass to human use.

In order to control this great natural system efficiently, we must first determine sensitive points. For example, wherever primary production is limited by the availability of nutrients, we can artificially add the required nutrients. This is only economical where there is a large source of nutrients readily available and/or the water mass involved is fairly stable and/or the limiting nutrients are only required in small quantities. Where these conditions hold, it may be economically feasible to directly affect primary production of biomass. These locations would be sensitive control points in the state space of the ecological system. Even here, the control dynamics have to be carefully investigated. We would not want a situation analogous to lake eutrophication to occur in particular areas of the ocean.

Similarly, the attempt to increase the economical harvest of biomass for human benefit involves a search for optimum control inputs. Predator species can be preferentially harvested in order to increase the production of desirable prey species. Depending upon the habits of the species involved, this approach may not be feasible. Other approaches should then be considered; for example, encouraging another species which feeds on the eggs or young of the predator. This would be a more sophisticated technique, and has inherent delays. For every possible control strategy we must determine the control dynamics as well as the cost/effectiveness. The overall value of each control approach will be strongly dependent on system stability.

A first approach to implementing marine ecological control would be to set up an international regulatory body to operate the control and regulate the fisheries. As past experience has shown, i.e., the case of the Antarctic whale fishery, human organizations have their own control dynamics which must be considered as part of the total control loop. Because organization dynamics are usually characterized by extreme inertia, it is probably best to design stable local control loops, through such socio-economic mechanisms as prices and alternative employment for the fishermen. The international control agencies would be primarily concerned with monitoring local control loops, adjusting set points (prices, taxes, artificial stocking, or similar control measures) and serving as a long-time-constant adaptive control element.

While optimizing the year-to-year operation of the fisheries we must not lose sight of very long time constant effects. The various life forms involved in the marine fisheries are of course subject to evolutionary effects. Some recent observations (9) indicate that evolution need not take millions of years. Much further research is needed before we can predict the possible impact of world-wide fishery control on the evolution of natural marine populations.

References

1. Beverton, R. J. H. and S. J. Holt. On the Dynamics of Exploited Fish Populations, Her Majesty's Stationery Office, London, (1957).

2. Brown, Lester R. "Human Food Production as a Process in the Biosphere", Scientific American, Volume 223 (September, 1970), Number 3.

3. Cohen, E. B. "Contingency Accommodation Planning", Technical Information Series 67SD287, General Electric Co., Phila., Pa. (1967).

4. Garfinkel, D. "A Simulation Study of the Effect on Simple Ecological Systems of Making Rate of Increase of Population Density-dependent", J. Theoret. Biol., Volume 14 (1967), 46-58.

5. Glaser, E. R. Population Interaction Models, with Computer Simulation Studies, Ph.D. dissertation, University of Pennsylvania Library (1969).

6. Hardin, G. "The Tragedy of the Commons", Science, Volume 162 (December, 1968), 1243-1248.

7. Haynes, C. V. Jr. "Elephant-Hunting in North America", Scientific American, Volume 201 (1959), Number 5.

8. Josephson, M. "The Invention of the Electric Light", Scientific American, Volume 201 (1959), Number 5.

9. Kettlewell, H. B. D. "A Survey of the Frequencies of Biston betularia and its Melanic Forms in Great Britain", Heredity, Volume 12 (1958), Number 51.

10. MacArthur, R. H. and J. H. Connell. The Biology of Populations, John Wiley and Sons, Inc., New York (1966).

11. Marsh, G. P. Man and Nature, The Belknap Press of Harvard University Press, Cambridge, Massachusetts (1965). *Originally published in 1864.

12. McVay, S. "The Last of the Great Whales", Scientific American, Volume 215 (1966), Number 2.

13. Rosenzweig, M. and R. MacArthur. Graphical Representation and Stability Conditions of Predator-prey Interactions, American Naturalist, Volume 97 (1963), 209-223.

14. Slobodkin, L. B. "Ecological Energy Relationship at the Population Level", American Naturalist, Volume 94 (1960), 213-236.

15. Watt, K. E. F. Ecology and Resource Management, a Quantitative Approach, McGraw-Hill Book Company, New York (1968).

A GRADIOMETER SYSTEM FOR GRAVITY ANOMALY SURVEYING

Milton B. Trageser
Advanced Technology Director
IL 3-404, 68 Albany Street
Massachusetts Institute of Technology
Charles Stark Draper Laboratory
Cambridge, Massachusetts 02139

ABSTRACT

A gravity gradiometer for use in a moving vehicle is feasible. Presently such a device is under development at the M.I.T. Charles Stark Draper Laboratory. A performance level of $\frac{1}{3}$ Eötvös Unit ($\frac{1}{3}$ X 10^{-9} sec^{-2}) can be projected for a properly designed instrument operating in a properly designed system. This performance level gives a survey accuracy of one milligal in 20 miles for a pure gradiometer system.

The paper presents the features necessary in a system to implement the above projection. Gravity anomaly indication is mathematically formulated. The effects of transient and slowly changing errors are analysed. Suitable gradiometer instrument concepts are presented. The measurement dynamics of the gradiometer feedback loop are studied. A data processing scheme for minimizing sensitivity to noise is developed. Requirements for excellent stabilization servos are derived. Methods of achieving excellent stabilization are disclosed. Vertical indication accuracy requirements are discussed. Necessary gradiometer compensations are evaluated with respect to their difficulty. The effect of Brownian motion noise is interpreted.

The paper also presents the features of the experimental gradiometer being built at the MIT Charles Stark Draper Laboratory. Rationalization is made for the selected support system. This instrument is compared with other instruments which incorporate related principles. The structural elements are described. Balancing provisions are treated. Details of the support system are revealed. The thermal design and temperature control system is explored.

1.0 PART 1: INTRODUCTION

The intention of this paper is to show the feasibility of making gravity measurements suitable for detailed geophysical surveys by using gravity gradiometers in a moving vehicle. A system is disclosed which is capable of producing free air gravity anomaly data of essentially the same quality as is currently obtained by fixed site gravimeter observations and leveling.

The question of feasibility can be resolved into two general areas. Is the operation of an instrument capable of measuring so small a stress as the gravity gradient possible in the acceleration and vibration environment of a moving vehicle? Is the measurement dynamics problem possible to solve in a practical system?

A gravity gradiometer instrument is presented in Part 3 of this paper. This instrument promises to be virtually insensitive to linear acceleration and vibration. The instrument is of a type which makes incorporation into a system having other inertial instruments natural. The results of many engineering calculations are given. All the calculations are compatible with a performance projection of $\frac{1}{3}$ Eötvös unit.

A system is developed for the application of the above gravity gradiometer instrument and is presented in Part 2 of this paper. The system contains a stabilized platform for the gradiometer and a data processing scheme for indicating the free air gravity anomaly from the measured gradients. The measurement dynamics problem is investigated in depth. Compensation for the mass of the survey vehicle is shown to be practical. Thermal Brownian Motion is shown to produce a negligible error. The features of the presented system give an accuracy which is compatible with the $\frac{1}{3}$ Eötvös unit performance projection for the instrument.

Gravity gradiometers are universally sensitive to angular vibration of the sensing mass. Angular vibration always causes rectification errors in the indicated gradient and sometimes causes noise. Gravity gradiometers generally require superb platform stabilization of roughly $\frac{1}{20}$" arc. The whole subject of angular vibration is belabored with mathematical rigor in Part 2. This difficult treatment was felt necessary to meet the objective of showing feasibility.

The gradiometer of Part 3 is cylindrical. A similar spherical gradiometer is mentioned in Part 2. This spherical gradiometer is unique among gradiometers. The precise degrees-of-freedom provided for gradient measurement also provide the

sensing mass with a second stage of angular vibration isolation. The requirements on the first
stage of isolation, the stabilized platform gimbals,
are thereby relaxed by two decades. This instrument will be the subject of a later paper.

The error in the free air gravity anomaly indicated
by a system using gradiometers has both fluctuations
and drift. The fluctuations result from platform
jitter noise and from dynamic lags in following the
actual gradient. The size of the fluctuations is
roughly proportional to vehicle speed. The drift
results from gradiometer unbalance or bias change.
The size of the drift is proportional to distance
traveled.

The most detailed surveys should be conducted with
a garden tractor-like vehicle traveling two knots
more or less. The fluctuations from the presented
system would then have a magnitude of .005 milligals.
The same sized error will result from the drift
error along 500 feet of traverse. Using a network
of interesting traverses and adjusting loop
closures should result in the capability of
surveying areas of several hundred acres with the
above accuracy.

A helicopter or a jeep traveling at 20 knots should
provide enough accuracy for most surveys. The
fluctuations would be .05 milligals. The drift
would give the same error in a mile of traverse.
The use of a network should enable the survey
of several tens-of-square miles with this accuracy.

The mobility of the gradiometer system is its
obvious big advantage over the current practice
of fixed site gravimeter observations. Data can
be gathered at a rapid pace with gradiometers.
Furthermore the precise leveling required for
gravimetry has no counterpart in the use of gradiometers. Gravimetry with an accuracy of .005 or .05
milligal requires knowledge of the elevation of
each observation site with an accuracy of better
than .05 or .5 feet in order to make the free air
reduction. A gradiometer system is shown in Part 2
to require knowledge of elevation only when significant vertical gradient anomalies occur. An
accuracy poorer than 5 or 50 feet gives errors
of .005 or .05 milligals in geophysically rough
environments.

The Eötvös correction limits the resolution in
marine gravimetry. The Eötvös correction counteracts the vertical component of Coriolis acceleration
which results from east-west ship velocity and the
rotation of the earth. To compute the Eötvös
correction accurate to .005 or .05 milligals requires knowledge of the east-west component of ship
velocity accurate to roughly .001 or .01 knot.
There is no counterpart for the Eötvös correction
in a gradiometer system.

The terrain effect is a well-known nuisance in geophysical surveying by gravity gradient measurements
made with the Eötvös torsion balance. Torsion
balance measurements are made at fixed sites. A
linear change in the gradient along the line
connecting two sites is assumed. The calculation
of the free air gravity anomaly change between
sites is based on this assumption. For this

assumption to be at all realistic requires that
the measurements be made at sites which can be
considered as representative of the area. Sites
are chosen on level ground well removed from all
large obstructions since the gradient measurements
are very sensitive to local masses. The terrain
is leveled with an accuracy of several
centimeters within a 50 or 100 meter radius
of the site in order to compute a correction to
the gradient measurements accurate to $\frac{1}{3}$ Eötvös
unit. This sensitivity to local masses is known
as the terrain effect.

There is no counterpart to the terrain effect with
a moving gravity gradiometer system. The gradient
is measured everywhere along the path of system
travel. As a massive obstruction is approached
the gradients it causes are measured and integrated
along the path. The indicated gravity disturbance
correctly includes the effect of the obstruction.
As the obstruction is departed its gradients are
integrated and cancel the effects of those measured
during approach.

There are many other interesting applications
of moving gravity gradiometer systems. They can
be used to indicate vertical deflections in an
inertial system. This data in turn can be used
for a direct indication of geoid height. Hybrid
gradiometer/gravimeter systems can be envisioned
for surveys which are both detailed and large
scale. A land vehicle surveying system using
inertial navigation components and gradiometers
can be envisioned to give second order survey
accuracy in elevation and position. Gradiometers
have interesting sampling properties in airborne
gravimetry for geodesy.

2.0 PART 2: THE SYSTEM

Suppose one had an instrument which could
measure gravity gradients in a moving vehicle.
How should a system be organized to indicate the
free air gravity anomaly? What unique properties
should such a system have? What physical effects
influence the measurement of the gravity gradients
in such a system? Answers to these questions are
developed in this part.

The mathematical framework for free air gravity
anomaly indication is developed. The effects of
instrument error and measurement noise are analyzed. A gradiometer concept and alternate
configurations are presented. The instrument
requires a torque-to-balance loop whose dynamics
are critical to the measurement process. Stabilized platform jitter causes noise in the gradient
measurements. Special precautions are necessary
for integrating the noisy gradients into clean
and accurate anomalies.

The jitter of a state-of-the-art stabilized platform causes potentially serious instability in
the gradient measurements as well as noise. The
present stabilization technology is discussed in
some detail. This discussion lays the foundation for the development of a minor stabilization servo modification which minimizes the effects
of the noise. Stabilization system modifications
to eliminate the measurement instability are

also suggested.

Several kinematic effects are analyzed which must be compensated in the system. The mass of the gradiometer system and the vehicle which moves with it affect the gradient measurements. Methods for compensating the effects of these local masses are discussed. Brownian Motion of the gradiometer element is studied and its effects are shown to be tolerable.

2.1 Free Air Gravity Anomaly Indication

The free air gravity anomaly, Δg_{ea} , is to be indicated or measured. The free air gravity[1,2] anomaly is the magnitude of the actual gravity vector, $\vec{\mathcal{G}}_a$, less the magnitude of the reference gravity vector, $\vec{\mathcal{G}}_e$. The actual gravity vector at some point is that which could be measured by an instrument at rest with respect to the earth. The reference gravity vector is defined by some reference gravity model such as the International Gravity Formula[1,2] and the International Ellipsoid (subscript e denotes ellipsoid).

The measured gravity anomaly, Δg_{em} , is intended to represent the free air gravity anomaly, Δg_{ea} . These quantities differ because of instrumental errors and approximations.

How do Δg_{ea} and Δg_{em} change with time as the sampling point moves with velocity $\vec{v}$ relative to the earth? Let $\vec{k}$ be a unit vector along the z-axis which is upward along the local vertical. Then

$$- \Delta g_{ea} = \vec{k} \cdot \vec{\mathcal{G}}_a - \vec{k} \cdot \vec{\mathcal{G}}_e \qquad (1)$$

$$- \Delta g_{em} = \vec{k} \cdot \vec{\mathcal{G}}_m - \vec{k} \cdot \vec{\mathcal{G}}_e \qquad (2)$$

Take time derivatives of the above.

$$- \frac{d \Delta g_{ea}}{dt} = \frac{d\vec{k}}{dt} \cdot \vec{\mathcal{G}}_a + \vec{k} \cdot \frac{d\vec{\mathcal{G}}_a}{dt} - \frac{d\vec{k}}{dt} \cdot \vec{\mathcal{G}}_e - \vec{k} \cdot \frac{d\vec{\mathcal{G}}_e}{dt} \qquad (3)$$

$$- \frac{d \Delta g_{em}}{dt} = \frac{d\vec{k}}{dt} \cdot \vec{\mathcal{G}}_m + \vec{k} \cdot \frac{d\vec{\mathcal{G}}_m}{dt} - \frac{d\vec{k}}{dt} \cdot \vec{\mathcal{G}}_e - \vec{k} \cdot \frac{d\vec{\mathcal{G}}_e}{dt} \qquad (4)$$

Let the gradient of the actual gravity vector, the gradient of the reference gravity vector, and the gradient of the measured gravity vector be represented respectively by dyadics G_a , G_e , and G_m . Each dyadic[3] has terms like $\vec{k}\vec{k} \frac{\partial g_{az}}{\partial z}$ and $\vec{k}\vec{i} \frac{\partial g_{az}}{\partial z}$ for components. The following differential equations follow from the definitions

$$\frac{d g_a}{dt} = G_a \cdot \vec{v} \qquad (5)$$

$$\frac{d g_e}{dt} = G_e \cdot \vec{v} \qquad (6)$$

$$\frac{d g_m}{dt} = G_m \cdot \vec{v} \qquad (7)$$

Substitute (5), (6), and (7) into (3) and (4).

$$- \frac{d \Delta g_{ea}}{dt} = \vec{k} \cdot \left[(G_a - G_e) \cdot \vec{v} \right] + \frac{d\vec{k}}{dt} \cdot \left(\vec{\mathcal{G}}_a - \vec{\mathcal{G}}_e \right) \qquad (8)$$

$$- \frac{d \Delta g_{em}}{dt} = \vec{k} \cdot \left[(G_m - G_e) \cdot \vec{v} \right] + \frac{d\vec{k}}{dt} \cdot \left(\vec{\mathcal{G}}_m - \vec{\mathcal{G}}_e \right) \qquad (9)$$

Equation (9) could be implemented completely to indicate the gravity anomaly. The components of G_m are measured by instruments which are mounted on a stabilized platform. The components of $\vec{v}$ can be resolved in this platform space. A scheme can be devised to keep this platform precisely aligned with local vertical $\vec{k}$. Thus the $\vec{k} \cdot \left[G_m \cdot \vec{v} \right]$ term can be computed.

G_e is determined in a space whose vertical axis is normal to the ellipsoid. To transform G_e into platform space requires knowledge of the vertical deflection. A scheme can be devised to accurately indicate this. The same type of vertical deflection data is necessary for the computation of the last term of (9). Such a system requires five gravity gradiometers and very precise gyroscopes and accelerometers.

The above complete implementation of equation (9) indicates a different free air gravity anomaly[1,2] than is ordinarily used. The free air reduction for this anomaly is based on elevations relative to the reference ellipsoid. The common free air reduction is based on elevations relative to sea level or the geoid. The two differ by the product of the vertical gravity gradient times the local geoid height.

Consider the following modification to equation (9). Drop entirely the $\frac{d\vec{k}}{dt}$ term. Bodily rotate G_e (not transform) from the ellipsoid space to the local vertical space. There are three motives for this modification. First, the dropped term and the erroneous transformation are equivalent to gradiometer instrument errors of only $\frac{1}{3}$ Eötvös unit when the deflection of the vertical is 20" arc. This abridgment seems like a worthwhile approximation since its error is comparable to that expected from the instruments. Second, the system complexity is reduced by not adding gradiometers to indicate vertical deflection. Third, it can be shown that the resulting equation almost perfectly gives the free air gravity anomaly as it is commonly defined. Dropping the term and erroneously transforming G_e are just what is required to account for the geoid height and the vertical gradient.

Equation (9) becomes

$$- \frac{d \Delta g_{em}}{dt} = \vec{k} \cdot \left[(G_m - G_e) \cdot \vec{v} \right] = \vec{k} \cdot \left[\Delta G_{em} \cdot \vec{v} \right] \qquad (10)$$

with a slightly different definition for Δg_{em} and G_e . In scalar form equation (10) is

$$\Delta g_{em} = \Delta g_{em_0} + \int \left[v_x \left(\frac{\partial g_{mz}}{\partial x} - \frac{\partial g_{ez}}{\partial x} \right) + v_y \left(\frac{\partial g_{mz}}{\partial y} - \frac{\partial g_{ez}}{\partial y} \right) + v_z \left(\frac{\partial g_{mz}}{\partial z} - \frac{\partial g_{ez}}{\partial z} \right) \right] dt \qquad (11)$$

A block diagram for implementing equation (11) is shown in Figure 1. The gradiometer information is first compensated for known effects. Examination

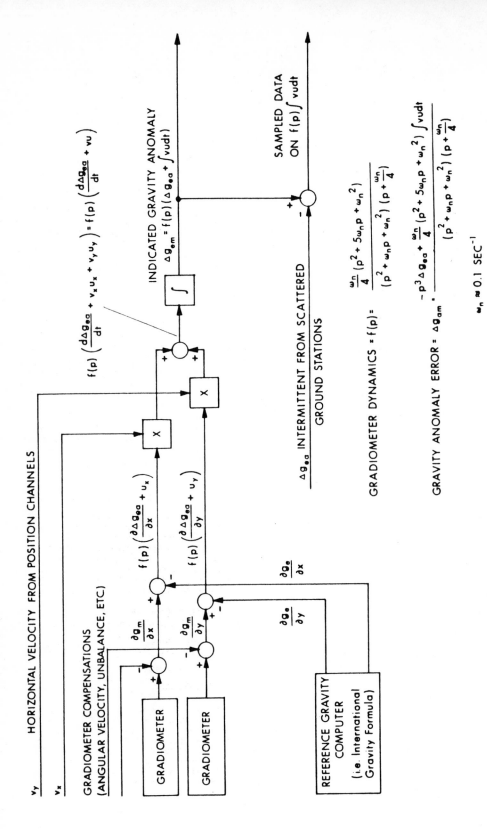

Fig. 1 Free Air Gravity Anomaly Indication

of these comes later. Gradients are accurately calculated from the reference gravity model and subtracted from the gradiometer information. The resulting components of the measured gravity anomaly gradient are multiplied by components of velocity and summed. This sum is the time rate of change of the free air gravity anomaly. Integration gives the indicated anomaly.

In Figure 1 the $v_{\dot{z}}$ term of equation (11) has been dropped. This should be acceptable for most gravity surveying applications. Consider a survey made by an aircraft at low altitude above relatively flat terrain. It should be feasible to fly the aircraft at constant altitude to within 50 feet for a distance of a mile or so. Gravity anomaly gradients typically have an order of magnitude of 30 Eötvös units. The product of altitude change times the gradient gives the order of magnitude of the potential error from dropping the $v_{\dot{z}}$ term.

$$\left(30\ E\ddot{o}tv\ddot{o}s\ Units\right)\left(\frac{10^{-9}sec^{-2}}{E\ddot{o}tv\ddot{o}s\ Unit}\right)\left(50ft\right)=1.5\times10^{-6}ft/sec^2\approx0.05\ milligal$$

This error is the same as would result from a gradiometer error of $\frac{1}{3}$ Eötvös unit over a mile of traverse.

2.2 Error Equation

It is of interest to examine the errors in the indicated gravity anomaly Δg_{em}. The counterpart of equation (10) can be written for actual gravity anomaly Δg_{ea} using the new definitions for Δg_{ea} and G_e.

$$-\frac{d\Delta g_{ea}}{dt} = \vec{k}\cdot\left[(G_a-G_e)\cdot\vec{v}\right] = \vec{k}\cdot\left[\Delta G_{ea}\cdot\vec{v}\right] \qquad (12)$$

Subtract (12) from (10).

$$-\frac{d\Delta g_{am}}{dt} = \vec{k}\cdot\left[(G_m-G_a)\cdot\vec{v}\right] = \vec{k}\cdot\left[\Delta G_{am}\cdot\vec{v}\right] \qquad (13)$$

Δg_{am} is the error in the indicated gravity anomaly. ΔG_{am} is the error in the measurement of the gravity gradients.

It is useful to integrate error equation (13) by two methods. The first form is most useful for the examination of low frequency errors in the gradient measurements.

$$-\Delta g_{am} = \int \vec{k}\cdot\left[\Delta G_{am}\cdot\vec{v}\right]dt \qquad (14)$$

Suppose a gradiometer instrument bias of $\frac{1}{3}$ Eötvös unit. What is the indicated gravity anomaly error per mile of traverse?

$$\left(\frac{1}{3}E\ddot{o}tv\ddot{o}s\ Unit\right)\left(\frac{10^{-9}sec^{-2}}{E\ddot{o}tv\ddot{o}s\ Unit}\right)\left(5280ft\right)=1.76\times10^{-6}ft/sec^2\approx0.05\ milligal$$

Integration of (13) by parts gives a form more useful for the examination of transient and dynamic errors.

$$-\Delta g_{am} = \int\vec{k}\cdot\left[\Delta G_{am}\,dt\cdot\vec{v}\right] - \int\int\vec{k}\cdot\left[\Delta G_{am}\,dt\cdot\frac{d\vec{v}}{dt}\right]dt \qquad (15)$$

The scalar form of the above equation is perhaps more enlightening. Letting $\Delta G_{am_{zx}} = \Delta G_x$ and $\Delta G_{am_{zy}} = \Delta G_y$ gives

$$\Delta g_{am} = v_x\int\Delta G_x dt + v_y\int\Delta G_y dt - \int\frac{dv_x}{dt}\int\Delta G_x dt\,dt - \int\frac{dv_y}{dt}\int\Delta G_y dt\,dt \quad (16)$$

It is interesting to speculate on the allowable order of magnitude of transients and noise in the $\int\Delta G\,dt$ quantities. Consider three vehicles moving at different but constant velocities. For velocities choose $\frac{1}{10}$, 1, and 10 g-sec. The first corresponds to a garden tractor moving at two knots. The second corresponds to a jeep, helicopter, or ship moving at 20 knots. The third is a 200 knot aircraft. Suppose the $\int\Delta G\,dt$ quantities are subject to transient noise errors whose order of magnitude is 10^{-7} sec^{-1} and whose frequency is in the neighborhood of one radian per ten seconds. In the garden tractor these transients cause noise in the indicated gravity anomaly of roughly .01 milligals with a scale in the neighborhood of 30 feet. In the helicopter and aircraft the corresponding noises are .1 milligal with a scale of 300 feet and one milligal with a scale of 3,000 feet.

Now consider accelerations in equation (16). The operator of each of the above vehicles attempts to maintain a straight course and a constant speed. Suppose each of their efforts meets with limited success and results in the equivalent of a $\frac{1}{20}$ g-sec maneuver every ten seconds. This corresponds to 30° course changes in the garden tractor for the circumnavigation of rocks and stumps. In the helicopter this could represent cross wind gusts which deflect the vehicles path by 3°. This probably represents flight of the aircraft on a medium calm day. There is no reason to assume a correlation between these maneuvers and the $\int\Delta G\,dt$ noise provided the stabilization gimbals have been carefully balanced. Each maneuver therefore contributes roughly

$$\left(\frac{1}{20}g\text{-sec}\right)\left(10^{-7}sec^{-1}\right)=\frac{1}{2}10^{-8}g\approx0.005\ milligal$$

to the error in the indicated gravity anomaly. These contributions will add in a root mean square manner. A maneuver rate of 360 per hour gives an error rate of .095 milligals per $\sqrt{hour}$. One third Eötvös unit gradiometer error matches the above rectified transient error on a two mile traverse by garden tractor, on a six mile traverse by helicopter, and on a twenty mile traverse by aircraft.

The above discussion shows that transients in $\int\Delta G\,dt$ of 10^{-7} sec^{-1} are near the borderline of allowability. This value will be used as a criteria in the discussion on dynamic errors which comes later.

2.3 Instrument Concept

The gradient sensing instrument is certainly the most critical feature of a gradiometer system for gravity anomaly surveying. What instrument concept has the greatest potential for yielding the performance assumed above in the acceleration and vibration environment of a moving vehicle? Extremely high performance gyros and accelerometers have been employed in far worse environments with great success. These inertial components owe their great success to the virtual insensitivity of their buoyant/visions/magnetic support system to high levels of acceleration and vibration. It is logical to look in this area of technology for the answer.

A gravity gradiometer can be made using a cylindrical float similar to that used in a high performance gyroscope. This is illustrated in Figure 2. This float is suspended inside of a housing by a buoyant/viscous/capacitive support system (not shown in Figure 2). Inside of this float is a mass configuration somewhat resembling that employed by Roland Eötvos in the "curvature variometer" he constructed at the end of the last century. The figure indicates that moment M is applied to the float by gradient $\frac{\partial g_y}{\partial x}$ acting on the difference between the transverse moments of inertia. References[1,4] are provided for a reader who does not find this intuitively obvious.

The above instrument must be mounted on a superb stabilized platform. The float rotates relative to the platform as a result of moment M. The rotation angle is precisely sensed. A minute torque is accurately applied by electronics to restore the float to its nominal orientation relative to the platform. This torque is taken as an indication of the gravity gradient. Several compensations must be made for kinematic effects.

The configuration shown in Figure 2 is axially symmetric. Two of these components are required to be mounted on the stabilized platform to make a gravity anomaly surveying system. Each component has its axis of cylinder horizontal. Their two axes are perpendicular. Thus $\bar{j}$ (the y-axis) in Figure 2 represents vertical on the platform. The two instruments then directly indicate $\frac{\partial g_z}{\partial x}$ and $\frac{\partial g_z}{\partial y}$.

2.4 Skewed Configuration

The skewed mass configuration shown in Figure 3 is an alternative. Now the axis of cylinder is mounted vertically on the stabilized platform. The measured moment is now the result of the action of two gradient components, $\frac{\partial g_x}{\partial z}$ and $\frac{\partial g_x}{\partial y}$. To separate these requires the use of three gradiometers on the platform as shown in Figure 4. In Figure 5 this instrument cluster is shown mounted on a three-degree-of-freedom stabilized platform. The platform also carries level sensing accelerometers and stabilization gyros.

The skewed mass configuration has three advantages with respect to the axially symmetric mass configuration. The gyroscope always performs more accurately with its axis of cylinder vertical; perhaps this will also be true of gradiometers. The gradient indicated by both symmetric and skewed sensor configurations is sensitive to platform angular acceleration about the axes of cylinder; inspection of the equations in Figure 5 shows

that this effect is cancelled out with this particular cluster of instruments if the gradiometers are well matched. The third advantage of the skewed configuration is that the inertia efficiency ratio can be made higher in the skewed configuration.

The inertia efficiency ratio is $\frac{I_{ACTIVE}}{I_{33}}$. This is a parameter for how sensitive the gradiometer dynamic error is to angle pickoff noise and to angular acceleration about the axis of cylinder. Consider all the mass of the float to be concentrated in two lines in the axially symmetric configuration. This limiting case gives an inertia efficiency ratio of unity. In the axially symmetric gradiometer which is being built at the Laboratory, this ratio is .65.

Now consider the skewed gradiometer with all the mass concentrated in two points. The limit of the inertia efficiency ratio is $\frac{\ell}{2r}$ where ℓ and r are float length and radius. In a unit of square cross section the ratio is again unity. However, the opportunity exists to double the ratio by multiplying the length and radius by $2^{\frac{1}{3}}$ and $2^{-\frac{1}{3}}$.

2.5 Other Configuration Alternatives

A third configuration alternative uses a similar mass arrangement to that employed in the early 1930's by Lancaster-Jones.[4] This design was a torsion wire-suspended "gravity gradiometer". This configuration is shown in Figure 6. The three weights at the edges of the cylinder are equal. They are arranged so that $I_{xx} - I_{yy} = 0$. Thus the unit is no longer sensitive to $\frac{\partial g_x}{\partial y}$.

The fourth weight shown lies on the axis of cylinder. This weight is roughly equal to each of the other three. The fourth weight provides end-for-end balance of the float. End-for-end balance prevents heavy loading of the buoyant/viscous/capacitive support system by transverse acceleration.

The Lancaster-Jones configuration is mounted with its axis of cylinder vertical. This is its advantage over the axially symmetric configuration. Only two instruments are required to measure $\frac{\partial g_z}{\partial x}$ and $\frac{\partial g_z}{\partial y}$. This is its advantage over the skewed configuration. The penalty is less effective use of the active mass. The active mass m is the sum of the four weights. It can be shown that the active product of inertia equals $\frac{1}{4}m\ell r$ for a Lancaster-Jones configuration using point masses. The active product of inertia for a skewed configuration is $\frac{1}{2}m\ell r$. The gradients therefore produce half the torque while the uncertainties from the suspension presumably remain the same. The limit of the inertia efficiency ratio for the Lancaster-Jones configuration is $\frac{\ell}{3r}$ compared to $\frac{\ell}{2r}$ for the skewed configuration.

A fourth configuration alternative is very attractive. It differs substantially from the above three. Inclusion in this presentation would be diversionary. Therefore it will be considered

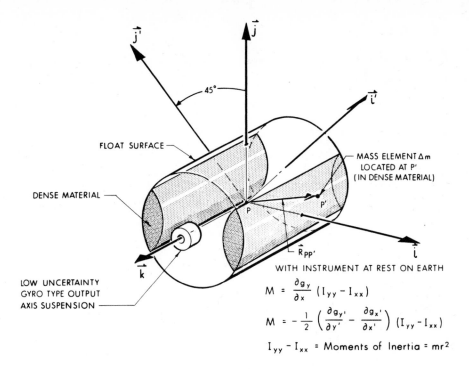

FLOAT SURFACE

DENSE MATERIAL

MASS ELEMENT Δm
LOCATED AT P'
(IN DENSE MATERIAL)

LOW UNCERTAINTY
GYRO TYPE OUTPUT
AXIS SUSPENSION

WITH INSTRUMENT AT REST ON EARTH

$$M = \frac{\partial g_y}{\partial x} (I_{yy} - I_{xx})$$

$$M = -\frac{1}{2} \left(\frac{\partial g_{y'}}{\partial y'} - \frac{\partial g_{x'}}{\partial x'} \right) (I_{yy} - I_{xx})$$

$$I_{yy} - I_{xx} = \text{Moments of Inertia} = mr^2$$

Fig. 2   Axially Symmetric Configuration

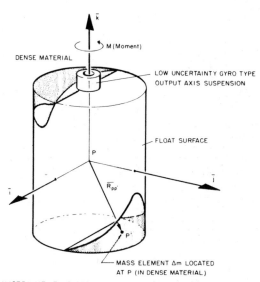

DENSE MATERIAL

M (Moment)

LOW UNCERTAINTY GYRO TYPE
OUTPUT AXIS SUSPENSION

FLOAT SURFACE

MASS ELEMENT Δm LOCATED
AT P (IN DENSE MATERIAL)

WITH INSTRUMENT AT REST ON EARTH

$$M = \frac{\partial g_x}{\partial z} I_{yz} - \frac{\partial g_x}{\partial y} (I_{xx} - I_{yy})$$

$$I_{xx} - I_{yy} = \text{Moments of Inertia} = mr^2$$

$$I_{yz} = \text{Product of Inertia} = -\frac{1}{2} m \ell r$$

Fig. 3   Skewed Mass Configuration

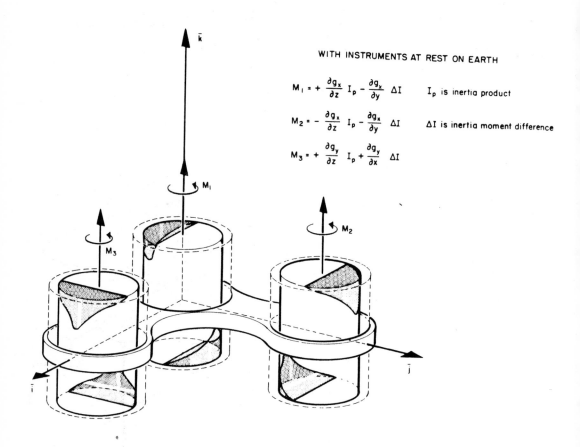

WITH INSTRUMENTS AT REST ON EARTH

$$M_1 = + \frac{\partial g_x}{\partial z} I_p - \frac{\partial g_x}{\partial y} \Delta I \qquad I_p \text{ is inertia product}$$

$$M_2 = - \frac{\partial g_x}{\partial z} I_p - \frac{\partial g_x}{\partial y} \Delta I \qquad \Delta I \text{ is inertia moment difference}$$

$$M_3 = + \frac{\partial g_y}{\partial z} I_p + \frac{\partial g_y}{\partial x} \Delta I$$

Fig. 4 Cluster of Skewed Gradiometers

$$\frac{\partial g_z}{\partial x} = \frac{\partial g_x}{\partial z} = \frac{1}{I_\rho} \frac{1}{2} (M_1 - M_2)$$

$$\frac{\partial g_z}{\partial y} = \frac{\partial g_y}{\partial z} = \frac{1}{I_\rho} (M_3 + \frac{1}{2} M_1 + \frac{1}{2} M_2)$$

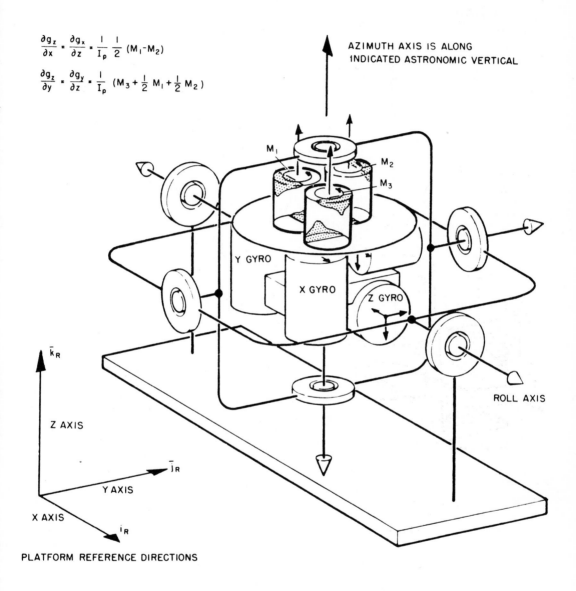

Fig. 5 Gradiometers on a Stabilized Platform

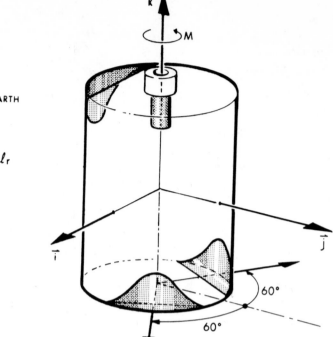

WITH INSTRUMENT AT REST ON EARTH

$$M = \frac{\partial g_x}{\partial z} I_{yz} = -\frac{\partial g_z}{\partial x} I_{yz}$$

$$I_{xx} - I_{yy} = 0$$

$$I_{yz} = \text{Product of Inertia} = \frac{1}{4} m\ell_r$$

Fig. 6   Lancaster-Jones Configuration

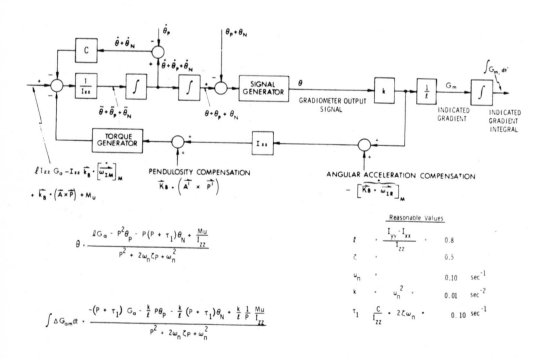

Fig. 7   Second Order Torque Feedback Loop

72

in some future paper.

Experience with the experimental axially symmetric gravity gradiometer which the Laboratory is currently building should enable the wise future selection of an appropriate sensor configuration for use in gravity anomaly surveying.

2.6 Torque Feedback Loop

The gravity gradiometer torque feedback loop is at the heart of the measurement dynamics problem. The loop has two functions. It must hold the float in a nearly constant orientation on the stabilized platform. It must deliver signals which can be accurately used as an indication of the gradient. Figure 7 shows the loop in its simplest form.

At the left is input gradient component G_a acting on an active inertia ℓI_{33}. The float structure accurately sums this torque, the fluid viscous shear torque, a purposely applied capacitive torque, and a small uncertainty torque. This sum is accurately scaled to angular acceleration by the axis-of-cylinder moment of inertia I_{33}. The angular acceleration is kinematically integrated to angular velocity. This of course is the source of the viscous shear.

At this point it is necessary to define the three θ's shown in Figure 7. Figure 8 defines the θ's. Space R is reference measuring platform space. Space R is smoothly rotating and has the orientation desired for the measuring platform. Space M is measuring platform space. Space M differs from space R principally because of inadequacies in the stabilization servos. θ_P is the axis-of-cylinder component of the angular displacement of space M from space R; it represents servo jitter and bias.

Space B is the body space of the gradiometer sensing mass. An angle sensor can be physically incorporated to read out the angular displacement of space B (float) from space M (housing). This angle is $\theta + \theta_N$. θ is the output indicated by the sensor. θ_N is erratic noise or bias disturbance in the sensor. This might result from structural instability or electronic inadequacy. Thus the angular acceleration of inertia I_{33} relative to space R is $\ddot{\theta} + \theta_P + \theta_N$. Space R is nearly inertial.

The buoyancy fluid damping C acts on the angular velocity of the gradiometer float relative to its housing, $\dot{\theta} + \dot{\theta}_N$. Characteristic time $\frac{I_{33}}{C}$ of the experimental gradiometer is slightly longer than 8 seconds.

The feedback loop in its simplest form multiplies indicated angle θ by an appropriate loop gain k. The desired angular acceleration to restore the float to null is $-k\theta$. This quantity is multiplied by known float inertia I_{33} and applied to the float as a capacitive torque. Figure 7 shows the differential equations for θ and the important transient error parameter $\int \Delta G_{am} dt$.

The dynamic and noise characteristics of the above loop have been studied for various gradiometer applications. An undamped natural frequency, ω_n, of $.1$ sec^{-1} has been found nearly optimum for many gradiometer applications. The 8 second damping characteristic time gives a damping ratio ζ near $.5$. An inertia efficiency ratio ℓ of $.8$ has been used in the plotted transient responses.

The transient responses of output signal θ to one microradian steps in θ_P and θ_N are plotted in Figure 9. These appear quite reasonable. Transient responses to a step of 10 Eötvös units and a ramp of one Eötvös unit per second are also plotted in the figure. These could be improved somewhat. It would be better if the float did not displace 2" arc in the presence of an extreme gradient of 100 Eötvös units. This average displacement could result in slightly changed average reaction torques in the support system.

The transient responses of the integrated gradient error $\int \Delta G_{am} dt$ for the same four disturbances are plotted in Figure 10. The response to a modest 10 Eötvös unit step is a marginal 10^{-7} sec^{-1} transient in the integrated gradient error. There is incentive for improving the loop.

2.7 Third Order Loop

Improvement can be accomplished by simply adding a rather low grade analog integrator as shown in Figure 11. The resulting transient responses of θ are shown in Figure 12. These are completely acceptable. The $\int \Delta G_{am} dt$ transient responses are shown in Figure 13. The response to transients in the gradient is much improved. However, they still give the impression of sluggishness. This sluggishness would be especially degrading to system performance in geophysical prospecting where detail is of interest. Inspection of Figure 11 shows that this sluggishness could be expected because of two integrations between the input and the output. Can one of these lags be practically eliminated?

2.8 Lag Compensation

A lag compensating signal is added outside the feedback loop in Figure 14. Transient responses of θ are still shown in Figure 12. The $\int \Delta G_{am} dt$ transient responses are shown in Figure 15. The response to a step in gradient is greatly improved. The gravity anomaly resulting from this step is sensed with a time lag of less than ten seconds.

The improvement in the response to a gradient ramp is even more spectacular. This improvement is very important since in nature the onset of a gradient change is better described by a ramp than by a step. For example, consider the one Eötvös unit per second ramp whose response is plotted in Figure 15. Over 100 seconds the gradient changes by 100 Eötvös units. The cause for such a large change would have to be a large mountain or geologic formation. It would require more than 100 seconds for a 300 knot vehicle to travel the 10 miles required to approach, pass, and depart the formation.

73

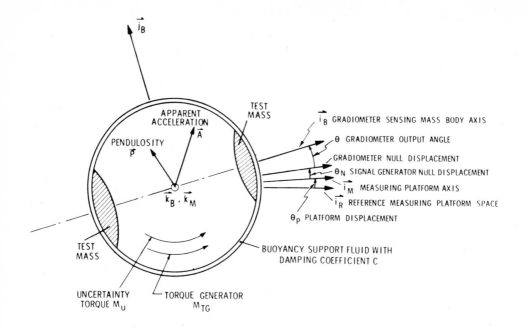

Fig. 8 Gradiometer/Measuring Platform Kinematics

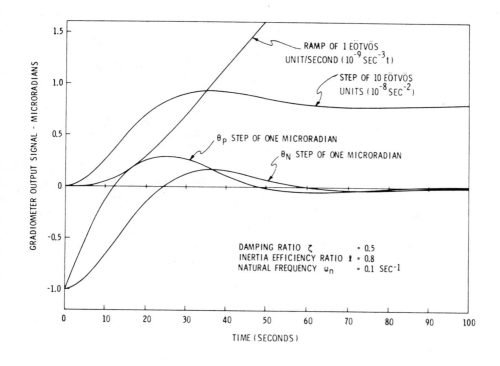

Fig. 9 θ Transient Response of Second Order Loop

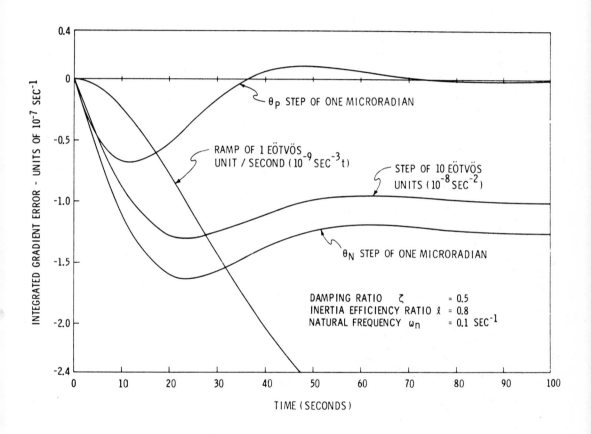

Fig. 10   Integrated Gradient Error Transient Response
of Second Order Loop

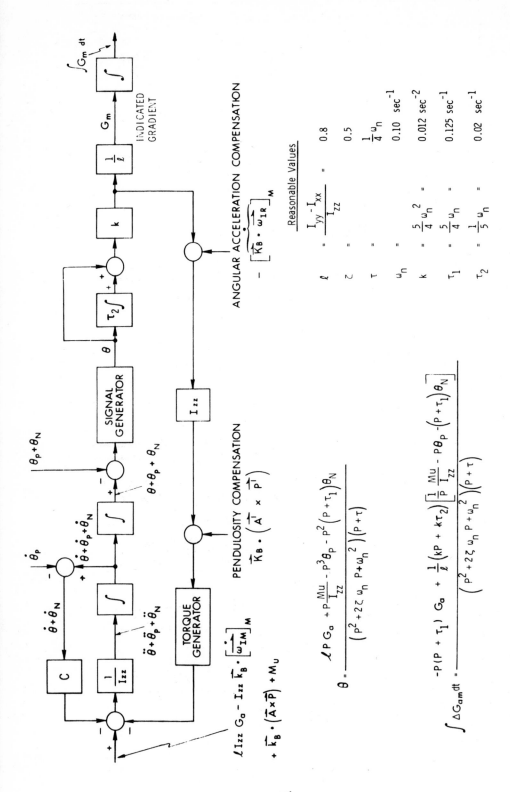

Fig. 11 Third Order Torque Feedback Loop

76

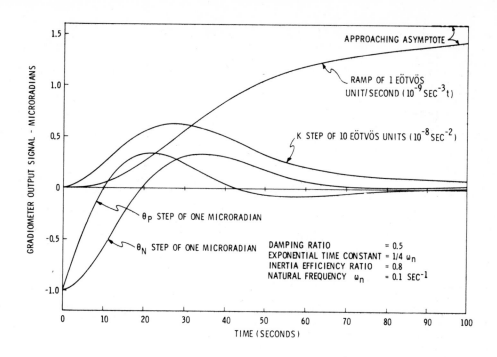

Fig. 12   θ Transient Response of Third Order Loop

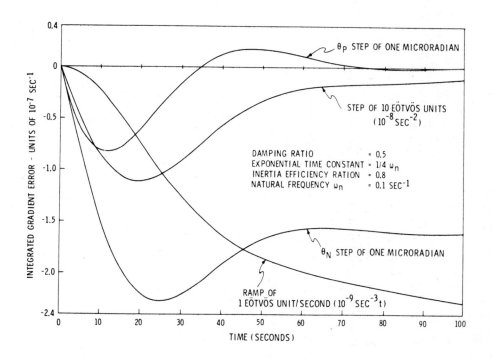

Fig. 13   Integrated Gradient Error Transient Response
. of Third Order Loop

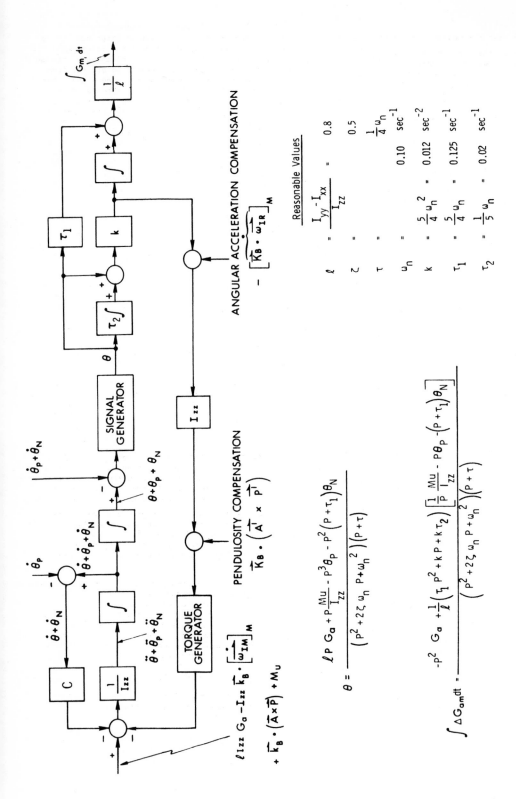

Fig. 14 Third Order Loop with Lag Compensation

78

It is seen that the response of $\int \Delta G_{am} dt$ to transients in the gradient are excellent using lag compensation. Was any penalty paid for this improvement? The high frequency attenuation in the response of $\int \Delta G_{am} dt$ to transients in θ_p and θ_N has been lost. Inspection of the differential equation for $\int \Delta G_{am} dt$ in Figure 14 shows that the high frequency components of θ_p and θ_N show up directly as indicated gradient noise with a gain of $\frac{\gamma}{\ell} = .156 \ sec^{-1}$

This situation poses no particular problem with respect to angle transducer noise θ_N. θ_N can have hardly any changes. The low frequency part of θ_N can only result from mechanical instability or slowly changing bias in the sensing electronics. It is hard to see how amplitudes of greater than a fraction of a microradian could occur during periods shorter than a thousand seconds. The high frequency part of θ_N is from noise in the sensing electronics. A detectability of 0.1" arc has already been demonstrated in the laboratory. This demonstration used the gradiometer electronics, simulated sensor capacities, a one volt excitation, and a 2 millisecond sampling time. Detectability levels of tenths of a microradian could possibly result with some averaging.

The situation is quite different with respect to stabilized platform noise $0p$. $0p$ can be rich in high frequency noise. The platform of a typical high performance inertial system jitters with amplitudes of around 2" arc (10^{-5} radian) at a frequency in the neighborhood of 25 cycles per second. This comes directly into $\int \Delta G_{am} dt$ as a noise amplitude of $15.6 \times 10^{-7} \ sec^{-1}$. The noise from this jitter in the indicated gradient after block "k" in Figure 14 is
$$(10^{-5} \ radian)(\tfrac{5}{4})(.01 \ sec^{-2})(\tfrac{1}{.8}) = 1.56 \times 10^{-7} sec^{-2}$$
$$= 156 \ E\ddot{o}tv\ddot{o}s \ units.$$

2.9 Integrations

How are the integrations $\int \nu \, G_m dt$ in equations (11) to be carried out with an accuracy of $\frac{1}{3}$ Eötvös unit when wideband noise exists in G_m of 156 Eötvös units? Will not the noise in ν and the noise in G_m produce ruinous rectifications? Careful attention must certainly be given to the integrations.

The integrated gradient $\int G_m \, dt$ in Figure 14 will be shown to be a very accurate and noise-free quantity. This quantity will be developed and directly used in performing the integrations.

A relatively minor modification to the usual stabilization servo is of major importance with respect to the above questions. The stabilization servo will be arranged to guarantee a magnitude of less than 4×10^{-7} radian-seconds for the quantity $\int \theta_P dt$. A scheme for implementing this will be discussed in a later section.

Examine first the question of the accuracy of the integrated gradient. The signal after box "k" in Figure 14 has fluctuations but is electronically very clean. It has reasonable voltage and impedance levels. This signal even exists in digital form in the experimental gradiometer. The signal consists of carrier cycles (100 KC) imposed on the capacitive torque generator. Each cycle corresponds to roughly .1 Eötvös unit-sec ($10^{-10} sec^{-1}$) when a one volt excitation level is used. This signal can be accurately integrated by counting cycles with a computer. Now follow this information around the torquing loop. It is also accurately integrated by kinematics. The cycle counting integral must accurately represent the integral of the gradient to the extent that the signal after "k" succeeds in keeping θ small.

How small can θ be kept? Satisfactory responses to changes in the gradient and in θ_N have already been established. A potentially serious disturbance of θ can result from noise in θ_p, the platform jitter. It is fruitful to regard θ as the sum of two parts, $\theta = \theta_R - \theta_p$. θ_R describes the motion of the float relative to space R. A relationship can be written for θ_R in terms of θ_p by using the equation for θ in figure 14. Using the value 4×10^{-7} radian-seconds for $\int \theta_p dt$ in this relationship gives a maximum value of 5×10^{-8} radians for θ_R. This noise is at relativity high frequency and can be ignored. The integrals $\int \theta_R dt$ and $\int \theta_p \, dt$ tend to be equal for low frequencies and thus cancel each other out.

How much noise in the integrated gradient can be produced by the remaining θp term in 0? Consider the main channel in figure 14. Its noise contribution in the indicated gradient is approximately $(4 \times 10^{-7} \ rad\text{-}sec) \frac{k}{\ell} = .06 \times 10^{-7} sec^{-1}$. Consider the lag compensation channel in figure 14. Its noise contribution is $(10^{-5} \ radian) \frac{\gamma}{\ell} = 15.6 \times 10^{-7} sec^{-1}$ with 2" arc of servo jitter, a quite unacceptable value. A low pass filter of one second characteristic time together with the error angle constraint gives the marginal value of (4×10^{-7} radian) $\frac{\gamma}{\ell} = 0.6 \times 10^{-7} sec^{-1}$ with negligible dynamic lag. A ten second filter gives the completely acceptable value of $0.06 \times 10^{-7} sec^{-1}$ with significant dynamic lag. At high frequencies the noise contributions from the two channels add coherently.

It has been established that $\int G_m dt$ can be obtained with a good accuracy and low noise level. How should the integration of $\int \nu \, G_m dt$ be accomplished? Let the computer determine a slowly, smoothly changing quantity G'_m. This quantity is determined in a manner which makes the integral $\int G''_m \, dt = \int (G_m - G'_m) dt$ bounded and relatively small. Let the integrals in equation (11) be represented by

$$\int \nu \, G_m dt = \int \nu \, G'_m \, dt + \int \nu \, G''_m \, dt \qquad (17)$$

The integration of the first term is straightforward. The second term is integrated by parts.

$$\int \nu \, G_m dt = \int \nu \, G'_m \, dt + \nu \int G''_m dt - \int \frac{d\nu}{dt} \int G''_m dt \, dt \qquad (18)$$

$\int G''_m dt$ consists of three parts. One part is from the computer and is noise free. The second part is from the main channel of Figure 14 and contains a little noise. The third part is from the lag compensation channel. This part contains little noise with a ten second filter and significant noise with a one second filter.

There is no opportunity for rectification of noise in the second term of equation (18). The dynamic response of this term to changes in the gradient should be optimized. Use the one second filter in the lag compensation channel. This nearly perfectly implements the lag compensated process for vehicles moving with constant speed. The error from θ_p transients is .66 X 10^{-7} sec^{-1}, mostly at high frequency. This matches well the error from step changes in the gradient of 10 or 20 Eötvös units. The overall result is roughly as described under "2.2 Error Equation."

The third term of equation (18) offers the opportunity for noise rectification. Use the ten second filter on the lag compensation channel. This gives a wideband noise level of .12 X 10^{-7}sec^{-1} in $\int G_m dt$. Suppose this rectifies once each ten seconds with 1.6 feet/sec of random velocity change. The resulting error is .01 milligal per hour. This compares favorably with gradiometer errors of $\frac{1}{3}$ Eötvös unit. The same error results from the rectification of .16 ft. per second noise at ten cycles per second.

The additional filtering causes an additional error in $\int \Delta G_{am} dt$ compared to the perfectly implemented lag compensated process. The maximum value of this error in following a ten Eötvös unit step is .4 X 10^{-7}sec^{-1}. Velocity changes can rectify with actual gradient changes.

A computer flow diagram for one channel of the integration scheme is shown in Figure 16. It can be seen that the implementation of this data process would be practical with digital differential analyzer techniques. It could also be implemented with an analog computer for certain applications.

A clean source of velocity and acceleration data is necessary at the higher frequencies. This can be obtained from the accelerometers and gyros of the stabilization system. The effects of low frequency gyro drifts can be removed by the introduction of supplementary navigation data in post-operation data reduction. This is the reason the quantity $\int G''_m dt$ is recorded along with the indicated anomaly.

2.10 Gradiometer Stabilization Requirements

It was assumed earlier that the gravity gradiometer was mounted on a stabilized platform. What must this platform do? How good must it be? How can it be built?

The three stabilization requirements of gradient resolution, noise level, and rectifying jitter are briefly stated. The remainder of this section mathematically develops the rectifying

jitter requirement. The current state of the art of stabilized platforms is briefly presented in the next section. Approaches are outlined for obtaining the necessary improvements in stabilization in later sections.

The proper resolution of the gravity gradient components is the most obvious requirement on the stabilized platform. The gradiometers must be held level and in some preferred azimuth orientation. An error in level causes the gradiometer to sense a component of $\left(\frac{\partial g_z}{\partial z} - \frac{\partial g_3}{\partial x} \right)$ This difference between the vertical and horizontal gradients of the vector field is a large 4600 Eötvös units. A leveling error of only 15" arc causes an error of $\frac{1}{3}$ Eötvös unit in the measurement of the gravity anomaly gradient. Accurate vertical indication is obviously essential.

The azimuth resolution of the gravity gradients and of the components of velocity must be in the same coordinate system. Suppose a large 100 Eötvös unit gravity anomaly gradient exists. An azimuth error of 0.2^{o} between the gradient and the velocity sensors can cause a resolution error of $\frac{1}{3}$ Eötvös unit.

Noise in the indicated gradient was shown to result from platform angular vibrations about the axis of cylinder of a gradiometer. It was earlier assumed that the integral of the platform jitter angle could be constrained. A maximum value for the magnitude of $\int \theta_p dt$ of 4 X 10^{-7} radian-seconds was shown to be acceptable. A scheme must be devised to implement this.

Platform angular vibration causes a second effect which is more serious. Small angular vibrations of the float about a transverse axis can produce rectifying torques. This effect requires that gradiometer floats be superbly stabilized. An order of magnitude improvement in the float jitter amplitude must be achieved compared to any stabilized platform known by this writer.

The above rectifying effect can be mathematically formulated by examining the nature of the actual gravity vector $\vec{g}_a$:[1]

$$\vec{g}_a = \nabla V + \vec{R}_{op} \, \omega_{IE}^2 - \vec{\omega}_{IE} \, (\vec{\omega}_{IE} \cdot \vec{R}_{op}) \qquad (19)$$

∇V is the gradient of the potential of the attracting masses of the earth. The remaining terms describe the centrifugal acceleration of the earth rotating with angular velocity $\vec{\omega}_{IE}$ about center of mass 0. $\vec{g}_a$ is measured at rest in earth space E.

Gravity gradient component $[G_{yx}]_E$ is measured at rest on the earth. Its value is found by operating on (19) with $\vec{j} \cdot \frac{\partial}{\partial x}$

$$[G_{yx}]_E = \vec{j} \cdot \frac{\partial \nabla V}{\partial x} - (\vec{i} \cdot \vec{\omega}_{IE})(\vec{j} \cdot \vec{\omega}_{IE}) \qquad (20)$$

Consider the nature of the gravity gradient measured by the instrument shown in Figure 2. The suspension system constrains the mass element to follow the measuring platform space M. The

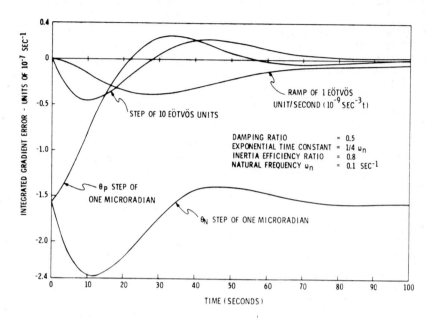

Fig. 15   Integrated Gradient Error Transient Response
of Lag Compensated Third Order Loop

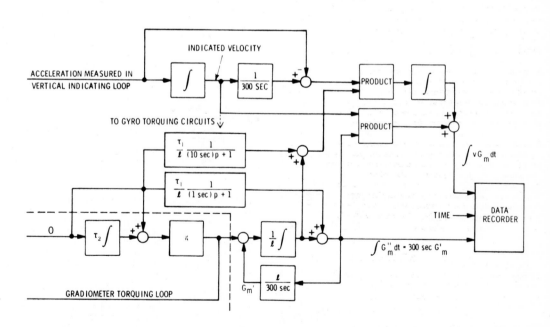

Fig. 16   Integration Computer Flow Diagram

gradient is measured at rest in space M rather than in space E.

$$\left[G_{yx}\right]_E = \vec{j} \cdot \frac{\partial \nabla V}{\partial x} - \left(\vec{i} \cdot \vec{\omega}_{IM}\right)\left(\vec{j} \cdot \vec{\omega}_{IM}\right) \qquad (21)$$

A measurement made at rest in space M can be transformed to correspond to a measurement made at rest in space E.

$$\left[G_{yx}\right]_E = \left[G_{yx}\right]_M + \left(\vec{i} \cdot \vec{\omega}_{IM}\right)\left(\vec{j} \cdot \vec{\omega}_{IM}\right) - \left(\vec{i} \cdot \vec{\omega}_{IE}\right)\left(\vec{j} \cdot \vec{\omega}_{IE}\right) \qquad (22)$$

The above transformation between rotating coordinate systems is a fundamental property of gravity gradients.

The effects of known measuring platform angular velocities will be compensated by employing equation (22) in the implementation of the gradiometer system. How accurately must this be accomplished? What about unknown angular velocity from platform jitter?

The following equation is consistent with the definitions in Figure 8.

$$\vec{\omega}_{IM} = \vec{\omega}_{IR} + \vec{\omega}_{RM} = \vec{\omega}_{IE} + \vec{\omega}_{ER} + \vec{\omega}_{RM} \qquad (23)$$

The actual orientation of the measuring platform is represented by space M. The desired (or reference) orientation of the platform is represented by space R. Space M has angular displacement $\vec{\beta}_{RM}$ relative to space R. $\vec{\beta}_{RM}$ represents the stabilization error of space M. High frequency disturbances are caused by gyroscope noise, electronic noise, gimbal bearing friction, and gimbal unbalance. Low frequency disturbances are caused by circuit bias changes and creep in the gradiometer mounting hardware. A magnitude of 10^{-5} radians (2'' arc) is typical for $\vec{\beta}_{RM}$.

Angular velocity $\vec{\omega}_{RM}$ results from the time rate of change of $\vec{\beta}_{RM}$. A good approximation for small angles is

$$\left[\dot{\vec{\beta}}_{RM}\right] = \vec{\omega}_{RM} \qquad (24)$$

The measuring platform is purposely given the angular velocity $\vec{\omega}_{IR}$ in the implementation of the gradiometer system. This angular velocity is intended to keep space R level and of correct azimuth as the vehicle travels over the earth. $\vec{\omega}_{IR}$ could be implemented by applying precision torques to the stabilization gyroscopes. Thus $\vec{\omega}_{IR}$ is internally available information.

$\vec{\omega}_{IR}$ has components $\vec{\omega}_{IE}$ and $\vec{\omega}_{ER}$. Both are smoothly and slowly changing quantities when resolved in platform space R. The magnitude of $\vec{\omega}_{IE}$ is 7×10^{-5} sec^{-1}. The magnitude of $\vec{\omega}_{IR}$ is roughly 10^{-5} sec^{-1} in a hundred knot vehicle.

An assessment of the implementation accuracy of equation (22) can be obtained by substituting (23) and using the above numerical values.

$$\left[G_{yx}\right]_E = \left[G_{yx}\right]_M + \omega_{IE_x}\omega_{ER_y} + \omega_{IE_y}\omega_{ER_x} + \omega_{ER_x}\omega_{ER_y}$$
$$+ \omega_{IR_x}\omega_{RM_y} + \omega_{IR_y}\omega_{RM_x} + \omega_{RM_x}\omega_{RM_y} \qquad (24)$$

The three terms on the top line of (24) can be explicitly calculated from internally available

information. Their orders of magnitude are one Eötvös unit. A nearly trivial computation in the integration computer will compensate for these terms.

Consider the terms on the second line of equation (24). Integration by parts gives the most insight to their error contributions.

$$\int \omega_{IR_x}\omega_{RM_y}\, dt = \omega_{IR_x}\beta_{RM_y} - \int \dot{\omega}_{IR_x}\beta_{RM_y}\, dt \qquad (25)$$

Suppose the magnitude of β_{RM_y} is 10^{-5} radian. The first term above can cause transients of only 10^{-9}sec^{-1}. This is negligible.

The largest value for $\dot{\omega}_{IR_x}$ results from horizontal vehicle acceleration. Its magnitude is 1.6×10^{-6} rad sec^{-2} for a one g acceleration. It can be seen that the second term above cannot contribute an error of more than .01 Eötvös unit. The terms in the second line of equation (24) can be ignored.

The bottom line of equation (24) involves the square of the unknown angular velocities of servo jitter. Suppose a previously quiet platform suddenly starts to jitter. By how much might the measured gradients be affected?

Assume a center-to-peak jitter amplitude of β_j. For ease in analysis suppose the jitter has a roughly sinusoidal wave form of frequency ω_j (or $2\pi f_j$). A jitter axis bisecting x and y gives the worst case. Then

$$\Delta G_{yx} = \overline{\omega_{RM_x}\omega_{RM_y}} = \tfrac{1}{2}\beta_j^2\,\omega_j^2\,\overline{\sin^2\omega_j t} = \tfrac{1}{4}\beta_j^2\,\omega_j^2 \qquad (26)$$

How large can jitter amplitude β_j be if the resulting indicated gradient shift is to be $\tfrac{1}{3}$ Eötvös unit or less?

$$\beta_j f_j = \left(\tfrac{1}{\pi}\sqrt{\tfrac{1}{3}\times 10^{-9}\text{sec}^{-2}}\right)\left(2.04 \times 10^{-5}\text{''arc/rad}\right) = 1.2\text{''arc cps} \qquad (27)$$

The above formula shows that jitter at one cycle per second must have an amplitude of one arc second or less. At ten cycles per second the jitter amplitude must be ten times smaller. State-of-the-art stabilized platforms have natural jitter frequencies near 25 cycles. At this frequency the jitter amplitude must be limited to $\tfrac{1}{20}$'' arc! Stabilization of gradiometer floats must indeed be superb compared to state-of-the-art platform jitter amplitudes of two arc seconds. Approaches for achieving this high performance are outlined later.

Gravity gradiometer stabilization requirements are not really quite so stringent as is indicated in the above paragraph. Two observations must be made on this subject. Most important, the earlier section on "Other Configuration Alternatives" alludes to an attractive fourth configuration. This configuration consists of a spherical float supported by the same type of buoyant/viscous/capacitive suspension as is applied in this paper to cylindrical floats. The same order of magnitude of ten seconds can be obtained for the characteristic time of inertia divided by viscosity. The spherical geometry gives the float three rotational degrees of freedom with respect to the platform. The platform can now jitter at high frequency and transmit almost no angular acceleration to the float. It can be shown that jitter amplitudes of one minute of arc at any frequency can cause no larger error than $\frac{1}{3}$ Eötvös unit.

The second observation requires speculation on the nature of servo jitter. Suppose servo jitter were symmetrical pure noise. Then ω_{RM_x} and ω_{RM_y} would be uncorrelated. The product of these two components would have negligible value when averaged for long integration times. Uncorrelated jitter of $\frac{1}{2}$" arc near 25 cycles per second can be shown to cause fluctuations in the gradient error of roughly 5 Eötvös units when averaged one second and $\frac{1}{3}$ Eötvös unit when averaged 200 seconds. The corresponding fluctuations in the integrated gradient error are 6×10^{-9} sec^{-1} and 10^{-7} sec^{-1}.

The above uncorrelated jitter conditions cannot be expected in practical servos. Servos generally tend to oscillate or jitter in a preferred direction. This results from unequal friction, unmatched gains, nonspherical inertias, gyro crosscoupling, and kinematic effects. Further, a tendency to oscillate in a given preferred direction cannot be expected to remain constant with changing gimbal geometry, vibration, acceleration, and time.

It is apparent that jitter amplitudes of $\frac{1}{20}$" arc or less should be sought in the design of the stabilization system for cylindrical gravity gradiometers. Any tendency for this jitter to be uncorrelated then represents a design margin. This design margin should be maximized by emphasizing symmetry, matched gains, and so forth in the stabilization system.

2.11 Stabilization Technology

The techniques of high performance inertial platform stabilization will be applied to gravity gradiometers. A state-of-the-art stabilization system is presented in somewhat simplified form. Modifications are then suggested for achieving the two properties of small jitter and of limited error angle integral which are uniquely required for gravity gradiometers.

The gravity gradiometers are mounted on a stabilized platform as shown in Figure 5. Three gyroscopes are also mounted on the platform. The gyros measure error in platform orientation. The platform is supported by gimbals relative to the vehicle. The gimbals provide three (or possibly four) angular degrees of freedom between the platform and the vehicle. The stabilization servos null the gyro errors by applying torques to the stable platform. These torques are applied about the gimbal degrees of freedom by means of motors.

Many high performance stabilization systems of the above kind have been built and operated. Figure 17 is a simplified block diagram of the typical high performance servo. Some torque disturbance T_D acts on the inertia of the platform causing an unwanted angular acceleration. The angular acceleration is kinematically integrated twice to platform error angle θ_P which is sensed by the gyros. Gyro noise θ_G is included in the error signal.

The gyro error signals are preamplified on the stable platform. They are then subjected to gimbal angle resolutions not shown in the figure. The resolved signals are fed via dynamic compensation circuits to the appropriate gimbal torque motors.

The direct drive gimbal torque motor (no gearing) is especially desirable for the gradiometer application. In this arrangement the stator and the armature are mounted on adjacent gimbal members coaxially with the degree of freedom between members. No gearing intervenes. This arrangement eliminates servo acceleration errors in tracking the motion of the vehicle. Servo velocity errors can also be virtually eliminated by driving this type of motor from a high impedance source. It should be noted that the direct drive torque motor allows stabilization against high frequency motions of the vehicle because the inertia of the platform provides high frequency stabilization without the participation of the servos.

The dynamic compensation of the servo signal is practically accomplished with lead and lag networks. These are approximated in Figure 17 by pure derivative and integral operators. Loop dynamics are determined by the values of k_1, k_2, and k_3 which can be achieved in practice. The platform error differential equation is shown in the figure.

Natural frequency ω_n is made as large as possible if the objective of the servo is minimum error angle. The upper limit on ω_n is determined in practice by dynamic lags in the gyros and other parts of the system. A natural frequency of 25 cycles per second is typical in high performance stabilization servos. The damping ratio ζ is usually near $\frac{1}{2}$.

Third order time constant τ should be made as large as possible to minimize low frequency errors. However, too large a value of τ causes stability problems. A value of five cycles per second is found to be a reasonable compromise in a servo having a 25-cycle-per-second natural frequency.

The error equation in Figure 17 shows a gyro noise term, θ_G. Most gyro noise has a frequency higher than several hundred cycles per second. This high frequency gyro noise is caused by dynamic unbalance in the gyro rotor, the balls, and the ball retainers. High frequency gyro noise must be considered with respect to circuit nonlinearities. However, it is not a source of servo jitter since it is easily filtered. Also, its effects are far above the natural frequency.

Low frequency gyro noise has not been widely studied. It is generally not a factor which determines servo performance. Experienced servo designers estimate that gyros have noise levels of less than $\frac{1}{10}$"arc in the frequency range of one-to-30 cycles per second. It is probable that gyro noise will not limit the stabilization of gravity gradiometers.

Minimizing torque disturbance T_D is apparently the key for obtaining superb stabilization. Coulomb friction is the primary source of torque disturb-

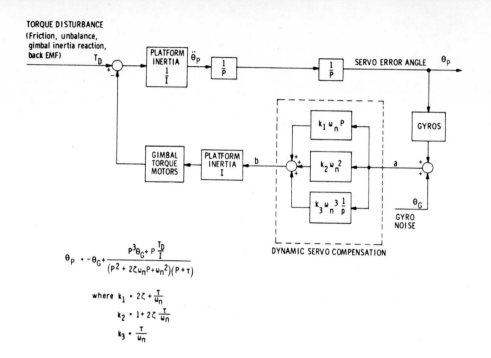

$$\theta_P = -\theta_G + \frac{P^3\theta_G + P\frac{T_D}{I}}{(P^2 + 2\zeta\omega_n P + \omega_n^2)(P+\tau)}$$

where $k_1 = 2\zeta + \frac{\tau}{\omega_n}$

$k_2 = 1 + 2\zeta\frac{\tau}{\omega_n}$

$k_3 = \frac{\tau}{\omega_n}$

Fig. 17 Simplified Direct Drive Servo Loop

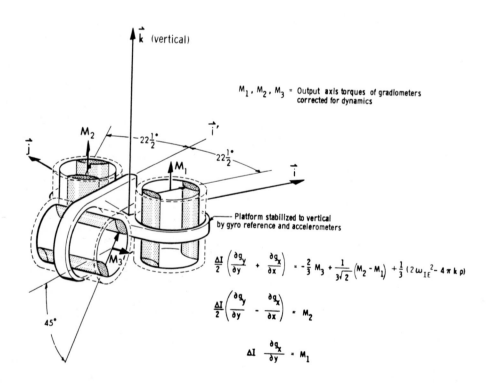

M_1, M_2, M_3 = Output axis torques of gradiometers corrected for dynamics

Platform stabilized to vertical by gyro reference and accelerometers

$$\frac{\Delta I}{2}\left(\frac{\partial g_y}{\partial y} + \frac{\partial g_x}{\partial x}\right) = -\frac{2}{3}M_3 + \frac{1}{3\sqrt{2}}(M_2 - M_1) + \frac{1}{3}(2\omega_{IE}^2 - 4\pi k \rho)$$

$$\frac{\Delta I}{2}\left(\frac{\partial g_y}{\partial y} - \frac{\partial g_x}{\partial x}\right) = M_2$$

$$\Delta I\,\frac{\partial g_x}{\partial y} = M_1$$

Fig. 18 Axially Symmetric Gradiometer Package

84

ance in state-of-the-art stabilization systems.
This friction originates in bearings and brushes.
Rather large-sized preloaded ball or roller
bearings are used between gimbal numbers to provide adequate stiffness. Each direct drive gimbal
torque motor uses a multi-segmented commutator.
Such a commutator requires power brushes located a
significant radius from the axis. Each gimbal
degree of freedom is bridged by fifty-to-one hundred slip rings carrying power and signals.

Table I gives the characteristics of a typical
state-of-the-art stabilization system. Several
systems having these general characteristics have
been designed, built, and tested. Friction levels
as low as 6 ounce-inches ($\frac{1}{32}$ ft-lb) are sometimes
achieved.

The nonlinear coulomb friction can cause a limit
cycle type oscillation. The amplitude of this
oscillation can be calculated using the error
differential equation in Figure 17. This calculation gives an oscillation amplitude of 1.5" arc
with frequency close to the undamped natural
frequency.

Oscillations near the natural frequency with amplitudes of one or two arc seconds are observed in
the laboratory. These observations involve several
state-of-the-art stabilization systems. The above
simplified model apparently adequately describes
the performance of state-of-the-art stabilization
systems. This simplified model will now be applied
to projecting stabilization improvements resulting
from design changes.

2.12 Error Angle Integral Constraint

An error angle integral constraint was assumed in
the earlier section on "Integrations." How can
$\int \theta_p dt$ be constrained to have a magnitude of less
than 4×10^{-7} rad-sec? What is the function and
the nature of the integration which is already
shown in the block diagram of Figure 17?

The integral channel operating on gyro error signal
"a" increases the servo stiffness against low
frequency disturbances. Friction or acceleration
acting on gimbal unbalance are such disturbances.
These disturbances can cause a platform angular
acceleration of $\frac{1}{8}$ radian per second^2 according to
the state-of-the-art system characteristics shown
in Table I. Counteracting these disturbances
requires an error signal at "a" if no integral
channel exists. The magnitude of this signal is

$$\left(\frac{1}{8} sec^{-2}\right)\left(\frac{1}{k_2 \omega_n^2}\right) = \left(\frac{1}{8} rad/sec^2\right)\left(\frac{1}{1.2}\right)\left[\frac{1}{(25 sec^{-1})(2\pi)}\right]^2 \approx 1" arc$$

The above small standoff error is eliminated by
the action of the integral channel. The error
angle is integrated. The error angle integral
is applied as an angular acceleration command.
Counteracting friction or gimbal unbalance requires
an error angle integral of

$$\left(\frac{1}{8} sec^{-2}\right)\left(\frac{1}{k_3 \omega_n^3}\right) = \left(\frac{1}{8} sec^{-2}\right)\left(\frac{1}{2}\right)\left[\frac{1}{(25 sec^{-1})(2\pi)}\right]^3 \approx 1.6 \times 10^{-7} rad/sec$$

It is seen that the standoff error quickly vanishes
since 1.6×10^{-7} rad-sec is only .03" arc-sec.

Static friction is another disturbance the effects
of which the integral channel minimizes. The
integral term builds up to match the friction level.
If static friction is significantly greater than
moving friction an overshoot will result. A limit
cycle oscillation is excited. Other system noises
also excite this oscillation. The frequency of
this oscillation is calculated to be slightly
higher than the undamped natural frequency. Its
amplitude is slightly larger (1.5" arc) than the
friction standoff error without the integral
channel. The integral channel improves the per-
fromance of the servo in the presence of friction.
Without the integral channel the platform would
experience erratic shifts of several arc seconds
from time to time. The integral channel makes
the servo much more active. The short term average
of the platform orientation accurately represents
the gyro reference orientation.

A third low frequency disturbance is perhaps more
important than the above two in servos designed
for less than the ultimate in performance. The
signal at point b in Figure 17 drives power
amplifiers. The amplifiers drive power motors which
have large permanent magnets, slots, and commutator
segments in their geometry. Amplifier input biases
can correspond to a fraction of a milliradian.
These biases can change slowly with time, temperature, and gimbal geometry. The error angle integral acquires a value which nearly perfectly
compensates for these biases.

Suppose the full scale of the integral channel is
chosen so that up to one milliradian of bias can
be matched. How good an integrator must be used?
The full scale of the integrator must correspond
to 3.2×10^{-5} radian-second. An integrator drift
of 10% of full scale per second causes a standoff
error of less than one arc second. Accomplishing
the integration with a low pass filter having a
ten second characteristic time produces a similar
error. The requirements on the integrator are
indeed modest. These requirements are generally
considerably exceeded in practice.

Can the desired error angle integral constraint
be obtained by merely changing integrator
requirements? Suppose the integration was
accomplished with a 1000-second low-pass filter
using an integrator whose drift is .1% of full
scale per second. Examine the integrated gradient
error equation in Figure 14. It can be shown that
the above drift rate provides an error angle integral constraint with enough accuracy to meet the
requirements in the earlier section on
"Integrations."

The operation of the above scheme begins with
energizing the servo. The error angle integrator
quickly settles to an average value which counteracts the amplifier input bias and the unbalances.
This average value has an order of magnitude of
10^{-5} radian-second. The 1.5" arc limit cycle
oscillation causes fluctuations of 4×10^{-7} radian-
second in the error angle integral about this
average value. The error angle integral constraint
is thus accomplished provided biases change slowly
compared to 2" arc with a frequency of one cycle
per minute.

The above scheme has three shortcomings. A 1000-second integrator is tough. Designing a system in which biases change slowly enough to fulfill the above requirements is difficult. The third shortcoming is a consequence of the resolver chain which is usually inserted at point "a" in Figure 17. Error angle integral stability of 4×10^{-7} radian-second is required for the ten second characteristic times of the integration computer filters. This requires a stability of .01" arc in dealing with the gyro error signal in the integral channel. It is obvious that the error angle integrator should be incorporated into the gyro error signal preamplifier. Separating these by a resolver chain is probably intolerable.

Transferring the integral compensation from the front end of the servo amplifier across the resolver chain to the gyro preamplifier has a disadvantage. The biases normally originate in the servo amplifier and the motor. In the new location the x-gyro error angle integrator could settle to a value which might counteract the pitch gimbal servo bias, for example. A vehicle heading change of 90° will now couple the x-gyro to the roll gimbal servo. The bias of this servo is presumably quite different. A transient of 10^{-5} radian-second could result.

It appears feasible to remedy both shortcomings by splitting the integral compensation. The high gain is applied to the error angle integrator at the gyro preamplifier. Probably a five-cycle-per-second first-order break point can be obtained. This integrator no longer counteracts the servo amplifier input biases. Its full scale can probably be reduced to 3×10^{-6} radian-second. Then the integrator can be implemented with a 100-second characteristic time low pass filter. Integrator drifts of 1% are allowable.

The second error angle integrator remains in the front end of the servo amplifier. Perhaps 20% as high a gain can be employed here. This would result in a second first-order break point in the neighborhood of one cycle per second. Full scale of 1.6×10^{-4} radian-second must be used because of the lower gain employed. The integration can be implemented with a 50-second characteristic time low pass filter having an integrator drift rate of 2% of full scale per second.

2.13 Angular Vibration Isolation

The gravity gradiometer float must be provided with nearly perfect angular vibration isolation. It was earlier pointed out that this could be accomplished by mounting a spherically configured gradiometer on a stabilized platform of modest accuracy. This is a unique virtue of the spherical configuration. All of the other gradiometer schemes known to this writer require superb stabilized platforms. This section is addressed to the general (non-spherical gradiometer) stabilized platform problem.

The direct drive stabilization system would be a perfect angular vibration isolator if it were not for disturbance torques from a variety of sources. These disturbance torques will be examined one

at a time. Ways will be suggested for eliminating or grossly reducing each of these torques.

A satisfactory stabilization system is shown as a projection of the current state of the art in Table 1. The projected system has the same dynamics as state-of-the-art systems. Further study could reveal a better choice. The added gradiometer components are assumed to increase the mass of the stabilized platform by 50%. Their volume is assumed to increase the radius of gyration by 50%. These changes more than triple the platform moments of inertia. The increased inertia is helpful according to the error equation in Figure 17.

How low must the disturbance torque level be? It has earlier been established that the amplitude of limit circle oscillations must be held down to $\frac{1}{20}$" arc for cylindrical gradiometers. The calculation which correctly gives the amplitude for state-of-the-art platforms can be scaled with the new numbers. Disturbance torques of roughly .002 ft.-lb. can be tolerated.

The disturbance torques are of three general kinds. There is a reaction torque on the stabilized platform from accelerating the outer gimbal in a three-degree-of-freedom stabilization system. Platform or gimbal mass unbalances cause torques when acted on by gravity or acceleration. Intergimbal assembly torques arise from bearings, motors, slip rings and so forth.

Outer gimbal inertia reaction torques occur only when the three-degree-of-freedom axes are not mutually perpendicular. Consider the gimbal system shown in Figure 5. The axes are orthogonal as shown. It is apparent that the platform inertia is self-stabilizing against small-amplitude high-frequency angular jiggles of the transporting vehicle.

Visualize now the vehicle climbing a grade of $\frac{1}{10}$ radian. The inner axis stays vertical. The outer axis is inclined from horizontal by $\frac{1}{10}$ radian. Angular acceleration of the outer gimbal is required to stabilize the platform against yaw jiggles of the vehicle. Suppose the yaw jiggles contain spectral components above the 25-cycle-per-second bandwidth of the servos. The torque to accelerate the outer gimbal must come from angular acceleration of the stabilized platform. The resulting platform jiggles are roughly equal to the product of the yaw jiggles, the sin of the middle gimbal angle, and the ratio of the outer gimbal inertia to the total inertia of the two inner gimbal members. Yaw jiggles are attenuated by a factor of roughly twenty in the $\frac{1}{10}$ radian illustration. The vehicle yaw jiggles must have an implausibly small 1" arc amplitude near the 25-cycle-per-second natural frequency to meet the $\frac{1}{20}$" arc requirement; and the amplitude must shrink with increasing frequency.

Outer gimbal inertia reaction torque is minimized by accurately maintaining the orthogonality of the three stabilization degrees of freedom. How accurately and by what means depends largely on the vehicle. In a submarine a fraction of a degree would probably be satisfactory orthogonality. This accuracy could be provided by a slowly acting, limited angle fourth degree of freedom. Thus the orientation of the gimbal base in Figure 5 could be adjusted in the vehicle to maintain a nearly horizontal outer gimbal axis as the vehicle changes its trim. The problem is more difficult for higher vibration levels and for more maneuverable vehicles.

Gimbal unbalance is acted on by linear vibration to produce angular vibration of the stabilized platform. Table 1 shows an assumed unbalance of .002 ft.-lb. for the projected servo. This value allows linear vibration levels of $\frac{1}{2}$ g to meet the desired $\frac{1}{3}$ Eötvös unit gradiometer performance level. Achievement of this unbalance level requires that the mass centers of the gimbal lie within .0007 inches of the stabilization axes. Stiff gimbal structures must be employed so that this value is not exceeded by the compliance of the gimbals under their own weight.

Intergimbal assembly torques are the principal problem. Table 1 shows a friction level of .002 ft.-lb. (.3 ounce-inch) causing a $\frac{1}{20}$" arc limit cycle oscillation. A number of innovations are possible to achieve this low level.

Obviously the large roller bearings customarily employed must be eliminated. Pressurized gas bearings are a practical substitution. These have been used in gimbal systems previously. It is known that great stiffness and very low torque can be obtained with properly designed pressurized gas bearings.

The second big offender is the commutator brush friction for the direct drive gimbal motors. A brushless resolver combined with solid state power modulators can perform the same function with virtually no torque. The details of this scheme have been worked out in this Laboratory for a different application.

Each gimbal degree of freedom is bridged by one hundred-or-so signal brushes and slip rings. Collectively these provide too much friction. Ten or so are allowable. It is possible to incorporate multiplex circuitry on the stable platform to transmit all of the signals on two wires. The details of this have also been worked out and applied in a system.

The above measures appear sufficient. However, if necessary, all brushes could be eliminated by using rotary transformers.

Angular vibration levels compatible with $\frac{1}{3}$ Eötvös unit gravity gradiometry are shown to be feasible by the above general plan.

2.14 Vertical Indication

The gradiometers must be leveled with an accuracy of 15" arc and held in azimuth with an accuracy of 0.2°. Three gyros are mounted on the stabilized platform to provide the information for the precise stabilization of the gradiometers in this preferred orientation. The gyros presumably were chosen for their low noise and good dynamic properties with respect to their stabilization chore. What other characteristics should they have?

It is logical to use the spatial memory of the same three gyros for vertical indication. Two accelerometers are also mounted on the stabilized platform to sense leveling errors. The acceleration information is combined with the gyro memory to implement the 84-minute Schuler-tuned second-order vertical-indicating loops which are required for this degree of accuracy. Many textbooks[5,6] exist on vertical indication and inertial navigation. This subject will not be further considered here.

The gyros and accelerometers are required to have accuracies comparable or slightly better than those in the typical one-mile-per-hour navigation system.

2.15 Compensation of Kinematic Effects

Three kinematic effects must be compensated in practical gradiometer systems. These effects are from stabilized platform angular velocity, from angular acceleration, and from residual pendulosity in the gradiometers. Each of these effects can be easily compensated by using information which is already internally available in the vertical indicating loops.

Platform angular velocity is compensated by the employment of the transformation given in equation (22). The discussion following the equation shows that this total effect is 7 Eötvös units for transonic vehicles. Thus compensation has nearly trivial accuracy requirements.

A platform angular acceleration compensation is indicated in Figure 7. Consider a gradiometer of the type shown in Figure 2 mounted on a stable platform with its axis of cylinder horizontal. The vertical indicating loops cause angular acceleration $-\dot{\omega}_{ER_2}$ of the stabilized platform as the vehicle accelerates in the x direction. The torque generator is required to supply an accelerating moment to the float of the gradiometer. Without proper compensation this moment would be mistaken for the effect of an applied gradient. What is the error in the integrated gradient which would result?

$$\int \Delta G \, dt = \int \frac{-\dot{\omega}_{ER_2} I_{\hat{3}\hat{3}}}{I_{active}} dt = \frac{\omega_{ER}}{\ell} = \frac{7 \times 10^{-5} \, rad/sec}{.8} = 10^{-4} sec^{-1}$$

A transonic vehicle and an inertia efficiency $\ell = .8$ were used above. Compensation accuracy of better than one part in one thousand is apparently required.

Balancing the gradiometer float with the sputtering pods described in section 3.6 is expected to be a very time-consuming process. There is little incentive to balance to lower torque levels than the gradients can cause. Thus the balancing procedure should be terminated, leaving a small residual pendulosity which can be accurately calibrated. The order of magnitude of 2000 Eötvös units per g would be appropriate for this residual pendulosity.

Consider the effect of vehicle acceleration along x on the gradiometer shown in Figure 2. Suppose the residual unbalance is along y. A torque is produced which could be mistaken for the effects of a gradient. What transients in the integrated gradient are possible?

$$\int \Delta G \, dt = \int \frac{a_x \, P}{I_{active}} \, dt = \frac{v P}{I_{active}} = v \, (2000 \; E\ddot{o}tv\ddot{o}s \; unit/g)$$

A value for v free of transients larger than one foot per second must be used in calculating the required compensation in order to keep transient errors in the integrated gradient less than 10^{-7} sec^{-1}.

2.16 Compensation for Vehicle Mass

A gravity gradiometer is very sensitive to local masses. This effect is well known from the procedures which are followed in making measurements with the Eötvös balance.[4] No site or terrain compensations are necessary with a moving gravity gradiometer system according to the discussion in Part 1, The Introduction. However, the effects of all the mass which moves along with the gradiometer system must be compensated. This section will give some ideas on how this compensation might be accomplished.

Fortunately the gravity gradients from point masses diminish with the inverse cube of distance. Table 2 shows the mass/distance combinations which give a gravity gradient of one Eötvös unit. Extreme sensitivity is observed to small masses within a radius of one meter of the instrument.

The masses closest to the gravity gradiometer in Figure 5 are the other gradiometers, the gyros, the accelerometers, the inner gimbal torque motors, and the structure comprising the stabilized platform. All of these immediate masses are in a fixed configuration relative to a given gradiometer. They will produce a substantial but constant bias in the indicated gravity gradient. This bias is easily calibrated and compensated.

The next closest assembly of masses to the gradiometer is the middle gimbal. The effect of middle gimbal mass on the gradiometer will obviously be a function of the inner gimbal angle as the vehicle changes its heading. Employment of symmetry minimizes the mass compensation. The inner gimbal should be made a spherical shell. Spherical shells produce zero gravity gradient in space within them. All that remains to compensate is the mass of a wiring harness and the middle gimbal torque motor. The motor is close enough to the gradiometer so that it is not a point mass. The gradiometer is large enough so that it is not a point probe with respect to such a close mass. The compensation is simplified by using two smaller motors, one on each end of the middle gimbal axis. Locating the gradiometer cluster as close as possible to the center of the gimbal system produces a further simplification. Rough calculations indicate that the resulting mass distribution can be compensated by computations based on point mass motors and an infinitesimal gradiometer size. Such computations are within the scope of a reasonable computer.

The above philosophy and comments apply also to the outer gimbal and the gimbal support structure.

Large, dense mass concentrations should be avoided within one or two meters of the gradiometer system. At these distances the gradiometers cannot be regarded as point probes for such severe disturbances.

All the rest of the vehicle mass is easily calibrated prior to operation. The vehicle is placed in a reasonably level open field. The valves of $\frac{\partial g_z}{\partial x}$ and $\frac{\partial g_z}{\partial y}$ are measured by the gravity gradiometers. The vehicle is maneuvered to place the gradiometer system in the same location with the vehicle having a reversed heading. New values of $\frac{\partial g_z}{\partial x}$ and $\frac{\partial g_z}{\partial y}$ are measured with the gradiometer platform stabilized in the same orientation relative to the earth. The change in the gradient measurements is twice the contribution of the vehicle to the gradients.

Operational compensation for the fixed mass configuration of the vehicle is calculated from the above two calibration quantities. The gradiometer system should be located in the tail of an aircraft, for example. This location could be isolated from the movements of personnel or equipment for a distance of three-or-so meters. The fuel in the wing tanks is remote but quite massive. A small correction based on fuel gauge information could be necessary. Also, a small approximate correction could be worked out for small vehicle trim changes.

2.17 Brownian Motion

Thermal noise can be a fundamental limit in the measurement of so small a stress as the gravity gradient. Dancing is experimentally observed behavior in small galvanometer mirrors. It is known that the same kinetic theory which correctly describes Brownian Motion can be profitably applied to predicting the motion of galvanometer mirrors. Might it not also give a result which is relevant to the gradiometer sensing mass described in Part 3 and Table 4?

The effects of thermal noise in the gradiometer torquing loop will first be considered. Examine the second order loop of Figure 7. It can be recognized that the feedback is equivalent to a torsion wire of spring constant $k I_{33} = \omega_n^2 I_{33}$. Suppose $\omega_n = .1 \; sec^{-1}$. The characteristics of the loop will be the same as a huge ($I_{33} = 2322 \; gm\text{-}cm^2$) galvanometer mirror on a damped one-minute period suspension. Energy can be stored either as kinetic energy in the sensing mass rotation or as virtual potential energy in the rotation θ against the torque of spring $\omega_n^2 I_{33}$. In the equilibrium state the potential and kinetic energies will each average $\frac{1}{2} kT$ according to the Equipartition Theorem (k is here the Boltzmann constant of 1.38×10^{-16} ergs/°K). The following equation for the average value of the potential energy can be written.

$$\frac{1}{2} I_{33} \omega_n^2 \overline{\theta^2} = \frac{1}{2} kT \qquad (28)$$

CHARACTERISTIC	STATE-OF-THE-ART	PROJECTED SERVO
ω_n	25 cps	25 cps
ζ	0.5	0.5
τ	5 cps	5 cps
Stabilized Mass	1 slug	1.5 slugs
Radius of Gyration	0.5 foot	0.75 feet
Inertia	0.25 slug-ft^2	0.84 slug-ft^2
Measured or Assumed Friction	0.03 ft-lb	0.0007 ft-lb (10 slip rings)
Measured or Assumed Unbalance	0.02 ft-lb	0.002 ft-lb
CG Displacement	0.010 in.	0.0007 in.
Calculated Oscillation	1.5"arc	0.05"arc
Measured Oscillation	1-2"arc	- - - -

Table 1 Projection of Servo Performance

$$\frac{\partial g_z}{\partial x} = \frac{1}{2}\left(\frac{\partial g_{z'}}{\partial z} - \frac{\partial g_{x'}}{\partial x'}\right) = 1 \text{ Eötvös unit}$$

Results from

Distance Meters	Mass Kilograms
1/2	1.25
1	10.00
2	80.00
3	270.00
5	1250.00
10	10000.00

Table 2 Gradients from Local Masses

The RMS value of θ due to thermal noise is

$$\theta_{RMS} = \sqrt{\frac{kT}{I\omega_n^2}} = \sqrt{\frac{(1.38 \times 10^{-16} \text{ergs}/°K)(336°K)}{(2322 \text{ gm cm}^2)(.01 \text{sec}^{-2})}} = 4.5 \times 10^{-8} \text{rad} \quad (29)$$

This small disturbance in gradiometer output certainty cannot be resolved in the presence of stabilization servo noise θ_p. It will nevertheless contribute something to the $_p$ indicated gradient noise. The RMS thermal noise contribution to the indicated gradient is

$$\Delta G_{RMS} = \frac{\omega_n^2}{\ell} \theta_{RMS} = (.01 \text{sec}^{-2})\left(\frac{2322}{1506}\right)(4.5 \times 10^{-8}) = .70 \times 10^{-9} \text{sec}^{-2}$$
$$= .7 \text{ Eötvös unit} \quad (30)$$

Although these results were derived for the simple second-order loop, it is intuitively obvious that the results qualitatively apply as well to the more elaborate loops. This error would be present even with ideal stabilization servos. It represents the lower theoretical limit of the noise.

Transient changes or noise in the integrated gradient have been shown to be of greater significance than noise in the gradient. Earlier section "2.2 Error Equation" shows that the effects of 10^{-7} sec^{-1} noise in the integrated gradient is marginal. It should be expected from the oscillatory nature of the loop that the noise given by (30) will be principally concentrated at the natural frequency of the loop. The order of magnitude of the RMS of the integrated gradient noise would therefore be given by

$$\int \Delta G dt \Big|_{RMS} = \frac{\Delta G|_{RMS}}{\omega_n} = .07 \times 10^{-7} \text{sec}^{-1}. \quad (31)$$

This value appears negligible.

A second viewpoint is interesting with respect to Brownian Motion. Can this thermal noise cause any average error in the measured gradients? It is known that the average position of a galvanometer mirror is quite accurate. Does its torsion wire supply any average torque? It must, for otherwise the orientation of the mirror would drift like a dust particle undergoing Brownian Motion.

Consider the low frequency aspects of the behavior of the gradiometer output angle θ. Over the long term θ remains a small angle. However, for low frequencies θ may be considered as the sum of two unbounded parts. One part is the result of the torque applied by the feedback loop. The second part is the result of the Brownian Motion drift of the gradiometer mass with the feedback loop open. In the absence of other disturbances these two parts of θ are of opposite sign and their magnitudes agree to within the 4.5×10^{-8} radian RMS derived earlier.

To estimate the Brownian Motion part, θ_B, the development attributed to Einstein in section 161 "Theory of the Brownian Motion" in <u>Kinematic Theory of Gases</u>[7] will be followed. Equation (223) of the reference becomes

$$I_{33} \ddot{\theta}_B = -C \dot{\theta}_B \quad (32)$$

Equation (224a) of the reference becomes

$$\overline{\theta_B^2} = \frac{2kT}{C} t \quad (33)$$

The RMS value of θ_B averaged over many time trials is therefore

$$\theta_{B_{RMS}} = \sqrt{\frac{2kT}{C} t} \quad (34)$$

The feedback part, θ_F, is a result of the applied torque encountering the inertia of the float and the viscous damping. The feedback torque is integrated and causes an error in the integrated gradient. The feedback part can be expressed as a function of the integrated gradient error.

$$\theta_F = -\frac{\ell I_{33}}{C} \int \Delta G \, dt \quad (35)$$

Recognize that $\theta_F \approx -\theta_B$. This gives a new equation for the integrated gradient error resulting from thermal noise.

$$\int \Delta G \, dt \Big|_{RMS} = \sqrt{\frac{2kTC}{\ell^2 I_{33}}} \sqrt{t} = \frac{1}{\ell} \sqrt{\frac{2kT\Upsilon_l}{I_{33}}} \sqrt{t}$$

$$= \left(\frac{2322}{1506}\right) \sqrt{\frac{(2)(1.38 \times 10^{-16} \text{ergs}/°K)(336°K)(.1 \text{sec}^{-1})}{2322 \text{ gm-cm}^2}} \sqrt{t}$$

$$= 3.1 \times 10^{-9} \sqrt{t} \text{ sec}^{-3/2} \quad (36)$$

Integration of the Brownian Motion gradient error for ten seconds is seen to give an RMS error of 1.0×10^{-8} sec^{-1}. This is an average gradient error of one Eötvös unit. It is interesting to note that this result corresponds closely to the .7 Eötvös unit effect of thermal noise given by equation (30) for the torquing loop.

Longer integration times give smaller average gradient errors. Values are shown in Table 3.

PART 3.1 THE INSTRUMENT

A concept suitable for a gravity anomaly gradiometer was discussed earlier and is shown in Figure 2. There is a striking similarity between the mass configuration used in this concept and that used by Baron von Eötvös in his excellent torsion balances. The instrument concept is not a consequence of following his idea however. Rather, it derives from a different instrument concept thought up for a different purpose.

The axially symmetric configuration is desirable for sensing the gradients required to indicate changes of the vertical deflection. A cluster of three such instruments shown in Figure 18 provides the data necessary for vertical deflection indication. The indication computer is similar to that for gravity anomalies which was developed in the previous part.

As many of you know, the Laboratory is most famous for making better and better gyros and accelerometers. These components have gotten so good that aircraft inertial navigation is potentially limited in accuracy by vertical deflections rather than by gyroscopic and accelerometer instrument performance. Gravity gradiometers can eliminate this inertial navigation performance limitation. This provided the motivation which led the Avionics Laboratory of the Air Force Systems Command to sponsor the gradiometer feasibility demonstration under the Laboratory's Advanced Inertial

Components Contract (F33615-68-C-1155). The experimental work which is reported on here has been conducted under this sponsorship. The design and construction of symmetric gradiometer is near completion. The design features embodied in it and its performance can be directly projected to the skewed and Lancaster-Jones configurations as well.

The conclusion was reached that some sort of gravity gradiometer was necessary for the solution of the vertical deflection problem in inertial navigation. With nearly two decades of experience with gyroscopic instruments it was natural to reach into this area of technology for the instrument concept. Figure 19 is a drawing of our best gyro design of several years ago modified to be a gradiometer. The figure shows a floated inertial component of the type for which the Laboratory is famous. Normally there would be a gyro rotor inside the float structure. The float is crosshatched.

3.2 Support System

The mass of the float structure is supported against the forces of gravity and acceleration by its buoyancy in a thin layer of fluid between the float and the housing. The gyro is designed so that the weight of the float is nearly exactly supported by its buoyancy. An elementary knowledge of mechanics shows that this buoyancy support is nearly perfect no matter what the strength of gravity or the imposed linear acceleration. To overcome the small residual buoyancy unbalance magnetic structures at each end are used to sense float displacement from its nominal position and to impose small trimming forces. These magnetic structures are also used to apply torques about the axis of cylinder and to measure angles about that axis. Notice that there is no frictional contact between pivots and jewels or the like.

An added feature in the support system bears comment. Between the float and the main housing is a thin layer of viscous fluid. To move the float about the axis of cylinder involves only shearing this fluid. To move the float in translation or to rotate it about a transverse axis requires the displacement of a significant volume of fluid through the narrow damping gap. Thus, the almost neutrally buoyant float is constrained solidly in translational degrees of freedom for high frequencies. It is apparently only necessary to apply forces in the magnetic suspension in the regime of low frequencies.

Suppose the moments of inertia of the float mass were exactly equal to those of the buoyancy fluid displacement by the volume of the float. The same statements could be made with respect to transverse rotations. However the inertias are not perfectly matched. But the inertias are not large. On the stable platform contemplated angular accelerations about the unit's center of geometry will be very small. Thus the viscous constraint on transverse rotations will be effective.

The above arrangement constitutes a buoyant/viscous

magnetic support system which constrains the float with respect to the main housing. The constraint is very stiff in five degrees of freedom. It allows easy motion in the sixth degree of freedom about the axis of cylinder. This arrangement has been very successful in low uncertainty torque inertial components.

3.3 Comparison with Gyro

The gyroscope float contains a spinning rotor. The rotor is supported on ball bearings. The bearings have balls which are separated by a ball retainer. This assembly is supported by a gimbal structure inside the float. A motor is contained in the assembly to provide the rotor spin. This necessitates four spring leads on the end of the unit to bring in power. To make a gradiometer of the above unit involves scooping out the rotor, the gimbal, and the bearings. The leads are eliminated. One is left with a very simple float structure. The removed mass is replaced with two elements of dense material which are well supported by the cylindrical can.

Table 4 compares this gyro and a gradiometer designed in a similar way. In the gyroscope very dense flotation fluid is desirable. High viscosity is also desired to give the gyroscope a short characteristic time. The high density is also desired in the gradiometer. However, the minute gradient torques must produce rotation about the axis of cylinder in order to be sensed. Therefore the characteristic time should be as long as possible so that the float inertia is accelerated to as high a speed as possible. This leads to the selection of a low viscosity fluid. The table shows a characteristic time of 1/2 millisecond for the gyro. This can be changed to nearly 10 seconds for the gradiometer. A penalty has been paid in density. In the gradiometer FC-78 is used because it is a chemically reasonable material having a low viscosity and a high density. The float weight must be reduced 25% to accommodate the loss of fluid density.

In the gyroscope the angular momentum of the rotor is the measurement effector. In the gradiometer the inertia difference about the two transverse axes is the measurement effector. It has already been stated that it is desirable to make measurements with an accuracy of one Eötvös unit or better. This requires that uncertainty torque about the axis of cylinder be comparable to or smaller than the $1.5\,\mu$dyne-cm. torque resulting from one Eötvös unit acting on this inertia difference. What gyro drift rate does this correspond to in the similar instrument? A gyro drift rate of 10^{-8} times the angular velocity of the rotation of the earth results from a torque of a similar size. (Meru in the table stands for milliearth rate unit.) In this unclassified paper an exact comparison with achieved gyro performance is not possible. However it can be stated that this performance is considerably better than is realized by any gyroscope. But the difference is not so great as to boggle the imagination.

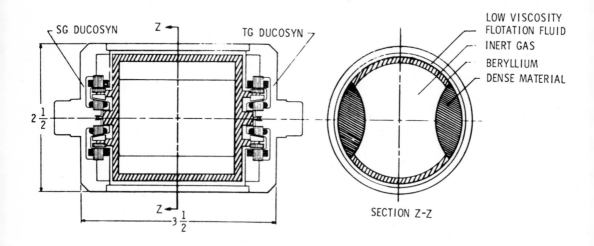

SG DUCOSYN   Z   TG DUCOSYN

$2\frac{1}{2}$

Z

$3\frac{1}{2}$

LOW VISCOSITY
FLOTATION FLUID
INERT GAS
BERYLLIUM
DENSE MATERIAL

SECTION Z-Z

Fig. 19 Gravity Gradiometer Based on 2 FBG 10 H Gyro
Design

Very simple float structure

No bearings or lubricant

No flex leads

Thin damping fluid - Easy to clean and out-gas

Microwatts internal energy dissipation - can be built in vacuum bottle

No gyroscopic torque ⎫   Very light support system loading
No pendulous torque ⎭   Capacity of 0.002 dyne-cm instead of 1000 dyne-cm

Fig. 20 Advantages Compared to Gyro

Integration Time sec.	$\int \Delta G \, dt \Big|_{\text{RMS Many Trials}}$ $10^{-7} \sec^{-1}$	Average $\Delta G_{xy} \Big|_{\text{RMS Many Trials}}$ Eötvös Units $= 10^{-9} \sec^{-2}$
1	0.031	3.10
10	0.100	1.00
100	0.310	0.31
1000	1.000	0.10

Table 3   Brownian Motion Drift

	Gyro	Gradiometer
Mass of Main Assembly	1320 grams	1430 grams
Mass of Float	430 grams	308 grams
Bouyancy Fluid	4500/125 Brominated	FC-78
Density	2.4 gm/cc.	1.606 gm/ cc at 145°F
Viscosity	4500 centipoises	0.43 centipoises at 145°F
Damping Gap	0.006 inches	0.010 inches
Coefficient of Damping Output Axis	2.8×10^6 dyne-cm/rad/sec	265 dyne-cm/rad/sec
Moment of Inertia Output Axis	1600 gm-cm^2	2322 gm-cm^2
Characteristic Time Output Axis	0.00057 sec	8.8 sec
Angular Momentum	1.5×10^6 gm-cm^2/sec	———
Inertia Difference	———	1506 gm-cm^2
Torque Produced by 10^{-5} meru	1.09 μdyne-cm	———
1 Eötvös Unit	———	1.56 μdyne-cm

Table 4   Comparison of Gradiometer With Gyro

3.4 Significant Differences from Gyro

There are many extremely significant differences between the gyroscope generically shown in Figure 19 and the gradiometer. Executing the design illustrated in Figure 19 would border on stupidity. Features will now be examined which enable the projection of gradiometer feasibility even though a gradiometer requires a much lower uncertainty level than is experienced in the best gyros. Figure 20 lists the most significant of these differences.

Most obvious is the simplification of the float structure by the reduction of parts and increased geometric simplicity. Much research in the past has concentrated on improving ball bearings, sloppy fitting ball retainers, migrating lubricants, spin motor mass instabilities, and flex leads. The gradiometer contains none of these potential sources of balance instability.

In gyros dirt and air bubbles in the viscous damping fluid have always been potential problems. The gradiometer flotation fluid has low viscosity and high vapor pressure. It can pass through filters with finer pores. Outgassing occurs much more easily.

Now come the important features. The gyro spin motor dissipates 5 watts. The gyro is a component in a system whose temperature is of the order of $100^{\circ}F$. Gyros are normally designed so that their floats operate at $145^{\circ}F$. Transferring 5 watts of rotor power through a $50^{\circ}F$ thermal gradient limits the amount of insulation that can be used to enshroud the gyro to protect it from environmental thermal gradients. Consider a gyro with horizontal axis of cylinder exposed to an environmental thermal gradient across its diameter. The flotation fluid layer heats on one side relative to the other. The resulting differential fluid expansion causes convection torque on the gyro float. The gradiometer will literally operate with internal dissipation of several microwatts. The gradiometer housing is being installed inside of a vacuum bottle with gold plating on the inner wall. The surface of the housing is goldplated. The gold surfaces minimize heat transfer by radiation. Protection from thermal gradients is certain to prove an important feature in a successful gradiometer. More detail on the thermal configuration will be presented later.

The second important feature the gradiometer has compared to a gyro is the scale of its muscles. Provisions must be made to apply torque to the gyro so that preflight alignment may be accomplished in a reasonable time. Full scale torquing rates of ten times the rate of rotation of the earth (150°/hour) is common and practical. This means that the magnetic suspension muscles in the gyroscope must have a full scale of 1,000 dyne-cm. The magnetic suspension muscles must also be strong to provide centering after periods of high torquing. In the gradiometer the largest torque needed is that required to balance the gradients. This allows a full scale of several millidyne-cm. The muscles in the gradiometer should obviously

be scaled down by this factor of a million compared to the gyro. Generally the uncertainty torque from muscles is proportional to the product of their full scale times the geometry errors in machining and material homogeneity. Not too much can be done to improve the geometry and homogeneity compared to well-designed gyros. However, it is entirely feasible to scale the muscles down by the factor of a million. More will be said about this later.

3.5 Characteristics of Experimental Gradiometer

The principal characteristics of the feasibility demonstration gradiometer are shown in Figure 21. The float structure is entirely of beryllium except for the dense weights. Beryllium is a material which has proven to be very stable in gyroscope applications. It is also a good thermal conductor which helps attenuate gradients. The weights in the float are made of spent uranium. Spent uranium has the advantage of high density and a thermal coefficient of expansion which is close to that of beryllium. These and other structural features can be seen in Figures 22, and 23, and 24. The plate between the two weights shown in Figure 24 is a structural stiffener. The dark pattern in Figure 23 is an array of slots milled in the beryllium float structure which have been back filled with epoxy. This provides a dielectric pattern around the plates (the unmilled sections between the slots) which are used in the capacitive sensor/torquer.

3.6 Balancing

Fine balance of the float must be achieved to the millidyne-cm. level in order to operate the capacity suspension with muscles which are also scaled to this level. Fine balance is accomplished with sputtering pods. In Figure 24 can be seen three cylindrical structures mounted on the end plate of the float. Each of these is a receptacle for a sputtering pod. A drawing of a sputtering pod is shown in Figure 25.

Coarse balance will be accomplished down to the level of several dyne-cm. before the float is assembled into the main housing. This balance between the center of mass and the center of buoyancy of the float can be measured much more accurately than this once the unit is assembled.

Inside the float there are six sputtering pods. To reduce the unbalance the proper sputtering pod is arced. A cam arrangement enables contacting the electrodes and the ground of the sputtering pods from outside the main housing. A glow discharge is established from the gold cathode to the anode. The discharge sputters gold from the cathode to the anode at the rate of roughly a milligram per hour. The first step in fine balancing can involve sputtering for several hours. The unbalance then again is measured with the suspension. Further unbalance reductions are affected with shorter and shorter periods of sputtering. Presumably this iterative process will converge in smaller and smaller steps toward an acceptable level of fine balance. The gold sputters most effectively from the button to the walls of the anode. It is clear

Float Structure is Beryllium with Uranium weights.

Fine Balance is accomplished in three degrees-of-freedom by translating gold via sputtering within the float of the assembled unit.

Suspension Geometry is measured in six degrees-of-freedom by capacity pickoffs with multiplexed excitation of one volt. The same circuits apply controlled torques and forces to float.

Thermal Configuration uses a thermal bridge structure to support the unit inside a gold plated thermal controlled vacuum jacket to isolate the unit from thermal gradients.

Temperature is controlled by measuring suspension forces to maintain neutral buoyancy within $20\mu^\circ C$.

Fig. 21 Features of Experimental Gravity Gradiometer

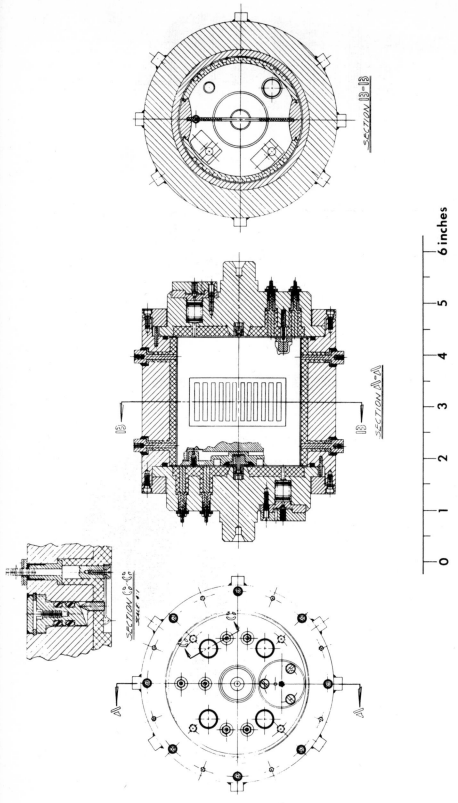

SECTION 13-13

SECTION A-A

SECTION C-C
SCALE #1

6 inches

Fig. 22   Gradiometer Element Assembly Drawing

Fig. 23 Assembled Float

Fig. 24 Pre-Assembled Float

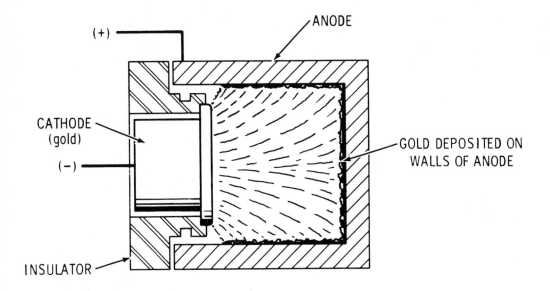

(+) ——————

ANODE

CATHODE
(gold)

(−) ——————

GOLD DEPOSITED ON
WALLS OF ANODE

INSULATOR ——————

- 1.5 milligrams/hr or 0.3 dyne-cm/hr balance change at 0.25 milliamp

- Plus and minus balance pods for each degree of freedom

- Cathode (gold) expended in 100 hrs @ 0.25 milliamp

Fig. 25 Fine Balance by Sputtering

that six pods are necessary to have plus and minus balance control of three degrees of freedom.

3.7 Main Housing

Figure 26 shows the parts of the main housing which are also made of beryllium. It is purposely designed with thick walls to enhance the attenuation of thermal gradients around the circumference. Figure 27 shows a view of the inside of the housing. It is worth noting the electrodes of the capacitive suspension. The shiny plates in the bottom of the housing are for radially suspending each end of the gradiometer. The pattern in the middle lays opposite the tooth pattern which has been cut in the float. These electrodes are plated on top of an epoxy lining. The geometry of the suspension system is better shown in the drawing of Figure 28.

3.8 Capacitive Support System

There are eight radial suspension electrodes altogether. A pair of diametrically opposite plates on one end of the housing is excited with a center tapped transformer. One hundred kilocycle alternating current is used. A low noise amplifier detects the signal between the two "common" plates connected in parallel and the center tap. All the other plates are grounded. Potential changes are induced on the float if it is closer to one excited plate than the other. The phase and amplitude of this alternating voltage is sensed through the common capacity. Thus the radial displacement in one degree of freedom is measured.

Data from the sense cycle above is used to control the force cycle which follows. Switches are thrown so that all plates except the appropriate one are grounded. A voltage is applied between ground and this one plate. The relatively high electric field strength between this plate and the float results in an attraction of the float toward it.

The above describes the operation of one channel for one cycle of the multiplex sense/force arrangement which is being employed. The functional block diagram for this arrangement is in Figure 29. The switches as shown are set in the sense position for one channel. Figure 30 shows the sense cycle in more detail. Figure 31 shows the force cycle in more detail. All six degrees of freedom are sensed and forced in a similar manner. There are four multiplex cycles per second. Each cycle consecutively operates six channels. The measurement of the gradient is derived from the torque applied by the axis-of-cylinder channel. This torque is accurately integrated from multiplex cycle to cycle.

The accuracy of the integrated torque determines how accurately the system will perform. Notice in the block diagrams that forcing voltages are clean and at relatively high voltage levels. This will be so even though the signal channels may be noisy. Thus noise in the sensing cycle does not affect the accuracy of the measurement of the integrated gradient. Further analyses have been carried out on the effects of gradiometer dyamnics on overall system performance. These are presented in Part 2 of this paper.

Provision has been made for a twenty volt excitation to the plates. This voltage level should be sufficient to enable the capacitive support to operate in the presence of the initial course float unbalances. This is necessary since the support is essential for measuring the unbalances. As the unbalance is reduced this voltage is decreased in several steps. One volt excitation is sufficient to suspend the float when the unbalances are at the millidyne cm. level.

It seems reasonable that sensing should be accomplished with roughly the same excitation on the plates as for forcing. A low noise sensing amplifier was therefore designed. It is required to sense 0.2" arc with reasonable signal-to-noise level with capacitor excitations of one volt. The electronic circuitry has been tested using precision capacitors to stimulate the gradiometer. It has demonstrated the desired performance.

3.9 Thermal Design

The thermal configuration of the gradiometer is shown in Figure 32. The inner circle represents the float with the two weights. The light annulus outside represents the flotation fluid. Containing the flotation fluid is the main housing with its thick beryllium walls. On each end of the housing is a portion of the trimming heater winding. These windings are used to dissipate a milliwatt to maintain a controlled temperature difference of $\frac{1}{2}$ F between the main housing and the vacuum jacket.

The vacuum jacket is represented by the outer dark circle. It is a rather thick-walled aluminum structure. The inside of the vacuum jacket and the outside of the main housing are both gold plated to minimize radiation heat exchange. The average temperature of the outside of the vacuum jacket is controlled with an accuracy of .001°F by a heater winding, sensor winding, plus insulation. Provision has been made to substitute a multisector array of heater windings should the experimental result indicate its necessity. The main housing is supported inside the vacuum jacket by means of relatively thin struts in tension. The strut configuration is a square. Two opposite corners are supported by the vacuum jacket. The other two corners support the main housing. These struts are carefully matched in cross section so that the configuration acts like a thermal wheatstone bridge. The heat from a temperature gradient across the diameter of the vacuum jacket is carried equally in the two branches of the strut network. Thus a temperature null exists across the attachment points on the main housing.

It is desired that the gradiometer be capable of operating with the axis of cylinder horizontal. The performance goal is $\frac{1}{3}$ Eötvös unit. The table at the bottom of Figure 32 is the sensitivity chain for thermal gradients. It shows that a gradient of one-third degree Centigrade across the thermal jacket is calculated to cause unbalance equivalent to $\frac{1}{3}$ Eötvös unit. It is anticipated that thermal vacuum jacket gradients will be controlled with an accuracy of several hundredths

Fig. 26 Housing Parts

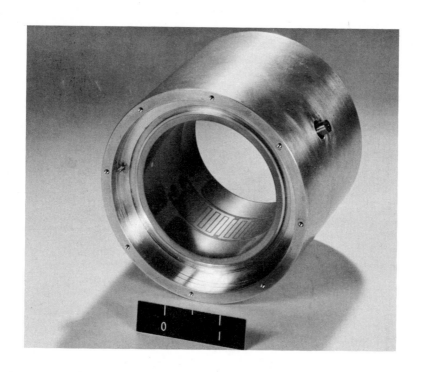

Fig. 27 Main Housing

100

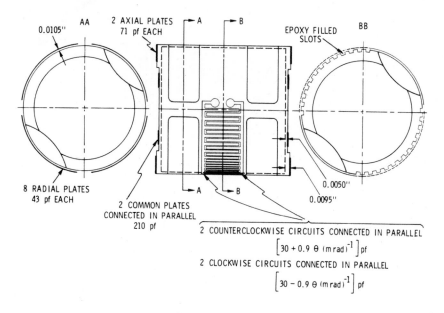

Fig. 28 Suspension Electrodes

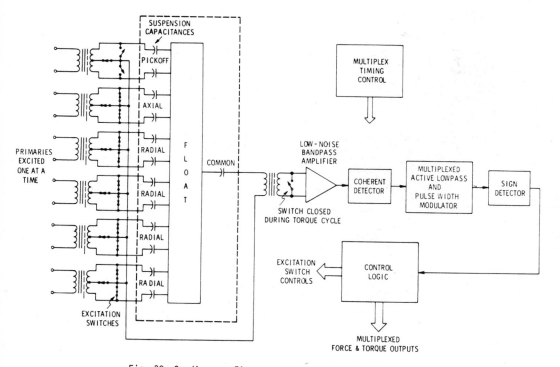

Fig. 29 Gradiometer Electronics Functional Block Design

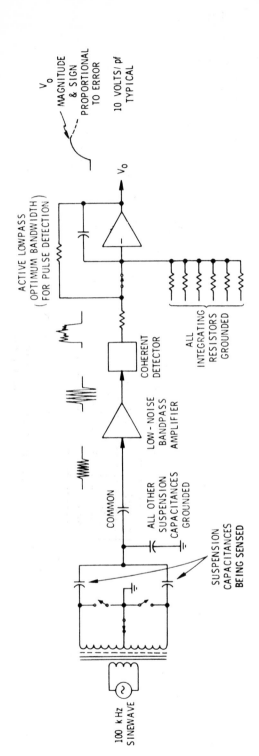

	NOMINAL CAPACITANCE	POSITION SENSITIVITY	BRIDGE SENSITIVITY
PICKOFF	30.6 pf	2.4×10^{-3} pf/sec	3.5 μV/sec/volt excitation
AXIAL	71 pf	7.7×10^{-3} pf/μin.	10.1 μV/μin./volt excitation
RADIAL	43 pf	4.1×10^{-3} pf/μin.	5.6 μV/μin./volt excitation

MINIMUM DETECTABLE SIGNAL IS ABOUT 0.5 μV.
TIME TO READ ONE AXIS IS 2 msec.

Fig. 30 Gradiometer Electronics Configuration During Sense Cycle

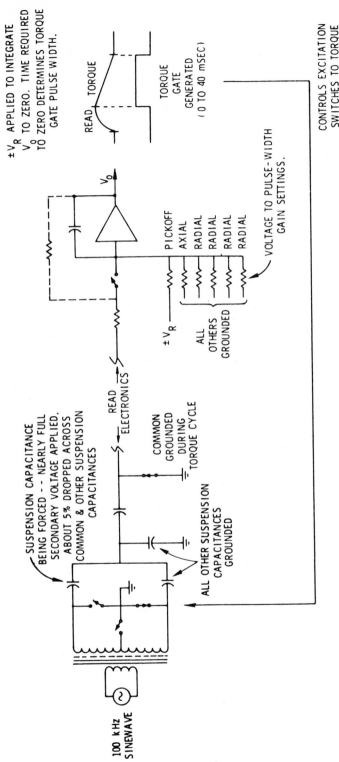

±V_R APPLIED TO INTEGRATE V_o TO ZERO. TIME REQUIRED TO ZERO DETERMINES TORQUE GATE PULSE WIDTH.

READ TORQUE

TORQUE GATE GENERATED (0 TO 40 mSEC)

CONTROLS EXCITATION SWITCHES TO TORQUE FLOAT.

VOLTAGE TO PULSE-WIDTH GAIN SETTINGS.

PICKOFF
AXIAL
RADIAL
RADIAL
RADIAL
RADIAL

±V_R

ALL OTHERS GROUNDED

V_o

READ ELECTRONICS

COMMON GROUNDED DURING TORQUE CYCLE

SUSPENSION CAPACITANCE BEING FORCED -- NEARLY FULL SECONDARY VOLTAGE APPLIED, ABOUT 5% DROPPED ACROSS COMMON & OTHER SUSPENSION CAPACITANCES

ALL OTHER SUSPENSION CAPACITANCES GROUNDED

100 kHz SINEWAVE

	FORCE/TORQUE SCALE FACTOR	AT 100 % DUTY CYCLE	
		@V = 20 V	@V = 1V
PICKOFF	0.01 V^2 dyne-cm	4 dyne-cm	0.01 dyne-cm
AXIAL	0.0151 V^2 dynes	6 dynes	0.015 dynes
RADIAL	0.00804 V^2 dynes	3.2 dynes	0.008 dynes

Fig. 31   Gradiometer Electronics Configuration During Force Cycle

THERMAL CONFIGURATION

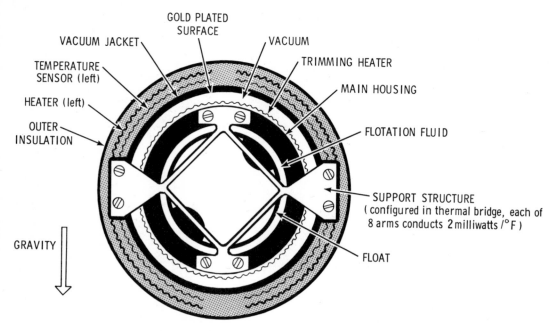

- Goal is 1/3 Eötvös unit $\left(1\overset{\circ}{\mathrm{E}} = 10^{-9}\,\mathrm{sec}^{-2} \right)$

- 1/2 μ dyne-cm unbalance gives error of 1/3 $\overset{\circ}{\mathrm{E}}$

- 1/3 μ°C flotation fluid temperature gradient gives 1/2 μ dyne-cm

- 2 μ watts flow between opposite quadrants on main housing causes 1/3 μ °C gradient

- 1/3 °C gradient in jacket wall causes 2 μ watts of radiation heat transfer

M.I.T. INSTRUMENTATION LABORATORY

Fig. 32 Thermal Configuration

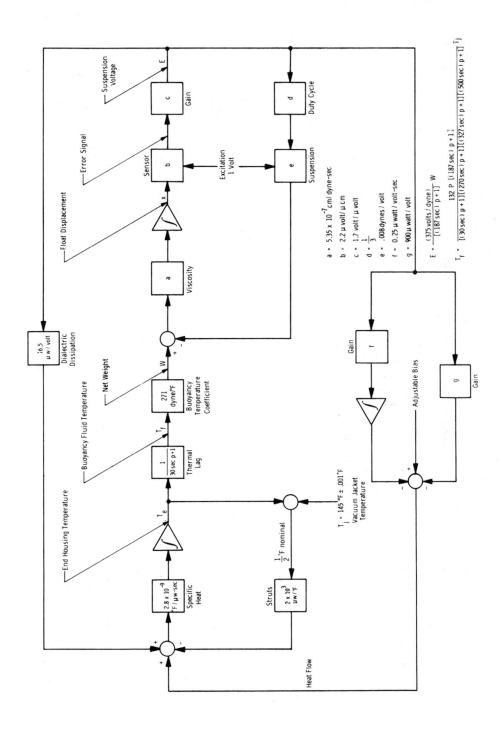

Fig. 33 Thermal Control System

$$a = 5.35 \times 10^{-7} \, cm/dyne\text{-}sec$$

$$b = 2.2 \, \mu \, volt/ \, \mu \, cm$$

$$c = 1.7 \, volt/ \, \mu \, volt$$

$$d = \frac{1}{3}$$

$$e = .008 \, dynes / volt$$

$$f = 0.25 \, \mu \, watt / volt\text{-}sec$$

$$g = 900 \, \mu \, watt / volt$$

$$E = \frac{(375 \, volts / dyne)}{[(187 \, sec) \, p + 1]} \, W$$

$$T_f = \frac{132 \, P \, [(187 \, sec) \, p + 1]}{[(30 \, sec) \, p + 1][(270 \, sec) \, p + 1][(327 \, sec) \, p + 1][(500 \, sec) \, p + 1]} \, T_j$$

of a degree. Thus a generous margin appears to be available.

Overall temperature control is another interesting feature. The buoyancy fluid has a much higher coefficient of thermal expansion than does the float assembly. Therefore the float tends to sink if the gradiometer is slightly warmer than it should be. A temperature control error of $20\mu^{\circ}C$ will require the full capability of the one volt excitation to support the float. Therefore it is necessary to control the temperature with somewhat greater accuracy than this!

It is fortunate that there is a very precise temperature sensor located at precisely the right place. The capacity suspension will be used to measure the net weight of the float. The same electronic scheme that is used to measure accurately the gravity gradient torques is available during other portions of the multiplex cycle to measure the suspension forces. The thermal control functional block diagram in Figure 33 shows the use of this weight information. The thermal control uses a proportional and integral channel to feed back the measured weight to modify the inner heater power by a fraction of a milliwatt.

The thermal control feedback loop has a bandwidth of roughly one cycle per hour. This is slow compared to the time lags in the weighing circuits. This is fast compared to the fifty- or sixty-hour time constant given by the quotient of the main housing thermal inertia divided by the conductance of the struts. The dynamics of the thermal control loop has been carefully designed to obtain over-damped behavior. This is desired to prevent the possibility of an overshoot. Overshoots are undesirable because thermal energy can be delivered by the inner heater but must escape through the long time constant of the struts. Temperature fluctuations of the vacuum jacket are attenuated by a factor of 400 in the critical frequency range of $\frac{1}{4}$ to 1 cycle per hour. Thus the average vacuum jacket temperature must be controlled with an accuracy of $.001^{\circ}C$ to achieve the desired buoyancy balance. Less stringent requirements of course apply outside the critical frequency range.

Theme

In designing this feasibility demonstration gradiometer we have attempted to anticipate all possible problems. The unit is most likely overdesigned in many respects. However, it is probably best to do everything possible to optimize the chance for success if the goal of $\frac{1}{2}\mu$dyne-cm. is to be achieved in a structure of this size.

Presently the float is being course balanced. The earliest experimental results are probably two months away.

KEY WORDS

gravity	geodesy
gradiometer	instrumentation
surveying	anomaly
geophysics	gravimetry

REFERENCES

(1) Heiskanen, W. A., Meinesz, F. A. Vening, The Earth and Its Gravity Field, McGraw-Hill Company, Inc., 1958.

(2) Grant, F. S. and West, G. F., Interpretation Theory in Applied Geophysics, McGraw-Hill Book Company, Inc. 1965.

(3) Goldstein, Herbert, Classical Mechanics, Addison-Wesley Publishing Company, Inc., 1950.

(4) Mueller, Ivan I., The Horizontal Gradients of Gravity in Geodesy, The Ohio State University Department of Geodetic Science, 1964.

(5) Wrigley, Walter, Hollister, Walter M. and Denhard, William G., Gyroscopic Theory, Design, and Instrumentation, M.I.T. Press, 1969.

(6) Draper, Charles S., Wrigley, Walter and Hovorka, John, Inertial Guidance, Pergamon Press, 1960.

(7) Kennard, Earle H., Kinetic Theory of Gases, McGraw-Hill Book Company, Inc., 1938.

APPLICATIONS OF SYSTEMS ENGINEERING
FOR SOLUTIONS TO SOCIAL AND ECONOMIC PROBLEMS

Robert R. Smith, George Priftis[*]

The application of a readily available aerospace technology to determine the solutions needed for social and economic problems, and the direction to take in obtaining these solutions, is thoroughly discussed in its potential for the solution of problems in the following fields:

1. Transportation

2. Fluid Waste

3. Solid Waste

4. Air Pollution

5. Water Pollution

6. Housing

7. Agriculture

8. Government Agencies

The solution to these and other problems dealing with humanity can only be solved once all of the knowns and unknowns along with the many variables affecting them have been determined. This can be accomplished through the application of Systems Engineering to the utilization of computer technology in the data handling field. This technology, Systems Engineering with computer supported collection, reduction and distribution of data will be used to conduct technically credible and comprehensive research and development projects in engineering and program management.

It can be seen in the ensuing paragraphs that there is a tremendous interdependence between the various fields covered. This essentially points out that the social and economic problems created by environmental pollution should be treated as a single system with each of the contributing elements as

---

[*] General Electric Co., Defense Programs Division, Washington, D.C. 20005

a subsystem inter-related by the interdependence of each upon the other as indicated in this article.

HOUSING

A most critical area and the subject of great importance in the federal budget is one of housing. Based on population trends and the current trend of housing units under or planned construction indicates severe shortages in the near future. This field is one in which many aerospace companies are already involved, but mostly on a component or subsystem basis.

The federal government's goal is to provide low-cost housing for low income groups. The technology of systems engineering can readily be applied here since this is more akin to the problems solved in the aerospace business - development of a low cost house.

Some of the detailed data necessary for the systems engineer in this field is listed in Table 1.   With this data as a start, the system parameters can be readily defined and subsystem requirements delineated.

Materials and Fabrication

The major expense in construction of a house lies in the materials and fabrication costs. Data on conventional, state-of-the-art and advanced state-of-the-art materials for house and apartment construction will be necessary. Conventional materials and construction techniques do not lend themselves to low cost housing techniques.

New materials data should be evaluated in conjunction with new fabrication or construction techniques. Modular construction, prefabrication and on-site manufacturing and assembly facilities are some of the possibilities.

The data accumulated in this area must be considered in the total system approach to housing.

Public Sector

The public sector is very varied from rural to urban, from new construction to refurbishment of old and from homes to apartments. Over all are zoning laws and building codes which are almost in as many varieties as flowers. Local, county and state zoning laws and building codes must be collected and evaluated for use in establishing realistic design criteria for housing that could be constructed, with only minor modifications throughout the United States. The accumulated data in zoning laws could be used to make recommended changes in keeping with total environmental planning. The inter-relationship between the housing, water pollution and air pollution fields can be controlled somewhat here by properly planning a community to maintain the balance necessary to satisfy the requirements of these fields. Building code data could possibly lead to more uniformity in this area from one locality to another.

Housing Developments

The latest developments in housing construction should be accumulated and catalogued for use in determining areas lacking in definition or areas in which research and development is needed. In the latter areas, systems engineering techniques developed in the aerospace industry can be applied to define specific areas for R&D effort and the parameters which should govern this effort.

On site manufacturing, fabrication and erection is an area which has and is being explored. With the data available and a systems analysis of this area, a more intelligent approach can be taken toward developing a new and unique method which will save both time and money.

Mobile homes or trailers permanently installed in what is now called a
"Mobile Home Park" appear to be an answer to the housing problem. Data on the
number manufactured, types available, costs, availability of space, acceptability
of this type home and general reaction of the public toward mobile homes must
be determined.

Systems Analysis

The data described in the preceding paragraphs and listed in Table 1 is
by no means all-inclusive. It primarily serves as a starting point for evaluating
the feasibility of realizing improved and more economical methods of providing
housing by application of modern technology and the systems approach. The systems
approach must take into consideration all of the parameters obtained in this
data handling process and place it in context with the inter-relationship of
housing with other environmental fields. Taking the system as a whole,
environmental planning methods can be applied through systems technology to
evolve housing which is low cost, provide for open spaces in community planning,
is esthetically appealing and includes sewage, water and solid waste management
planning.

TRANSPORTATION

Todays Travel Patterns

Transportation has made great advances since the end of World War II. A
greater mobility is available today and this mobility is highly valued by the
urban and suburban resident. Toll highways and expressways allow motorists to
travel long distances in a relatively short time. This short travel time has
caused a transition of the urbanite into the suburbanite where travel into the
city for employment by motor vehicle or commuter train takes a comparatively short
time.

The advent of jet aircraft has made transcontinental and intercontinental travel a matter of hours, not days or weeks. Businessmen think nothing of flying from New York to California in the morning and possibly returning late the same day, a thing unheard of as recent as twenty years ago.

Transportation of products from fruits and vegetables to pies and perishable foods are rapidly moved to the market place. Airplanes have further reduced freight shipment times adding to the rapid accessibility of our market place to the entrepreneurs of agriculture and business.

Effects of the Travel Pattern

This boom in transportation has its adverse affects in that jobs along with people have moved out of the city to avoid the congestion prevalent there. This leaves those who have no private means of transportation with fewer opportunities to find meaningful and compensable employment. The result is higher unemployment and welfare in the cities and a correspondingly higher rate of crime. As the urban city creeps out into the suburban areas, these problems tag along. Another adverse effect is that the tremendous number of motor vehicles on the roads and in the congested cities has created an air pollution problem that may be approaching a critical stage.

Urban Problems

Although some industries have moved from the cities and much new industry has been located outside the city, there is still a great deal of travel to and from the metropolitan areas from the suburbs. It is estimated that for most major metropolitan areas at least 50% of the traffic flow is due to people going to and from work or traveling on business.

Congestion, noise, rapid transit, lack of open spaces, and community planning are just a few of the problems facing the urban center in the transportation sector. For convenience, a great many people employed in the cities use automobiles as their primary mode of transportation. Public transportation in the form of buses, streetcars, subways or trains either may not be conveniently located for these commuters or they may not travel close enough to their places of employment. Rapid transit systems may be overcrowded, lack air-conditioning, not conform to published schedules, have poor facilities at their access points, cost more than is considered fair under existing conditions and not be as rapid as the name implies.

Data concerning transit or mass transportation systems covering the problems mentioned above in addition to advanced methods of transport, transport centers, rehabilitation and redevelopment efforts to ease congestion and overall community planning needs to be accumulated. This accumulated data can be studied by the systems engineer to achieve a transport system which encompasses these and other problems which may evolve in the analysis. Table 2 presents data deemed necessary as a minimum to define the parameters and systems requirements to lead towards the solution or solutions to this urban problem. Additionally, data on noise and congestion caused by transportation media has to be evaluated along with information on methods to alleviate these problems.

Systems engineering can be applied in this area to examine the entire problem, recommend modifications based on background data and propose completely new methods of transportation that will adequately meet the requirements of the total environmental system. The goal being to make the city more attractive to industry and people and reverse the flow out to one of flowing in. This could lead to an increase in employment opportunities, a lessening in the number of people unemployed and in welfare and possibly a decrease in the crime rate.

Suburban Problems

The primary transportation problem associated with suburban and rural areas is one of access to the city in the minimum amount of time. Automotive travel is the most highly used means of transportation into the city. This is due to the convenience factor involved. The inconvenience comes from congestion which causes delays or traffic to move slowly, inadequate parking facilities and the air pollution or smog conditions created in the city.

As mentioned previously, the inconvenience associated with rapid transit or commuter trains possibly deters the driving commuter from using these modes of transportation. Outlying transportation centers with adequate parking facilities, modern ticketing methods, conveniently scheduled modes of transportation and less crowded conditions may lure commuters to other modes of transportation. Data should be accumulated in this area in conjunction with data on transport patterns within the suburban and rural areas. Information on suburban community planning to control the sometimes unsightly communities, housing developments and shopping centers within the transport system should be obtained.

These data along with information on inter-city transportation of people and goods can be evaluated on a regional or meglopolitan basis taking into consideration problems of several cities and the area between. This may be the more ideal case for the systems engineer to establish the requirements for a transportation systems approach. It is not expected that the total system problem would be solved at one time, but instead by breaking the requirements down to subsystem and even lower levels, solutions could be achieved.

Through the application of modern technology, systems engineering techniques and effective program management tremendous advances can be made in the transportation field.

WATER POLLUTION

The basic aim in any water resource management effort is to maintain an adequate supply of potable water that meets modern standards of chemical and biological purity. Accumulation of the necessary data on water standards and the current methods in use to meet these standards is discussed below. In the accumulation, sorting, and evaluation of the collected data, the shortcomings and, hopefully, the remedies necessary to rectify existing treatment methods will be determined.

Since the available fresh water on the earth is only 0.325% of the earth's entire water supply, it is apparent that environmental planning must be employed treating water pollution as a system being affected by many subsystems (e.g., sewage, disposal, industrial dumping, etc.).

The data bank established for the water pollution field should consist as a minimum of all of the available information in the categories listed in Table 3. This information once collected, sorted and evaluated will provide us with a more intelligent base from which to work in solving some of the problems in the water pollution field.

The First Step - Standards and Regulatory Controls

First and foremost, it will be necessary to determine what standards for water quality are really necessary and if they should apply to the nation as a whole or only to geographical areas or regions of the country. Having this information available and comparing it with current and proposed restrictions within the states, more effective federal and state regulatory controls can be devised to meet the necessary water quality standards.

This can be accomplished by taking the existing restrictions and regulations, comparing them with requirements and standards that are necessary and then

114

transforming the results into meaningful legislation which establishs regulations that can realistically be achieved. These controls and restrictions would, of course, have to take into consideration the contributing elements and their respective contribution to the water pollution problem, such as changes in local zoning laws to restrict developers from filling in swampy or tidal water areas which are a part of the total watershed system.

Sewage and Water Treatment

Since sewage is the largest contributor to water pollution, the status of sewage treatment equipment will provide valuable information on what is commercially available today, under design or being tested and what is being proposed for the future. Selection of the proper course to take in developing new sewage treatment equipment will be based on this information along with that determined in the fluid waste field. Interdependence between the residuals from water treatment and their effects on, or additions to, another field of pollution are important and should fall out of this sewage status survey, industrial treatment equipment survey and the other areas listed in Table 3.

The state-of-the-art of sewage treatment facilities from which the waste water and other residuals can be recycled back into the productive process or recovered for useful purposes will be investigated. Sewage treatment systems such as the reversed osmosis and closed cycle systems will be searched out in depth for their current usage, treatment residuals effects and the future planning for usage of these systems. Water retreatment requirements and the feasibility of incorporating the sewage treatment facility in with the water purification facility will be evaluated as to its current and planned usage. Current defects and drawbacks of these and other systems will be determined to provide an insight into the problems which need solutions. Age and efficiency of existing treatment facilities will be among the data accumulated and will provide an indication of the overall status of our sewage treatment facilities throughout the country. With this information available, pinpointing specific problem areas, and the subsystem requirements surrounding these problem areas, the aerospace engineer and scientist can readily apply his technological background to obtaining the needed solutions.

Based on the data accumulated in this area, a more desirable approach toward water treatment facilities and their interrelationship with sewage treatment facilities can be realized. Using the accumulated data, water systems specifications can be developed based on regional, rural, and urban requirements and economics. The affects of water treatment residuals can be defined along with possible or achievable solutions to the residuals problem.

Utilizing the information gathered on the age and efficiency of existing water treatment facilities, their location and size of the community or communities they are serving, a report for federal and state government water pollution authorities can be issued. With a report of this type, more intelligent planning can be used by our government officials for the allocation of their monies such that they are allocated on the basis of need and not on the basis of political agrandizement.

Specific equipment problems such as corrosion problems, pumps, chemicals, filtering media, controls, all will be delineated and their interrelationship within the water treatment system defined to insure that future designs are more systems oriented than product or component oriented with no thought to the remainder of the system. Specifications more in line with the particular requirements of water treatment plants and water reuse systems can be developed. Areas can be defined for new or continuing research in effluent treatment to

further reduce residuals which when introduced into our waterways, further
reduce the BOD (biological oxygen demand) generated.

Industrial Waste Water Treatment

Industrial pollution constituents will be determined in the data accumulation
process. These constituents will most likely be more varied than the industries
which generate them as waste residuals. Current, state-of-the-art, and advanced
state-of-the-art equipment for industrial waste water treatment, conditioning and
quality control will be investigated to obtain all of the data available on these
types of equipment. In particular, the needs and requirements for thermal
conditioning equipment and the affects of thermal conditions on marine life are
of extreme importance. Radiation detection not only in the vicinity of the nuclear
power plant, but also in the soil, plants and even milk, must be investigated for
the methods, equipment and most desirable locations for devices to monitor this
pollution hazard.

Reference 3   states that in many industries, the reverse osmosis process
is currently in use. It will be necessary to determine exactly how many. It
will be necessary to determine the constituents that can be treated by this
process for extension of its use to other industries. The utilization of ion
exchange processes must be determined, the industries in which it is utilized and
for what result.

Public and Civil Areas

Past and present effects of landfill operations on the reduction of marine life
breeding grounds, marine life population, local water tables and other related
results will be examined for all pertinent data available. This information will
be applied to better planning for both land and water use on both a local and
regional level. The overall effects of reclaiming swampy land through landfill

on both the ecological and social environments must be determined. Man must have clean air to breath and fresh water to drink, but he also must have his recreational facilities. The latter may be most affected by landfill reclamation projects.

The inter-relationship of the various local, state and federal agencies which have a responsibility for water quality control will have to be determined. Their current involvement, power or authority and coordination with each other is of primary importance. This information is necessary in order to establish the regulatory controls mentioned previously and supply these agencies the wherewithal to police and enforce them at all levels of government without needless jurisdictional disputes over responsibilities or authority.

Since most of the burden of regulation and prosecution lies on the backs of the states and local governments, it is in these areas primarily that data must be accumulated.

Taking all of the contributors and the various elements contributed towards polluting our streams and rivers; reasonable restrictions and realistic legislation can be drawn up. It will be the specific duty of these agencies to police these restrictions and enforce the legislation. It will also be up to these agencies, utilizing information at their disposal on current water conditions, to update or modify restrictions and propose amendments to existing legislation reflecting improvements in the current water condition.

Water Quality - Control

Knowing everything about the problem and its treatment, it will be necessary to monitor and control the quality of the water and the affects of its treatment residuals on the external environment to maintain the standards desired. Collection and storage of all available data relating to these categories will provide sufficient information on which to determine needs for new or better equipment to sample, measure, and report the results of tests on water quality. This, of course, would most likely have to be broken down into classifications such as sewerage, industrial, etc., and in particular, the industrial; further broken down into the type of industry (e.g. chemical, textile, steel, etc.). It is possible that, once all of the data has been collected and evaluated, that a single monitoring or measurement device would be capable of use under several conditions, thus eliminating two separate pieces of testing equipment being built where one would suffice. This area will be a key one and extreme care will have to be taken to determine precisely what the requirements are and what the deviations could be from one part of the country to another.

Technology Application

Armed with all of this information, it will be much easier to determine where the technologies can be applied and specifically what technology to apply, as has been discussed in the preceding paragraphs in many areas for which data should be collected. This, of course, is of little or no value unless a monitary value can also be placed on the problem and its proposed solution. Therefore, further data will be needed on costs of pollution caused damage which has occurred to date. Utilization of this data and the costs to provide the solutions, intelligent decisions can be made at the government and industry level as to which problem or problems affecting water pollution to attach first. A relationship of return on investment involving the cost of the cure and its resultant anticipated results will have to be developed to aid government and industry in their decision making.

The primary area of application will be in the total environmental system as it affects the social and economic environment in which we live. All of this information can be used in a total environmental planning approach wherein all aspects of water pollution can be evaluated for a local area at the regional or national level and considered in a master plan for water pollution control.

Guidelines, based on factual data, can be published on the total environmental planning approach for use by both urban and rural communities. These guidelines will provide communities with a systematic approach to watershed protection through a total community zoning approach based on esthetic, economic, social and recreational, education, water availability, sewage containment or treatment, space and population considerations.

AIR POLLUTION

Pollution of the atmosphere comes about through burning fuels to produce energy, by waste incineration, and by discharge of gas and aerosol by-products from chemical processing, manufacturing, construction, and demolition. Air pollution, although a worldwide problem, is primarily one of municipalities. It is here that pollutants are concentrated and become entrapped in small geographical areas that are densely populated. However, if a systematic approach to solving our air pollution problems is not followed, the urban heat island dome will eventually expand from our cities into the rural areas of the surrounding country side.

The data to be accumulated for use in the systems analysis of this source of pollution is tabulated in Table 4. The inter-relationship with other fields such as transportation, housing or building, and solid waste disposal should also be determined in the data accumulation process.

Air Quality Standards and Restrictions

The Clean Air Act as amended in October 1965, authorized the Secretary of HEW to set emission standards for new motor vehicles sold in the U.S. Standards were set for complete control of crankcase emissions and partial control of hydrocarbons and carbon monoxide from the exhaust by 1968. Nitrogen oxide standards have been tightened for 1971 with a waiver given to California for tighter standards and tightened nationally for 1973 and later vehicles. Under discussion are proposed national standards for 1975 which appear to be really pressing the internal combustion engine in terms of design capabilities and performance.

Data should be obtained first on the local levels of air pollution constituents, their localized affect on health and other medical aspects of the pollutants. Local quality standards and timetables should be researched and categorized by state and geographic location or air quality region as defined by the Department of HEW.

These standards and timetables by law must meet the national criteria mentioned previously. Comparisons of the pollution constituents and their percentages along with the contributing elements and the percentage they contribute can be compared with the air quality criteria. This criteria is based on dosages of air pollutants which cause adverse effects on people and property and are issued by the National Air Pollution Control Administration (NAPCA). This comparison will indicate whether on the local level the standards and timetables set to meet these standards are adequate. Statistical analysis of data accumulated on pollutants also can contribute to the air quality criteria which now only covers the following:

1. Sulphur Oxides

2. Gross Particulate Matter

3. Photochemical Oxidants

4. Carbon Monoxide

5. Hydrocarbons

There is sufficient medical data available on toxic or harmful dosages of most every known element which can have an affect on the respiratory system. It is a matter of accumulating and cataloguing this information through the data handling process so that in the overall systems analysis of the problem, it can be incorporated into the standards, then into the specifications for control equipment and into the control and measurement equipment.

Local and state ordinances against various means of air pollution, such as: open burning or incineration of trash and solid wastes should be catalogued and grouped within the air quality regions. This data when compared with the pollution constituents, air quality criteria and standards currently in effect will indicate if restrictions are adequate or if any are in effect at all in the critical areas.

Energy Conversion

At the moment, the major contributor to air pollution is the internal combustion engine. Data, by air quality region, should be accumulated on total tonnage of air pollutants contributed by the combined effects of automobile, buses and trucks. This data should further be broken down to establish the levels of gaseous pollutants and particulate matter in the emissions of these motor vehicles. Taking this data long with total tonnages of pollutants in a region, critical regions can be defined. The inter-relationship of air pollution and transportation must also be considered here since it is modes of transportation which are contributing to air pollution.

Contributions from space heating and power generation must be determined and controls currently in use and necessary in the future ascertained. More efficient fuel combustion processes must be the result and hopefully data accumulated here will point the way towards these processes.

Home and Industry

Incineration systems for both home and industrial use, to reduce the content of pollutants emitted, should be evaluated for their efficiency, effectivity and costs. Use of fuels other than high sulfur coal and oil for home and industrial heating is of primary importance.

The materials balance and flow concept for homes and particularly for industries appears to be an approach for determining the input and the various outputs from these sectors which possibly can be reused or more effectively disposed of.

The Urban Problem

Of most concern is the air pollution problem that exists in our large urban areas. The large concentrations of motor vehicles, industry and homes introduce huge volumes of pollutants into the air every day. Nature through its natural processes cleans and filters the air through changes in weather conditions. In the urban center, large buildings, closely spaced, do not allow air currents to flow through and cleanse the air. Also, the buildings retain and generate heat which traps the air tending to rise from the ground through normal means. This creates the heat dome mentioned previously.

In attempting to achieve solutions to the air pollution problem, this along with those areas discussed previously and those others listed in Table 4   must be evaluated as a whole system.

Systems Solution

In evaluating the air pollution field as a total system, the external costs imposed by residuals discharged to the environment must be compared and judged against the costs of controlling the amount of these residuals. This should also consider external costs associated with increased levels of residuals in another environmental medium as a result of air pollution control.

The data obtained would be examined in all facets of the problem to obtain the parameters encompassing the total system and subsystem requirements with the ultimate goals delineated. These system parameters and subsystem requirements, of course, need to be factored into the entire air pollution control program. With them, each area or subsystem can be analyzed and solutions evolved as a small part of the whole but within the systems requirements of the whole.

A direction which most probably will result will be that of the research and development activity conducted by both government and industry. Joint solutions are more desirable than none. Air pollution control systems designs and the program to foster these designs must be one of national scope that also recognize the needs of the future.

FLUID WASTE

Treatment and disposal of liquid pollutants poses a major problem in the United States today. Currently there are three ways to rid water of the solids and solutes it captures through use by industry and the consuming public. These are listed below:

1. Physical

2. Chemical

3. Biochemical

These liquid pollutants are divided into three classes:

a. Floating material

b. Suspended matter

c. Dissolved impurities

and there is a further distinction between organic and inorganic pollutants.

The specific treatment for a given waste material actually depends on the kind and amount of pollutants, their assimilation by the water resource involved, the ability to remove the material and can the purified liquid be reused or sold. The requirements of the regulatory agencies and existing legislation on both local and state levels also come into the picture.

Data pertaining to these and other problems in the fluid waste field, as listed in Table 5,   should be obtained for systems evaluation in approaching solutions to the total problem of fluid waste disposal.

Purification Standards and Regulatory Agencies

Quality standards for purified water as they currently exist should be collected and catalogued as to urban areas, rural areas, coastal regions, interior regions, arid and wet climates, and geographic locations. Since no one standard conceivably could apply to the nation as a whole, a breakdown such as this must be made. With this data, reasonable standards can be adopted on state and local levels. Legislation to enforce these standards, which would also cover storage and transport of fluid waste, can then intelligently be proposed and passed into law.

Data accumulation should also consider industrial waste water standards both separately and in conjunction with the sewage requirements and standards. These data can be accumulated on a coordinated basis with a water pollution study since the areas are interdependent.

Evaluation of the data accumulated here will lead to more well defined quality standards and system specifications for fluid waste treatment equipment and facilities to meet these standards. Tolerable levels of degradable organic materials, specified in terms of the five-day biochemical oxygen demand (BO D5), contained

in the purified fluids can be set. Systems analysis of the data accumulated also

will determine maximum allowable plant nutrients, nitrogen and phosphates that

can be tolerated in purified liquids being discharged into the waterways.

The regulatory agencies involved, their jurisdiction and authority as well

as their inter-relationship with water pollution control agencies is an important

area for systems analysis by accumulating this data for evaluation. Broader

powers, wider jurisdiction and centralization into a single agency, such as a

fluid resources management agency to handle both water and fluid waste pollution

problems may be the result of the systems analysis. It would appear that this is

the direction to take at this point in time even without the data to substantiate

such a move.

Current Treatment Methods

Most liquid waste treatment involves screening, sedimentation, flocculation,

flotation and/or filtration. Chemical additives also play an important part

through their usage in the processes mentioned above to aid the mechanics of these

processes. These are examples of the physical processes mentioned previously

which can be used in combination with chemicals. Since these processes are either

used singly or in combinations with each other, data should be accumulated on

usage, material removed, amount of sludge created, quality of effluent from process,

subsequent processes used, number of like systems in use, age, efficiency and

volume of liquid waste treated.

Industrial wastes are treated by biological means widely used for sewage

disposal. Material suspended in solution is readily attacked by bacteria producing

carbon dioxide and water with inorganic by-products which produce a sludge. These

treatment methods consist of aerobic biological processes or activated sludge process,

anaerobic biological process (Figure   1), trickling filter (Figure 2),
and shallow pond or lagoon. Data on the usage, material removed, amount of sludge
created, BOD reduction, quality of effluent, subsequent processes used, number of
like processes in use, age, efficiency and volume of liquid waste treated.

Chemicals added to neutralize acids or alkalis are frequently part of the
additives in processes already described. Chemical treatment also considers not
only adding to but also removing from the fluid waste water undesirable chemicals.
Physio-chemical processes consist of chemical addition, adsorption, ion exchange,
continuous ion exchange, dialysis, electrodialysis and reverse osmosis (Figure 3).
The same data collected on the physical and biochemical processes should be
collected on the physio-chemical processes.

The evaluation of all this data collected in the various treatment methods
can lead in many directions. From the systems standpoint, the data will lead
to treatment systems specifications, based on operational data, for advanced
treatment systems. Effectivity of current processes can lead to systems design
approaches utilizing combinations of these processes to produce a fluid which can
either be sold as a liquid fertilizer or reused by recycling it into the water
treatment system. Projections, based on efficiency, volume of fluid treated and
volume of fluid waste generated can be made on local levels for requirements
in the future. In addition to the fluid waste generated, the amount of sludge
which is predominately water, generated will be known for subsequent treatment.

The range of treatment methods and the data accumulated and evaluated is by
no means all inclusive. It serves as a starting point for evaluating the
feasibility of realizing improved and more economic treatment methods by the
application of modern technology and the systems approach.

Solids Extraction and Reuse

The residue from the treatment methods described above are solid and liquid. The liquid can be discharged to a nearby water-course, solid, however, cannot. This solid or sludge can be used as landfill, and in fertilizers. In any case, it must be treated to make it relatively unobjectionable and to facilitate disposal.

All data available on sludge treatment methods, dewatering, gases generated during treatment, potential value of dry sludge and percent water reduction during treatment should be collected and evaluated for possible applications of an aerospace technological development.

Fluid Waste Collection

At present, most fluid waste is collected from the home and industry through sewer systems or in septic tanks. The waste material reaches these points in an untreated condition. Through systems analysis of existing methods of collection and pretreatment, new methods may be devised. Complete systems from home to complete treatment and disposal should be the ultimate goal. This may possibly require pretreatment in the home, treatment during transport in the sewers such that the waste material upon reaching its destination requires relatively little final treatment.

Costs for most all of the treatment methods for sewage and industrial fluid wastes should be readily available for existing systems. In determining systems solutions for either area, these costs and contemplated costs for advanced state-of-the-art systems should be compared. Initial, operating and labor costs all included.

Using all of the information gathered, as suggested in Table 5 , the systems engineer can then define the requirements for a totally integrated fluid waste management program.

128

AGRICULTURE

Current Trends

At this time, agricultural production in the United States is more than
adequate to meet the demands created internally with surplus crops in many areas
for export sales. There appears to be no shortages in fruit and vegetable
production. Livestock and poultry shipments to the market place are at or above
prior years levels. These are all due to increased yields per acre, more
efficient farming methods, more enriching livestock and poultry feeds and less
spoilage in shipment to the market place.

If the current rate at which land is being taken out of production continues
or increases, shortages may occur sometime in the future. Since environmental
planning for social and economic improvement must be based on some time in the
future, it will be necessary to plan agricultural needs on this basis. Population
throughout the U.S. and the world is on the increase which has two effects,
first more space will be needed to accommodate the population increase, and
second more foodstuffs will be necessary to feed the increased population. An
increase in space requirements creates an adverse effect on agriculture by taking
up ground normally used in farming.

Farmland Utilization

More adequate utilization of existing farmland to provide greater crops
yields will be necessary, Table 6.   This can be assisted through the development
of better fertilizer and soil enrichment programs. Seed development programs
producing more disease resistant strains, crops more suitable for mechanized
harvesting methods, and higher yields per planting can also provide some
assistance in the future. Year round growth possibilities of hardier strains

129

of existing agricultural products and dual crop studies evaluating the advantages or disadvantages of such successive plantings need to be carried out.

Systems engineering applied to data obtained on farmland utilization information would be of most benefit in the areas of mechanical picking apparatus. Here systems requirements and specifications tailored to meet the parameters associated with each crop suited for mechanical harvesting can be developed. Programs leading to research and development on new strains for mechanized harvesting can result from the systems studies.

The resistance of agricultural products to insects, disease, and fungus and the controls developed and under development need to be determined. Hardiness or ability to withstand extreme environments and the hybridization of hardier strains has to be researched and the data used by the systems engineer to evaluate the necessity for additional programs.

Data on the efficiency of farming operations covering dairy farming, harvesting of all types of crops by mechanical means, shipment to market, on-site product packaging, general use of operational and maintenance equipment, and equipment distribution.

Regulatory and Advisory Agencies

The federal government plays a huge role in the agricultural field through the Department of Agriculture. Crop reports, estimates of harvest volume, research and development grants, acreage allocations and price support levels are all functions of this agency. On the local or state levels are the state agricultural extension centers, a function connected with a state college of agriculture.

An interchange of information must take place between these agencies and the farmers for the benefit of both. The effectiveness of these organizations needs to be evaluated on the basis of the advantages offered to the entire system. The type of information distributed and data received by these agencies needs to be studied to determine if it is adequate or more and different data and information is necessary.

Data Utilization

The systems engineer in applying his technology to the data accumulated, as listed in Table 6, through evaluation of external and internal conditions can establish requirements for future development. In conjunction with agriculture specialists and agencies, farm management control programs can be delineated. Improvement in distribution systems, reduction in labor costs through better implementation of equipment and the establishment of more farm centers or cooperatives for the benefit of farmers can be some results. The application of systems engineering technology to the agricultural field can mean improvement and profit to the farmer.

SOLID WASTE

The Problem

It is estimated that at present 500,000 tons of solid wastes are produced daily at an annual cost of somewhere near 5 billion dollars for disposal. This expenditure for solid waste disposal in the United States places it third behind education and road construction in costs to local governments. The disposal methods currently in use do not effectively reflect 20th century technology.

The most common methods of disposal are open dumping and burning, incineration and sanitary landfill. In open dumping, the waste is dumped at a site selected for this and then burned. Incineration is burning in a furnance or combustion chamber under controlled conditions. Sanitary landfilling consists of burial of the waste products which in time undergoes slow anaerobic degradation. These are all methods which have been used for centuries with very little improvement. Considering the technological advances of the past 25 years, this is a sad state of affairs.

Contributing Elements

The primary contributing element is the consumer who generates a tremendous quantity of garbage, rubbish and ashes as illustrated by Figure 4   from Reference 1. Breakdowns are available on the composition of the solid waste from households and are included in the data requirements of Table 7.   Industrial contribution run from animal carcasses to paper waste. Composition on a general scale of industrial wastes is also available.

Detailed data at the various sources such as households, manufacturing plants, chemical plants, oil refineries, meat packing plants, and pulp mills to mention a few is necessary. This data should consist of contribution and percentage of solid waste generated for each contributing element. Evaluation of this data by the systems engineer should result in materials flow charts with which recommendations can be made to industrial concerns on uses for the solid wastes resulting from their processes. It is more than likely that a good deal of the waste generated can be recycled back into the economy. Firestone Tire and Rubber Company for example is building a pilot plant to reclaim chemicals and raw materials from worn out disposed tires.

Collection and Disposal

Collection is primarily done by truck either on open dump truck or closed truck with a mechanical compactor. Disposal has been discussed in a previous paragraph.

Data needs to be accumulated on recent developments in collection methods, problems associated with collection, separate collection or separation of waste constituents (e.g. paper, bottles, cans, etc.), labor costs, standardized containers, precompaction at the source and any other related information. Systems analysis of this data can lead to specifications and performance requirements for collection vehicles. Research and development activity in the development of a more automated collection system can be defined with parameters, which will meet systems requirements, based on the data accumulated.

Data on developments in the area of disposal methods such as high density mechanical compaction (Japanese process), pyrolsis, incineration, land and minefill, and salvage. Evaluation of the data accumulated by the systems engineer can lead to disposal methods tailored to specific waste materials, disposal methods which yield reusable chemicals, materials and energy, and disposal methods which consist of reprocessing the waste material for reuse.

Application of the systems engineering approach to waste disposal first must tackle the problem of sorting before the disposal methods discussed in the preceding paragraph can even be considered. The systems engineer, based on the data accumulated on waste material composition, arrive at the requirements for automatic sorting equipment. These requirements will lead to the design of rapid, highly selective and economical sorting devices. This coupled with salvage or conversion processes can be considered a total system for disposal of solid wastes.

Of all of the disposal methods in current use, the open dump is the worst pollution menace, among other things. The systems engineer must come up with alternatives that eliminate or reduce the use of this method of disposal which breeds insects, rodents, causes odors, are unsightly and must be burned to control these problems and reduce volume. The burning contributes to air pollution and drainage through these dumps contributes to water pollution.

Through systems analysis of the constituents of solid waste, collection and disposal recommendations to industry and to government for disposible designs for packaging. Some industries have started working in the area of making disposal a product design consideration and research projects have been carried out, Reference 2. This is just a small step in the right direction and with the application of the technology of systems engineering giant steps can be taken.

CONCLUSIONS

The information presented in this paper provides just a base from which to start towards the solution of social and economic problems through environmental pollution control. To develop an understanding of the social-economic system, it will be necessary as the starting point to identify the key elements involved; that is, those elements whose relationships and interaction define and give special character to the system. It has been attempted in this paper to do just that in as broad a manner as possible.

The pollution potential in the U.S. can be visualized as a product of the number of people times the standard of living. Based on past and present trends, it appears the population will double and the standard of living quadruple over the next 50 years. The future implications are obvious if modern technology and the systems approach are not applied to deal with the future potential pollution load.

An essential technique which must be implemented is the integration of pollution control into the production process. This has been advanced in this paper and through application of the systems engineering technology developed in the aerospace industry can be achieved. This must be accomplished so that pollution tonnages will not incindate society in the future. A general acceptance of the idea that it is cheaper to control pollution than to content with it should be incorporated in existing industrial processes and new industrial plants to be built.

Concern for arriving at some overall indicator of the quality of the environment in which the various interrelations and trade-offs can be included leads toward the concept of net social benefit - that is, total (or incremental) social benefit less social cost! This is pictorially indicated in Figure 5 which is taken from Reference 1. This concept of social benefit can be applied to a particular environmental disturbance or to any large range of environmental effects.

Harvey S. Perloff in Reference 1, states that one view of the urban environment is as a contained (but not closed) highly interrelated system (or subsystem) of natural and man made elements in various mixes. This is the manner in which the subject has been approached in the discussion of the systems engineering approach to the social and economic problems.

The capacity to deal effectively with the enormously complex problems of the urban environment will be increased if the concepts can be sharpened through the means discussed in this paper. This capacity can also be increased by the data accumulated through clarification of the problems, improvement of the measurement tools and an increase in the capacity to be inventive about new institutional arrangements to cope with new situations as they arise.

TABLE 1

HOUSING DATA REQUIREMENTS

1. Materials Development

   a. Conventional
   b. Ferrous and Non-Ferrous
   c. Fibers
   d. Plastics and Foams

2. Fabrication Techniques

   a. Joining and Fastening
   b. Subassemblies
   c. Walls
   d. Floors
   e. Ceilings
   f. Wiring
   g. Plumbing
   h. Foundations
   i. Roofing

3. Construction Techniques

   a. Conventional
   b. On-Site Manufacturing
   c. Modular Concepts

      (1) Walls
      (2) Rooms
      (3) Others

   d. Prefabrication Methods

4. Mobile Home Development

5. Zoning Laws and Building Codes

   a. Local
   b. County
   c. State

6. Housing Requirements

   a. Apartments
   b. Houses
   c. Rural and Urban

7. Environmental Control System Development

TABLE 2

TRANSPORTATION DATA REQUIREMENTS

1. Modes of Transportation Within Cities

   a. Rapid Transit
   b. Trains
   c. Airplanes

2. Noise

   a. Levels of Various Media
   b. Zoning Regulations
   c. Noise Suppression Devices
   d. Areas of High Concentration

3. Traffic Congestion

   a. Areas of High Concentrations
   b. Contributing Elements
   c. Effects of Redevelopment
   d. Community Planning

4. Transportation Centers

   a. Currently in Use
   b. Ticketing Methods
   c. Schedules
   d. Convenience
   e. Travel Conditions
   f. Availability of Parking
   g. Proposed for Future Use

5. Transportation into the Cities

   a. Motor Vehicles
   b. Commuter Trains
   c. Airplanes
   d. Convenience of Transportation Centers
   e. Highway Availability
   f. Land Availability for Advanced Systems
   g. Underground
   h. Over-head (Monorail)

6. Transportation of Goods

   a. Truck
   b. Train
   c. Airplane
   d. Waterborne

7. Population Distribution

8. Employment Distribution

9. Traffic Flow Patterns

   a. Into City
   b. Within City
   c. Out of City
   d. Suburban

10. Transportation of Fuels

    a. Gas and Oil Pipelines
    b. Leak Detection Systems

11. Highway and Road Construction Materials

    a. Durability
    b. New Materials Development

12. Transportation Between Cities

    a. Motor Vehicles
    b. High Speed Trains
    c. Airplanes
    d. Waterborne

TABLE 3

WATER POLLUTION DATA REQUIREMENTS

1. Water Quality Standards

   a. National Level
   b. States
   c. Geographic Location (Northeast, Middle Atlantic, etc.)
   d. For Human Consumption
   e. To Support Marine Life

2. Water Pollution Restrictions

   a. Current
      (1) States
      (2) Federal

   b. Proposed or In Legislation
      (1) States
      (2) Federal Government

3. Water Needs and Availability

   a. Regional
   b. National

4. Treatment Equipment

   a. In Current Use
      (1) Sewage
      (2) Industrial
          (a) Chemicals
          (b) Acid Mine Drainage
          (c) Pulp Mill Effluent
          (d) Other Industrial Wastes
          (e) Thermal Conditioning

   b. State-of-the-Art
      (1) Sewage
      (2) Industrial
      (3) Home Use

   c. Advanced-State-of-the-Art
      (1) Sewage
      (2) Industrial
      (3) Home Use

5. Water Quality Control Equipment

   a. In Current Use

   b. Measurable Quantities
      (1) Sewage Treatment
      (2) Industrial

6. Pollution Detection Devices

   a. Detectable Elements
      (1) BOD (Biochemical Oxygen Demand)
      (2) Acidity/Alkalinity (pH)
      (3) Hardness
      (4) Organisms or Bacteria
      (5) Dissolved Solids

   b. Current Methods
   c. State-of-the-Art Methods
   d. Laboratory Techniques

7. Governmental Activities

   a. Responsibilities
   b. Authority
   c. Coordination
   d. Long-Range and Short-Range Goals
   e. Interrelationships and Interdependence

8. Environmental Planning

   a. Landfill Activity
   b. Regional Water Transfers

9. Cost Effectiveness

   a. Costs Associated with Pollution Caused Damage
   b. Costs of Water Treatment Equipment
   c. Operational Costs of Existing Equipment
   d. Operational Efficiency of Existing Equipment
   e. Proposed Equipment
      (1) Costs - Initial
      (2) Cost - Operating
      (3) Efficiencies Expected

TABLE 4

AIR POLLUTION DATA REQUIREMENTS

1. Air Quality Standards
   a. National
   b. States
   c. Geographic Location
   d. Health and Medical

2. Air Pollution Restrictions
   a. Proposed as in Legislation
      (1) Federal Government
      (2) States
      (3) Local Ordinances

3. Energy Conversion - Fossil Fuels
   a. Internal Combustion Engine
      (1) Automobile
      (2) Buses
      (3) Trucks
   b. Space Heating
      (1) Fossil Fuels
          Gaseous and particulate emissions
   c. Power Generation
      (1) Fossil Fuels
          Gaseous and particulate emissions
   d. Aircraft Engines

4. Incineration Systems
   a. Home
   b. Industrial
   c. Solid Waste Disposal

5. Industrial Pollution
   a. Chemical Industry
   b. Petroleum Refining
   c. Metal Refining and Fabricating
   d. Manufacturing

6. Motor Vehicle Emission Control
   a. Automobile Pollution Control Devices
      (1) Types Available
      (2) Advanced Development Status
      (3) Effectiveness
      (4) Efficiency
      (5) Reliability Factors
      (6) Suitability for Vehicles in Current Use
      (7) Cost/Price
      (8) Installation Costs
   b. Power System Development
      (1) Internal Combustion Engine
      (2) Turbine Engine
      (3) Electric
      (4) Others
   c. Carburation System Development
   d. Fuel Development
      (1) Reduction of Non-Combustible Harmful Elements
      (2) Lead-Free Gasoline
      (3) Aircraft Fuels

7. Industrial Pollution Control Equipment
   a. Particulate Recovery
      (1) In Current Use
      (2) Under Development
   b. Absorption
      (1) In Current Use
      (2) Under Development
   c. Absorption and Particulate Recovery
      (1) In Current Use
      (2) Under Development

8. Development Status of Industrial Pollution Control Equipment Other Than Item 7
   a. Fuel-Complete Combustion Processes
   b. Flue Gas Control Equipment
   c. Stack and Chimney Recycle Systems
   d. Secondary Uses Developed for Gases and Particulates Generated Through Combustion

9. Air Quality Control Equipment
   a. In Current Use
   b. Measurable Quantities and Equipment
      (1) Exhaust Emissions
      (2) Industrial Emissions
      (3) Ground Level Air
      (4) Higher Altitude Air

10. Pollution Detection Devices

11. Governmental Activities

12. Environmental Planning

13. Cost Effectiveness

TABLE 5

FLUID WASTE DATA REQUIREMENTS

1. Fluid Waste Water Purification Standards
   a. Urban Areas
   b. Rural Areas
   c. Coastal and Interior Regions
   d. Geographic Locations

2. Regulatory Agencies
   a. Local
   b. State

3. Treatment Methods

4. Fluid Waste Collection Methods

5. Use of Residual Solids and Liquids

6. Use of By-Products of Treatment Process
   a. Heat
   b. Gases

7. Pre-Treatment Units for Homes
   a. Availability
   b. Unit Costs
   c. Compatibility with Existing Systems
   d. Installation and Operating Costs

8. Development of New Treatment Processes

TABLE 6

AGRICULTURE DATA REQUIREMENTS

1. Utilization of Existing Land

2. Fertilizer Development

3. Seed Development

4. Insect, Disease and Fungus Control
   a. Germicides
   b. Fungicides
   c. Pesticides
   d. Organic Methods
   e. Use of Predators
   f. DDT Usage and Effects

5. Year Round Growth Possibilities

6. Dual Crop Studies
   a. Soil Enrichment Crops
   b. Soil Depletion Crops
   c. Combinations

7. Animal Feeds
   a. In Current Use
   b. Under Study

8. Farm Efficiency
   a. Dairy
   b. Harvesting of Crops
      (1) Hand
      (2) Mechanized Methods
   c. Development of Mechanized Harvesting Equipment
   d. Transportation of Products to Market
   e. On-Site Preparation for Market
   f. Plowing, Planting, and Maintenance Equipment
   g. Equipment Distribution

9. Agricultural Agencies
   a. Effectiveness
   b. Information Flow
      (1) To Farmer From Agencies
      (2) To Agencies From Farmers
   c. Utilization of Information

10. Crop Development
    a. New Strains for New Areas
    b. Hardiness for Extreme Climates
    c. Disease Resistance

11. Farming Center Distribution

12. Land Availability
    a. For Farming
    b. Current Plans
    c. Future Uses

TABLE 7

SOLID WASTE DATA REQUIREMENTS

1. Collection Methods

2. Disposal Methods

   a. Dumping and Burning
   b. Incineration
   c. Landfill

3. Contribution of Disposal Methods to Air and Water Pollution

4. Sorting and Processing

5. Status of Industrial Compactors

   a. Metal Scrap
   b. Refuse
   c. Garbage

6. Reprocessing Equipment Status

   a. Scrap Metal
   b. Building Products
   c. Non-Metallic Scrap
   d. Garbage
   e. Others

7. Uses for Reprocessed Waste

8. Status of Disposible Packaging Design

9. Reusable Containers or Packages

10. Constituents of Solid Wastes

    a. Percentages by Weight
    b. Percentages by Volume
    c. Weight and Volume Breakdown

11. Contributing Elements

    a. Breakdown of Constituents by Contributing Elements

12. Material Flow Data

    a. Households
    b. Industry

13. Re-Use of Waste by Recycling into Industrial Process

— SURFACE OF GROUND

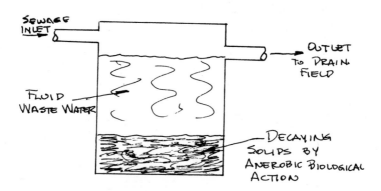

SEWAGE INLET

FLUID WASTE WATER

OUTLET TO DRAIN FIELD

DECAYING SOLIDS BY ANEROBIC BIOLOGICAL ACTION

ANEROBIC BIOLOGICAL PROCESS
SEPTIC TANK SYSTEM
FIGURE 1

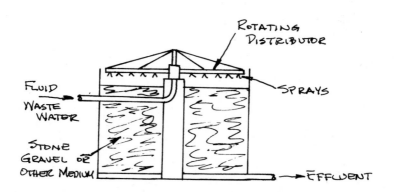

ROTATING DISTRIBUTOR

FLUID WASTE WATER

SPRAYS

STONE GRAVEL OR OTHER MEDIUM

EFFLUENT

TRICKLING FILTER
FIGURE 2

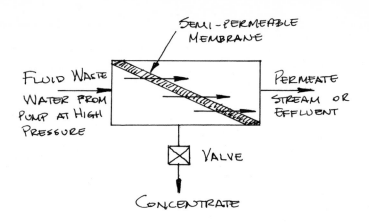

SEMI-PERMEABLE
MEMBRANE

FLUID WASTE
WATER FROM
PUMP AT HIGH
PRESSURE

PERMEATE
STREAM OR
EFFLUENT

VALVE

CONCENTRATE

REVERSE OSMOSIS PROCESS
SCHEMATIC

FIGURE 3

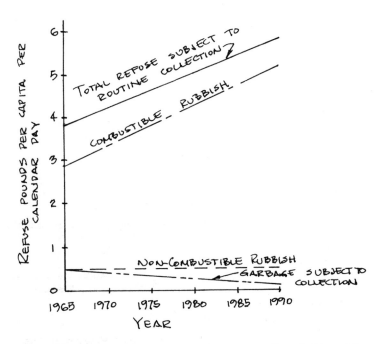

PROJECTION OF REFUSE PRODUCTION
TRENDS FOR HOUSEHOLDS

FIGURE 4

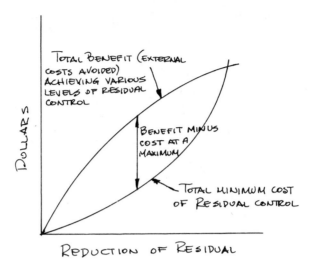

Net Social Benefit Cost

Figure 5

REFERENCES

1. "The Quality of the Urban Environment," edited by H. S. Perloff,
    Johns Hopkins Press, 1969.

2. Cooper, M. M., Fain, C. C., Hulbert, S. F., "Design of Water-Disposable
    Packaging Container," ASME Paper No. 69-WA/PID-16, Presented at 1969
    Winter Annual Meeting.

3. Myers, J. H., "Reverse Osmosis for Industrial Water and Waste Treatment,"
    ASME Paper No. 70-PEM-21, Presented at 1970 Plant Engineering and Maintenance
    Conference, Fort Worth, Texas, March 1970.

ON PROPERTIES OF MATURE SEVERE VORTICAL STORMS[†]

P. Dergarabedian[*] and F. E. Fendell[**]
TRW Systems
Redondo Beach, California

Abstract

Estimates of the maximum swirling speeds in fully developed violent atmospheric vortices are deduced from normally available data. For a tornado, knowledge of the ambient cloud deck height and the distance to which the funnel cloud tip has descended yields the maximum swirl; for a hurricane, a tephigram for the ambient atmosphere in which the storm was generated yields upper and lower bounds on the swirl speed. These calculations suggest that typical swirling speeds achieved rarely much exceed two hundred miles per hour. Since the Mach number is much less than unity, an incompressible model suffices for examining vortex dynamics. Then the boundary layer under a rapidly swirling vortex is numerically integrated by Galerkin's method to corroborate aspects of a novel structure for fully developed hurricanes proposed by Carrier. First, all the radial influx in a mature quasi-steady storm is confined to the surface boundary layer, where the no-slip boundary condition leaves an uncompensated radial pressure gradient. The results indicate that the source of the flux up the eye-wall is fluid that sinks slowly into the surface boundary layer from the large mass of rapidly swirling air which forms the bulk of the storm. Further, although nonlinear convective effects are dominant in part of the boundary layer, the divergence under swirls distributions actually encountered in storms is well approximated by the classical divergence-swirl relation for linear Ekman layers. Weighted-residuals calculations often yield a premature eruption of the boundary layer into the eye-wall; the reason for this artifact of the calculation is believed to be failure to account fully for the inflow-layer thickness near the axis. Friction is important across much of the boundary layer far from the axis of rotation, but near the axis frictional effects are significant only very near the wall and most of the inflow layer is controlled by inertia and pressure forces.

I. Introduction

The paucity of reliable measurements has delayed the development of satisfactory theories of the mass, momentum, and energy balances in severe vortical storms of the lower atmosphere. However, all such storms involve the interplay of (1) large updrafts and downdrafts generated in the atmosphere by strong enough (effective) thermal instability, and (2) the attainment of large swirling speeds under the conservation of angular momentum.[1-3] The convective motion can be engendered, for example, by conflagration (firestorms) or by warm moist air lying under cold dry air (thunderstorms). Less violent convection leads to thermals, occasionally created by solar heating of the desert floor or condensation of water vapor near the ocean surface. When the inflow-updraft pattern persists in the presence of enriched ambient vorticity (as the horizontal shear of a horizontal wind), then the thermal may transform suddenly into a waterspout or dustdevil. The analogous local transition of a temperate-zone thunderstorm into a tornado or a firestorm into a firewhirl is potentially more destructive. Suddenly the primary and secondary flows interchange roles: the reverse-stagnation flow in the presence of minor swirling becomes a rapid swirling with smaller radial inflow and axial updraft. The transition of a tropical depression from a weak low-pressure area into a hurricane may require weeks rather than minutes because the source of vorticity is the rotation of the earth, but the basic process bears much resemblance. In all these vortices fluid particles move toward their axis of rotation (under convectively induced advection); their swirling speed increases in inverse proportion to their distance from the axis, in the absence of frictional forces. While electrical effects may accompany some intense atmospheric vortices, electrical effects are not basic to the phenomena, which may be accounted for by the laws governing the thermo-hydrodynamics of (usually moist) air.

No comprehensive theory for even one member of the class of vortical storms is attempted here; rather, simple models elucidating points of primary engineering interest will be developed. For example, the ability to estimate rapidly, from normally available data, the maximum swirling speed of a tornado or hurricane is frequently useful to pilots of seacraft and aircraft. Further, accumulated evidence on such speeds is frequently valuable to structural engineers in storm-prone areas. Such estimation procedures will be undertaken in the next section. They have the useful by-product that since the maximum swirling speeds computed rarely exceed about one-quarter of the sonic speed for sea-level air (i.e., the Mach

[†]The authors are deeply indebted for indispensable advice, guidance, and assistance generously given during this work by Prof. G. F. Carrier of Harvard University, consultant to TRW Systems. Suggestions on numerical analysis by Prof. D. G. M. Anderson of Harvard University are also gratefully acknowledged. The computer programs were written by Messrs. P. Feldman and M. Bilyk of TRW Systems. The authors benefited greatly from discussions with Drs. A. Hammond and O. George, who were simultaneously conducting research on aspects of the hurricane problem for their doctoral theses at Harvard University under the supervision of Prof. Carrier. This research was supported by the U. S. Army Reserach Office (Durham, North Carolina) under contract DAHC04 67 C 0015 and by TRW Systems under its Internal Research and Development Program.

[*]Director of Launch Vehicle Studies, Systems Engineering and Integration Division.

[**]Staff Engineer, Science and Technology Division.

number rarely reaches 0.3) incompressible theory ought to describe the dynamics adequately, even though the driving mechanism involves consideration of the energetics.

Later sections will attempt to elucidate certain points concerning the structure of mature, fully developed severe vortical storms; these points have implications on storm modification procedures. Little will be said concerning the genesis of such storms, which requires a time-dependent treatment[4] outside the scope of the quasisteady analyses presented here.

Finally, the authors find it useful to emphasize the similarities, rather than the differences, among the various types of violent atmospheric vortices--at least at the current stage of understanding. Also, for the simple analyses presented here, essentially laminar models are taken as adequate, although larger (eddy) values may be ascribed to the dynamic viscosity (taken constant) than are appropriate for description of laminar flow. Further, although the approximation obviously is better for a tornado than for a hurricane, the curvature of the earth will be neglected throughout this report and attention will be confined to a plane tangent to the earth's surface at the point of interest.

II. Estimates of Maximum Swirling Speeds

A. A Method for Tornadoes Requiring a Photograph

A steady flow exists above the ground plane $z = 0$; the flow is modelled as axisymmetric about a vertical axis so cylindrical polar coordinates (r, θ, z) are adopted. (Axisymmetry should be adequate for severe rotating storms except near the outer edge of the vortex where translational speed is on the same order as the azimuthal velocity component v.) The hydrostatic and cyclostrophic balances, together with adiabatic flow of an ideal gas, are taken as adequate:

$$\frac{1}{\rho}\frac{\partial p}{\partial z} + g = 0, \qquad (1)$$

$$\frac{1}{\rho}\frac{\partial p}{\partial r} - \frac{v^2}{r} = 0, \qquad (2)$$

$$p/\rho^\gamma = p_0/\rho_0{}^\gamma \rightarrow p/p_0 = (T/T_0)^{\gamma/(\gamma-1)}. \qquad (3)$$

The formulation is complete if the azimuthal velocity component v is specified. For a tall thin vortex such as a tornado a circulation distribution independent of distance above the ground is taken to suffice, except in a frictional layer near the ground where axial gradients are large. If $v = v(r)$ only, then the pressure p is the sum of an axially invariant dynamic portion plus a radially invariant hydrostatic portion. It is perhaps worth iterating that because of hydrostatic contributions, the pressure axially varying even though the azimuthal velocity component is not. Also, the frictional layer, in which the swirl relative to the earth decreases to

zero at the ground, is neglected here because an estimate of the maximum swirl is sought.

If temperature $T(r \rightarrow \infty, z = 0) = T_0$ by choice of datum, Eqs. (1)-(3) imply immediately an equation describing the isotherm T_*:

$$z = \frac{c_p (T_0 - T_*)}{g} - \frac{1}{g}\int_r^\infty \frac{[v(\rho_1)]^2}{\rho_1} d\rho_1. \qquad (4)$$

If the vorticity has an axial component only, then retention of the nonlinear convective terms in (1) and (2) would subtract a term $(u^2 + w^2)/2g$ from the right-hand side of (4), where u and w are the radial and axial velocity components, respectively; this correction would only slightly modify the estimate of $(v)_{max}$ given below. The isotherm $T_* = T_d$, the dew-point temperature, marks a boundary which is taken to be coincident with the funnel cloud. The only discrepancy is likely to occur near the ground where sucked-up debris and dust mark the edge of the funnel cloud, but the calculation is not very accurate near $z = 0$ anyway. The small variation of the dew point with pressure is here neglected. The dry-air form (3) is retained even though the air is saturated right at the condensation boundary; the intractability of the moist adiabat[5] for analytic manipulation will be evident when it is introduced below.

The azimuthal velocity component v is found from the conservation of angular momentum, here a balance of radial convection and radial diffusion. The most satisfactory simplification is to adopt the familiar Rankine vortex model for v, a matching of rigid rotation near the axis to a potential vortex far from the axis:

$$v(r) = \begin{cases} kr/2\pi a^2 & 0 \le r \le a \\[2mm] k/2\pi r & a \le r \le \infty, \end{cases} \qquad (5)$$

where the circulation approaches k as $r \rightarrow \infty$. Of course, any $v(r)$ may be substituted in (4). Substituting (5) in (4) for $T_* = T_d$ gives, non-dimensionally,

$$Z = 1 + \begin{cases} K\left(\frac{R^2}{2} - 1\right) & R \le 1 \\[3mm] -\frac{K}{2R^2} & R \ge 1, \end{cases} \qquad (6)$$

where

$$Z = \frac{z}{c_p (T_0 - T_d)/g}, \quad R = \frac{r}{a}, \quad K = \frac{k^2}{4\pi^2 a^2 c_p(T_0 - T_d)}. \qquad (7)$$

A cross-sectional plot of the family of curves described by (6) is given as Fig. 1. The use of different scales to nondimensionalize the radial and axial coordinates is appropriate. In fact, borrowing from aerodynamic wing theory, one may define the ratio of the vertical scale height $c_p(T_0 - T_d)/g$ to the horizontal scale length a as an aspect ratio for tornadoes. The larger the ratio, the better the two-dimensional model for azimuthal velocity component holds over a wide range of Z. Furthermore, K is the ratio of the primary-flow circulation to the instability which generates the secondary flow. For a given tornado storm $c_p(T_0 - T_d)/g$, a conventional approximation of the ambient cloud height, and a are taken as known from photographs. From (6), r = a (i.e., R = 1) at Z = 1 - K/2; thus for $K \leq 2$ (and $K \geq 2$ is rare), a is the radius of the funnel cloud at height Z = 1 - K/2. Since for K < 1, from inspection of (6) at R = 0, K is the fraction of the distance from the cloud deck to the ground to which the funnel cloud tip has descended, for $K \leq 1$ one finds a to be the funnel cloud radius at a height half-way between the cloud deck and the funnel cloud tip. In other words, for K < 1, the right-circular-cylindrical locus of maximum swirl points intersects the funnel cloud in a circle of radius a at height midway between cloud deck and the funnel cloud tip.

From (5) and (7), if one denotes the ambient cloud deck height $c_p(T_0 - T_d)/g$ as h,

$$(v)_{max} = v(a) = \frac{k}{2\pi a} = [K\, c_p(T_0 - T_d)]^{1/2} = (Kgh)^{1/2} \tag{8}$$

For funnel clouds that do not reach the ground or just touch the ground, the value of K has been discussed. For very destructive twisters with funnel clouds of finite radius on the ground (i.e., for K > 1), K must be chosen by fitting (6) to a funnel-cloud photograph. From knowledge of K and a, one finds

$$k = 2\pi a \,(v)_{max}, \tag{9}$$

so for $K \leq 1$, knowledge of the cloud deck height h and the fraction K of the distance to the ground to which the funnel cloud tip descends not only readily gives the maximum swirling speed but also the ambient circulation.

Golden has published photographs of a waterspout off Key West, Florida on 10 September 1969, for which K > 1 and h = 2000 feet.[6] For a lower bound on $(v)_{max}$ one may take K = 1, so (8) implies $(v)_{max} > 173$ mph. Furthermore, inspection of the photograph gives $a \simeq 100$ ft. so $k > 1.6 \times 10^5$ ft²/sec (although later it will be implied that $k < 2.2 \times 10^5$ ft²/sec when this case is discussed again below).

The theory has been applied to several other tall thin vortices[1]; Golden provides useful data on other waterspouts.[7-9]

B. A Method for Hurricanes Requiring a Tephigram

This method is primarily designed for the two-cell structure of hurricanes (in which an eye centered about the axis of rotation with downdraft and outflow lies within an inflow and updraft), but it proves adaptable to one-cell vortices as well (inflow and updraft everywhere near the axis of rotation, as seemingly occurs in many tornadoes). The method yields an upper and lower bound on the maximum swirling speed in a two-cell vortex, as opposed to the lower bound given by using the clearly visible funnel in the previously described method. This technique requires as input a tephigram of the ambient air in which the vortex was formed (temperature and relative humidity vs. pressure).

The method is based on a four-part model of the structure of a mature hurricane proposed by G. F. Carrier.[10] The four-region subdivision is based on different physical processes being dominant in different regions of the storm (see Fig. 2). In region I there is a warm moist air typical in stratification of the ambient atmosphere in which the hurricane was generated. This air spun up under conservation of angular momentum as it moved in toward the axis of symmetry during the formative stage. As the mature stage was approached, a gradient-wind balance of pressure, Coriolis, and centrifugal forces choked off any further inflow; the inflow is only enough to prevent the eye-wall III from diffusing outward, and that requires only a very small radial flow. The air in I, then, is rapidly swirling, with a small downflux into the frictional boundary layer II. The small downflux leads to a large net mass flux into the frictional layer because of the area involved. Furthermore, the downdraft is only a gross average because transiently and locally there is intense convective activity by which clouds form and rain falls. The clouds are strained into the spiral band pattern seen on radar screens by the rapid swirl.

In the frictional boundary layer II, the only region in which angular momentum is not conserved but is partially lost to the sea, there is appreciable influx. In fact, the azimuthal and radial velocity components are of comparable magnitude, and the vertical velocity component is much smaller. The reason is that the no-slip boundary condition reduces the centrifugal force, and a relatively uncompensated pressure gradient drives the fluid toward the axis of symmetry. Far from the axis in II the classical balance of the linear Ekman layer (friction and Coriolis forces) suffices and actually three-quarters of the flux through II comes from downflux across the outer half of the interface between II and I. Closer in to the axis the nonlinear accelerations, especially the centrifugal acceleration, must enter.

As the pressure gradient in I lets more air sink into II, the influx in II drives the boundary layer air moderately rapidly up a cloudy eye-wall. Here hydrostatic and cyclostrophic approximations hold; since the heat of condensation is released as the moist air rises, the gas retaining the heat but the water falling out, the sequence of thermodynamic state traversed is that of a moist adiabat based on sea-level ambient conditions. The swirl near the top of III is so reduced that the air seems to an observor on earth to be rotating opposite in sense to the rotation in I and II (which is cyclonic in the Northern Hemisphere, and anticyclonic in the Southern). The air in III slips over the air in I with no interaction.

At low altitudes the eye-wall flushes moist air out of IV, and at high altitude rained-out air is entrained into IV. In time an eye forms, in which relatively dry air is warmed by compressional heating as it sinks. The entrainment of air continually out of the bottom of the eye column lets new air sink and be warmed; otherwise, transport processes in time would let the eye lose heat and cool. The eye permits much greater pressure deficits from ambient and hence supports much higher swirling speeds. At a fixed altitude, the density in the eye is less than that in the eye-wall, which in turn is less than that of the ambient gas at the storm edge.

Carrier's novel model thus pictures the hurricane as a once-through process in which a "fuel supply"--the warm moist air in I--is slowly exhausted. The storm weakens because the air drifting down into the frictional layer toward the end is typical of the higher tropical environment and hence of lower equivalent potential temperature. Eventually the "fuel supply" is exhausted and the boundary between III and I sinks toward II.

Carrier's model avoids a shortcoming common to other models[11], in which it is taken that the enthalpy is constant in a boundary layer and that the flow through II is radial inflow from the outer edge, and not downflux from I to II. These other models must postulate arbitrarily a three-order-of magnitude increase in sensible heat and a two-order-of-magnitude increase in latent neat from the ocean to the contiguous atmosphere in a hurricane over the normal transfer in the tropics. The postulated increase is to permit the air, drawn from the edge, to be sufficiently moist but cloud-free until the eye is approached.[12] In fact, Hammond[13] has shown that it is the total stagnation enthalpy (the sum of static enthalpy, latent heat, gravitational potential energy, and kinetic energy components) that is conserved at roughly the ambient stratification throughout regions I and II. Only near the eye-wall does the updraft become strong enough to give a total stagnation enthalpy profile constant with height (as opposed to the ambient total stagnation enthalpy profile that holds outside the eye-wall--a profile that decreases with altitude for a couple of miles, then increases, owing to the interaction of cumulus convection, turbulent transport, and radiative transfer). Thus the enthalpy flux from sea to atmosphere is about the same in a hurricane as outside; further by plume and radiative mechanisms not understood in detail, Hammond[13] shows that the total stagnation enthalpy that is added is not deposited directly into the boundary layer, but is deposited in region I above the boundary layer. In this way the flux compensates for rain-out in the "fuel supply" of region I; when the storm passes over land this compensatory flux from the sea is eliminated, and the storm weakens on the scale of half a day to several days.

An upper bound on the central pressure deficit achievable in a known spawning ambient atmosphere will now be set forth by use of the hurricane model just presented, of hydrostatics, and of the thermodynamics of moist and dry air. This central pressure deficit can then be translated into an estimate of maximum swirl speed through dynamics (the radial momentum equation), once a realistic radial distribution of the azimuthal velocity component is adopted. The first step is to neglect the frictional boundary layer II, which is relatively thin and across which the pressure does not change to lowest order according to lowest-order boundary-layer theory (see Fig. 3).

The variation of pressure p, density ρ, and temperature T with height above the ocean z, for any ambient tropical atmosphere in which a hurricane forms, may be computed from

$$p_a = \rho_a R_a T \qquad \text{(a = dry air)} \qquad (10)$$

$$p_v = \rho_v R_a T/\sigma \qquad \text{(v = water vapor; } \sigma = 0.622), \qquad (11)$$

$$p = p_a + p_v, \quad \rho = \rho_a + \rho_v, \quad p_v = P(T)\,(RH), \qquad (12)$$

$$\frac{dp}{dz} = -\rho g, \qquad (13)$$

$$T = f(p), \quad (RH) = g(p), \qquad (14)$$

where the temperature profile $f(p)$ and the relative humidity (RH) profile $g(p)$ are taken as known through measurement. The saturation pressure $P(T)$ is well-tabulated for vapor and liquid phases above freezing, and vapor and solid phases below freezing.[14] The integration proceeds from sea level upward: data typically extend from 1000 mb to 150 mb. This latter pressure may well be taken to be the top of the storm since little convective instability exists above this height and motion relative to the earth is usually small at around 150 mb, which will be taken to correspond to height z_1. The pressure at height z_1, denoted p_1, will be taken to be the pressure at z_1 for all radial positions, not just in the ambient. Furthermore, the sea-level ambient state is denoted by a subscript s.

In a fully developed storm the air rising up the eye-wall in Carrier's model follows a moist adiabat based on the ground-level ambient state (until late in the storm when an ambient state above sea-level should serve as the reference state for the moist adiabat, but by then the storm has weakened from the maximum intensity level of interest here). Thus for the eye-wall one integrates

$$\frac{dT}{dp} = \frac{\dfrac{R_a T}{p_a} + \dfrac{L\sigma}{p}\dfrac{p}{p_a}}{c_p + \left(\dfrac{L\sigma + R_a T}{p_a}\right)\dfrac{dP}{dT}} \qquad (15)$$

where $T(p_s) = T_s$, together with Eqs. (10)-(12) with (RH) = 1. The heat released by condensation warms and lightens the gas, but the rain so formed falls out. The integration proceeds in the direction of decreasing pressure to p_1; $T(p_1) \equiv T_m$. Then, to associate an altitude with each thermodynamic state so calculated, one integrates Eqs. (10)-(13) (RH) = 1, and (15) subject to $p(z_1) = p_1$, $T(z_1) = T_m$; the integration proceeds in the direction of increasing pressure; $p(z = 0) \equiv p_e$, $\rho(z = 0) \equiv \rho_e$. If no eye existed in a vortex, the pressure at the storm center would be p_e--the air on the axis of a one-cell vortex is then described by a moist adiabat, as just presented. Such is the case in some tornadoes and waterspouts.

In a mature hurricane a pressure deficit in excess of $(p_s - p_e)$ is achieved by having the air

148

in a relatively dry eye sink slowly under an adiabatic recompression. Thus in a hurricane $(p_s - p_e)$ is a lower bound on the central pressure deficit. For an upper bound on the deficit that may be achieved, one may adopt the model that the eye is completely dry and that the air entrained into the eye is drawn from the top of the eye-wall (or at least has that state at height z_1). Such a model gives the maximum recompression with no heat loss to re-evaportion of moisture--certainly an idealization of the actual situation. The governing laws are, of course, Eqs. (3), (10) and (13), $(\dot{RH}) = 0$, integrated in the direction of decreasing z subject to the initial conditions $p(z_1) = p_1$, $T(z_1) = T_m$; $p(z=0) \equiv p_c$, $\rho(z=0) \equiv \rho_c$, where $p_c < p_e < p_s$ and $\rho_c < \rho_e < \rho_s$ (although the density discrepancies are at most on the order of twenty-five percent and thus not important for the calculations to be now presented for maximum swirl speed). In fact, in actual hurricanes the central pressure is greater than p_e but less than the p_c given here.

If one adopts the cylostrophic balance (2), holds ρ constant (at, say, its ambient value), and adopts the Rankine-like vortex $(0 < n \bar{<} 1)$

$$v(r) = \begin{cases} (v)_{max} \, (r/R) & 0 \bar{<} r \bar{<} R \\ \\ (v)_{max} \, (R/r)^n & R \bar{<} r \bar{<} \infty, \end{cases} \quad (16)$$

one obtains

$$(v)_{max} = \left[\frac{2n}{n+1} \left(\frac{p_s - p_e}{\rho_s} \right) \right]^{1/2}. \quad (17)$$

In practice $0.5 \bar{<} n \bar{<} 1$ according to the sparse evidence available.[15] Further, the cores of only one-cell vortices rigidly rotate, so Eq. (17) is limited to the case when no eye exists and a moist adiabatic ascent describes particles near the axis of symmetry.

When an eye exists, the core is observed not to rotate so one adopts

$$v(r) = \begin{cases} 0 & 0 \bar{<} r \bar{<} R \\ \\ (v)_{max} \, (R/r)^n & R \bar{<} r \bar{<} \infty, \end{cases} \quad (18)$$

and obtains from (2)

$$(v)_{max} = \left[2n \left(\frac{p_s - p_c}{\rho_s} \right) \right]^{1/2}. \quad (19)$$

Actually, the Coriolis force should be retained in a hurricane [for a minor correction of a few percent in $(v)_{max}$]:

$$\rho_s \left(\frac{v^2}{r} + fv \right) = \frac{\partial p}{\partial r}, \quad f = 2\Omega_e \cos \theta \quad (20)$$

where Ω_e is the rotation of the earth and θ is colatitude. For $n = 1$, the case of primary interest,

$$(v)_{max} = fR \ln\left(\frac{r_o}{R}\right) \left\{ -1 + \left[1 + \frac{2(p_s - p_c)}{\rho_s f^2 r_o^2 \left[\ln\left(\frac{r_o}{R}\right)\right]^2} \right]^{1/2} \right\} \quad (21)$$

where r_o characterizes the radius of the entire extent of the storm (~500 mi.) and R characterizes the radius of the eye-wall (~25 mi.). For $n < 1$, the formula corresponding to Eq. (21) is

$$(v)_{max} = \frac{f R_o n}{1 - n} \left\{ -1 + \left[1 + \frac{2(p_s - p_c)(1 - n)^2}{\rho_s n f^2 R_o} \right]^{1/2} \right\} \quad (22)$$

where no estimate of r_o is required. This method has also been applied to a variety of cases in Ref. 1.

While this method is primarily designed for hurricanes, it may be used in conjunction with the previous photograph method on tornadoes and water-spouts. For example, Golden[6] has furnished a tephigram with relative humidity data for the Key West waterspout discussed earlier; the data extends to 400 mb only; the sea-level ambient pressure was 1020 mb. Calculations show that in the absence of an eye the pressure at the center would be 999.8 mb; with an eye, 952 mb. The smaller (no eye) deficit with a rigidly rotating core would give $(v)_{max} = 76$ mph for $n = 0.5$ and 93 mph for $n = 1$. The larger deficit gives, from Eq. (19), $(v)_{max} = 170$ mph for $n = 0.5$ and $(v)_{max} = 241$ mph for $n = 1$. Since the photograph method gave a lower bound of 173 mph, one can assert

$$173 < (v)_{max} < 241 \text{ mph}$$

and that the waterspout was of two-cell structure with a non-rotating core joined to a potential vortex. Because the lower bound was based on a rigid core with $K = 1$, it is not a tight bound and the waterspout was swirling over 200 mph in all probability. The upper bound of 241 mph places bounds on K: $1 < K \leq 2$. (See Figs. 4-6.)

For the typical ambient West Indies tephigram given by Jordan[16] (extending to the 130 mb level) for September--the peak of the hurricane-spawning season--one finds a pressure deficit of 58 mb for a one-cell storm and 137.5 mb for a two-cell storm. For a storm at 80° colatitude with eye at 25 mi. and of total extent 500 mi., one finds for a storm with an eye, retaining Coriolis force, $(v)_{max} = 242.5$ mph for $n = 0.5$ and $(v)_{max} = 339.4$ mph for $n = 1$. If one disregards the Coriolis force, the corresponding results are 244.8 mph and 346 mph, so the correction is indeed small. For a storm without an eye, the 58 mb deficit is equivalent to $(v)_{max} = 130.2$ mph for $n = 0.5$ and 159.5 mph for $n = 1$, where the Coriolis force has been neglected. (See Figs. 7-9.)

Carrier's model thus permits the differing weights of various columns of air in the storm (based on differing moisture content and thermo-dynamic processes) to be translated readily into upper- and lower-bound estimates of the maximum swirling speed. Furthermore, reasonable bounds are so calculated without requiring large enthalpy transfer from the ocean to the air in the boundary layer.

III. The Frictional Boundary Layer

A steady axisymmetric flow of an incompress-ible constant-property fluid is now studied to confirm the crucial point that, under observed swirls, sufficient downflux enters the surface frictional layer to account for the mass flux up tne eye-wall.[17] The analysis will be carried out in a noninertial coordinate system rotating at the constant speed of the component of the rotation of the earth normal to the local tangent plane.

Because the boundary-layer divergence under an impressed swirl (the major constraint furnished by the boundary layer on the invisicid flow above it) is relatively small in magnitude, quite precise solution of the coupled quasilinear parabolic partial differential equations governing the layer is required.[18] Numerical integration by finite-difference methods is formidable because the flow component in the time-like direction is, in successively thinner strips lying parallel to the boundary, alternately in the direction of inte-gration and reversed to it. Though the longitudinal flow is, on net, in the direction of integration, the integration is marginally stable and very few results have been reported.[19]

Here Galerkin's version of the method of weighted residuals[20,21] will be applied to the surface boundary layer; while integral methods have been tried in the past[22-29], special attention will be paid here to residuals and to impressed swirls of interest in hurricanes.

A. The Boundary-Value Problem

The dimensional governing equations are under the previously stated model:

$$\nabla \cdot \vec{q} = 0, \tag{23}$$

$$\nabla(q^2/2) + (\nabla x \vec{q}) x \vec{q} + 2\vec{\Omega}_e x \vec{q} = -\nabla \bar{p} - \nu \nabla x (\nabla x \vec{q}), \tag{24}$$

where $\bar{p} = p/\rho_o + (\vec{\Omega}_e \times \vec{r})^2/2 + gz$, the gravitational acceleration $\vec{g} = - g\hat{z}$, the velocity in noninertial coordinates $\vec{v} = \vec{\Omega}_e \times \vec{r} + \vec{q}$, the component of the rotation of the earth normal to the local tangent plane is $\vec{\Omega}_e$, and the kinematic viscosity (later given eddy-diffusivity values) is ν. Also, $\vec{\Omega}_e = \Omega \hat{z}$.

Nondimensionalization is effected by letting

$$\vec{q}' = \vec{q}/(\Psi_o\Omega)^{1/2}, \quad p' = \bar{p}/(\Psi_o\Omega), \quad \vec{r}' = \vec{r}/(\Psi_o/\Omega)^{1/2}, \tag{25}$$

and $E = \nu/\Psi_o$ where the Ekman number $E \ll 1$ and Ψ_o characterizes the circulation away from the boundary (such as the maximum swirl speed times the radius at which it occurs). Dropping primes, one has

$$\nabla \cdot \vec{q} = 0 \tag{26}$$

$$\nabla(q^2/2) + (\nabla x \vec{q}) x \vec{q} + 2\hat{z} x \vec{q} = -\nabla p - E\nabla x(\nabla x \vec{q}). \tag{27}$$

In axisymmetric cylindrical polar coordinates

$$\vec{q} = u \hat{r} + v \hat{\theta} + w \hat{z}, \quad \vec{r} = r \hat{r} + z \hat{z}. \tag{28}$$

In scalar components these equations are

$$(ru)_r = (rw)_z = 0, \tag{29}$$

$$uu_r + wu_z - 2v - r^{-1} v^2 + p_r = E\{u_{zz} + [u_{rr} + (r^{-1} u)_r]\}, \tag{30}$$

$$u(rv)_r + w(rv)_z + 2ru = E\{(rv)_{zz} + r[r^{-1} (rv)_r]_r\}, \tag{31}$$

$$uw_r + ww_z + p_z = E\{w_{zz} + r^{-1} (rw_r)_r\}, \tag{32}$$

where subscript denotes partial differentiation.

Away from the boundary (i.e., in region I) the following expansions are adopted:

$$p = \pi(r, z) + \ldots, \quad u = EU(r, z) + \ldots,$$
$$v = V(r, z) + \ldots, \quad w = E^{1/2} W(r, z) + \ldots. \tag{33}$$

Substitution of (33) in (29)-(33) yields the gradient-wind equation:

$$\pi_z = 0, \quad W_z = 0, \quad \pi_r = 2V + V^2/r. \tag{34}$$

The axially invariant solution is complete when $\pi(r)$ or $V(r)$ is specified [here $V(r)$ will be given]; $W(r)$ is found by matching the solution of (34) to the frictional layer solution near the wall and in this sense $W(r)$ is determined by the boundary-layer dynamics.

If $\zeta = z E^{-1/2}$ [which implies that the fric-tional layer is $O(E^{1/2})$ in thickness] and if near the boundary

$$u = u_b (r, \zeta) + \ldots, \quad v = v_b (r, \zeta) + \ldots,$$
$$w = E^{1/2} w_b(r, \zeta) + \ldots, \quad p = p_b (r, \zeta) + \ldots, \tag{35}$$

then the axial component of the momentum equation (32) degenerates to $(\partial p_b/\partial \zeta) = 0$ so the pressure field in the boundary layer is known from the solution of (34). If

$$\psi = r v_b, \quad \Psi = r V, \quad \phi = r u_b, \quad x = r^2, \quad \tilde{w} = 2^{-1/2} w_b,$$
$$\tilde{\zeta} = 2^{1/2} \zeta, \tag{36}*$$

---

*For convenience, the relation between the quantities introduced in (36) and dimensional physical variables (denoted in this footnote only by a subscript asterisk) is noted: $\phi = r_* u_*/\Psi_{o*}$, $\psi = r_* v_*/\Psi_{o*}$, $\Psi = r_* V_*/\Psi_{o*}$, $\tilde{w} = w_*/(2\Omega_* \nu_*)^{1/2}$, $\tilde{\zeta} = z_*/(\nu_*/2\Omega_*)^{1/2}$, and $x = r_*^2 \Omega_*/\Psi_{o*}$.

150

then, dropping the tildes, one has from substituting (35) and (36) in (29)-(31):

$$\phi_x + w_\zeta = 0, \tag{37}$$

$$L_1[\phi, \psi; \Psi; x, \zeta] \equiv \phi\phi_x + w\phi + (\psi^2 - \psi^2 - \phi^2)/2 -$$

$$(\psi - \Psi) - \phi_{\zeta\zeta} = 0, \tag{38}$$

$$L_2[\phi, \Psi; x, \zeta] \equiv \phi\psi_x + w\psi_\zeta + \phi - \psi_{\zeta\zeta} = 0 . \tag{39}$$

Matching of the inner and outer expansions requires

$$\zeta \to \infty: \quad \phi \to 0, \ \psi \to \Psi(x), \text{ given}, \tag{40}$$

and at $\zeta = 0$ no-slip conditions are adopted:

$$\zeta = 0: \quad \phi = w = \psi = 0. \tag{41}$$

Formulation is completed by specifications of initial conditions; for now it suffices to state that when $x \to \infty$ a solution is given by discarding all nonlinear terms in (37)-(39). Solution of the Coriolis-friction forces balance that results, when subject to (40) and (41), gives the classical result due to Ekman:

$$\phi = - [\Psi(x)] \sin (2^{-1/2} \zeta) \exp (-2^{-1/2} \zeta) , \tag{42}$$

$$\psi = [\Psi(x)] [1 - \cos (2^{-1/2} \zeta) \exp (-2^{-1/2} \zeta)] , \tag{43}$$

$$w = 2^{-1/2} [\Psi_x(x)] \{1 -$$

$$[\sin(2^{-1/2} \zeta) + \cos(2^{-1/2} \zeta)] [\exp(-2^{-1/2} \zeta)]\}. \tag{44}$$

The boundary-value problem given by (37)-(44) is invariant under a special affine transformation that permits one to generate other solutions from a known solution. Specifically, if a solution is given by $\phi(x, \zeta)$, $\psi(x, \zeta)$, $w(x, \zeta)$, and $\Psi(x)$, then a solution is also given by $b\phi(\sigma, \zeta)$, $b\psi(\sigma, \zeta)$, $w(\sigma, \zeta)$, and $b\Psi(\sigma)$ where $\sigma = x/b$ and b is any finite constant (real and positive).

B. Application of the Method of Weighted Residuals

An easily executed approximate solution to the boundary-value problem is attained by letting(30)

$$\phi(x, \zeta) = \sum_{n=1}^{N} a_n(x) \ \omega_n(x, \zeta)$$

$$\hat{\psi}(x, \zeta) = \sum_{n=1}^{N} b_n(x) \ \omega_n(x, \zeta) , \qquad \left.\right\} \tag{45}$$

$$\hat{\psi} = \psi - \Psi(x) \{1 - [\cos (a[\lambda(x)]^k \zeta)] \cdot$$

$$[\exp (-b [\lambda(x)]^k \zeta)]\} ,$$

where a, b are positive constants, $\lambda(x)$ is a known function of x discussed below, and $k = 0$ or 1, depending upon which choice of authors adopted as intuitively superior in a given case. Thus, the dependent variables ϕ and $\hat{\psi}$, chosen because they conveniently obey homogeneous boundary conditions at $\zeta = 0$ and $\zeta \to \infty$, are each approximated by a product series of N terms in which $\omega_n(x, \zeta)$ is a member of a (preferably orthonormal) set of

functions adopted for their appropriate behavior. Since N is held small in practice, emphasis on the completeness of the set $\omega_n(x, \zeta)$ is specious. Actually here a selected set of base functions $\Lambda_j(n)$ are rendered orthonormal by the Gram-Schmidt procedure; the choice

$$\Lambda_j(n) = [\sin (jn)] [\exp (-jn)] , \tag{46}$$

where

$$n = \lambda(x) \ \zeta, \ \lambda(x) = \{[1 + \psi(x)/x] \cdot$$

$$[1 + d\psi(x)/dx]\}^{1/4}/2^{1/2} , \tag{47}$$

is motivated and evaluated in Appendix A.

It follows that one may write

$$\omega_n(x, \zeta) = \omega_n(n) = H_n^{-1/2} \sum_{j=1}^{n} g_{nj} \Lambda_j(n) ,$$

$$n = 1, 2, \ldots, N, \tag{48}$$

where the triagonal matrix of weighting constants is here taken to have all its diagonal elements equal to unity and the factor $H_n^{-1/2}$ effects the normalization:

$$H_p^{-1/2} H_n^{-1/2} \sum_{j=1}^{n} \sum_{k=1}^{p} g_{nj} g_{pk} \int_0^{\infty} \Lambda_j(n) \Lambda_k(n) \ dn =$$

$$\delta_{pn}, \begin{cases} p = 1, 2, \ldots, n \\ n = 1, 2, \ldots, N. \end{cases} \tag{49}*$$

Clearly the weighting function over the semi-infinite domain has been taken as unity.

The approximate solution is known once $a_n(x)$, $b_n(x)$, $n = 1, 2, \ldots, N$ are known. These are found here by Galerkin's variation of the method of weighted residuals, i.e., the residuals obtained by substituting (45), subject to (46)-(49), in (38) and (39) are required to be orthogonal to each member of the orthonormal set ω_n employed:

*Since an algorithm is unwieldy, the elements g_{ij} are found from the following sets of simultaneous algebraic equations:

$$\sum_{k=1}^{n-1} a_{jk} g_{nk} = -a_{nj}, \ j = 1, 2, \ldots, n - 1,$$

where $n = 2, 3, \ldots, N$ and

$$a_{jk} = a_{kj} = \int_0^{\infty} \sin(jn) \sin(kn) \exp[-(j+k)n] \ dn =$$

$$\frac{jk}{2(j+k) (j^2+k^2)}$$

and $g_{nk} = 1$ for $n = k$. However, a simple algorithm gives H_n:

$$H_n = \sum_{i=1}^{n} a_{ii} g_{ni}^2 +$$

$$2\left\{\sum_{i=1}^{n-1} a_{ni} g_{nk} + \sum_{i=1}^{n-1} \sum_{k=i+1}^{n-1} a_{ki} g_{ni} g_{nk}\right\} .$$

$$\int_0^\infty L_i[\phi, \hat{\psi}; x, \eta] \, \omega_n(\eta) \, d\eta = 0; \quad i = 1, 2;$$

$$n = 1, 2, \ldots, N. \tag{50}$$

(The continuity equation relates w to a_n.) The resulting set of 2N coupled quasi-linear ordinary differential equations, each of the first order, may be numerically integrated by marching from some initial value x_1 (discussed below) toward the axis of symmetry (i.e., by marching in the direction of decreasing x). Hopefully, retention of successively more terms in the approximating series (adopting larger values of N) will suggest a convergent solution; in any case, calculation of residuals by substituting the proposed approximate solution into the partial differential equations should indicate the accuracy achieved.

C. The Derivative Initial-Value Problem

Under (45)-(49) the continuity equation (37) becomes

$$w(x, \eta) = \frac{\lambda'}{\lambda^2} \int_0^\eta \phi(x, \eta_1) \, d\eta_1 - \frac{1}{\lambda} \int_0^\eta \frac{\partial \phi(x, \eta_1)}{\partial x} \, d\eta_1$$

$$+ \frac{\lambda' \, \eta \, \phi(x, \eta)}{\lambda^2} \tag{51}$$

and the divergence (since $\eta \to \infty$ when $\zeta \to \infty$, except where $\lambda = 0$)

$$w(x, \eta \to \infty) = \frac{1}{\lambda^2} \sum_{n=1}^{N} \frac{\lambda' a_n - \lambda a_n'}{H_n^{1/2}} \sum_{j=1}^{n} \frac{g_{nj}}{2j}, \tag{52}$$

where the prime denotes ordinary derivative with respect to the streamwise coordinate x. Also, the dimensionless net radial influx is given by

$$\delta(x) = -\int_0^\infty \phi(x, \zeta) \, d\zeta = -[\lambda(x)]^{-1} \int_0^\infty \phi(x, \eta) \, d\eta =$$

$$-[\lambda(x)]^{-1} \sum_{n=1}^{N} \frac{a_n(x)}{H_n^{1/2}} \sum_{j=1}^{n} \frac{g_{nj}}{2j}. \tag{53}$$

To obtain the divergence and flux, one must solve the 2N equations (50), which will be given here schematically as (m = 1, 2, . . . , N):

$$\sum_{p=1}^{N} \{c_{pm}[a_n, b_n; x] + d_{pm}[a_n, b_n; x]\} a_p'(x)$$

$$= G_m [a_n, b_n; x]; \tag{54a}$$

$$\sum_{p=1}^{N} c_{pm}[a_n, b_n; x] b_p'(x) =$$

$$\sum_{p=1}^{N} e_{pm}[a_n, b_n; x] a_p'(x) + F_m[a_n, b_n; x] . \tag{54b}$$

The explicit expressions for c_{pm}, d_{pm}, and e_{pm} will not be given here for brevity; they are tedious but completely straightforward to derive. In writing

(54), one assumes that $a_n(x)$, $b_n(x)$, $n = 1, 2, \ldots, N$, are known at x. Except where $c_{pm} = 0$ or $d_{pm} = -c_{pm}$, one may obtain $a_p'(x)$ from (54a) and then $b_p'(x)$ from (54b); thus decoupling permits handling half the equations at one time. However, $c_{pm} = 0$ does occur at one point, the starting point x_1, for the impressed swirls ψ of interest here and hence the imposed angular momentum distributions to be studied are now discussed.

One interesting class of impressed swirls, in dimensional terms, is

$$V = \begin{cases} \bar{C} \, r^{-n} & 0 < r \le r_2 \\ D \, (r_1 - r) & r_2 \le r \le r_1 \end{cases} \tag{55}$$

where V is the azimuthal velocity component in the inviscid region outside the frictional layer and $\bar{C}$, D, n, r_2, and r_1 are positive constants. In fact, r_1 is in some sense "large" because it represents the outer edge of the storm, a radial distance beyond which the vortex does not interact with its environment; the swirl is taken to vanish linearly near this outer edge. The power-law decay for $r < r_2$ is inspired by measurements and deductions reported by Miller.[15] Requiring continuity of V and its first derivative at $r = r_2$ (to be determined) leads to the following three-parameter $(\bar{c}, n, x_1)$ family of impressed swirls in nondimensional variables:

$$\psi(x; \bar{c}, x_1) = \begin{cases} \bar{c} \, x^{(1-n)/2}, & 0 < x < x_1/(1 + n^{-1})^2 \\ n\bar{c} \left(\dfrac{x_1^{1/2}}{1 + n^{-1}}\right)^{-(n+1)} [(x_1 x)^{1/2} - x], \\ \qquad x_1/(1 + n^{-1})^2 \le x \le x_1 . \end{cases} \tag{56}$$

The solution cannot be meaningfully carried in all the way to x = 0 because (56) is singular there (since n > 0), but also because the scaling adopted in (35) may be suspect because radial stress derivatives may no longer be negligible relative to axial stress derivatives.

Another swirl distribution demonstrated by Carrier[4,17] to be of interest to both the mature and the intensifying hurricane is

$$\psi(x; \bar{D}) = \bar{D}(1 - x/x_1), \quad 0 < x \le x_1 . \tag{57}$$

For $\bar{D} = x_1 = 1$, (57) gives $\psi_x = -1$ and hence $\lambda = 0$ at all $0 < x < 1$; since $\bar{D} = 1$ and $x_1 = O(1)$ for a typical tornado, the choice of base function adopted in Appendix A may be infelicitous; for a hurricane $x_1 = O(20)$ and no such problem arises.

The swirls described by (56) and (57) vanish at the starting point x_1. If (42)-(44), which hold as $x \to \infty$, are applied at x = x_1, then $\phi = \psi = 0$ at x = x_1 and the singular behavior of the governing equations is evident from (38) and (39). More explicitly $c_{pm} = 0$ at x = x_1 in (54) when $\psi(x_1) = 0$. However, there is no reason to believe precisely (42)-(44) have any special merit as starting conditions at the finite point x_1. Thus, the initial conditions for (54) invoked here for convenience are:

$$a_1(x_s) = -\Psi(x_s)/2^{3/2}; \; a_n(x_s) = 0, n = 2, 3, \ldots, N; \qquad (58)$$

$$D_n(x_s) = 0, n = 1, 2, \ldots, N, \qquad (59)$$

where $x_s = x_1 - \epsilon$, $0 < \epsilon \ll 1$. Trials conducted reveal the solution obtained for $0 < x < x_s$ is suitably invariant of ϵ over a large range of ϵ $(.01 \le \epsilon < 1)$ and $x[0 < x < (x_s - 0.5)]$. The starting requirements (58), (59) let ϕ, ψ obey linear-Ekman-layer-like starting conditions. In fact, for (56) with $n = \bar{c} = 1$, $x_1 = 20$, $\lambda(x_1)$ $2^{-1/2}$--the error is less than 3%.

D. Discussion of Results

Integration of (54), subject to (56) [or (57)], (58), and (59) for $x_1 = O(20)$, must be carried out under stringent error bounds to preclude spurious oscillatory behavior in $w(x, \eta \rightarrow \infty)$. A one-term approximation (N = 1) requires about twenty seconds on a CDC 6500 computer under a predictor-corrector integration routine with a fourth-order Runge-Kutta starting procedure; two-term approximations require about four minutes; three-term approximations, over thirty minutes. The model does not warrant precise solution (no-slip conditions at a flat boundary, axisymmetry, constant eddy viscosity are high idealizations); also, the results obtained for $w(x, \eta \rightarrow \infty)$, as will be indicated below, are for practical purposes the same for N = 1, 2, or 3 in several cases tested. In fact, the function subtracted off from ψ by (45) is so adequate an approximation (except at small x) that ψ makes little contribution. Thus a preponderance of results presented below will be for N = 1. Retention of more terms in the series (45) accomplishes little under the set of base functions adopted, because additional terms cannot appreciably extend the x domain where the series permit a good representation of the solution (see Appendix A).

Figures 10, 11, and 12 reveal typical results for the divergence $w(x, \zeta \rightarrow \infty)$ and the radial volumetric flux $\delta(x)$ for the swirl distribution (56) with $\bar{c} = 1$, $x_1 = 20$. The effect of varying a, b slightly from $2^{-1/2}$ or of setting k = 0 or k = 1 [see (45)] is slight; all the results are about the same, and throughout the region of downdraft the Ekman result for linearized theory, $w(x, \zeta \rightarrow \infty) = \Psi_x/2^{1/2}$, remains an excellent approximation to the computed divergences. This is true even though in some of the boundary layer nonlinear convective terms are of dominant importance. The results given are mainly for n = 1; increasing n slightly defers the eruption [e.g., decreases the value of x for which $w(x, \zeta \rightarrow \infty) = 0$], but eruption is still premature [see Appendix A]. If $\Psi_0 = 5 \cdot 10^3$ mi^2/hr in an intense hurricane and $\Omega = 0.06$ hr^{-1} in the Tropics, one sees that a substantial updraft is predicted at x = 1, or about 200 miles from the center of a hurricane; eye-walls actually occur at about 25 miles from the center. Since $w(x, \zeta \rightarrow \infty)$ varies slowly in x for x > 1, the radial volumetric flux of the surface frictional layer at $x = x_2$ is proportional to the area included in $x_2 \le x \le x_1$. Since the area involved in

x < 1 is less than five percent of the total area through which fluid settles into the boundary layer, only a small error in total transport to the eye-wall is incurred. Carrier[17] through approximate analytic (Oseen-linearization) treatment of the incompressible boundary layer equations confirms the adequacy of the results given here for the down-draft region. Figures 13, 14, and 15 give the axial profiles, at several radial positions, of the dependent variables ψ, ϕ and w, respectively, for one of the cases plotted in Figure 11.

Figures 16, 17, and 18 give the divergence and flux for the swirl distribution (57) for $x_1 = 20$, 10, and 4, respectively (with $\bar{D} = k = N = 1$); decreasing x_1 confines the updraft from the boundary layer to a region close to the axis. Again the linear divergence relation due to Ekman is quite accurate throughout the extensive region of down-draft from the inviscid flow into the boundary layer, and correctly indicates that the magnitude of the downflux increases as x_1 decreases. For the case plotted in Figure 16, Figs. 19, 20 and 21 give the axial profiles, at several radial positions, of the dependent variables ψ, ϕ, and w, respectively. If kinematic viscosity is given an eddy value appropriate for turbulent shear flow [i.e., $\nu = O(10 \; m^2 \; sec^{-1})$], the thickness of the friction layer is $O(\nu/\Omega)^{1/2} \simeq O$ (1 mi) and, according to Fig. 16, the downdraft in the boundary layer in the outer half of the hurricane is hardly even $O(10^{-2}$ mph). The near constancy of $w(x, \zeta \rightarrow \infty)$ for x > 3 in Fig. 16 is noteworthy; since the radial volumetric flux δ is fed by a constant downdraft $w(x, \zeta \rightarrow \infty) \simeq -0.035$, it is not surprising that $|d\delta/dx| \simeq 0.035$. If $\Psi_0 \simeq O(5 \cdot 10^3$ mi^2 $hr^{-1})$, the dimensional volumetric flux eruption up the eye-wall is $(2\pi^2 \; \Psi_0^2 \; \nu/\Omega)^{1/2} \delta \simeq O(7.3 \cdot 10^3 \; mi^2 \; hr^{-1})$. Since the density is $O(10^{-4}$ gm $cm^{-3})$, the associated mass flux radially inward through the boundary layer just before eruption $\simeq O(10^9$ kg $s^{-1})$. The mass initially in the boundary layer at the time of reaching the mature stage provides the throughput for about a week and the mass stored in region II easily sustains the storm for more than a week more. Figure 20 shows that the maximum of the radial velocity component is roughly one-third as large as the impressed azimuthal velocity component at a given radial position.

Figure 22 presents the residuals and the error (defined as the absolute value of the residual divided by the largest term in absolute value) for the azimuthal momentum equation for typical cases; the accuracy clearly degenerates as x decreases.

Finally, the spin-up time for the boundary layer is $O(\Omega^{-1})$, or about sixteen hours at 15° latitude, where hurricanes form. Carrier[4,15] has shown that this is the longest (rate-controlling) time associated with the intensification process; thus a transient boundary layer analysis is required for the intensification process for hurricanes (but quite possibly not for tornadoes).

IV. Concluding Remarks

Although further work is required before the model is sufficiently developed to predict the effect of seeding, the model warrants this attention because sufficient features of the essential physics are included. The model may be "seeded" ultimately by examining the alterations induced by assuming local transient heat addition (to simulate the effects of artificially induced phase transition). Of course, one would seek a four-to-six hour cycle of mitigation-reintensification from "seeding" high in the eye-wall to recover the purported effect of actual 1969 field seeding operations.[31,32] This will be a subtle goal because merely expanding the eye-wall (the supposed goal)[33] will not in itself increase the central pressure; somehow the eye itself must be altered.

Finally, the freezing of supercooled water may not be the only means within current technology by which "seeding" may alleviate a hurricane. The use of warm-fog dispersal methods to cause premature rain-out in the "stored fuel" region I of Figure 2 deserves consideration. In fact, getting the frictional boundary layer to run all the way into the axis before erupting would surely weaken the vortex. Also, seeding to alter direction as opposed to diminishing intensity and/or lifetime should not be prematurely dismissed.

Appendix A. Selection of the Base Functions

Of particular interest is the divergence in or out of the surface boundary layer, i.e., $w(x, \zeta \to \infty)$. While it is not clear that $w(x, \zeta \to \infty)$ is governed by the behavior of the boundary layer at large ζ, still a starting point is to adopt a series suitable for the boundary layer for $\zeta \gg 1$:

$$\phi = \phi_1(x, \zeta) + \ldots, \quad \psi = \Psi(x) + \psi_1(x, \zeta) + \ldots,$$

$$w = W_0(x) + w_1(x, \zeta) + \ldots \qquad (A1)$$

where $\Psi(x)$ is given, $w(x, \zeta \to \infty)$ is sought, and ϕ_1, ψ_1, $w_1 \to 0$ as $\zeta \to \infty$. Substitution of (A1) in the equations governing the surface frictional layer and linearizing gives

$$\phi_{1_x} + w_{1_\zeta} = 0, \qquad (A2)$$

$$\Psi_x \phi_1 + W_0 \psi_{1_\zeta} + \phi_1 = \psi_{1_{\zeta\zeta}}, \qquad (A3)$$

$$W_0 \phi_{1_\zeta} - \Psi \psi_1/x - \psi_1 = \phi_{1_{\zeta\zeta}}. \qquad (A4)$$

Equtions (A3) and (A4) combine to yield

$$\psi_{1_{\zeta\zeta\zeta\zeta}} - 2W_0 \psi_{1_{\zeta\zeta}} + W_0^2 \psi_{1_{\zeta\zeta}} + (\Psi/x + 1) \cdot$$

$$(\Psi_x + 1) \psi_1 = 0 , \qquad (A5)$$

in which x enters parametrically only. If $\psi_1 = \chi(x) \exp(-c\zeta)$, $Re(c) > 0$ by the boundary condition. In fact,

$$c^4 + 2W_0 c^3 + W_0^2 c^2 + (\Psi/x + 1) (\Psi_x + 1) = 0 , (A6)$$

so

$$c = -\frac{W_0}{2} + \left\{ \left(\frac{W_0}{2}\right)^2 \pm i \left[\left(\frac{\Psi}{x} + 1\right)(\Psi_x + 1)\right]^{1/2} \right\}^{1/2} \quad (A7)$$

Thus, for any W_0, oscillatory behavior with exponentially rapid decay is expected at large ζ

for all x. If $\psi = \text{const.}$, as $x \to \infty$, one expects $W_0 = 0$ and $c = (1 \pm i)/2^{1/2}$--the classical result of Ekman. In general, for $W_0 \to 0$

$$c = (1 \pm i) [(\Psi/x + 1) (\Psi_x + 1)]^{1/4}/2^{1/2}$$

and the base functions adopted are

$$\sin[j\lambda(x)\zeta] \exp[-j\lambda(x)\zeta], \quad j = 1, 2, 3, \ldots, (A8)$$

where $\lambda(x) = [(\Psi/x + 1) (\Psi_x + 1)]^{1/4}/2^{1/2}$.

When $\Psi_x \to -1$, $x \to 0$, or W_0 gets large, clearly the choice of base functions is poor. Consideration of these restrictions makes it evident that the base functions serve well at large x but not at small x. The choice forces the characteristic thickness of the frictional layer λ^{-1} to get thinner as x decreases, although the radial mass transport gets larger. The choice of base functions precipitates an early disgorging from the incompressible boundary layer of flux it can no longer transport. The difficulty in adopting one set of base functions is that a set (such as the present one) that suffices at large x performs poorly at small x, and vice versa. The difficulty arises because, while friction and Coriolis forces dominate at large x, friction plays a role only near $\eta = 0$ at small x; the bulk of the boundary layer at small x is controlled by radial convective, centrifugal, and pressure forces and this portion, which transport most of the radial flux, is discarded by (A8).

However, the preponderance of the downflux occurs at large x, where the base functions permit an adequate representation. As long as the premature updraft is recognized as an artifact of the method of solution under (A9) and is not taken literally as the solution, a good characterization of the mass flux through the bulk of the boundary should be achieved by use of the adopted base functions. If, for example, $w(x, \zeta \to \infty)$ is fairly constant in x--as turns out to be the case for swirl distributions of geophysical interest--three-quarters of the throughput sinks into the surface boundary layer at $(r_1/2) \leq r \leq r_1$ [or $(x_1/4) \leq x \leq x_1$, where $x \sim r^2$ and r_1 is the outer extremity of the storm].

If, in (A1)-(A7), one sets $W_0 = 0$ and seeks a solution to the linearized equations (A2)-(A4) valid at all ζ (i.e., subject to no-slip conditions at $\zeta = 0$ and the requirements ϕ_1, $\psi_1 \to 0$ as $\zeta \to \infty$), one finds the divergence to be

$$w(x, \zeta \to \infty) = \left\{ \frac{\Psi}{2^{1/2}} \left[\frac{(1 + \Psi/x)^{1/4}}{(1 + \Psi_x)^{3/4}} \right] \right\}_x . \qquad (A10)$$

Of course, near $\zeta = 0$, ψ_1 cannot really be taken as a small perturbation to Ψ. Nevertheless, the result does suggest that for swirl distributions of interest for hurricanes, wherever the divergence is small (i.e., at large x), the classical linear result [cf. Eq. (44)]

$$w(x, \zeta \to \infty) = (\Psi/2^{1/2})_x \qquad (A11)$$

might well be valid. Indeed, the computations described in the main text confirm this very important point. Of course (A11) implies efflux from the boundary layer where the outer swirl increases with increasing radius; and influx to the boundary layer where it decreases with increasing radius. For a potential vortex, $\Psi = K$ (a const.), (A11) gives no divergence, but (A10) gives a finite downflux at all $x > 0$.

References

1. Dergarabedian, P. and Fendell, F., "On Estimation of Maximum Wind Speeds in Tornadoes and Hurricanes," The Journal of the Astronautical Sciences, Vol. 17, No. 4, January-February 1970, pp. 218-236.

2. Tribus, M., "Physical View of Cloud Seeding," Science, Vol. 168, No. 3928, 10 April 1970, pp. 201-211.

3. Dergarabedian, P. and Fendell, F., "Parameters Governing the Generation of Free Vortices," The Physics of Fluids, Vol. 10, No. 11, November 1967, pp. 2293-2299.

4. Carrier, G. F., "The Intensification of Hurricanes," August 1970, Report 99994-6085-RO-00, TRW Systems, Fluid Mechanics Laboratory, Redondo Beach, California (to be published in J. Fluid Mech.).

5. Eliassen, A. and Kleinscnmidt, E., "Dynamic Meteorology," Encyclopedia of Physics, Vol. 48 (Geophysics II), edited by S. Flugge and J. Bartels, Springer-Verlag, Berlin, 1957, pp. 1-154.

6. Golden, J. H., "The Lower Florida Keys Waterspout Project, May-September 1969," Bulletin of the American Meteorological Society, Vol. 51, No. 3, March 1970, cover photograph, pp. 235-236 (also private correspondence).

7. Golden, J. H., "Waterspouts at Lower Matecumbe Key, Florida, 2 September 1967," Weather, Vol. 23, No. 3, Marcn 1968, pp. 102-114.

8. Golden, J. H., "The Dinner Key 'Tornadic Waterspout' of June 7, 1968," Mariners Weather Log, Vol. 13, No. 4, July 1969, pp. 139-147.

9. Golden, J. H., "Waterspouts and Tornadoes over South Florida," Monthly Weather Review, to appear.

10. Carrier, G. F., "Singular Perturbation Theory and Geophysics," SIAM Review, Vol. 12, No. 2, April 1970, pp. 175-193.

11. Riehl, H., Tropical Meteorology, 1st ed., McGraw-Hill, New York, 1954, chapter 11.

12. Malkus, J. S. and Riehl, H., "On the Dynamics and Energy Transformations in Steady-State Hurricanes," Tellus, Vol. 12, No. 1, Feb. 1960, pp. 1-20.

13. Hammond, A., "On the Energy Supply of Hurricanes: A Model of the Boundary Layer," Ph.D. thesis, June 1970, Harvard University, Cambridge, Massachusetts.

14. Keenan, J. H. and Keyes, F. G., Thermodynamic Properties of Steam Including Data for the Liquid and Solid Phases, John Wiley, New York, 1936.

15. Miller, B. I., "Characteristics of Hurricanes," Science, Vol. 157, No. 3795, 22 September 1967, pp. 1389-1399.

16. Jordan, C. L., "A Mean Atmosphere for the West Indies Area," National Hurricane Research Project Report No. 6, May 1957, U. S. Department of Commerce, Washington, D.C., 17 pp.

17. Carrier, G. F., "Swirling Flow Boundary Layers," August 1970, Report 99994-6086-RO-00, TRW Systems, Fluid Mechanics Laboratory, Redondo Beach, California (to be published in J. Fluid Mech.).

18. Fendell, F. and Dergarabedian, P., "On the Structure of Mature Severe Storms," AIAA Paper No. 69-671, 16-18 June 1969 (AIAA Fluid and Plasma Dynamics Conference, San Francisco, California).

19. Anderson, O. L., "Numerical Solutions of the Compressible Boundary Layer Equations for Rotating Axisymmetric Flows," Ph.D. thesis in Aeronautical Engineering, October 1966, Hartford Graduate Center of the Rensselaer Polytechnic Institute of Connecticut, East Windsor Hill, Connecticut.

20. Finlayson, B. A. and Scriven, L. E., "The Method of Weighted Residuals - A Review," Applied Mechanics Reviews, Vol. 19, No. 9, September 1966, pp. 735-748.

21. MacDonald, D. A., "Solution of the Incompressible Boundary Layer Equations via the Galerkin Kantorovich Technique," Journal of the Institute of Mathematics and Its Applications, Vol. 6, No. 2, June 1970, pp. 115-130.

22. Smith, R. C. and Smith, P., "Theoretical Flow Pattern of a Vortex in the Neighborhood of a Solid Boundary," Tellus, Vol. 17, No. 2, May 1965, pp. 213-219.

23. Turner, J. S., "The Constraints Imposed on Vortices by the Top and Bottom Boundary Conditions," Journal of Fluid Mechanics, Vol. 25, Part 2, June 1966, pp. 377-400.

24. Barcilon, A., "Inflow Layer in a Mature Hurricane," Report R67SD59, October 1967, General Electric Space Sciences Laboratory, King of Prussia, Pennsylvania.

25. Smith, R. K., "The Surface Boundary Layer of a Hurricane," Tellus, Vol. 20, No. 3, September 1968, pp. 473-484.

26. Leslie, L. M. and Smith, R. K., "The Surface Boundary Layer of a Hurricane. II.," Tellus, Vol. 22, No. 3, 1970, pp. 288-297.

27. Wippermann, F. W., Berkofsky, L., and Szillinsky, A., "Numerical Experiments on the Formation of a Tornado Funnel Under an Intensifying Vortex," _Quarterly Journal of the Royal Meteorological Society_, Vol. 95, No. 406, October 1969, pp. 689-702.

28. Kuo, H. L., "Axisymmetric Flows in the Boundary Layer of a Maintained Vortex," Planetary Circulation Project Report 15, 30 April 1969, Department of Geophysical Sciences, The University of Chicago, Illinois.

29. Chi, S. W., Ying, S. J., and Chang, C. C., "The Ground Turbulent Boundary Layer of a Stationary Tornado-Like Vortex," _Tellus_, Vol. 21, No. 5, 1969, pp. 693-700.

30. George, O., "The Boundary Layer Dynamics Under Swirling Flows in a Rotating System," Ph.D. thesis, June 1970, Harvard University, Cambridge, Massachusetts.

31. Gentry, R. C., "Project Stormfury, 1969," presented at the Sixth Technical Conference on Hurricanes, 2-4 December 1969, Miami, Florida, 8 pp.

32. Gentry, R. C., "Project Stormfury," _Bulletin of the American Meteorological Society_, Vol. 50, No. 6, June 1969, pp. 404-409.

33. Simpson, R. H. and Malkus, J. S., "Experiments in Hurricanes Modification," _Scientific American_, Vol. 211, No. 6, December 1964, pp. 27-34.

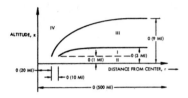

Fig. 2. This conjectured configuration of a mature hurricane with rough order-of-magnitude dimensions is not drawn to scale. The subdomains are: I, region of rapid swirl and slow downdraft; II, frictional boundary layer; III, eye-wall; and IV, eye.

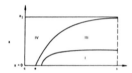

Fig. 3. This cross-sectional diagram shows a hypothetical cylindrical solid, cut out of the atmosphere and taken to contain a mature axisymmetric hurricane. The surface frictional layer II of Fig. 2 has been omitted, so subdomain I is taken to extend to z = 0.

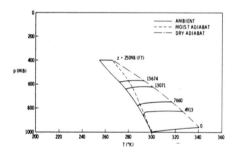

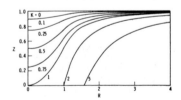

Fig. 1. The family of funnel-cloud configurations compatible with a Rankine vortex, in dimensionless coordinates.

Fig. 4. This tephigram for the Key West, Florida waterspout of 10 September 1969 shows the sequence of thermodynamic states occupied by a column of air near the vortex (ambient curve); the states occupied by sea-level ambient air expanded while kept just saturated (moist adiabat curve); and the states occupied by sea-level air which, after being expanded moist-adiabatically to the height of the top of the ambient curve, is then recompressed without any heat loss to re-evaporation of water (dry adiabat curve). Constant-altitude curves are noted parametrically. The efficacy of the method is here hampered by the absence of ambient data above 400 mb.

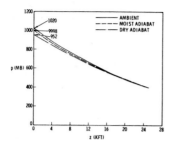

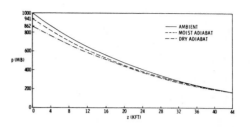

Fig. 8. Pressure-altitude plots corresponding
to the curves of Fig. 7.

Fig. 5. Pressure-altitude plots corresponding
to the curves of Fig. 4.

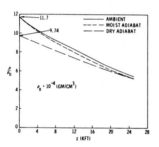

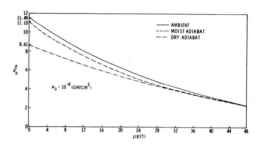

Fig. 9. Density-altitude plots corresponding to
the curves of Fig. 7.

Fig. 6. Density-altitude plots corresponding to
the curves of Fig. 4.

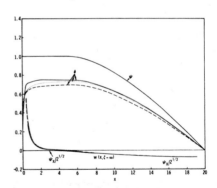

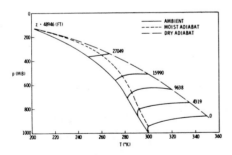

Fig. 7. Tephigram based Jordan's data for the
typical West Indies ambient atmosphere in the hurricane spawning season. The curves are analogous
to those of Fig. 4.

Fig. 10. The divergence $w(x, \zeta \to \infty)$ and the volumetric
flux δ for the swirl (56) with $\bar{c} = n = 1$, $x_1 = 20$.
All results are for one-term series ($N = 1$). The
volumetric flux varies slightly depending whether
$k = 1$ [see Eq. (45)], $a = b = 2^{-\frac{1}{2}}$ (solid curve);
$k = 0$, $a = b = 1$ (dotted curve); $k = 0$, $a = b$
$= 2^{-\frac{1}{2}}$ (dashed curve). However, the divergences
for all these cases are indistinguishable on the
scale adopted, and Ekman's result $\psi_x / 2^{\frac{1}{2}}$ well
approximates the divergences computed for the
region where downdraft is predicted.

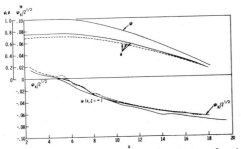

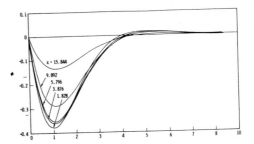

Fig. 11. The divergence $w(x, \zeta \to \infty)$ and the volumetric flux δ for the swirl (56) with $\bar{c} = n = 1$, $a = b = 2^{-\frac{1}{2}}$ and $x_1 = 20$. The solid curves of δ and $w(x, \zeta \to \infty)$ are for $k = N = 1$; the dashed curves are for $k = 0$ and $N = 1$; and the dotted curves are for $k = 0$ and $N = 2$. Clearly these variations make no qualitative differences. Common to all three cases is the same impressed swirl profile Ψ and hence the same linearized result for the divergence $\Psi_x/2^{\frac{1}{2}}$, which turns out to approximate the computed divergences $w(x, \zeta \to \infty)$ very well throughout the region in which a downdraft is predicted.

Fig. 14. The axial profiles of effectively the radial velocity component at several radial positions for the case plotted with solid lines in Fig. 11.

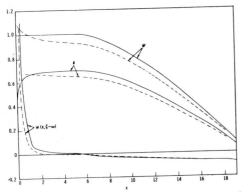

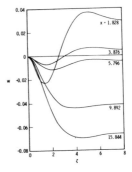

Fig. 12. The divergence $w(x, \zeta \to \infty)$ and the volumetric flux δ for the swirl (56) with $k = 0$, $N = \bar{c} = 1$, $x_1 = 20$. The solid curve is based on $n = 1$ and the dashed, on $n = 1.1$. Here $a = b = 2^{-\frac{1}{2}}$.

Fig. 15. The axial profile of the axial velocity component at several radial positions for the case plotted with solid lines in Fig. 11.

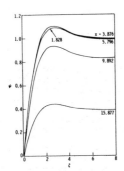

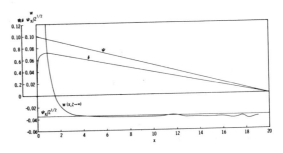

Fig. 13. The axial profile of effectively the angular momentum at several radial positions for the case plotted with solid lines in Fig. 11.

Fig. 16. The divergence $w(x, \zeta \to \infty)$ and the volumetric flux δ for the impressed swirl Ψ given by (57) with $\bar{D} = 1$, $x_1 = 20$, $k = 1$, $N = 1$. Again, except near the axis where nonlinear effects dominate, the linear Ekman layer result, $w(x, \zeta \to \infty) = \Psi_x/2^{\frac{1}{2}}$, is an excellent approximation to the numerical results.

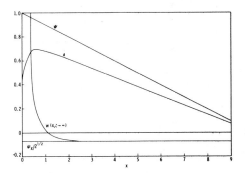

Fig. 17. The divergence $w(x, \zeta \to \infty)$ and the volumetric flux δ for the swirl (57) with $\bar{D} = k = N = 1$, $x_1 = 10$. For the smaller storm a stronger downdraft occurs (as predicted by Ekman's linear result); the eruption is deferred until closer to the axis.

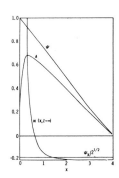

Fig. 18. The divergence $w(x, \zeta \to \infty)$ and the volumetric flux δ for the swirl (57) with $\bar{D} = k = N = 1$, $x_1 = 4$.

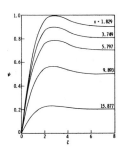

Fig. 19. The axial profile of effectively the angular momentum at several radial positions for the case plotted in Fig. 16. The overshoot of the swirl above its ambient value is common to all cases run.

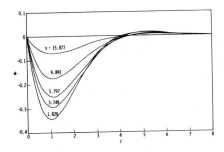

Fig. 20. The axial profile of the modified radial velocity component at several radial positions for the case plotted in Fig. 16. The net flux is clearly inward, although a layer of substantial outflow occurs in the reversing profiles.

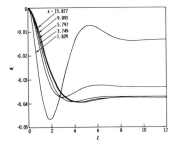

Fig. 21. The axial profile of the axial velocity component at several radial positions for the case plotted in Fig. 16. The vertical speeds are an order of magnitude smaller than the effective angular momentum plotted in Fig. 17.

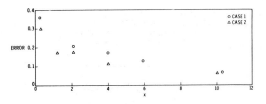

Fig. 22. The increase in the error of the weighted-residuals calculation as x decreases, for the radial momentum equation (38). The error is here defined as the absolute value of the ratio of the residual to the largest term. The point $\zeta \approx 1.5$ has been taken as a reasonable position for evaluating the characteristic error. Case 1 refers to the swirl (56) with $n = N = \bar{c} = K = 1$ and $x_1 = 20$. Case 2 refers to the swirl (57) with $\bar{D} = 1$, $x_1 = 20$, $N = 1$, and $k = 1$. Errors at $x \approx 10$ of about 6% are tolerable for present purposes, but errors of about 20% at $x \approx 2$ cast doubt on the solution.

AAS70-073

PORTABLE MASS SPECTROMETER/COMPUTER FOR AIR POLLUTION ANALYSIS AND MONITORING

By: John C. Pernicka and Gerald F. McGowan

King Resources Company
Special Projects Laboratory
Denver, Colorado 80202
August, 1970

Abstract

Since over 90% of what we refer to as air pollution consists of gaseous pollutants, we felt that a system which could detect and monitor these gaseous pollutants would have considerable value in air pollution control. Presently, systems exist which can detect two or three selected gases, but in general, no single system is available which can determine the composition of the atmosphere in a rapid and efficient manner. There are many approaches which could be investigated to determine the composition of the atmosphere ie, optical emission-absorption, chemical reaction, gas chromatography, mass analysis, etc.

Our decision to pursue the investigation of one or more approaches to atmospheric analysis was determined quite objectively and influenced only by minor circumstances, namely the availability of equipment and funding to investigate mass analyzer/computer systems. Our objective in this investigation is to stimulate interest in applying the latest aerospace techniques in mass spectroscopy and computer systems to the air pollution control problem.

A mass analyzer is generally a rapid tool used in gas analysis and if coupled to a computer system can be made efficient in terms of data reduction, but there are many inherent limitations to the system. The two most important limitations are: (1) limited partial pressure sensitivity, and (2) inability to separate and detect minute quantities of gases which exhibit the same mass to charge ratios as extremely abundant gases in the same mixture. These two limitations are not insurmountable particularly if one is willing to use gas chromatography techniques for preconcentration and preseparation. However, we have limited our discussions in this paper to mass analyzers and computers since our investigations are by no means complete. We feel that the mass analyzer connected to a real time computer is an excellent detection system and warrants considerable discussion at this time. The ideal system which we hope to achieve will be discussed at some future date after we have expanded the system to include additional control capability and evaluated the system in extensive field tests.

This paper describes a portable Mass Spectrometer/Computer system for air pollution analysis and monitoring, and includes discussions of high vacuum techniques, mass analyzer technology, electronic systems design and packaging, real time computer systems, signal processing techniques, and mass analyzer data reduction techniques. Each section contains a description of the relevant technology, the present state-of-the-art, and the application of the technology to the specific problem.

Introduction

Air pollution has been defined as the presence in the air of substances generated by man which interfere with his comfort, safety, and/or health. The problem was recognized as early as 1315, when King Edward I tried to prohibit the burning of sea coal because of the noxious fumes given off. He was not successful in preventing the use of coal since there was no cheap substitute to provide the energy required by the populace. Conditions have not improved over the centuries. As long as man demands cheap sources of energy and continues to utilize fossil fuels to provide this energy, we are faced with a growing problem. Air pollution levels and frequency have increased to a point of real concern with the growth in size and activity in many metropolitan areas. Any attempt to reduce the current burden of air pollution or to prevent a further increase is clearly a socio-economic problem which will affect entire communities.

In order to control air pollution, we have to first define it explicitly and then establish levels and quantities which are either acceptable or unacceptable. King Edward I probably never thought about defining air pollution, yet he had definite ideas about what was discomforting to him. He had the power and authority to make a subjective judgement as to the degree of pollution but he was unable to provide the technology to do anything about it or to provide an alternate solution to the problem.

We have come a long way in technological development applied to the reduction of pollution in certain processes but in the majority of cases economic factors restrict the implementation of these techniques. Similarly, the choice of fuels to provide us with energy is governed in most cases by the cost. Here we are, over four centuries later still burning fossil fuels and polluting the very air our future existance depends on. What is an acceptable level of pollution? How much discomfort should people be required to endure? To what extent should we jeopardize the safety and health of man? Just ask any one of the many millions of people living in the megalopolises of the world today. Man, equipped with a sensor system scientists find hard to duplicate (the eyes, ears, and nose) coupled to a data storage and processing system unsurpassed by none, the brain, can very easily determine the presence of air pollution. In fact, to a certain extent, he can even tell how discomforting the pollution is and where it might be coming from. Yet we do not trust man's subjective judgement. We would rather have an unemotional machine make a quantitative and qualitative analysis of the situation, and based on some logical "thinking" process we gave it, reach a conclusion.

It is quite obvious at this point that instrumentation to detect, analyze and monitor air pollution play an important role in effective pollution control. After all, how can we be certain our pollution control measures are effective if we can not monitor the resulting trend of our efforts? Our scientific community faces a moral as well as social obligation to aid man in solving one of his most perplexing and elusive problems, air pollution control. Sometimes it is not obvious how a major portion of our scientific research, namely the space program, will directly help us solve socio-economic problems on earth. But, if we consider the earth as Richard Buckminster Fuller does, the "space ship earth", then we can see a direct correlation of the problems of air pollution on a spacecraft verses those on earth.

Let us take a closer look at the composition of air pollution. Less than one-tenth of the total man-made air pollution consists of suspended particulates, where as, over nine-tenths consists of gaseous material, namely: carbon monoxide, nitric oxide, nitrogen dioxide, sulfur dioxide, hydrogen chloride, multiple oxidents, hydrocarbons, and ozone. Most air pollution sources are extremely complex and their emissions may contain any number of the above mentioned pollutants. Thus, to effectively control pollution, we must be able to detect, analyze and monitor all the constituents of air pollution, not just a few.

Over the past fifteen years, air pollution monitors have been developed which are

based on classical chemical analytical methods. In general, these instruments are limited to the investigation of at least one compound and at best a single class of compounds. Thus, to monitor a large number of pollutants, a number of separate instruments are required. In order to achieve minimum detectable limits of 0.01 parts per million, many of the systems must collect and preconcentrate air samples over periods as long as one hour for one measurement. A number of physical methods are being studied which would provide a quick analysis of some of the more difficult pollutants, but again a separate technique is usually required for each particular compound or sub-group of compounds.

The utility of present air pollution monitoring stations is considerably restricted because of present instrumentation. In order to obtain the maximum amount of useful data, fixed stations have been constructed in some cities which house the many different sensors required and in some cases are operated remotely from a central location. Since it is difficult if not impossible to monitor the pollution emitted from fixed sources throughout a city with a limited number of fixed stations, mobile vans have been instrumented in some cases to provide a means of spot checking compliance with local air pollution regulations. Most of these mobile monitoring stations are limited in the number of compounds which they can effectively analyze because of the limitations of available instrumentation. Perhaps one of the most important factors influencing the validity of indirect measurements is a thorough knowledge of the meteorological conditions which existed before, during, and after the air pollution measurement period. Obtaining reliable weather information over a large area is in many cases a monumental task which we would only speculatively consider less difficult than obtaining air pollution measurements.

Ideally, we would like to make rapid, instantaneous measurements of air pollution throughout the air volume of interest. If we had a small, lightweight instrument which could rapidly detect and analyze all of the air pollutants of interest mounted in an aircraft, we could obtain measurements which would provide virtually an instantaneous picture of the situation relative to the time and speed scale of meteorological movement. The advantages of an aircraft-mounted air pollution monitoring station are too numerous to do justice to in this short paper, but if we consider the operating costs relative to the coverage provided over a large metropolitan area, we will find the aircraft technique worthwhile as well as economical. The major difficulty with the aircraft technique is that with present instrumentation the aircraft would have to be very large and slow moving, such as a dirigible. Of course, now with a slow speed we get involved in the meteorological problem again.

A possible solution to our instrumentation problem has been brought to our attention recently during a planning phase of our space program. The problem was quite straight forward: Find out what the atmosphere is surrounding a planet during an unmanned fly by. The instrument chosen for this task was a small, lightweight, remotely operated mass spectrometer. We should take notice of this space age instrument, for even though it was never intended to achieve the sensitivity required for air pollution detection, the technological advancement of the state-of-the-art has been significant.

It is difficult to discuss mass spectrometry without becoming involved in a discussion of vacuum systems, electronic systems, data recording systems, and particularly computer systems if we are speaking of a practical system for air pollution detection, analysis and monitoring. However, in view of our limited space, time, and the attention span of the average reader, we will concentrate our discussion on those items which we feel are essential in understanding the technique involved and the operation of the total system as applied to the air pollution problem.

Mass Spectrometry Technology

Mass spectrometry has been used since its inception in 1913 by J. J. Thomson for chemical analysis. Its use was first applied to the identification of naturally occurring isotopes, and in fact the list of all naturally occurring isotopes was virtually complete by 1939. Scientists have reported the usefulness of mass spectrometry applied to the measurement of atmospheric pollution as early as 1953 with successful determination of a wide variety of organic materials even earlier in 1950. Mass Spectrometric Analysis was even applied to the study of internal combustion engine exhaust gases by 1954. As with all analytical techniques, the art of mass spectrometry has progressed only as fast as the development of the instrumentation ie, the mass spectrometer.

A mass spectrometer is basically a device which can distinguish between particles of matter in a gaseous state according to their mass-to-charge ratio (m/e). Thus, one might guess that some sort of method of sample ionization is required and is a common characteristic of all mass spectrometers. Generally, the gas sample at reduced pressure is ionized by electron bombardment. The electron beam is produced by a hot filament (usually tungsten) and accelerated to a particular energy of about 75 ev.

The ionized gas sample is separated on the basis of mass-to-charge ratio by the interaction of the charged particles with magnetic and/or electric fields. The different types of mass analyzers are characterized by the particular electric/magnetic interaction utilized to provide mass separation. The following discussion is concerned with the different types of mass analyzers, their characteristics, and advantages/disadvantages.

Magnetic Analyzer

The magnetic analyzer which was the first mass separation technique employed (Fig. 1), produces positive ions in an ion source located generally outside the main magnetic field. The ionizing electrons in the ion source are mono-energetic and confined to a narrow beam. A small permanent magnet is sometimes used to focus the electron beam. The positive ions formed by the electron beam drift out through a slit at the end of the ionization chamber. An accelerating electrostatic field in conjunction with an ion-repeller electrode assists in the extraction of the ions from the ion source. The resultant accelerated monoenergetic ion beam is deflected into an arc of a circle by means of a homogeneous magnetic field directed at right angles to the velocity of the ions.

The magnetic field segregates the ions into different m/e ratios. The ion beams which satisfy the conditions of the instrument pass through a collector-defining slit and are detected at the ion collector. To focus ions of a given m/e value on the collector, either the ion accelerating voltage or the magnetic field strength is varied. Varying the accelerating voltage to scan the mass spectrum generally reduces the sensitivity for heavier ions. A reduction of accelerating voltage results in a smaller fraction of heavy ions being drawn from the ion source than if a fixed voltage is employed and the strength of the magnetic field is varied. In the latter case, the extraction efficiency from the ion source would be constant. The sensitivity is also limited by the loss of ions at the defining slit. Resolution, in turn, is limited by alignment errors in the analyzer, the energy spread in the beam entering the analyzer, and instabilities in the control voltages and in the magnetic field. Since magnetic analyzers exhibit no energy-focusing properties, ion sources with a low energy spread must be used.

Advantages/disadvantages of the magnetic analyzer are:

1. Has the highest resolution capability and, therefore, the greatest useful mass range.

2. Obtains high resolution, but at the expense of an increase in size.

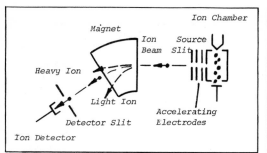

Figure 1, Magnetic Analyzer.

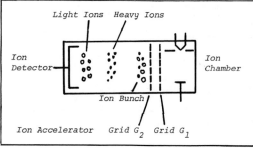

Figure 2, Time of Flight Analyzer.

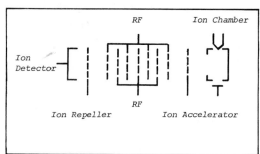

Figure 3, Radio Frequency Spectrometer.

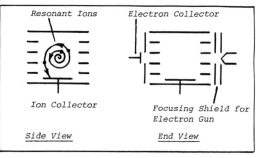

Figure 4, Omegatron Analyzer.

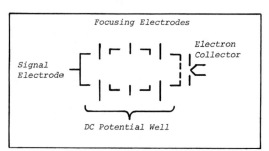

Figure 5, Farvitron Analyzer.

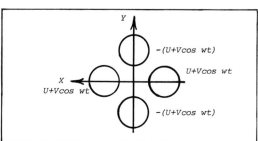

Figure 6, Quadrupole Analyzer.

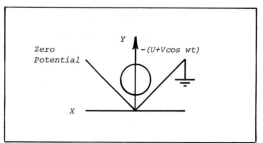

Figure 7, Monopole Analyzer.

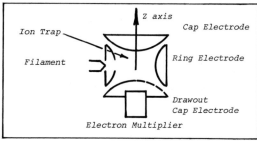

Figure 8, Three Dimensional Quadrupole.

3. Has approximately the same sensitivity as resonance analyzers.

Time-of-flight Analyzer

The time-of-flight analyzer (Fig.2) consists of a pulsed electron gun ion source and a grid system which draws ions out of the ion source and accelerates them as a packet through a field-free drift tube. The field-free drift tube is used for containing the ion packet and supplying the required distance for separating the ions according to their mass-to-charge ratio (m/e). An ion collector to detect the ions is located at the end of the drift tube. The time-of-flight analyzer measures the time required for an ion to traverse a certain specified distance. In this fixed distance of travel the time of travel of the ions will vary with their mass. The lighter masses will travel more rapidly, and reach the ion collector in a shorter period of time. The rest of the ions follow in increasing order of mass.

The acceleration fields used to extract the ions from the ion source and accelerate them toward the ion collector are either applied continuously or are pulsed at the end of the ion formation. All the ions receive essentially the same momentum if, with a single constant accelerating field, the pulse cuts off before any of the ions leave the ion source; all the ions receive essentially the same energy if the accelerating pulse lasts until all ions have left the ion source. In either case the velocity of the ions in the field-free drift space is a function of their mass-to-charge ratio (m/e).

The resolving power of the time-of-flight mass spectrometer is dependent upon the source delivering the ions of a given m/e ratio to the ion collector in a sharp pulse, even when the ions vary in initial position and velocity.

Advantages/disadvantages of the Time-of-flight Analyzer are:

1. Especially suitable for high-speed operation.

2. Eliminates critical magnetic fields.

3. Limited resolving power.

4. Has no narrow slits in the ion source and detector which allows one dimension of the ion beam to be much larger than is possible in magnetic analyzers, and thus allows a more effective utilization of any given electron beam in producing useful ions.

5. Produces mass spectra slightly more abundantly in the heavier ions and slightly less abundantly in the lighter ions than in the magnetic analyzer.

6. Possesses so-called "harmonics" which tend to confuse the data.

Radio Frequency Analyzer (The Bennett Tube)

The Bennett radio frequency analyzer (Fig. 3) is a nonmagnetic analyzer which separates ions of different mass-to-charge ratio by means of electric potentials applied to grids. Ions emerging from the ion source are all accelerated to the same energy in an electro-static field, where they then enter one or more rf stages. Each stage is a series of three equally spaced parallel grids. The control grid is charged with an alternating rf voltage applied with respect to the outer grids which are at ground potential.

To obtain a maximum energy increment, the ions must start with the correct velocity at the optimum phase of the rf field. For any given frequency, only ions of a given mass-to-charge ratio will travel from grid to grid in time to benefit from another acceleration. That is, the resonant ion passes through the grids just as the rf grid changes polarity relative to the adjacent grids. Heavier ions fail to reach the grid in time, and lighter ions pass through the grid too soon. The out-of-phase ions lose energy, and the ions in phase with the rf field will accelerate and emerge with maximum energy and speed toward the detector. The ion beam is accelerated continuously, and the mass spectrum is scanned by varying the frequency of the accelerating voltage. The resolution of the analyzer can be increased by increasing the number of times energy is imparted to the ion. This is accomplished in multi-stage rf analyzers which consist of two or more rf analyzer stages separated by equipotential drift spaces. Multi-stage rf analyzers are identified by the number of stages and the number and order of rf cycles between successive stages.

Advantages/disadvantages of the Radio Frequency Analyzer are:

1. Simple construction and lightweight.

2. Mass analysis capability without a magnetic field.

3. The ion beam cross section is limited only by grid size and the linear mass-to-voltage relationship.

4. Requires a fair amount of circuitry, and tends to produce ghost signals which can be confusing.

5. The resolution is not very high and decreases with increasing mass.

6. Can be developed for rapid reproduction of the spectrum because of
   its high sensitivity.

7. A disadvantage of all rf analyzers
   (as compared to the corresponding
   magnetic analyzers) is the more complicated electronic system.

8. Using grids as the rf electrodes gives
   higher current efficiency than the
   equivalent magnetic analyzer.

Omegatron Analyzer

This instrument (Fig. 4) employs the cyclotron principle to effect mass separation. In
other words, ion resonance is used for mass
selection. An omegatron differs from a cyclotron only in the manner of application of the
ac field. In the omegatron, the field tends
to be uniform in space while in the cyclotron
it is concentrated at the junction of two
"D's". The electron beam in the omegatron is
directed parallel to a magnetic field, ionizing
the gas in the central region of the analyzer.
Ions are prevented from escaping axially by a
dc field. An rf electric field perpendicular
to the magnetic field extracts the ions.
When the rf field is in resonance with the cyclotron oscillating frequency of the ions, the
ions gain energy with each circulation and spiral
outward until they impinge upon the ion collector. In the ideal case, the ion trajectory is
an Archimedes spiral with the radius increasing
at a constant rate. Nonresonant ions have
no continuous buildup of energy and remain in
the vicinity of the central axis. Of course,
these nonresonant ions will be present in the
accelerating phase of the rf field for a
limited number of circulations but they do not
reach the ion collector. A small draw-out
voltage imposed on the rf electrodes slowly
forces the nonresonant ions out of the center
where they are caught on the electrodes. The
mass spectrum is scanned by varying either the
rf frequency or the magnetic field.

There is a guard ring stack on the omegatron
which serves to make the rf field homogeneous
and thereby brings the best possible agreement
between theoretical and experimental resonant
frequency. However, since ions have thermal-
velocity components in the direction of the
magnetic field, axial drifts are superimposed
on the spiral motion already considered. Nonresonant ions benefit from this because they
are intercepted by the guard ring stack which
reduces the axial space charge. In turn, to
prevent excessive loss of the resonant ions,
it is usually necessary to apply a trapping
voltage to the guard-ring stack. However,
this trapping voltage and the space charge
give rise to a radial electric field, and
thus cause the orbital frequency to differ

slightly from the cyclotron frequency.

The resolution of the omegatron decreases
with increasing ion mass. The resolution
can be improved by either increasing the
magnetic field or by reducing the rf voltage.
This is not always practicable, however, because reducing the rf voltage below a certain
point creates difficulties of contact potential variation, and increasing the magnetic field becomes very expensive.

No harmonic peaks are produced by the omegatron in its operation because an ion in the
omegatron is accelerated continuously rather
than at discrete intervals. This is in contrast to the cyclotron, which produces harmonic peaks.

Advantages/disadvantages of the Omegatron
Analyzer are:

1. Can be built in very small dimensions and is easily degassed.

2. Is very sensitive due to its volume
   and the fact that the ion current
   is not limited by any slits.

3. The pressure is accurately proportional to the reading. Since all resonant ions reach the collector, absolute partial pressures can be calculated from the geometry of the electron
   beam and the known ionization cross
   sections of the gases.

4. The resolving power is high and can be
   adjusted.

5. The disadvantages are that it requires
   a large magnet and is sensitive to
   small changes of surface potential in
   the measurement system, which easily
   give rise to spurious signals.

6. Has space charge difficulties which
   interfere with its use with heavier
   atoms.

7. The ratio of ions collected at the ion
   collector after separation to the total
   number of ions produced is high.

8. Employs small dc potentials to keep
   the ions on their long spiral path in
   the region of the collector, which,
   like the unavoidable space charge,
   lead to a deviation of the resonant
   frequency from the theoretical value,
   and limit the precision of the measurement.

Farvitron

The Farvitron (Fig. 5) is a type of rf analyzer in which ions execute linear oscillations in an electrostatic potential well maintained between two parallel electrodes. The Farvitron consists of a cylindrically symmetrical electrode system which includes a cathode, an ion cathode electrode, focusing electrodes, and a signal electrode. Located between the ion cathode electrode and the signal electrode is a dc potential well. Ions are produced by an electron beam originating from the cathode and directed axially along the analyzer. The ions formed by the electron beam are accelerated toward the ion cathode electrode and oscillate axially in the potential well. Around this axis a tubular shaped ion cloud builds up in which ions of various frequencies and phase angles relative to the field exist. If an rf voltage is now superimposed on the dc potential of the ion cathode electrode, then the electron current is modulated along with the production of ions. Therefore, only a certain group of ions will oscillate in phase, and a continuous energy exchange takes place between the rf field and the ion oscillation. Ions which exchange energy with the rf voltage enter unstable paths and are dispersed quickly, being discharged at the electrodes. The ions in resonance with the rf voltage exchange virtually no energy, and thus develop an ac voltage of high frequency on the signal electrode. The amplitude of this induced voltage is proportional to the number of ions oscillating in phase. The high-frequency signal thus produced is amplified, demodulated, and recorded.

The oscillation frequency of the ions is governed by the mass-to-charge ratio and is independent of the amplitude. The whole mass spectrum can be scanned by varying the frequency of the rf voltage applied to the ion cathode electrode.

Advantages/disadvantages of the Farvitron are:

1. Has a small, handy gauge head which needs no adjustment.

2. Presents fast response, easy amplification of ion currents, and rapid recording possibilities.

3. Has a high scanning frequency of the mass spectrum. Therefore, it is especially suitable for direct observation of rapidly changing processes.

4. Uses low rf power.

5. Has no magnetic field.

6. The neutral particles are ionized within the analyzing section. Therefore, they do not have to pass through complex physical structures before analysis.

7. Has low resolution.

8. Has harmonic peaks. Ghosts caused by higher and lower harmonics of the rf field appear at masses of 1/4 and 4 times that of a given ion.

9. Does not allow for quantitative determination of gas composition or for measurement of total pressure because of its measuring principle. Gas components, present in small proportion, can be detected only if their share of the total pressure is at least three percent.

10. Discriminates in favor of higher masses (lower frequencies) so that the height of the peaks in the mass spectrum obtained gives only a rough indication of partial pressures.

11. Does not allow a quantitative analysis of the gas composition because of space charge limitation.

12. Has relatively low sensitivity, because of high background noise.

Quadrupole Analyzer

The Quadrupole (Fig. 6) uses an rf electric field for mass analysis. A two-dimensional quadrupole field is established between four parallel rod-shaped electrodes. Ideally, the four parallel rods should be hyperbolic in cross section, but, in most quadrupoles, they have been approximated by rods that are circular in cross section. This is accomplished by making the round rods slightly larger than the instrument radius. Both a dc voltage and an rf voltage are applied to this quadrupole array. The axis of the rods lie along the edges of an imaginary rectangular prism, thus establishing a time varying potential distribution in the region between the rods. Beyond the four-pole system, ions are injected from an ion source and proceed down the axis of the analyzer section (Z axis) to an ion detector located at the far end. There are no forces acting in the Z direction. The ions continue in the Z direction with the constant velocity at which they were injected into the quadrupole rf field while their x and y amplitudes vary. The ion beam is usually restricted in cross section and angular divergence by circular apertures placed at the entrance to the analyzer. No defining aperture is necessary for the ion detector. Thus, this type of analyzer separates ions of different mass-to-charge ratio by means of a high-frequency electric quadrupole field. For a given field, only the mass-to-charge ratio of an ion determines whether the path is stable or unstable since there is no focusing in the analyzer. The trajectory of ions injected into such a field is described by Mathieu's differential equations, which have well-known properties of solution. These equations are second order linear differential equations with periodic coefficients.

The mass spectrum is scanned by varying either the magnitude of the rf voltage or the frequency while maintaining the ratio of the dc and rf voltage constant. Usually the voltage is varied, yielding a linear mass scale. The dc voltage field alone has a focusing effect for the ions in the X direction. Therefore, stability in the Y direction must result from the interaction of the ion and the rf field. When the rf field is superimposed, the motion of the ion in the X direction is similar to the amplitude of an oscillatory system excited by a frequency close to its resonant frequency. In the Y direction the ion's motion is roughly synchronous with the rf voltage.

The ion must be stable in both X and Y directions if it is to reach the ion detector. Whether or not an ion strikes a rod is controlled not only by the stable or unstable nature of its trajectory but also by the initial position and angle of motion of the ion as it enters the quadrupole region.

Advantages/disadvantages of the Quadrupole Analyzer are:

1. Can be used at high pressures because the stable ions are subjected to focusing forces along their whole path length in the analyzer. Therefore, line-width broadening and intensity reduction suffered by conventional analyzers as a result of gas collisions is reduced in the quadrupole analyzer.

2. Is lightweight, and has a small volume.

3. It can accept a large spread of ion energies entering the analyzer region without loss of resolution.

4. Does not need a magnetic field.

5. Has a linear mass scale which is derived from a linear voltage sweep.

6. The resolution can be increased by lowering the injection energy of the ions. However, the increase of resolution is employed at the expense of transmission. The resolution can also be changed by varying the ratio of dc to rf voltages.

7. Only the resolution and transmission is affected by the initial conditions; the mass spectra are uniquely related to the gas under analysis. This is in contrast to analyzers which depend on the time of flight.

8. Offers the possibility of making the separation of masses ineffective when the dc potential is switched off. In this manner, a measurement of total ion-current, and, thereby, total pressure can be performed.

9. The main experimental difficulty in the construction of a high-resolution quadrupole stems from the fact that the electrode rods must be uniform in cross section and parallel over their length with a tolerance of only a few microns.

10. Extremely sensitive to contamination.

Monopole Analyzer

The monopole analyzer (Fig. 7) is a variation of the quadrupole analyzer. The principles of its operation are essentially the same as those of the quadrupole. In the quadrupole configuration, if one draws equipotential lines in the cross section of the assembly, there is a region defined by the intersection of the two lines which is always at zero potential.

The monopole consists of a single rod of circular cross section held parallel to a right angled electrode. The angled electrode is grounded, while a combined dc and rf potential is applied to the single rod. Mathieu's differential equations for the quadrupole are the same type which describe the field between the grounded angled electrode and the single rod in the monopole. However, there is an important distinction in the solution of the equations of motion in the monopole. In addition to requiring that an ion have trajectories which are stable in the X and Y direction, the ion also must not strike the angled electrode. In the case of the monopole, the angled electrode lies along the Z axis, so that the Y direction is of special interest. Now the motion of the ion in the Y direction of the monopole represents a beat, and the high frequency oscillations within the beat are not oscillations about the Z axis as is the case in the X direction. Therefore, Y stable solutions represent a beat of finite amplitude in the Y direction. An ion which is stable in the quadrupole can now only reach the ion detector in the monopole provided $Y > |X|$ and the monopole field length is less than half the length of the total beat. As in the quadrupole, the ions travel with a constant velocity in the Z direction. The field length and the ion velocity in the monopole are chosen so that the X and Y stable ions traverse the analyzer during the time that the field length is less than half the beat length of the ions.

The relation between ion mass and beat length is such that ions of greater mass have longer beats and ions of lower mass have shorter beats. The ions of lower mass are X and Y stable, but collide with the angled electrode before they can reach the ion detector. Ions of higher mass are unstable in the Y direction. About 50 percent of all ions entering the analyzer enter at the wrong phase of the rf cycle and are lost by being driven into the angled electrode.

The mass spectrum is scanned by varying the frequency of the rf field or the voltage amplitude. However, the ion injection voltage in the monopole is held constant, although it is not necessary that the ratio of applied voltage be maintained constant, as is required in the quadrupole. In addition, as the frequency is varied in the monopole to scan the mass spectrum, all ions that reach the detector will experience the same number of rf periods in the analyzing field. Therefore, a constant resolving power over the entire mass range is obtained. The number of rf periods the ions require for a given resolution in the monopole is nearly a factor of three less than the number of periods necessary in the quadrupole.

Advantages/disadvantages of the Monopole Analyzer are:

1. Construction is simpler in the monopole. Only one rod must be aligned rather than the four rods in the quadrupole.

2. Requires that the injection energy be kept fairly constant. Therefore it does not share the advantage of the quadrupole in that it is insensitive to a large spread in ion entrance energies.

3. The resolving power is practically independent of the ratio of applied voltages for ions reaching the detector. This is not the case for the quadrupole.

4. Is extremely sensitive to contamination. A similar effect has been observed in the quadrupole.

5. In the quadrupole, the mass peaks are equally spaced, and their width is proportional to their mass. Therefore, a light mass will have a narrower peak compared with the peak of a heavier mass. However, in the monopole the mass peaks are equally spaced, but their width is nearly constant regardless of the mass.

6. Exhibits severe mass discrimination that varies with operating conditions. Changing the operating frequency affects the relative amplitudes of the mass peaks.

7. Monopole's sensitivity is a function of the resolution.

Three-Dimensional Quadrupole (Ion Cage Analyzer)

The quadrupole field with cylindrical symmetry can be extended to a three-dimensional rotational symmetrical field (Fig. 8). In the two-dimensional quadrupole, the stable ions were stable with respect to the X and Y directions. Motion was force-free in the Z direction. In the three-dimensional quadrupole, the stable ions are stable with respect to all three coordinate axes. The ions are bound quasi-elastically to the origin, about which they describe three-dimensional Lissajous figures. In the absence of interfering effects, the ions can be confined to a region around the origin for an arbitrary length of time (ion cage).

Three electrodes are used to generate the rotationally symmetric quadrupole field, each of which is a hyperboloid of revolution. The structure is rotationally symmetrical about the Z axis. The so-called ring and cap electrodes are complementary hyperboloids whose relative dimensions are set by Laplace's equation so that the square of the minimum distance from the center to the ring is equal to twice the minimum distance from the center to the end-caps. That is, the asymptotes are chosen so that the potential satisfies the Laplace equation at all points. The end-caps are maintained at the same potential and both a dc voltage and an rf voltage are applied between the caps and ring. The equations of motion of the ions again lead to the Mathieu equations with the typical stability behaviour of its solutions. For the three-dimensional quadrupole, an r term is used in place of the X or Y direction since they are equivalent and perpendicular to the Z direction.

In the three-dimensional quadrupole, molecules are ionized inside the analyzer by injecting an electron beam through one of the end-caps. Ions which are oscillating in a stable mode can be detected by a resonance method based on the damping of an oscillating circuit. In other words, the existing oscillating ions are excited in their fundamental frequency. The ions absorb energy from the oscillatory circuit and damp the circuit until they collide with the electrodes as a result of their increasing amplitude. Therefore, only some of the existing oscillating ions can fulfill the resonance condition required for detection.

A further development of the above-mentioned resonance method in the three-dimensional quadrupole is the technique of periodically pulsing the stored ions out through one of the end-caps to an electron multiplier. The electron gun can be pulsed off before the ion drainout pulse. This allows the ions of unstable trajectories to be lost and avoids effects of soft x-rays. The magnitude of the rf voltage is scanned, while the ratio of rf to dc voltage remains constant.

For small devices, a "stable" ion may not be stored because of collision with the electrodes. This is caused by the stability limits being dependent on the amplitude of the oscillation and not on the initial ion velocity. However, the amplitude of oscillation increases in proportion to the initial ion velocity. In this regard, a small device will discriminate more against energetic ions as the mass resolution is increased.

The resolving power is approximately equal to the number of resonant field periods experienced by a resonant ion which originated in the XY-plane. The finite transit times of the resonant ions up to the time of discharge on the electrodes, or the mean time of two collisions of the ion with neutral gas atoms, results in the limiting of the resolving power. As the resolution is increased, the sensitivity is decreased. Resolution is also limited because of space charge effects.

Because of the space charge effects, the three-dimensional quadrupole exhibits all the advantages and disadvantages of the ion accumulation principle.

Mass Spectrometer System

The mass spectrometer system used in our tests is a commercially available system with a number of unique features. The mass analyzer (Fig. 9) employs three stages of mass separation in order to achieve a partial pressure sensitivity as low as 1 to 20 parts per billion. Two tandem, opposed direction, magnetic deflections are followed by an electrostatic high pass energy filter that suppresses low energy ions which would otherwise contribute to low mass peak tailing. The first magnetic stage provides mass focusing, where as, the second magnetic stage provides for efficient momentum filtering and is extremely effective in eliminating the effects of ion-molecule scattering.

Ionization and ion beam acceleration are

achieved as previously described in the magnetic analyzer section. A mass scan range from 1 to 500 AMU is available and can be achieved either by scanning the electro-magnet current or the ion accelerating voltage. Since a rapid scan is desireable, a fixed electro-magnet current is used with a variable accelerating voltage to provide mass scans. A resolution of 250 AMU is obtainable with this system.

The beam tube region is separated from the ion source region by the source defining slit so that differential pumping may be employed. A liquid nitrogen trapped oil diffusion pump vacuum system is used to provide a high pumping speed for all gases which flow through the system. Ion pumps, for example, will not remove noble gases as fast as active gases and result in large argon and helium background levels. The LN_2 trapped diffusion pump system in conjunction with an inlet throttle valve and internal molecular orifice insure a nonfractionating gas flow necessary for accurate analysis. A digital motor drive on the throttle valve is controlled by servo system which maintains a constant pressure in the ionizer chamber.

In order to measure levels of mercury in the air, which are from 100 to 1000 times less than the partial pressure sensitivity of the system, a gold plated heater wire was inserted in the inlet system of the mass spectrometer. A ten to fifteen minute collection period was required in some cases to see an identifiable mercury spectra. At the end of the collection period, the gold wire was isolated from the atmosphere by closing two valves and evacuating the chamber. No noticeable mercury was given off until the wire was heated to at least 150^0 C and a helium carrier gas was implemented to facilitate moving the mercury molecules into the ion chamber.

Although the dual magnet system is large and somewhat heavier than desireable, by packaging the vacuum system, analyzer, and inlet system in one light-weight aluminum module 22 inches wide, 30 inches high, and 36 inches long, we were able to obtain a total system weight which was less than 500 pounds.

During extensive field tests earlier this year, we have noticed that there is a pronounced reduction in ionization efficiency due to prolonged operation at relatively high pressures in the ion chamber ($5X10^{-4}$ torr). Also, with a high through-put, it is difficult to keep background levels in the system sufficiently low to facilitate continuous rapid data collection. It would be interesting to apply a modulated beam technique utilized in a commercial quadrupole analyzer to the magnetic system we used in our tests. In the modulated beam technique, the sample gas is introduced in the form of a modulated molecular beam. Besides a reduction in

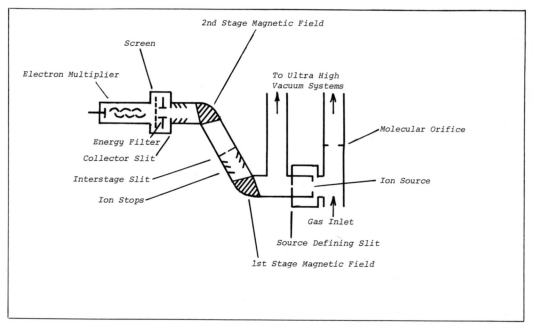

Figure 9, Double Focused Magnetic Analyzer.

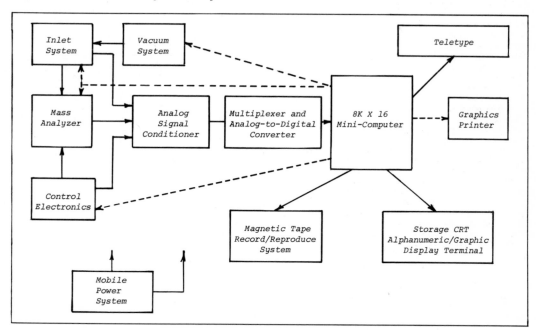

Figure 10, Block Diagram of Mass Spectrometer Computer System.

ionizer contamination, the most significant
advantage to this technique is the complete
distinction made between the gas being introduced to the ionizer and the residual
gases in the mass spectrometer vacuum system.

Data Acquisition Systems Technology

As we have seen how man has been able to extend
his own sensory perception through the development of such sophisticated instruments as mass
analyzers, it is also interesting to observe
the development of the digital computer which
is basically an extension of mans' intelligence.
The first significant development in the quest
for artificial intelligence resulted in the
abacus which was introduced over 2500 years
ago. Then, approximately 500 years later,
in attempting to devise means of telling time
more accurately such large special purpose
computers as the Stonehenge were created.
This noteable achievement of ancient as-
tronomers is believed to have been capable of
establishing calendar time to seconds of
accuracy from the moon and sun positions. A
considerable amount of time evolved until Pascal
developed the first digital adding machine
in the 1600's and George Boole discovered the
concepts of Boolean algebra in the 1800's.
Finally, in 1947, John Von Neumann established the concepts of a stored program
computer and from that point we have rapidly
evolved through the first generation computers
of the 1950's, the second generation in the
first half of the 1960's, the third generation
of the late 1960's, and the eagerly anticipated fourth generation of the 1970's.

The culmination of our aerospace research and
development activities in the moon landing of
1969 is probably more largely attributeable to
the development of computer technology--both
hardware and software--than any other single
technology. That same technology which resulted in the ultra-miniature, reliable, and
low-power components which controlled everything involved in that historic flight from
the spacecraft atmosphere to the flight path
has resulted in machines which can also make
life on earth more desireable. Today, the
mini-computer, combining second and third
generation computer technology, has become a
powerful extension of mans' intelligence which
can be economically used to solve many of our
trivial and complex problems.

Before the output of a mass analyzer can be
reliably interpreted in a meaningful manner for
control and monitoring of air pollution, the
actual data must be processed to reduce noise
and other imperfections and to enhance those
characteristics which are of interest. Although a certain amount of useful information
can be gleaned from a mass spectra with such
tools as a measuring scale and slide-rule;

the ultimate capabilities of this atmospheric
analyzer can only be achieved through rapid, precise reduction of mass spectral data via a
digital computer. Such an achievement is also
dependent on the application of advanced signal
conditioning, multiplexing, analog-to-digital
conversion, data display and storage technologies.

The output of a mass analyzer, even after it has
been appropriately conditioned in both amplitude
and frequency, is not easily interpreted since
the output indication at any specific mass number
is a function of many variables--predominantly
the quantitative composition of the input gas at
all other mass numbers and the instrument background. It is relatively simple to display,
record, and store the instrument background spectra and the spectra of interest; however, it is
much more difficult to accurately determine the
quantitative composition of the input gas sample.
This is achieved by individually calibrating the
mass analyzer with known amounts of each gas component of interest. Then, by solving the resultant partial-pressure sensitivity matrix for a
given composite spectra, a calculated quantitative contribution of each gas for the assumed
spectra can be obtained. Other variables which
can be included in the data analysis include:
accelerating voltage, magnetic field, leak rates,
temperature, system pressures, ionizing voltage,
humidity, altitude, etc. Many of these variables,
as well as other process control parameters, can
be placed under direct digital control to eliminate the inconsistencies inherent in human control.

Additional data enhancement can be achieved
through matching of the unknown mass spectra to
known mass spectra of interest. Ultimately,
the computer can be used to calculate the exact
contribution of each known source of atmospheric
pollution through the solution of a 2-dimensional
matrix involving the spectra of each known source
and the instrument partial pressure sensitivity
coefficients. This knowledge can then be used to
define a mathematical model of the atmosphere
which will enable us to predict the composition
of our atmosphere and control those sources of
importance to our national well-being. Such an
analysis is more practical when conducted at a
local level although the ultimate goal consists
of a world-wide model and air-pollution monitoring and control system. Such a system is dependent on accumulating a significant amount of
real-time data. On a local basis this is best
accomplished with a mobile atmospheric data
collection system.

Computer Hardware

A basic system of the type implied above has been
developed to prove the feasibility of this data
collection processing and display technique.
Although this system is just one of the first
steps in the evolution of the ideal instrumen-

tation system it does indicate some of the problems and capabilities inherent to this type of system. The block diagram of this system is shown in Figure 10. The dotted lines in this illustrate the expanded capabilities which have not yet been implemented and tested.

The heart of this system is a minicomputer with a 2.6 microsecond 8K x 16 bit memory. This 16 bit machine is capable of single-precision accuracy far exceeding all computational requirements and has a basic instruction repertoire of about 40 different instructions. Additionally, it has a very flexible I/O structure with up to 16 different priority levels and a direct memory access channel whereby external data can be inserted directly into memory without conscious program control.

The man-machine interface is accomplished with a conventional teletypewriter and a Storage CRT display terminal. The teletypewriter provides hard-copy output of program listings and data and, in addition, contains a keyboard, paper-tape punch and reader. Since most computer manufacturer supplied software is in paper-tape form some type of paper-tape I/O is required. The storage CRT display terminal contains a storage type CRT display and keyboard. This device is primarily used for inputting program information and displaying graphic information resulting from the data acquisition and processing functions. The graphic display area is approximately 16cm by 21cm and contains over 10^6 computer addressable points. The storage type of CRT display has several advantages over the conventional refresh type CRT display in that there is no practical limitation on the complexity of the graphic display, and it is much more reliable since there is no refreshing memory as the memory is actually in the CRT. Additionally, built-in devices are now available which allow one to obtain a hard-copy printout directly from the CRT display. The particular display terminal which was selected also contained hardware character and vector generators thereby relieving the computer from some time consumming housekeeping chores.

The permanent data storage medium was selected to be magnetic tape. There are a variety of magnetic tape record/reproduce systems available, however, placing considerable emphasis on field applicability and reliability narrowed the field significantly. The device selected is based on a unique tape cartridge which contains two endless-loop reels of 1/4" tape. The transport itself accepts two cartridges thereby resulting in the capability to read and/or write on any two reels simultaneously. The cartridge itself is strongly constructed and contains a built-in dust cover for pro-

tecting the tape. No threading is required, thereby making it easy to use with non-skilled personnel. The recording/playback scheme utilizes two independent data tracks and evaluates the flux reversals for a third vote in a triple-redundant process. Resulting bit error rates are less than one in 10^9 at a bit rate of 6000 bps. Each tape reel can contain up to 180,000 8-bit characters resulting in a system capacity of 720,000 8-bit characters. Besides using the tape system for atmospheric data recording, a tape operating system has been designed for this equipment, making it extremely valuable for program development. Since this tape system is not IBM compatible it cannot be played back into standard, larger data processing equipment without a special interface. IBM compatible tape equipment is not very well suited to this application because of the requirement for skilled operators, separate large tape storage containers, and a clean environment. Phillips cassette type tape equipment is progressing very rapidly and may also be considered for this application.

The analog multiplexer and analog-to-digital converter which was selected to sample and digitize the analog atmospheric analyzer data contains a 64 channel solid-state MOS-FET multiplexer with a sample-and-hold device for freezing fast moving data. The sampled data is then quantized to a resolution of 12 bits with a 50 kc throughput rate. Although the digital output can be transferred into the computer under program control, a feature which has been most useful in this application, is the ability to scan a group of channels under direct memory access control. In this mode, the scan is started under program control, however, the actual data transfer of each digitized sample is accomplished on a cycle stealing basis without conscious program control. As a result, the computer can be working high priority tasks while waiting for the multiplexer and converter to complete their tasks.

Before the data from the mass analyzer is input to the multiplexer, it is conditioned by a group of signal conditioning amplifiers. These amplifiers convert differential signals to single-sided ground referenced signals, amplify the level to a common ± 10 volt range, and limit the bandwidth of the channels to reduce the effects of wide-band noise. Many integrated circuit and modular amplifiers are available today which possess the low-drift, low-noise, high common-mode rejection ratio, high input impedance and low input current characteristics which are required in this application. Since the signal conditioner and multiplexer are both differential input devices, excellent ground noise rejection is achieved.

Additional digital inputs, digital outputs, and analog outputs are planned to extend the

computers capability to control the mass analyzer, vacuum and inlet systems. An additional graphic hard-copy printer is also to be included for making geographical atmospheric-
pollution contour maps.

A discussion of the hardware involved in this
system would not be complete without some comment on the power system. Since this system
was assembled in a 4-wheel drive vehicle, the
power sources were limited to internal combustion motor-generator sets. Both 3600 and 1800
RPM models are available, however, the 1800
RPM motor has a much longer time between over-
hauls. Then, considering the number of cylinders, one should observe that a single-cylinder,
4-cycle, 1800 RPM motor coupled to a 60 hz
generator will produce one power-stroke every
fourth electrical power cycle resulting in
significant variation in voltage and instantaneous frequency within the 4-cycle power frequency period. Alternately, the twin-cylinder,
4-cycle, 1800 RPM motor produces a power stroke
every other cycle of the electrical power cycle,
resulting in considerable more voltage and frequency stability. Since most motor control
systems are mechanical, the instantaneous voltage and frequency regulation are relatively
poor. As a result some form of electrical
regulation is normally required. Ferroresonant and parametric transformers are often
used for this application because of their
simplicity, good voltage regulation, insulation, and assumed efficiency. Care must be
exercised, however, in calculating efficiency
since both of these devices have a very poor
input power factor when conservatively
loaded. This is true even though their input
power factor is relatively good at rated load.
Thus, their specified efficiency of 75-85%
must be interpreted carefully. In addition,
the ferroresonant transformer will operate
satisfactorily over a larger input voltage
range although the parametric transformer has
much better high frequency noise rejection.
Both devices also exhibit output voltages which
vary approximately proportional to input frequency. As a result, it is not a simple matter
to design a satisfactory power system for a
complex and sensitive instrumentation system.
Perhaps a fuel cell, with electronic regulation
and inversion, will be the ultimate solution
if the price can be reduced to a competitive
level.

In the system which has been field tested, a
7.5KVA twin-cylinder, 1800 RPM motor-generator was used to power the major portion of
the complex electronic gear. A separate 4KVA
single-cylinder, 1800 RPM motor-generator was
used to power the vacuum pumps, resistance
heaters, and other equipment where waveform
irregularities are relatively unimportant.

Computer Software

The software which is used with this system includes the following: diagnostics, standard
assembler, editor, and debugger programs, a
variety of utility programs, and some special
applications oriented programs--Sniff and Resniff. Sniff is the primary program which is
used to request variable test parameters from the
operator, acquire mass analyzer data, sort the
mass analyzer data and discard the redundant or
erroneous data, store the resultant acceptable
data on magnetic tape, and display the mass spectra in real time on a linear set of X-Y axes on
the CRT display terminal. Resniff is the program which is used to recall data from magnetic
tape that was recorded under Sniff program control. In addition, an auxilliary program allows
the pertinent mass peak amplitudes to be listed
on a hardcopy printout.

Operating under Sniff program control, the computer first requests the following test data to
be input from the keyboard:

1. If the data is to be recorded on magnetic tape, on which reel and at what
   block location is it to be recorded.

2. The identifying run number.

3. Date.

4. The beginning and ending mass numbers
   of the desired spectra.

5. The calibration constant, or the mass
   number at which it is to be self-cali-
   brated.

6. The type of Y-axis display requested--
   high-gain linear, low-gain linear, or
   logarithmic.

7. The quantum level to be used in the test
   for acceptable data.

8. The threshold level to be used in the
   test for acceptable data.

At the completion of this data entry procedure the
computer draws the grids for the display and labels
them according to the keyed-in parameters. The
computer then halts, allowing the operator to
set-up the mass-analyzer and sense switch 0. If
sense switch 0 is set, the computer will record
the following mass spectra, otherwise it will
only be displayed and not recorded. When the
system has been properly set-up the operator in-
structs the computer to proceed and also starts
the mass spectra scan. The computer then begins
acquiring data from the mass analyzer and processing it according to the following tests:

1. Is the mass number within the specified range?

2. Is the mass number within an allowable tolerance from the previous sample?

3. Is the mass amplitude greater than the keyed in threshold?

4. Does the current mass amplitude differ from the previous mass amplitude by more than the keyed in quantum level?

If the current set of data passes all of the above tests, it is considered valid and the point is both plotted and recorded. If the data does not pass all the above tests it is considered invalid and the computer acquires additional samples until a set of data is acquired which passes all of the above tests. The point is then plotted and recorded and the procedure repeated until the run is completed. The run may be prematurely terminated at any point in the scan by setting the end sense switch--bit 15. At the end of the scan the sense switches are again read to determine which of the following options is to be executed:

1. Reinitialize the display by erasing and drawing a new set of grids before starting the next scan.

2. Overlay or superimpose the following mass spectra on the preceeding data.

3. Return to the test parameter entry procedure before starting the next run.

In a similar manner, additional mass spectra are processed or the operator may set up for a different mass range by executing option 3 above. A set of data, as used above, actually implies a group of 8 individual data samples. Three of these channels are mass analyzer amplitude output, scan voltage and magnetic field intensity. The remainder are associated with calibration, pressures, and temperatures. The complete set of 8 data words are recorded for each valid data point.

It should be noted that the mass number is calculated from the equation $m = \frac{K B^2}{V}$ where m = mass number, K = calibration constant, B = magnetic field intensity, and V = mass analyzer scan voltage. In addition, this equation is accurate only over a small mass range and additional compensation terms are included if a wide mass range is specified.

Also, a significant portion of the Sniff program is consumed in diagnostic and defensive programming procedures. These procedures are used to make it very difficult for the operator to enter erroneous data and to ensure that all data which is recorded and/or displayed is valid experimental data.

Resniff primarily allows the operator to recall mass spectra from magnetic tape according to Run number. An additional feature allows the operator to read the first run on a tape in case the exact run number is unknown. The requested mass spectra is displayed exactly as it was when actually recorded. All data necessary to recreate the original conditions are recorded and may be examined by a list instruction. Additional capabilities are built-in to this program to allow mass spectra or runs on different tapes to be overlayed for comparative purposes or a run to be repeated with the operators choice of a high-gain linear, low-gain linear, or logarithmic Y-axis display.

The auxiliary program for printing out mass peak numbers and respective amplitudes operates in two different modes--tabular and continuous. In the tabular mode the program requests the pertinent mass peaks to be input from the keyboard. Then during the scan the program determines the peak amplitude which occurred at the keyed in mass number $\pm1/2$ mass number. This peak amplitude and mass number are then stored in a buffer area until the scan is complete at which time the mass spectra data is typed out. The continuous mode operates in a similar manner except that each peak amplitude in the scan is determined, stored, and then typed out at the completion of the scan.

Summary

The preceeding discussions have shown that a solution to the atmospheric pollution problem is clearly dependent upon economical and practical means of pollution monitoring, analysis and control. In the past, pollution measurement systems were limited to fixed sites with instruments which had very limited capability, but the results of these first measurements have shown us what initial steps must be taken for effective pollution control. Today through the exploitation of aerospace technology we have shown that the mass spectrometer/computer system is undoubtedly a potential method for monitoring air pollution with accuracy and speed heretofore unavailable. The economic utilization of this system necessitates its installation in a mobile laboratory--either ground or airborne. Through the size, weight, and power reductions which have been achieved, an airborne installation is a practical technique for monitoring air pollution over a large metropolitan area at minimal cost. The resultant data after being reduced through real-time data processing techniques can be objectively displayed in a timely intelligible manner. Air pollution prediction and source identification could be ultimately achieved through efficient computer utilization. Through our discussion of the practical problems encountered in the development and field testing of a prototype system, we hope to have generated an interest in continuing the investigation of this approach to air pollution monitoring and analysis.

Bibliography

1. Bachler, W. and Reich, G.: *Some Examples of the use of the Farvitron for Plotting Rapidly Changing Processes.* Proc. 7th Symposium AVS, pp. 401-406, 1960.

2. Beynon, J. H.: *Mass Spectrometry and its Applications to Organic Chemistry,* Elsevier, New York, 1960.

3. Blauth, Erich W.: *Dynamic Mass Spectrometers.* Elsevior Publishing Company, New York, 1966.

4. Brubaker, Wilson M.: *Short Course - "Mass Spectrometry Theory and Applications."* University of California, Los Angeles, February 6-10, 1967.

5. Clark, George L.: *The Encyclopedia of Spectroscopy.* Reinhold Publishing Corporation, New York, 1960.

6. Dawson, P. H. and Whetten, N. R.: *Quadrupoles, Monopoles and Ion Traps.* Research/Development, February, 1968, pp. 46-50.

7. Dawson, P. H. and Whetten, N. R.: *Ion Storage in Three-Dimensional Rotationally Symmetric Quadrupole Fields, I. Theoretical Treatment.* G. E. Research and Development Center, Rpt. No. 67-C-287, July, 1967.

8. Dawson, P. H. and Whetten, N. R.: *Ion Storage in Three-Dimensional Rotationally Symmetric Quadrupole Fields, II. A Sensitive Mass Spectrometer.* G.E. Research and Development Center, Report No. 67-C-287, July, 1967.

9. Ettre, L. S., and Zlatkis, Albert: *The Practive of Gas Chromatography,* Inter-Science, New York, 1967.

10. Goode, H. H. and MacHol, R. E.: *System Engineering.* McGraw-Hill Company, Inc., New York, 1957.

11. Gruden, K. R.: *Varian Associates, Analytical Instrument Div. Report 52-G-001-37: Sector Instruments versus Cycloidal,* March, 1967.

12. Gunther, Karl-Georg: *A Partial Pressure Vacuum Gauge Working According to the Principle of the Electrical Mass Filter.* Vacuum, Vol. 10, no. 4, Pergamon Press, Ltd., 1960, pp. 293-309.

13. Hill, H. C.: *Introduction to Mass Spectrometry.* Sadtler Research Laboratories, Inc., Philadelphia, Penn., 1966.

14. Hudson, J. B. and Watters, R. L.: *The Monopole-A new instrument for Measuring Partial Pressures.* IEEE Trans. Instr. and Meas., Vol. lM-15, No. 3, September, 1966.

15. Husson, S. S.: *Microprogramming: Principles and Practices.* Prentice-Hall, Inc., New Jersey, 1970.

16. Inghram, Mark G. and Hayden, Richard J.: *A Handbook on Mass Spectroscopy.* Nuclear Science Series Report Number 14, National Academy of Sciences - National Research Council, Washington, D. C., 1954.

17. Jayaram, R.: *Mass Spectrometry, Theory and Applications.* Plenum Press, New York, 1963.

18. Johnson, L. R.: *System Structure in Data, Programs and Computers.* Prentice-Hall, Inc., New Jersey, 1970.

19. Kiser, Robert W.: *Introduction to Mass Spectrometry and its Applications.* Prentice-Hall, Inc., New Jersey, 1965.

20. Leck, J. H.: *Pressure Measurement in Vacuum Systems.* Chapman and Hall, Ltd.

21. Leite, R. J., Kasper, A. R., and Mason, C.J.: *Development of a Farvitron Mass Spectrometer for Space Applications.* Technical Proposal to NASA, submitted by High Altitude Engineering Laboratory, University of Michigan, March, 1967.

22. Lichtman, David: *Ultra-High Vacuum Mass Spectrometry.* Research/Development, February, 1964.

23. Luxenberg, H. R. and Kuehn, R. L. : *Display Systems Engineering.* McGraw-Hill Company Inc., New York, 1968.

24. Martin, J. T.: *Design of Real-Time Computer Systems.* Prentice-Hall, Inc., New Jersey, 1967.

25. McDowell, Charles A.: *Mass Spectrometry.* McGraw-Hill Company, Inc. New York, 1963.

26. McLafferty, F. W.: *Interpretation of Mass Spectra,* Benjamin, New York, 1967.

27. Niemann, H. B. and Kennedy, D. C.: *Omegatron Mass Spectrometer for Partial Pressure Measurements in Upper Atmosphere.* Rev. Sci. Instr., vol. 37, no. 6, June, 1966.

28. Parslow, R. D., Prowse, R. W., Green, R. E.: *Computer Graphics.* Plenum Publishing Corp., New York, 1968.

29. Reed, R. I.: *Mass Spectrometry.* Academic Press, New York, 1965.

30. Reich, R.: *The Farvitron - A New Partial Pressure Indicator without a Magnetic Field.* Proc. 7th Symposium AVS, pp. 396-400, 1960.

31. Roboz, John: *Introduction to Mass Spectrometry,* Interscience, New York, 1968.

32. Schaefer, E. J. and Nichols, M. H.: *Mass Spectrometer for Upper Air Measurement.* ARS Journal, American Rocket Society, Inc., December, 1961.

33. Shinskey, F. G.: *Process Control Systems Engineering.* McGraw-Hill Co., Inc. New York, 1957.

34. Stenhagen, E., Abrahamsson, S., and McLafferty, F. W.: *Atlas of Mass Spectral Data,* Interscience, New York, 1969.

35. Stimler, Saul: *Real-Time Data-Processing Systems.* McGraw-Hill Company, Inc., New York, 1969.

36. Van Atta, C. M.: *Vacuum Science and Engineering,* McGraw-Hill Company, Inc., New York, 1965.

37. Vedeneyev, V. I., Gurvich, L. V., Kondratyev, V. N., Medvedev, V. A., Frankevich, Y. L.: *Bond Energies Ionization Potentials and Electron Affinities,* Edward Arnold Ltd., London, 1966.

38. Wiley, W. C. and McLaren, I. H.: *Time-of-Flight Mass Spectrometer with Improved Resolution.* Rev. Sci. Instr., vol. 26, no. 12, December, 1955.

39. *1969 ASTM Standards,* Part 23, Water; Atmospheric Analysis, American Society for Testing and Materials, Philadelphia, 1969.

ROVER – AN APPLICATION OF AEROSPACE TECHNOLOGY TO GROUND TRANSPORTATION

W. A. DeTally
Senior Scientist

J. A. Benson
Avionics Manager

Douglas Aircraft Company
McDonnell Douglas Corporation
Long Beach, California

Abstract

The need for improved obstacle detection is a critical issue in providing the degree of safety required by future High Speed Ground Transportation vehicles. This paper describes a definition process used to develop a design concept for an electronics subsystem to provide obstacle detection for modern ground transportation vehicles.

By application of the methodology and understanding gained from aerospace solutions to the problem of obstacle detection, an a priori solution to the ground transportation problem is effected. A conceptual configuration for this electronics solution is evolved and has been classified as a Radiating Obstacle Viewer (ROVER).

Introduction

The Douglas Aircraft Company has been actively investigating the application of aerospace technology to social and economic problems. In so doing it has become obvious that the technology and management capabilities developed in the aerospace industry could find application in many areas within these categories. Transportation Secretary John Volpe has pointed the way for the application of aerospace technology to the transportation technology. It is his belief that future solutions of transportation problems are through aerospace technology applications and "lies in a new technology that will provide a quantum jump in both the speed and comfort of ground transportation." Douglas has recognized the challenge of providing this new technology.

The implementation of significant increases in the speed and comfort of ground transportation is severely constrained by the attendant requirement for maximization of safety. Accidents not only diminish public acceptance but also impose a heavy financial drain upon vehicle manufacturers and users. This problem has been inherent to and an inhibitor of "safe" travel throughout the evolution of all transportation systems. Developments currently underway in the field of High Speed Ground Transportation (HSGT) vehicles brings this problem into even sharper focus. Specifically, the Federal Railroad Administration (FRA) office of HSGT has identified the problem of obstacle detection as critical to providing safety in these new transportation systems.

The human eye has been an important element of obstacle detection in ground transportation systems. Adverse weather and high vehicle speeds impose such severe constraints on the eye's capability to adequately detect and resolve objects, that safe operation even in today's transportation environment has been difficult to obtain. Obstacle detection performance commensurate with future HSGT systems requires that the capability of the eye be significantly augmented. Aerospace avionics technology has developed electronic and optical devices that provide such a means of supplementing the eye. The adaptation of such devices to ground transportation vehicle utilization suggests one possible approach to improved obstacle detection for the HSGT regime. Douglas has coined the term "grionics" to identify these electronic devices used in ground transportation in the same context that avionics is applied to aerospace applications.

This paper describes the definition process used to develop a design concept for an electronics sensor subsystem to provide obstacle detection commensurate with the requirements being developed for HSGT vehicles. The end item of the definition process is a recommended subsystem configuration that has been titled ROVER – Radiating Obstacle Viewer. In the body of the paper the definition process is first summarized, to concisely present the logical progression from subsystem requirements to recommended configuration, and then each step of the process is discussed in detail.

Definition Process

The tasks utilized in the concept definition process for the obstacle detection subsystem (ROVER) are based upon a system engineering approach. The process tasks and their organizational relationship are shown in Figure 1. As illustrated in this figure, the development of the recommended configuration utilized both a sequential and cyclic progression of the following tasks:

1. Requirements definition
2. Functional organization
3. Functional design analysis
4. Configuration analysis
5. Cost-benefit analysis
6. Recommended configuration

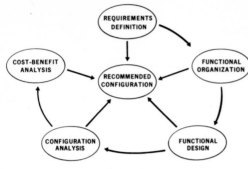

FIGURE 1. TASKS

The first and one of the more important steps in this program was the determination of a proper set of subsystem requirements. Data from the literature available on high speed ground transportation studies were used to identify applicable operational parameters and bracket their expected values for the regime within which the subsystem would be required to operate.

With this compilation of requirements it was then possible to make an initial identification of major program risk areas. This first identification of potential problem areas was of prime importance in the definition of functional task allocations for the study. An additional expansion of this stage of requirements identification was the development of general functional block schematics to provide an intrasystem control basis for detail component studies.

The next step in the process was the development of a functional organization of task assignments of the people, vehicle, and station elements with respect to subsystem requirements. Given this organization, subsystem functional designs were implemented independently but within a common network of functional factors. Generally these factors are a set of simply stated but comprehensive constraints. This step was particularly useful in isolating and identifying, within each candidate subsystem concept, the proper relationship between man and machine functions. This task also provided data for the first estimates of magnitude, complexity, and cost of the concepts under consideration.

From these functional subsystem concept definitions it was possible to identify the principal areas of technical risk. These risk areas were then emphasized in the configuration analysis considering factors of convenience, time, safety, comfort, frequency, and ecology.

The configuration analysis of the subsystem concept development process provided identification of all significant elements of the subsystem. Subsystem element definitions were then synthesized into candidate subsystems and reviewed with respect to cost and benefit. From the cost-benefit analysis results a single recommended subsystem configuration concept was established.

Task 1: Requirements Definition

A set of requirements for an obstacle detection subsystem operating in the high speed environment of ground transportation is developed in this section. Consideration of both current and predicted vehicle design and performance was addressed with particular emphasis placed on the tracked air cushion vehicle (TACV) concept. This required a review of the operational scenarios of these vehicles to compile a set of their performance characteristics. These performance parameters were then used to identify a general set of performance categories that would influence the requirements for the obstacle detection subsystem. For this study the selected categories were environment, sensor measurement capability and platform characteristics. Within each of these categories several parameters and associated values were selected as a bounding set of requirements or goals for the subsystem.

Table 1 presents the generic classification of parameters selected as applicable to obstacle detection and avoidance. With this general set of requirements established, the transport vehicle scenarios were once again reviewed to obtain representative values for the category parameters. Table 2 lists the specific values established for use in this study.

ENVIRONMENT	SENSOR	PLATFORM
RAIN	VELOCITY	VELOCITY
WATER VAPOR	SIZE	ACCELERATION
WIND	LOCATION	STABILITY
TEMPERATURE	PATH INTEGRITY	PROPULSION
TERRAIN	MATERIAL	
LIGHTING		
OBSTACLE DETECTION DISTANCE		

TABLE 1. GENERAL REQUIREMENTS

ENVIRONMENT	SENSOR	PLATFORM
RAIN: 8 MM/HOUR	VELOCITY: 0 TO 700 MPH	VELOCITY: 350 MPH
WATER VAPOR: 0.1 MM OR LESS	SIZE: 2 cm^3 MINIMUM	ACCELERATION:
WIND: 60 MPH CROSSWIND	LOCATION: WITHIN 360° (SPHERICAL)	LONGITUDINAL ±5.0g
		VERTICAL ±0.1g
TEMPERATURE:	PATH INTEGRITY*:	LATERAL ±0.1g
−40 TO +125°F OPERATING	VERTICAL ACCEL. < 0.01 grms	STABILITY:
−60 TO +150°F NON-OPERATING	LATERAL ACCEL. < 0.007 grms	ROLL ANGLE ±11 DEGREES
TERRAIN: CONTINENTAL U.S.A.	MATERIAL:	PITCH ANGLE ± 3 DEGREES
LIGHTING: FULL SUN TO QUARTER MOON	ANIMAL OBJECTS	YAW ANGLE 0.5 DEGREES
OBSTACLE DETECTION DISTANCE:	MINERAL OBJECTS	PROPULSION: LIM
3 MILES OR GREATER**	VEGETABLE OBJECTS	

*INDICATES ACCELERATIONS RESULTING FROM TRACK DISCONTINUITIES
**DEPENDENT UPON TRANSPORT VEHICLE DECELERATION CAPABILITY

TABLE 2. ROVER REQUIREMENTS

Initially the philosophy was to develop a design concept that would comply with all of the requirements. However, as the full set of requirements was defined it was apparent that some of the values selected placed conflicting requirements on ROVER. In order to best resolve these conflicts it was necessary to plan for multisensors with large dynamic ranges and detection capability under high acceleration and velocity conditions.

Within the vehicles studied the acceleration and deceleration capabilities varied dependent upon specific vehicle configurations. The vehicle weight, frontal area, braking system, and propulsion system significantly affect the stopping distance and time parameters. In order to account for stopping times of several minutes and stopping distances of several miles, it is required that obstacle detection be accomplished when the obstacle is many miles from the transport vehicle. For the types of TACV considered during the study, 3 miles is representative of the maximum distance difference required between the transport vehicle and the obstacle at time of detection.

The primary requirement for ROVER is to prevent transport vehicle collision with obstacles along the pathway. The speed regime of the transport vehicles coupled with the range performance of sensors in this near ground operating environment dictate that ROVER must in effect extend the range of the sensors in order to provide the 3-mile detection distance difference. This requires that ROVER be placed far enough ahead of the transport vehicle to effect obstacle detection within the time constraint of safe deceleration of the transport vehicle. Therefore, ROVER will move relative to the transport vehicle.

The high speed operation required for compatibility with the transport vehicle requires that ROVER can decelerate at 5g's to prevent its collision with small objects detected at short range. This requirement is also imposed by the need to prevent collisions with other transport vehicles, and with ROVERS since closing speeds of 700 mph are attained in "head-on" conditions. Utilization of the same track as the transport vehicle is a desirable goal. This will reduce the requirements for directional control of ROVER, permit utilization of the track power by ROVER and facilitate the implementation of the track integrity measurement mode of ROVER.

To prove fully effective, ROVER must be able to sense objects of any composition and under a variety of constraints including day and night lighting conditions and all weather conditions. To account for terrain elevation changes, ROVER requires a capability to move vertically. Sensing must also be accomplished through a full 360° in azimuth to provide detection of obstacles that may interdict the pathway between ROVER and the transport vehicle.

Subsequent to the definition of these particular requirements the subsystem critical design area was identified. By proper focus from the "desired" to the "required" it was possible to pinpoint the critical design area for the surveillance functional group, i.e., the detection of obstacles under obscured viewing situations. Within the ROVER subsystem, this critical design area is represented by the sensor dynamic range. The effects of animal, mineral, and vegetable detection and 700 mph closing rates during detection have proven to be the coup de grace design items.

Task 2: Functional Organization

The functional organization for obstacle detection and avoidance includes the sensor subsystem, the transport vehicle, the operator, and the supporting transportation network. Major functions have been assigned to each of these parts of the organization. Such decisions as which functional groups would be

assigned to ROVER and which to other subsystems and what sensor functional class best fits the tasks assigned to ROVER had to be completed. As a natural result of the critical design identification a functional description of the people and equipment, and their organization with respect to one another was evolved. All of the parts of the organization work as a unit toward the stimulus-response decisions and actions of the operator. Figure 2 illustrates this functional organization. The operator exercises sensor control and processing decisions, and may be located on board the vehicle, at control stations, at terminal stations, at wayside stations or at some central traffic control station. He initiates and deactivates ROVER, controls the operational modes, monitors the status of ROVER, controls the transport vehicle motion and exercises decisions used on ROVER data.

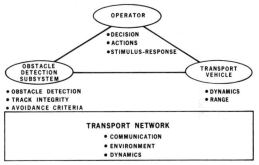

FIGURE 2. FUNCTIONAL ORGANIZATION

The sensor subsystem, as its name implies, views the objects within the path of the vehicle and is, in fact, the prime element of ROVER. Potentially it includes electromagnetic-optical devices across a wide range of the spectrum. The ROVER platform is the vehicle that houses the ROVER sensor and associated grionics. It is dynamic relative to the transport vehicle and self-stabilizing. The supporting member that completes organization is the transport network. Since the transport networks considered for ROVER include large variations of concepts, it was mandatory that significant independence exist between the network functional definitions and the other components of the functional organization. This independence was emphasized to allow development in depth of the operator, sensor and platform components. The dynamics, environment, and communication peculiarities of the network were defined in a normalized fashion, thereby representing the conglomerate of existing and future networks.

The performance of the total functional organization is dependent on the interrelationship of all vehicles, stations, and people for the particular network, their dynamics and environment. Inspection of the surveillance problem while attempting to account for the transport network would be too difficult, so the design solution has been approached with specific emphasis on the sensor-platform-operator triad keeping the transport network as the general design modifier.

Task 3: Functional Design

Four categories of configurations have been established for the ROVER subsystem candidates. These are remote fixed, remote mobile, associated fixed, and associated mobile. Within each of these categories both continuous and discrete operating systems have been considered. It is within the context of these categories that potential risks were investigated, and as more insight was obtained into the potential concepts for ROVER the critical areas for configuration evaluation were selected. This task was in essence a refinement of the critical area identification accomplished during the functional organization task.

For this study a method was implemented by which each candidate configuration for the ROVER subsystem could be analyzed independently but within the common constraints developed during the requirements definition and functional organization determinations. A standardized categoric grouping of simple but comprehensive set of identifiers was sought. Configuration elements were reviewed for signal flow and interface identification. The goal was to obtain a definitive division of these candidates into a standard set of functions. As the particulars of each subsystem element became more and more familiar, the grouping of functions became more and more defined. Furthermore, the number of functional groupings decreased as their definitions were expanded. Gradually four factors became definitive of the functional groupings inclusive of all subsystems. These factors were the forcing function (i.e., the environment), the communication or interface linkage, the sensing, and the display. While these factors are not unique to this study they were the key to further insight into the integration and design of the subsystem. Figure 3 presents an example of how the four factors were applied to a candidate configuration utilizing a radar sensor subsystem concept for ROVER.

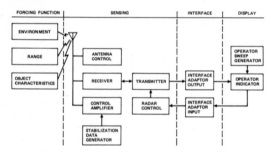

FIGURE 3. FUNCTIONAL DESIGN

For all obstacle detection candidate configurations some forcing functions are dependent while others are independent of the particular configuration. Generally the terrain and weather environment varies independently of the transport network but is bounded by the geographical situation. The dynamics associated with the particular transport vehicle and the ROVER platform are examples of responses to environmental sources that are dependent on the particular ROVER subsystem.

The choice of the sensing element for ROVER required examination of a wide variety of devices. Table 3 presents those elements initially considered as potential sensors. The electromagnetic frequencies included by these sensors are 10^{-1} Hz to 10^7 GHz. Each sensor has been analyzed with reference to the quality of detection of animal, mineral, and vegetable objects with respect to several environmental factors.

Considerations for communication interfaces for ROVER included those with stations and those with the transport vehicle. In both cases radio transmission is considered the optimum candidate since telemetry and broadcast receive packages currently in use in many aerospace programs could be readily adapted to ROVER. Even though the interface distance is expected to be only 0 to 3 miles, line of sight transmission is considered unlikely due to the interference from urban and terrestrial objects within the operating environment. Interface data will include all display, decision, and some control parameters since the ROVER utilization concept dictates that

CAPACITANCE	RADAR
ELECTROMAGNETIC	INFRARED
ELECTROSTATIC	RADIOMETRY
SEISMIC	LASER
RADIO FREQUENCY	VISUAL
ULTRASONIC	PHOTO-ELECTRIC
TELEVISION	PRESSURE DIFFERENTIAL

TABLE 3. ROVER SENSOR ELEMENT CATEGORIES

these functions would be accomplished somewhere other than on board the ROVER.

Historically the problem of obstacle detection and avoidance in the transportation environment has been solved by human observation of objects, identification of the objects as obstacles, stopping of the vehicle and removal of the obstacle. This process has proven cumbersome even in yesterday's environment. For the high speed systems planned for the future this historical concept of obstacle detection and avoidance appears unrealistic from the probable impact on scheduling, support and service. While detection of obstacles is not technically difficult without modifiers, it does become a problem of the first magnitude when obscured viewing, long ranges and high speeds are considered. When avoidance is coupled with detection the risk of meeting this total objective becomes high. At the high speeds and mass values expected for future transport vehicles it will be difficult to accomplish timely removal of obstacles and well near impossible to attempt avoidance.

During the configuration analysis both obstacle detection and obstacle avoidance were considered. The subsystem concepts for ROVER were optimized to accomplish detection and aid in the process of avoidance.

Task 4: Configuration Analysis

The configuration analysis was conducted with respect to optimizing ROVER for assistance to vehicle response upon obstacle detection. The primary objective of ROVER is detection but the primary motivation to the design definition has been vehicle response to detection, the design function with the highest technical risk. The "remote fixed" and "remote mobile" configuration categories refer to those configurations "remote" to either the vehicles or stations and either "fixed" or "mobile" with respect to the vehicles or stations. The "associated fixed" and "associated mobile" analogously refer to those configurations "associated" with either the vehicles or the stations and either "fixed" or "mobile" with respect to the vehicles or stations.

For remote fixed configurations, fences, beacons, and Exospace satellites were considered. For remote mobile both primary and secondary tracked devices, and airborne devices (both Aerospace and Exospace) were investigated, while track embedded, vehicle mounted and station positioned configurations were considered for the associated fixed category. While each of these configurations has some qualities which tend to optimize vehicle response to detection it was found that the fourth category, associated mobile, was most appropriate for the "response-to-detection" goal. This category was used to establish the baseline configuration for ROVER.

The sensor, being the detecting device, is the crucial element of the ROVER equipment. Several programs for the application of sensors to obstacle detection in the ground transportation environment are currently in development. Both capability and probable cost will be established during their design development. The approach being investigated for utilization of these sensors has been for the associated fixed category defined in this study. Douglas is studying the potential for utilization of these sensors on ROVER. One sensor, an optical laser being developed by RCA, can identify a 1-inch-diameter object from a distance of 200 feet. Another sensor utilizing electrostatic sensing properties has been studied by General Applied Science Laboratories. The goal for object detection size for these sensors is on the order of 2 cm³. Both sensors rely on the reflecting and scattering properties of obstacles placed in the path of the radiated energy and as such are wayside surveillance sensors. A comparison of these and other sensors illustrates the difficulty of obtaining a sensor that satisfactorily detects under all conditions. Table 4 presents some sensor classes and makes a comparison of their quality of detection under several conditions. Figure 4 presents the relative detection capability for some of the sensors being considered for ROVER.

In consideration of the baseline subsystem for ROVER such questions as the following were answered:

1. What constitutes adequate performance in terms of the variety of transport networks?

2. If two or more subsystems appear capable of performing detection, what measures are needed to determine which subsystem will better meet detection requirements?

3. How shall cost and benefit factors associated with subsystem procurement be computed in order to maintain a like basis for comparison?

4. What are the selected baseline configuration sensitivities to detection measurement, to detail design, and to component availability?

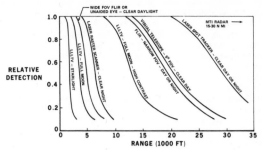

FIGURE 4. SENSOR PERFORMANCE COMPARISON

The specific benefit parameters evaluated included:

1. Detection capability

2. Response

3. Reliability

4. Availability

5. Maintainability

Task 5: Cost-Benefit Analysis

Subsequent to the determination of requirements, allocation of functions, and configuration evaluations, the above indicated parameters were analyzed according to a cost-benefit philosophy. As stated above, response-to-detection must be optimized. The subsystems of the associated-mobile category optimize response by minimizing time of detection and maximizing communication with the transport vehicle. In consideration of each of the other categories several configurations were investigated. Fences, including everything from simple wire mesh to electrified surface tunnels were analyzed. While the benefit of fences, especially surface tunnels, is significant from

SENSOR	OBJECT			ENVIRONMENT					
	ANIMAL (MAN)	VEGETABLE (LOG)	MINERAL (TRUCK)	RAIN	FOG	TERRAIN	DAY	NIGHT	COMMENTS
DOPPLER RADAR	N/A	N/A	30,000 FT	POOR	FAIR	BAD	GOOD	GOOD	ONLY AGAINST MOVING OBJECTS
ULTRASONICS	2,000 FT	1,000 FT	5,000 FT	FAIR	GOOD	BAD	GOOD	GOOD	
LLLTV	3,000 FT	2,000 FT	9,000 FT	BAD	BAD	BAD	GOOD	FAIR	
SEARCH RADAR (MTI)	N/A	N/A	15-30 N MI	POOR	FAIR	BAD	GOOD	GOOD	
SEISMIC SENSOR	300 FT	N/A	1,500 FT	FAIR	GOOD	GOOD	GOOD	GOOD	GROUND INSTALLATION (MOVING TARGET)
LASER (SPOT TRACKER)	4,000 FT	3,000 FT	22,000 FT	FAIR	BAD	BAD	GOOD	GOOD	
INFRARED (FLIR)	4,000 FT	1,000 FT	12,000 FT	FAIR	FAIR	BAD	GOOD	GOOD	
MAGNETIC	N/A	N/A	300 FT	GOOD	GOOD	GOOD	GOOD	GOOD	GROUND INSTALLATION (METALLIC TARGET)
RADIOMETER	600 FT	1,000 FT	1,000 FT	GOOD	GOOD	BAD	GOOD	GOOD	
PHOTO-ELECTRIC	300 FT	300 FT	300 FT	POOR	BAD	BAD	GOOD	GOOD	
ELECTROSTATIC	0 FT	0 FT	0 FT	GOOD	GOOD	GOOD	GOOD	GOOD	GROUND INSTALLATION (REQUIRED CONTACT)
PRESSURE SENSOR	0 FT	0 FT	0 FT	GOOD	GOOD	GOOD	GOOD	GOOD	GROUND INSTALLATION (REQUIRED CONTACT)
CAPACITANCE	100 FT	100 FT	200 FT	GOOD	GOOD	GOOD	GOOD	GOOD	

N/A — USE OF SENSOR NOT CONSIDERED APPLICABLE

TABLE 4. RELATIVE DETECTION CAPABILITY

the standpoint of restricting obstacles from vehicle pathways, the cost of installation and maintenance of such fences is prohibitively high compared to other subsystem approaches. Centrally located beacons or beacons periodically placed along the path provide excellent detection benefit but again are significantly costly. This configuration could be considered more attractive if the function of surveillance were a part of some centralized transportation command and control network. This configuration is being further investigated by Douglas. The use of Exospace satellites for the complete obstacle detection function is both technically beyond the state of the art and presents enormous costs of acquisition and operation. Its attractiveness is in coverage per subsystem and as such has the highest probability of becoming the configuration of the future.

Remote-mobile configurations exemplified by random running track detectors can be configured for use on the primary track or on secondary tracks constructed separate from the primary tracks. Such detection subsystems would require costs equivalent to ROVER but would lack the benefit of individual vehicle association. If a transportation system of vehicle control were tied into this type of detection subsystem, some higher level of benefit results. Such a configuration also demands costs associated with the control system far greater than ROVER. Remote mobile airborne devices include both aircraft and spacecraft. While detection benefit is good and coverage is widespread and continuous, acquisition and operational costs are currently prohibitive.

Track embedded configurations tend to be low cost subsystems on a per unit basis but are such that many units are required for continuous path coverage. Therefore, the cost of continuous detection is significant. In addition, a larger degree of processing and control would be required as compared to the ROVER configuration further increasing the configuration costs. Vehicle mounted detection systems would be the most beneficial for obstacle detection and could be made least costly. Unfortunately, the high speed requirement for the transport vehicles dictates an obstacle sensing capability that extends to three or four miles ahead of the transport vehicle location. This requirement coupled with the weather constraints and terrain irregularities prohibits mounting the subsystem detection sensor on the vehicle. In considering station fixed configurations the problem of small object detection dictates multiple stations. As such the cost of this configuration would be significantly more than ROVER.

Several parameters were identified as to their influence on the cost of ROVER. These parameters are presented in Table 5. Of the listed parameters, detection range and velocity environment are among the more influential parameters. Figures 5 and 6 present the variation of cost with variation of range and velocity

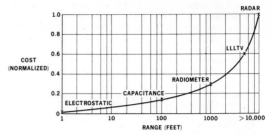

FIGURE 5. COST PER SUBSYSTEM – RANGE

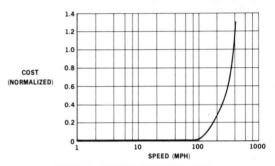

FIGURE 6. COST PER SUBSYSTEM – SPEED

respectively. Range variation is associated with the type sensor utilized. As such, particular costs can be normalized using the most expensive sensor as the norm. Miniaturized electrostatic sensors would represent the lowest cost per unit sensor. In Figure 6 the cost sensitivity to speeds beyond 100 mph is acute and can be approximated by a cubic function. As such, ROVER vehicle speeds of 350 mph or less seem to be reasonably cost-beneficial, whereas speeds in excess of 350 mph should be avoided to remain cost-beneficial.

Since the other parameters considered for the cost-benefit analysis are dependent on the dynamic range and closing velocity parameters, Figures 5 and 6 can be considered representative of all other parameters.

Task 6: Recommended Subsystem Configuration

This paper thus far has dealt with a process used in the definition and justification of functional and performance requirements. To develop a description of how ROVER would perform in its intended environment, it was necessary to review the foregoing analysis in the context of a total functional subsystem. This task consisted primarily of an element-by-element examination to determine the primary characteristics of ROVER.

Within the scope of this paper it is not practical to display the detail system schematics and information flow diagrams developed during the definition process. However, the significant features of ROVER as developed from the synthesis of the configuration studies are reviewed for correlation to the established obstacle detection tasks.

The ROVER subsystem is utilized in conjunction with a primary transport vehicle. In its initial concept ROVER is specifically applied to tracked high speed ground transportation vehicles. While physically independent of the primary vehicle, it remains associated to the vehicle at all times. Information flow between ROVER and the primary vehicle is carried over a short

•	DETECTION RANGE
•	VELOCITY
•	DATA QUANTITY
•	STATION FREQUENCY
•	DETECTION RESOLUTION
•	PROPULSION
•	OBSTACLE SIZE

TABLE 5. ROVER COST PARAMETERS

range VHF radio linkage. ROVER will precede the transport vehicle along the track by a distance proportional to the stopping distance associated with the speed of the transport vehicle plus a fixed safety factor. The ROVER will be self-stabilized and will have the capability to move vertically on its support to compensate for moderate changes in terrain height. This concept for ROVER is pictorially presented in Figure 7.

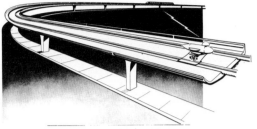

FIGURE 7. ROVER

The ROVER subsystem elements required for successful performance of the obstacle detection and surveillance function, as shown in Figure 8, include all of the necessary sensing, control, and propulsion equipment. The interfacing functions to integrate ROVER with the environment and associated transport vehicle are also identified.

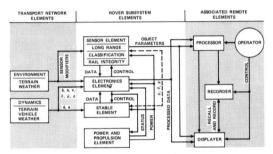

FIGURE 8. ROVER BLOCK DIAGRAM

Successful performance of the ROVER subsystem functions is obviously dependent upon integration of these elements. The stable element is conceived as an element possessing the characteristics and capabilities of a gyro stabilized platform. Its class of performance will be commensurate with the pointing accuracies of the sensors and the stabilization of ROVER in its movement over the ground track.

The electronics element provides the control and reporting functions within the ROVER subsystem. As such, it contains the electronic circuitry necessary to implement functions associated with the velocity command requirements of ROVER, the sensors mode of operation, and the correction factors for the stable element and then initiates the proper commands to these elements. Further, it performs monitoring of the status of the elements and activates communication of this information as well as portions of the sensed information not directly relayed by the sensors.

In the application of ROVER to a tracked high speed transport vehicle, the propulsion element is considered to be a low power linear induction motor driving the ROVER through an attachment to the track. If ROVER is applied to a non-tracked vehicle, the propulsion unit becomes more complex if the source of energy as well as the propulsive unit must be incorporated into the subsystem. In this type of application the electronics element also increases in complexity, as it must control these additional propulsion elements as well as provide guidance and control signals for positioning of ROVER over the desired roadway in both height and direction.

The sensor element for ROVER will require high resolution, track-while-scan and weather penetration characteristics. This may require the utilization of several sensors operating in different frequency bands to provide all functions simultaneously. The long range detection function of the sensor should penetrate through all weather and lighting conditions for up to 3 miles and have an obstacle resolution of 25 square feet. In this operating mode the sensor should also be able to track detected obstacles while simultaneously scanning through 360°. The need to provide enough specific information on detected obstacles to permit action decisions for obstacle removal or avoidance dictates different sensor performance than for the long range detection function. In addition, track integrity sensing must also be performed.

These considerations coupled with the operating speed regime strongly suggest that a single sensor would not be capable of providing realtime data for all functions even if capable of milti-mode operations. Therefore, the initial concept of ROVER includes three separate sensors:

1. Long range obstacle detector and 360° scanner sensor

2. Obstacle classification sensor

3. Track integrity sensor.

It is anticipated that a combination of information from the three sensor elements will be utilized in the actual functions of obstacle classification.

The associated elements within the primary transport vehicle are not necessarily unique to the definition of ROVER. They provide, as shown in Figure 8, the facility for utilization of the information developed in the ROVER and are similar to the control and display devices utilized in many existing aerospace and geospace systems. The display unit would be a multi-mode storage CRT capable of displaying both processed alphanumeric and raw sensor data. With this device, the operator, through control of the computer and recorder, can correlate obstacle data for action decisions. He will also be able to interrogate ROVER directly or command specific modes of operation.

Summary

System analysis and methodologies have been used in a relatively small number of areas. Virtually all of these have been in connection with problems of national defense. Douglas is practicing the concept that system analysis will find even wider application in the planning and solution of non-defense problems. Some of these problems are inherent in transportation. The ROVER study emphasizes the application of grionics to the surveillance function in a systematic manner and with respect to the total problem of portal to portal high speed mass ground transportation.

The preceding configuration determination process clearly formulates a problem-solution relationship and is in essence the definition phase in a three-phased systems analysis approach. The three phases being pursued by Douglas are identified as definition, research and analysis, and design and validation. Further investigation of the surveillance function is proceeding. The current analysis is of the baseline configuration with respect to the requirements of various transport vehicles. Hardware implementation is being emphasized.

Prior to ROVER, the investigation of grionics has been random and mainly one of requirement definition. With the beginning of the ROVER study, Douglas has focused on a problem that has received too little emphasis – the role of grionics in ground transportation. Design of grionics for ground transportation systems is not an insignificant task. To so state is to present a premature solution.

The definition activities presented herein have encompassed data collection, requirements analysis, function analysis, configuration analysis and the preliminary definition of ROVER. An important step in these activities was that of detail subsystem functional analysis. This activity provided detail insight into subsystem. operations, implementation risks, and bounded all design decisions. The specific trade-off studies conducted on a cost-benefit philosophy for high risk areas provided initial substantiation that led to the preliminary recommended configuration. While it is unlikely that ROVER will reduce the overall geospace transportation system complexity, it is nonetheless an important design concept. Unique compared to previous approaches of obscured viewing and obstacle detection, ROVER offers several significant advantages. For example, given vehicles currently under development, ROVER can be built from existing aerospace avionics. Further, since ROVER would utilize a building block component approach, modifications for new transport vehicles could easily be implemented. Being small in size, weight, and power, ROVER is easily powered and propelled, and can most likely share in the transport vehicle generation of these items.

Acknowledgement ──────── It was not possible to conduct the type of definition program described in this paper without the aid and cooperation of a great many people. In this respect the authors express their sincere appreciation and gratitude for the support supplied by the many Department of Transportation personnel and our fellow engineers and scientists of the Military Systems Engineering department of Douglas Aircraft Company.

Bibliography

1. *Defining Transportation Requirements*, ASME Transportation Engineering Conference, 1968 Proceedings.

2. *Transportation, The Pressure for Balance*, Design News, February 17, 1969.

3. *Urban Mass Rapid Transit, 1970 – 1980*, by D.L. Henry, N.E. Jones, C.H. Parmelee, L.N. Thunstrom, McDonnell Aircraft Corporation.

4. *Transportation Research at Douglas*, by Corporate Planning, Douglas Aircraft Company of McDonnell Douglas Corporation.

5. *Emerging Patterns of Urban Growth and Travel*, by Alexander Ganz, M.I.T. Project Transport, January, 1968.

6. *The Aerotrain System*, by Francois L. Giraud, Societe Bertin and Cie, 1968.

7. *The Glideway System*, from M.I.T., M.I.T. Report No. 6.

8. *The Guideway System for Automated Transportation*, by D.M. Baumann, M.I.T., 20 January 1969.

9. *Study in New Systems of Urban Transportation*, M.A. Sullcin, et al., Los Angeles Division of North American Rockwell Corp., 5 January 1968.

10. *Tracked Air Cushion Research Vehicle*, Grumman Aircraft Engineering, March 1969.

11. *Tracked Air Cushion Research Vehicle Preliminary Design Study Reports*, General Electric Co., 17 March 1969.

12. *Air Transport, Rapid Transit, and High Speed Rail System for Future Taiwan Transportation*, by Dr. Lewis Li-Tang Au, Douglas Aircraft Company, July 1970.

AEROSPACE-DEVELOPED ENTROPY CORRELATION
APPLIED IN EVALUATING COMBUSTOR-INCINERATOR DESIGN

C. J. HARRIS, STAFF SCIENTIST
GENERAL ELECTRIC COMPANY
VALLEY FORGE, PA.

ABSTRACT

A better understanding of the fundamental processes in the combustion of waste and fossil fuels should lead to better control of the effluent from such combustors and a subsequent reduction in air pollution. At present, simple analyses are not available which can be readily used in fully characterizing the gases produced for the wide spectrum of combustors in use; much less analyses for predicting particulate production. The extensive chemical kinetic analytical techniques developed in earlier aerospace studies should be directly applicable in aiding in specifying some of the processes controlling the gaseous species production in combustors of current interest. One such analytical technique is the entropy correlation of the chemical species composition for nonequilibrium expanding air flows. This paper discusses the application of this analytical approach to combustor problems as they relate to air pollution. In particular it looks at the production of NO and indicates some pertinent criteria to be kept in mind in future combustor design geared to reduce NO production to a minimum.

I. INTRODUCTION

The phenomena associated with the expansion of high temperature-high pressure air from a reservoir or plenum have been studied by several authors. Early analytical work on flow expansions and nonequilibrium effects was carried out by Bray (1)(2) on monoatomic gases. Lordi and Mates (3) did a detailed numerical analysis-computer program study on high enthalpy air flows with nonequilibrium effects present. Harris (4) utilized the results of Reference 3 and similar computer calculations by Boyer (5) and Eschenroeder et al (6) to show that the nonequilibrium chemical composition in the expanding nozzle air flow could be readily correlated as a function of plenum or reservoir entropy. Harris et al (7) also showed that a similar "entropy correlation" was valid for specifying the nonequilibrium electron concentration values in an expanding air flow and in specifying the chemical species concentrations in the shock layer flow about a slender blunt conical body (8). Both Harney (9) and Ring and Johnson (10) have made extensions to the entropy correlation concept offered in References 4 and 11.

More recently Reddy and Daum (12) used a similar solutions analytical approach to evaluate nonequilibrium nozzle flows and again found that entropy was the dominate correlating parameter.

II. DISCUSSION

For high temperature-high pressure air expanding from a chamber, such as the plenum with the converging-diverging nozzle in Fig. 1, it was found that the flow soon "freezes" (8)(11), has a nonequilibrium chemical composition, and over a very wide range of plenum steady state conditions this frozen nonequilibrium composition can be correlated based on the corresponding equilibrium steady state entropy value (S/R) in the plenum. This entropy correlation for air chemical species concentrations is also shown in Fig. 1. The corresponding steady-state equilibrium temperature, pressure, and enthalpy values in the plenum are tabulated at the top of Fig. 1. These are for the steady state conditions at which the numerical calculations (3)(5)(6) were made. And it is upon these calculations that the correlation is based. This entropy correlation of the chemical species concentrations also appears to be valid over a nozzle physical scale range of approximately 5, i.e. ℓ = 1 cm to 4.74 cm, where ℓ is as defined in Reference 3, based on $A/A* = 1.0 + (\frac{x}{\ell})^2$.

Fig. 1 shows one species that is produced in the air system that is of particular interest in the photochemical smog - air pollution problem (13). That is NO or NO_x. The prime chemical reactions for NO production used in the analyses upon which the entropy correlation is based are,

$$N_2 + O \rightleftharpoons N + NO \qquad (1)$$

$$N + O_2 \rightleftharpoons NO + O \qquad (2)$$

The slower $N_2 + O_2 \rightleftharpoons 2$ NO reaction is considered, but as in the work of Eyzat and Guibert (14), Lavoie et al (15), and others, this reaction is felt to play a minor role in NO production. When water vapor is present an additional reaction and an extremely rapid reaction is,

$$N + OH \rightleftharpoons H + NO \qquad (3)$$

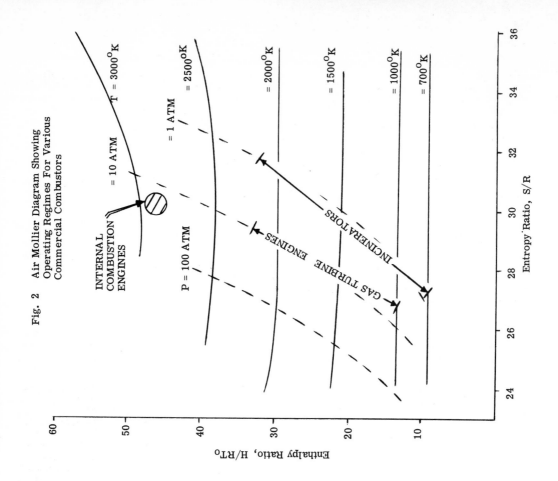

Fig. 2 Air Mollier Diagram Showing
Operating Regimes For Various
Commercial Combustors

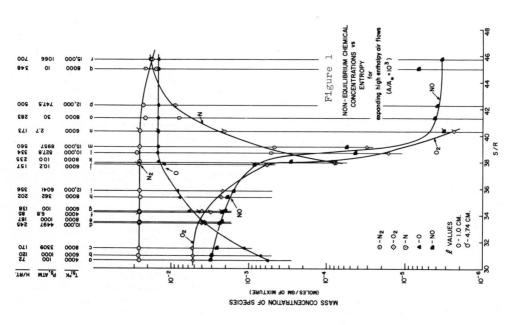

And recently in work reported by Johnson and Hilt (16), Fenimore points out the atomic nitrogen producing reaction in combustors,

$$CH + N_2 \rightleftharpoons N + HCN \qquad (4)$$

This reaction produces NO by way of reaction 3 above. This combination or chain leads to the formation in a combustor of what Fenimore (17) calls "prompt NO".

For a pure air system the entropy correlation of Fig. 1 readily shows that for plenum operation at S/R values below 38 to 30 there is a high concentration of NO produced. Further, at S/R values between 33 and the previous stated value of 38 there are both large concentrations of NO and O atoms, but very little N atoms. Above an S/R value of 38 the NO concentration rapidly diminishes, but the O atom and N atom concentrations are quite high.

The entropy correlation of Fig. 1 may be used almost directly in those combustors where air is the predominant compound heated and very little of any other chemical species, such as CH radicals, are introduced in the process. However, as shown in Fig. 2, most present day combustors do not operate in the thermodynamic regime where the entropy correlation has been fully substantiated (4)(10)(11). For the group of commercial combustors shown in Fig. 2, operation takes place in the entropy ratio, S/R, regime from 26 to 32. The municipal incinerators operate at an ambient peak pressure of close to 1 ATM and at maximum steady state temperatures up to 2000°K. Gas turbines operate at steady state maximum pressures of 7 to 10 ATM and in the temperature range from 1000° to 2200°K. The internal combustion engine operates at the highest pressure, i. e. up to 20 ATM and at maximum steady state temperatures of 2700°K.

No additional numerical calculations were carried out in this particular study on combustor-incinerator design. The previous work (Fig. 1) however does suggest a judicious extrapolation of the previous numerical results for entropy ratio, S/R, values less than 30. This extrapolation is offered in Fig. 3. These extrapolated entropy correlation results may be used to imply what type of effluent or gaseous species production may be expected from the commercial combustors listed in Fig. 2. Again, the initial assumption made is that only high temperature air is being exhausted. For nitrogen and nitrogen compounds Bartok et al (18) show that the fuel contributed nitrogen only dominates at the lowest portion of the temperature operating regime for combustors. The extrapolated results (Fig. 3) show that the entropy ratio regime from 26 to 32 is the regime of max. NO production. There is some O atom production, but negligible N atom production. To decrease the NO production the combustor maximum steady state entropy ratio value must be decreased (<20)

or increased (>38). Fig. 2 shows that to accomplish this best with the existing commercial combustors requires changing the steady state operating pressure rather than the temperature. But, to decrease the entropy ratio to values close to S/R ~20 will require orders of magnitude increases in pressure and this seems highly impractical. Increasing the entropy ratio towards an S/R value of 38 or greater means a substantial reduction in the combustor maximum steady state pressure. This may be possible and practical, but calls for radically new combustor engineering design. Whereas, operation at low S/R values (~20), if possible, essentially solves the problem of NO production and eliminates the presence of other dissociated air species, operation at S/R ~38 introduces other problems.

Analytically, this results in low NO concentrations in the combustor exhaust. However, there will be a very large concentration of O atoms and N atoms. These may react downstream in the expanding flow system to form NO, particularly by way of the atomic oxygen reaction with the molecular nitrogen, i. e. Reaction 1. Therefore, for a system operating at these high plenum S/R values it may be desirable to develop an overall combustor-exhaust system design that allows either or both the atomic oxygen or nitrogen to be promptly trapped or collected immediately downstream of the combustor. The presence of large concentrations of atomic nitrogen further suggest that while downstream "quenching" (18) of the flow with cool air may lower the stream temperature, it may also encourage Reaction 2 to take place to an undesired degree. The entropy correlation when used, as here, to merely evaluate the pure air case is very helpful in quickly revealing the complexity of problems that will exist when operating combustors at various S/R values.

The remainder of this paper speculates on how the entropy correlation might be further applied as a sound analytical tool for giving quick performance estimates on combustor performance where gaseous species in addition to those of air are produced.

As in the aerospace air case, the chemical constituents of the fuel or waste oxidized in the combustor should be identified first. The equilibrium chemistry for these chemical constituents would then be defined and used over a range of thermodynamic conditions to construct a Mollier Diagram (19) for the resulting gaseous products. Next, the non-equilibrium chemistry for these gaseous products would be modeled and where necessary reaction rates acquired from existing work or by experimentation (20)(21). As in the pure air case, a limited number of high speed computer (3)(22) solutions would be carried out for the chemical kinetic system over a range of entropy, S/R, values in order to determine if the chemical species concentrations correlate

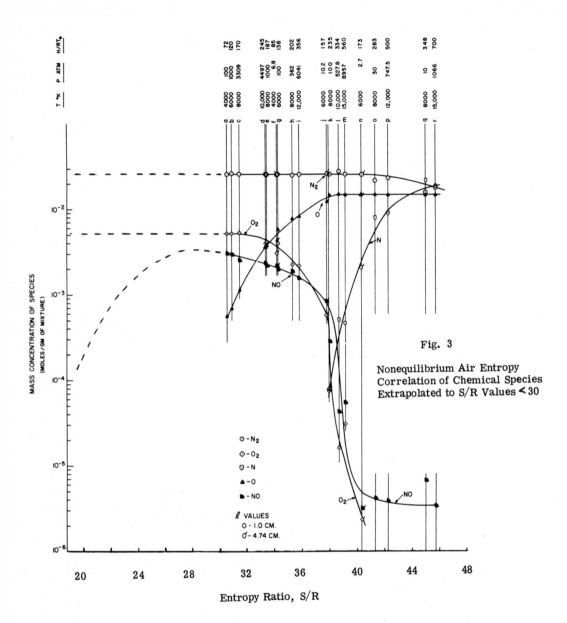

Fig. 3

Nonequilibrium Air Entropy
Correlation of Chemical Species
Extrapolated to S/R Values < 30

as a function of combustor or reservoir entropy. A hypothetical result is offered in Fig. 4. From such a correlation one can attempt to pick a combustor equilibrium steady state entropy value that will lead to the minimum production of all toxic gaseous species. Having chosen that S/R value, it is next required to pick from the spectrum of possible combustor operating conditions, as specified on the corresponding Mollier Diagram (Fig. 5), those which are practical as regards the present and future state-of-the-engineering art for combustors. From this analysis rather well defined boundary conditions are established which aid in the design of the optimum combustor, the expanding flow section, and any downstream flow processing devices (Fig. 6) for both reducing particle effluent and preventing the combining of otherwise non-toxic single gaseous components into toxic compounds.

SUMMARY

In the fashion discussed above, both for the pure air case and for the hypothetical case with other toxic and non-toxic gaseous species produced, "the Entropy Correlation" may be used to pre-design a complete combustor system so as to optimize its operation by reducing gaseous pollutant production in the first stage (Fig. 6), rather than undertaking inadequate preventive measures in the final effluent stage. The extrapolation to S/R values < 30 needs to be rigorously analytically verified. Also, it is desirable to carry out the complete procedure suggested for the "hypothetical" case. This represents future work to be done, but the direction of this work is well defined and is grounded in a well-proven, simple, and easy-to-use basic concept.

REFERENCES

1. Bray, K. N. C., "Atomic Recombination in a Hypersonic Wind Tunnel Nozzle", J. of Fluid Mech. 6, 1959.

2. Bray, K. N. C., "Sudden-Freezing Analysis for Nonequilibrium Nozzle Flows", ARS Journal, June 1961.

3. Lordi, J. A. and Mates, R. E., "Non-equilibrium Expansion of High Enthalpy Air Flows", CAL Report No. AD1716-A-3, March 1964.

4. Harris, C. J., "Comment on Nonequilibrium Effects on High-Enthalpy Expansion of Air", AIAA Journal, June 1966.

5. Boyer, D. W., "Nonequilibrium Nozzle Expansion Calculations for the Space Sciences Lab., GE Co.", CAL Order No. 640, July 1962.

6. Eschenroeder, A. Q., Boyer, D. W. and Hall, G., "Exact Solutions for Nonequilibrium Expansions of Air with Coupled Chemical Reactions", CAL Report AF-1413-A-1, May 1961.

7. Harris, C. J., Marston, C. and Warren, W. R., "MHD Generator and Accelerator Experiments in Seeded and Unseeded Air Flows", R66SD50, Sept. 1966.

8. Harris, C. J., "Correlation of Inviscid Air Nonequilibrium Shock Layer Properties", GE Report R68SD333, Dec. 1968, also AIAA Paper 70-866.

9. Harney, D. J., "Similarity of Nonequilibrium Expansions in Hypersonic Nozzles", FDM-TM-67-1, May 1967.

10. Ring, L. E. and Johnson, P. W., "Correlation and Prediction of Air Nonequilibrium in Nozzles", AIAA Paper 68-378, 3rd Aero. Testing Conference, April 1968.

11. Harris, C. J. and Warren, W. R., "Correlation of Nonequilibrium Chemical Properties of Expanding Air Flows", GE R64SD92, Dec. 1964.

12. Reddy, N. M. and Daum, F. L., "Similar Solutions In Vibrational Nonequilibrium Nozzle Flows", AIAA Fluid and Plasma Dynamics Conference, 1970.

13. Westberg, K. and Cohen, N., "The Chemical Kinetics of Photochemical Smog as Analyzed by Computer", AIAA Paper #70-753.

14. Eyzat, P. and Guibert, J. C., "A New Look at Nitrogen Oxides Formation in Internal Combustion Engines", SAE Paper 680124, 1968.

15. Lavoie, G. A., Heywood, J. B. and Keck, J. C., "Experimental and Theoretical Study of Nitric Oxide Formation in Internal Combustion Engines", MIT, Fluid Mechanics Lab, Report 69-10, November 1969.

16. Johnson, R. H. and Hilt, M. B., "Formation and Measurements of Nitrogen Oxides in Gas Turbines", GE-70-GTD-9, March 1970.

17. Fenimore, C. P., "Formation of Nitric Oxide in Premixed Hydrocarbon Flames", 12th Combustion Symposium.

18. Bartok, W., et al, "Systems Study of Nitrogen Oxide Control Methods for Stationary Sources", GR-2-NOS-69, November 1969.

19. Wachman, H. Y. et al, "Equilibrium Chemical Composition and Thermodynamic Properties of Air-Carbon Mixtures at High

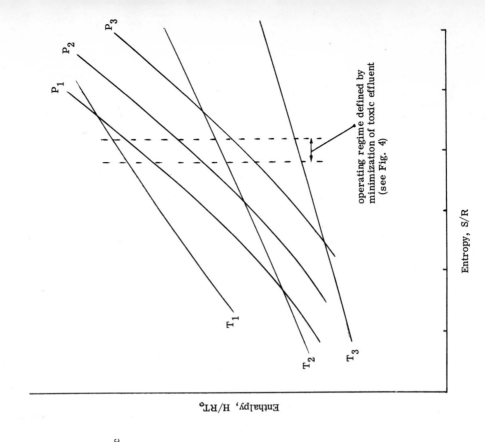

Fig. 5   Hypothetical - Mollier Diagram for the Gaseous Species
          Produced in the Combustor

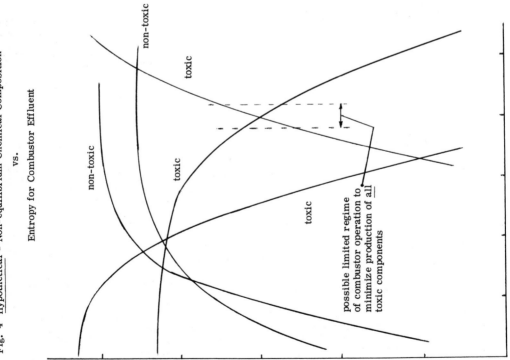

Fig. 4   Hypothetical - Non-equilibrium Chemical Composition
                              vs.
          Entropy for Combustor Effluent

190

Fig. 6 - Diagram of prime stages in a Combustor-Exhaust system

COMBUSTOR	INITIAL GAS AND PARTICLE EXHAUST	GAS AND PARTICLE PROCESSOR	STACK AND STACK FILTERS	REACTION WITH ATMOS. (SUN, WIND, RAIN, ETC.)
1	2	3	4	5

Temperature", Journal of Chemical and Eng. Data, Oct. 1960, Vol. 5, No. 4.

20. Browne, W. G. et al, "A Study of Acetlylene-Oxygen Flames", 12th International Symposium on Combustion, Pittsburgh, Pa., 1969.

21. Browne, W. G. et al, "A Study of the Chemical Kinetics of Shock Heated $H_2/CO/O_2$

Mixtures", 12th International Symposium on Combustion, Pittsburgh, Pa., 1969.

22. McMenamin, D. and O'Brien, M., "The Finite Difference Solution of Multicomponent Nonequilibrium Steady Influscid Stream Tube Flows Using a Novel Stepping Technique", GE67SD241, April 1967.

AN ISOTOPE X-RAY DEVICE

D. R. Russell
Senior Research Scientist
General Dynamics
Ft. Worth, Texas

Abstract

This paper discusses a non-electrical, multipurpose x-ray device which is small, lightweight, and portable. Areas of biomedical applicability are identified, and several characteristic radiographs obtained with the device are presented and discussed.

Introduction

The General Dynamics Isotope X-ray Device (patent pending) is a small, portable, non-electrical x-ray machine. There are many areas of biomedical applicability including: (1) examining patients who cannot be moved to a hospital x-ray room and/or are located where electrical power sources are not readily available, such as disaster areas, battlefield front lines, the scene of an accident, airborne hospital facilities, in orbital flight, or in a lunar shelter; (2) use in remote areas where electric power does not exist and where the transportation of fuel for generator-driven x-ray machines is impractical; (3) backup for conventional x-ray equipment in hospitals in the event of a power failure; (4) where the small size and complete portability characteristics make a non-electrical x-ray machine (isotope x-ray device) attractive, eg., for field tests and geometric situations where use of standard x-ray machines is difficult or impossible.

Criteria for suitable isotopes include availability, cost, high specific activity, appropriate photon energy, and suitable half-life.

Several isotopes (promethium-147, ytterbium-169, iodine-125, thulium-170, and others) have been investigated in an attempt to develop a portable, non-electrical x-ray machine. These investigations have met with varying degrees of success.[1,2,3,4]

Promethium-147 is a bremsstrahlung source, which requires that the source size be quite large (several millimeters in diameter), therefore impairing the resolution of the developed x-ray film.[5] Ytterbium-169 and iodine-125 have half-lives of 32 and 60 days, respectively, thereby requiring that these sources be replaced frequently.

Evaluation of these criteria indicated that sufficiently pure thulium-170 would adequately fulfill the source requirements for an isotope x-ray device. Thulium-170 has a half-life of 129 days and an 84 keV gamma ray, plus some higher energy bremsstrahlung radiation.

Initially, the thulium-170 sources were contaminated with tantalum-182, which has a 115 day half-life and four gamma rays with energies between 1.12 and 1.23 MeV. This problem has now been solved and the additional shielding that was used for the tantalum-contaminated thulium sources is no longer required.

Experimental Results

The protection of personnel was considered to be of paramount importance during each phase of the design, fabrication, and testing of General Dynamics' Isotope X-ray Device. The structure of the shielding is such that the encapsulated source is exceptionally well protected against exposure by physical damage; for example, dropping the device could not cause exposure of the source. As a result, the isotope x-ray device is radiologically safe for the person being x-rayed as well as for the x-ray technician.

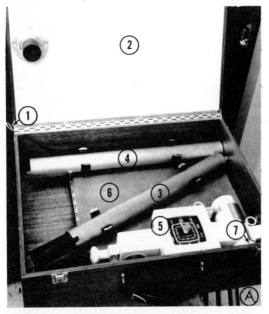

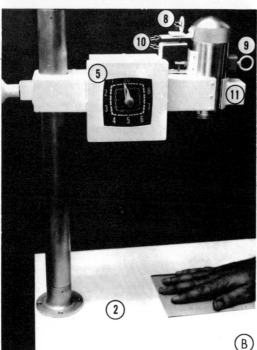

FIGURE 1. PROTOTYPE ISOTOPE X-RAY DEVICE

Figure 1 shows two photographs of the prototype isotope x-ray device. This device is lockable, rugged, and has adequate shielding. The operation of this device is as follows: the locked attache' case is opened and hinge pen ① is removed. The top of the case ② serves as the x-ray film holder. Vertical braces ③ and ④ are then placed upright as shown in ⑧. The mechanical timer-shutter-source housing is placed on the vertical braces and adjusted to the appropriate height for the x-ray film size being used (5" x 7", 8" x 10", or 14" x 17"). Cap ⑦ is removed and placed in the film compartment ⑥ of the attache' case. The lockable pen ⑧ is removed, spring loaded shutter ⑨ is pulled out and pen ⑧ is placed through brackets ⑩ and the end of shutter ⑨ and locked, as shown in ⑧. Mechanical timer ⑤ is set for the proper exposure time, after which shutter ⑪ is manually opened by a knob (not shown) on the back of the timer system. After the exposure time has elapsed, shutter ⑪ automatically closes. The source housing was designed such that replacement of depleted sources is a routine procedure.

Figure 2 is a photograph that was made with the isotope x-ray device shown in Figure 1. This photograph is the positive of an x-ray negative of the hand phalanx 3-2 (middle knuckle of the middle finger) and a reference aluminum wedge. The original negative has sufficient resolution and contrast for densitometric purposes, i.e., to determine bone mass.[6]

FIGURE 2. POSITIVE OF AN X-RAY NEGATIVE OF A HAND PHALANX 3-2

Figure 3 is the positive of an x-ray negative of a cracked femur bone from a cadaver. The contrast and resolution of this negative are of excellent diagnostic quality.

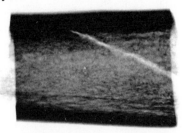

FIGURE 3. POSITIVE OF A NEGATIVE OF A CRACKED FEMUR BONE

Figure 4 is a positive of an x-ray negative of the author's right foot. The negative was recorded on Cronex 2 x-ray film with Par Speed Intensifying Screens. The resolution and contrast are more than adequate for diagnostic uses.

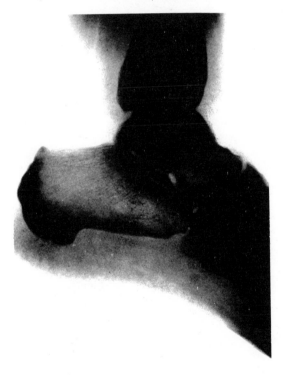

FIGURE 4. POSITIVE OF A LATERAL FOOT RADIOGRAPH

Conclusions

Results presented in this paper show that a non-electrical x-ray machine (isotope x-ray device) is a practical, workable solution in certain problem areas where complete portability, non-electrical, and small size requirements eliminate the use of conventional x-ray machines. X-ray negatives of good diagnostic quality are obtainable with the isotope x-ray device (thulium-170) described in this paper.

References

1. J. J. Ezop, "Study of the Capability of Isotopic Source of Secondary Radiation," IIT Research Institute, Report No. IITRI 1209-9, (1963).

2. E. W. Phelan, "Radioisotopes in Medicine," U. S. Atomic Energy Commission, Div. of Technical Information, 27, (1967).

3. F. L. Green, "Portable Devices for Isotope Chest Radiography and Other Applications," Proc. of Symposium on Low-Energy X and Gamma Sources and Applications, ORNL 11C-5, 309, (1964).

4. W. G. Myers, "On a New Source of X-Rays," The Ohio State Medical Journal, 772, (1962).

5. D. R. Russell, "General Dynamics Isotope X-Ray Device," General Dynamics Report FZP-948, March 1968.

6. P. B. Mack et. al., "New Development in Equipment for the Roentgenographic Measurement of Bone Density," Am. J. Roentgenol. Radium Therapy Nucl. Med., 82, 303, (1959).

MEASUREMENT AND ANALYSIS OF VIBRATION IN TRANSPORTATION SYSTEMS

Sherman A. Clevenson and John J. Catherines
NASA Langley Research Center
Hampton, Virginia

Abstract

An application of aerospace instrumentation and data reduction techniques is utilized in the development of a portable, low-frequency, low-amplitude vibration measuring, recording, and data reduction system. The measuring/recording system consists of commercially available components including a stereo home-type tape recorder. Necessary playback and data reduction equipment are indicated. Some examples of vibration measurements and analyses of a STOL and a CTOL aircraft, a high-speed train, and an automobile are given.

Introduction

A significant factor in the public acceptance of any mode of transportation is the quality of the ride. This includes not only comfort, but the ability to do simple tasks such as reading and writing. Little quantitative information on ride quality exists from which to develop meaningful criteria for public transportation systems, because of the difficulty in measuring the complex environment of passenger vehicles and in correlating these measurements with the subjective responses of the passengers. Part of the difficulty in developing ride criteria and/or acceptable vibration levels stems from problems in measuring, recording, and analyzing the relatively low-level vibration environment associated with passenger vehicles in the low-frequency (0-30 Hz) regime.

Langley Research Center has an ongoing program to examine one aspect of ride criteria, namely, the effect of vibration on human comfort. As part of this program, a measurement/recording/data reduction system has been developed as an application of aerospace instrumentation and data reduction techniques. This paper describes the measuring, recording, and data reduction system developed at Langley Research Center. In addition, the application of these techniques for measuring the ride quality of such mass transportation systems as high-speed-rail vehicles, STOL aircraft, and automobiles is given.

Application of Aerospace Technology

Basic Concepts of Flight Telemetry

In the development of a portable, low-frequency, vibration measuring and recording system for obtaining ride-comfort vibration measurements, concepts of flight telemetry instrumentation used in recording analog (continuous) data from spacecraft are utilized and are indicated in Figure 1. The parameter to be measured (e.g., vibration) is detected with a transducer whose electrical output controls a voltage controlled oscillator (VCO), which has a preset center frequency. A voltage input from the transducer causes a proportional change in the output frequency of the VCO. The VCO's typically use standard IRIG center frequencies that vary from 400 Hz (Channel 1) to 70 000 Hz (Channel 18). The outputs from all 18 channels are multiplexed with a reference frequency of 200 000 Hz and transmitted

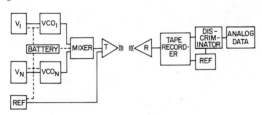

Figure 1.- Schematic diagram of system for obtaining flight data.

to earth. A receiving station with its sensitive antennae obtains the multiplexed signals and records them on a high-speed tape recorder. The multiplexed signals are directed to 18 discriminators tuned to the 18 center frequencies of the VCO's. The discriminator operation is opposite that of the VCO, that is, the output voltage of the discriminator is directly proportional to the frequency of the input signals and, hence, is directly proportional to the amplitude of the input vibration.

Requirements of Ground-Based System

Basic requirements for the measurement/recording system are given in table 1. The first consideration was its portability and capability to measure and record low frequencies ($\to 0$ Hz) and low amplitudes. This requirement indicated the need for some type of frequency modulation (FM) recorder. FM multichannel tape recorder systems were investigated and, in general, were found to be neither self-contained nor portable. In addition, FM recorders are expensive compared to direct-record tape recorders. For example, the most appropriate system commercially available was a seven-channel, battery-operated portable recorder which weighed 30 lb and cost approximately $10 000. Therefore, a lighter weight, less expensive, but high quality measuring recording system was developed utilizing the aforementioned concepts of space flight measurement techniques(1). The system consisted of a home-type audio (direct record), 8-lb stereo tape recorder in conjunction with servo-accelerometer small VCO's, and associated batteries totaling about 21 lb (Fig. 2). The basic combination system weighs 29 lb, as compared with 51 lb when the commercial FM recorder is used.

Measuring System

The measuring system (Fig. 3) consists of three vibration transducers (28 V servo-accelerometer sensitive in frequency range down to 0 Hz) which are mutually perpendicularly oriented, and whose electrical outputs control the frequency outputs of three VCO's. The outputs of the VCO's are resistively coupled and multiplexed on one track of the stereo recorder. The wiring diagram of the measuring system is shown in Figure 4. As noted in the figure, batteries supply power to energize the vibration transducers and VCO's. In addition to the three data channel VCO's whose center

Figure 2.- Portable battery-operated vibration
measuring and recording system.

Figure 3.- Portable measuring system with cover
removed.

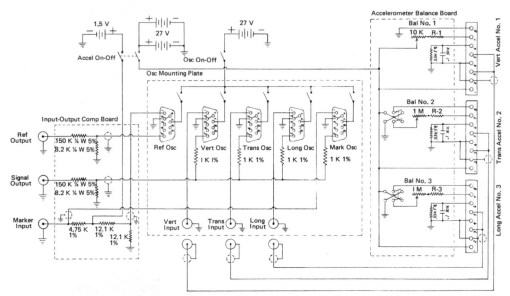

Figure 4.- Wiring diagram of the vibration measuring system.

frequencies are 5400 Hz, 3900 Hz, and 3000 Hz, one additional VCO whose center frequency is 7350 Hz is included for insertion of reference markers in the data, and one reference oscillator whose frequency is 12 500 Hz is included as a reference frequency standard. A functional diagram of the measuring/recording system is shown in Figure 5.

The instrument package has various features to overcome measuring difficulties that could lead to misleading conclusions. Rocking frequencies that occurred when the instrumentation container was placed on uneven surfaces or on soft areas, such as carpets, were eliminated by attaching three pointed legs to the container, two at the ends of one long side and one at the middle of the other side. These legs were approximately 0.1 in. in diameter and either 1/2 in. or 1 in. long, depending on the

thickness of the carpet. Resonant frequencies of the mounted transducers were increased above the frequency range (0-30 Hz) of the human comfort studies by attaching them to a steel block which, in turn, was fastened to an aluminum alloy base plate 7 in. by 11 in. by 3/4 in. thick. The batteries were also mounted directly to the base plate to keep the center of gravity as low as possible. The rest of the components were mounted on low shelves. To keep the upper portions of the container lightweight, the sides, top, and handle were made of aluminum alloy. To allow the measuring system to be flown on test aircraft, modifications such as steel helicoil inserts and safety wiring were installed and the equipment was certified as flightworthy.

198

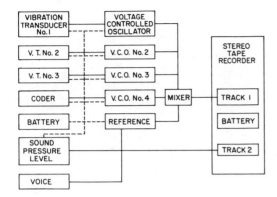

Figure 5.- Functional diagram of the measuring/
recording system.

Marker Indicators

Two types of marker indicators were developed
for use in automated data reduction to eliminate
the necessity in identification of real-time voice
annotation playback. One marker utilizes a small
box with six pushbuttons. Each pushbutton is
connected to a different resistor in a circuit
between the battery and the VCO. When the button
is depressed, a fixed voltage is applied to the
system and the voltage is detected during data
recovery. Only six coded signals are available in
this system. The second marker utilizes a BCD
(binary coded digital) encoder capable of indicating
999 numbers (Fig. 6). A logic diagram of the encoder
is shown in Figure 7. The encoder basically consists
of a switch (pushbutton) battery, pulse generator,
thumb-operated three-digit indicator with numerals
from 0-9 (3 decade switch), 12 bit shift register,
and a one-shot control that allows only one series
of 12 pulses to pass. In the operation of the
encoder, the desired code (number) is set into the
switch. The switch is closed by depressing the
pushbutton which resets the shift register and
starts the pulse generator. The register interro-
gates, in turn, each switch of the 3 decade
digiswitch and sends a shifted pulse to the one-shot
control. The output of the one-shot control is a
pulse train of 12 narrow or wide pulses. Each
series of four pulses correspond to one digit. The
three-digit number represented by the generated
signal shown on Figure 7 is 431.

Tape Recorder

The tape recorder selected (Fig. 8) is a
battery-operated direct record, stereo home-type
recorder whose speed is controlled by an
11-transistor circuit and whose wow and flutter are
rated at 0.2 percent. Recording can be made at
tape speeds of 15/16, 1-7/8, 3-3/4, and 7-1/2 in./sec
with frequency responses of 3000, 6500,
10 500, and 14 000 Hz, respectively. The recorder
uses 1/4-in.-wide magnetic tape on 5 in. reels. It
has two microphone inputs, recording level meters,
volume controls, stereo input, and separate stereo
outputs. The recorder uses five 1.2-V nickel-
cadmium batteries for 6 hr continuous operation,
weighs 8 lb including batteries, and costs approximately $400. The recorder is usually operated at
3-3/4 in./sec to accommodate a reference frequency of

Figure 6.- Binary coded digital (BCD) encoder.

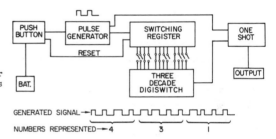

Figure 7.- Logic diagram of the binary coded
digital encoder.

Figure 8.- Tape recorder.

12 500 Hz required by the existing data recovery system. The outputs of the multiplexed VCO's and reference frequency are recorded on one track and voice annotation, and sound pressure levels (noise) are recorded on the second track (see Fig. 5).

Data Recovery System

A functional diagram of the data recovery system is shown in Figure 9. The same recorder-player that was used for recording vibration data is used during data recovery. The outputs of the track containing multiplexed data are directed through a band-pass filter to isolate the reference frequency and also to four discriminators tuned to the four center frequencies of the VCO's. When using narrow-band (±7-1/2 percent center frequency) IRIG VCO's, as is done in this system, compensation for the wow and flutter of the tape recorder is accomplished with the reference frequency. During playback, the reference frequency signal is directed to a compensation module which detects any deviation from the set frequency. When a deviation occurs, an inverse percentage correction is applied to the discriminators. Thus, errors due to wow and flutter are minimized and the overall accuracy of the system is within 2 percent.

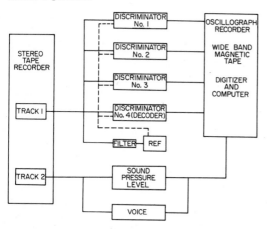

Figure 9.- Functional diagram of the data recovery system.

The discriminator outputs are directed to an oscillograph recorder for real-time records, to a wide band FM tape recorder for future analysis and storage, and to a digitizer and CDC 6600 digital computer from which statistical parameters defining the ride environment are obtained. When the BCD encoder is used, the output of the discriminator is directed to a decoder to obtain the coded numbers. The outputs of the digital computer are in the form of power spectral density plots, histograms, auto-correlation values, cross-correlation values, root-mean-square values, and peak acceleration values in excess of given acceleration levels. Examples of the results of vibration measurements are given in the next section.

Measurement Examples

Measurements of vibration levels have been made on a number of vehicles used for transportation (table 2) including CTOL (convention take-off and landing) and STOL (short take-off and landing) aircraft, high-speed trains, and automobiles. The measuring/recording system has fulfilled all the initial preset requirements and has been used to obtain excellent results. An example of real-time data is shown in Figure 10. This figure illustrates a sample of a vibration record measured on a STOL aircraft during a 25° banking maneuver at 210 knots while flying 2000 ft above the ground. These measurements were made during an evaluation of the aircraft operation characteristics in the New York City area. The vehicle is a four-engine turboprop, deflected slipstream aircraft capable of take-offs and landings over 50-ft obstacles within a distance of approximately 1000 ft. The three traces in the figure show the vertical, longitudinal, and lateral accelerations in g (gravity) units of acceleration as a function of time. The steady-state 1g component that is always present in the vertical direction has been biased out electronically. Considerable low-frequency, high accelerations (above 0.1g) occur in the vertical direction, whereas higher frequencies (3-4 Hz) at lower accelerations occur in the longitudinal and lateral directions.

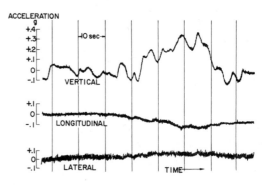

Figure 10.- Sample vibrations measured on STOL aircraft, 210 knots, banking maneuver.

Maximum Acceleration Levels

From real-time records, maximum acceleration levels can be determined for various times and conditions. Examples of maximum accelerations in the vertical and lateral directions for a STOL and a CTOL (three jet commercial transport) are shown in Figure 11. The data on the STOL were obtained by averaging the acceleration measurements for six take-offs, cruise, and landing exercises and the data for the CTOL were obtained during one flight from New York City to Newport News, Virginia. Although the figure indicates that the acceleration levels during cruise condition are considerably lower for the CTOL than for the STOL, it should be noted that the operating environments for the flights were different. For example, air turbulence and gust conditions were not measured, the speeds of the two aircraft were not the same, and the altitudes were very different. These data are shown only to give an indication of typical peak acceleration levels encountered on routine flights of STOL and CTOL aircraft.

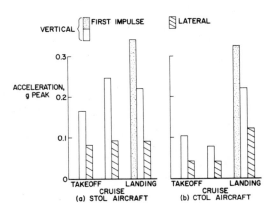

FIRST IMPULSE ▓ LATERAL

VERTICAL

Figure 11.- Maximum accelerations measured on STOL and CTOL aircraft.

Data Reduction

As mentioned earlier, the data can be digitized for programing on a digital computer to obtain various statistical results. An example of some of the exceedance values obtained from vibration measurements of a high-speed train during a track identification program is shown in printout form in Figure 12. The data are sampled at 50 times per sec (real time). The time (hr, min, sec, and hundredths of sec) is used only for reference and is recorded at four times true time, since the data are digitized four times faster (200 times per sec) than they were obtained. The interval samples in the listing are the total samples between mile-posts. Mileposts are listed on the far right of the figure. The three values listed (0.050, 0.060, and 0.150) at the top of the columns, are instan-taneous minimum g levels. The numbers listed in the three columns are the percentages that these g levels are exceeded. For example, the number 4.4 (first number in 0.050 column) indicates that of the 3218 samples of acceleration between the previous milepost and milepost 251, 4.4 percent of these samples had g values greater than 0.05g. Similar sets of numbers are shown for exceedance values in the vertical direction where the selected g values are 0.080, 0.100, and 0.150. Asterisks are program-printed beside any number greater than 5 percent. Various city names are program-printed beside selected numbers. For example, the code 240 causes Wilmington to be printed and indicates that the train is at the incoming station marker, and 241

NASA–DOT TRACK RIDING QUALITY PROGRAM

DATE 3 / 19 / 70   SYSTEM   LKHD .1   TRAIN NO.   107

CAR NO. 851   (NUMBER 1 OF 6 CARS IN TRAIN)

TIME	INTERVAL SAMPLES	LATERAL			VERTICAL			MILE POST	
		.050	.060	.150	.080	.100	.150		
11:48:50.65	3218	4.4	4.1	2.5	3.5	3.2	2.4	251	PHILLY
11:49:30.15	7900	4.2	2.6	.1	6.1 *	2.3	.3	3	
11:50: 8.10	7590	1.3	.8	0.0	10.7 *	3.9	.1	5	
11:50:20.96	2572	.2	0.0	0.0	9.1 *	3.8	.4	6	
11:50:33.77	2562	1.8	1.2	0.0	7.9 *	4.0	.4	7	
11:50:45.08	2261	.5	.3	0.0	2.5	.1	0.0	8	
11:50:54.15	1815	.9	.4	0.0	3.1	.6	.1	9	
11:51: 2.96	1762	6.1 *	3.6	.5	4.7	1.4	0.0	10	
11:51:11.78	1764	5.2 *	2.7	0.0	4.5	1.1	.1	11	
11:51:20.79	1802	11.7 *	7.3 *	0.0	6.4 *	2.8	.2	12	
11:51:29.49	1740	26.1 *	19.6 *	.3	14.3 *	7.6 *	1.9	13	
11:51:38.55	1811	13.7 *	8.7 *	.1	21.8 *	13.5 *	3.6	14	
11:51:47.41	1773	12.8 *	9.6 *	.2	19.6 *	12.1 *	3.4	15	
11:51:56.55	1828	3.7	1.5	0.0	10.8 *	5.3 *	1.3	16	
11:52:13.23	3336	2.2	.8	0.0	9.7 *	3.8	.3	17	
11:52:28.20	2994	.3	.0	0.0	1.0	.4	0.0	18	
11:52:38.22	2003	2.8	1.6	0.0	1.7	.7	.1	19	
11:52:45.77	1511	15.9 *	12.5 *	.5	6.0 *	2.1	.3	20	
11:52:53.53	1551	11.5 *	9.6 *	.1	5.6 *	2.6	.6	21	
11:53: 1.39	1573	7.7 *	5.0 *	.4	5.6 *	2.5	.3	22	
11:53:10.23	1767	16.5 *	12.0 *	.6	9.2 *	4.8	.3	23	
11:53:20.15	1985	.5	.2	0.0	.5	.1	0.0	24	
11:53:28.98	1766	3.1	1.9	0.0	3.3	1.5	.5	25	
11:53:40.20	2243	8.6 *	6.0 *	.2	19.7 *	11.9 *	3.7	26	
11:53:53.48	2657	3.3	2.2	0.0	9.3 *	4.5	.8	240	WILMINGTON
11:54: 2.99	1902	2.1	1.1	.2	2.5	.5	0.0	754	
11:54:16.38	2677	6.3 *	6.0 *	4.1	5.5 *	5.0 *	4.2	241	WILMINGTON
11:54:39.06	4536	3.1	1.3	0.0	24.9 *	15.9 *	4.6	28	
11:54:50.73	2335	5.7 *	3.5	0.0	9.3 *	4.1	.4	29	

Figure 12.- Data printout.

indicates that the train is at the outgoing station marker. From data such as these, particularly bad sections of track can be identified which contribute to a rough ride.

A typical example of vibration measurements on a late model, medium weight station wagon is given in Figure 13. The instrument package was placed on the floor on the front right side of the automobile. Data points for 15 or more occurrences were averaged to obtain the peak acceleration levels indicated for each typical operating mode, that is, cruise, acceleration, braking, bumps, and turns. These automobile rides were typical, and although it was impossible to write legibly on a data board at various times, the rides were considered typical of American automobiles of this class. Although the frequencies of occurrences were not studied, it is assumed that the peak levels occurred only sporadically and are thus accceptable.

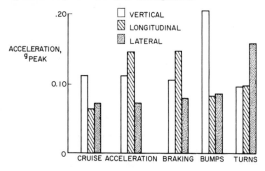

Figure 13.- Peak acceleration during automobile ride.

For determining the vibration frequency at which the maximum acceleration energy occurs, power spectral density (PSD) analyses can be made. Examples of typical PSD plots are given in Figure 14 in which vertical acceleration vibration data for a STOL aircraft, a CTOL airplane, and a passenger railroad train are shown (see ref. 2). It may be noted that the maximum energy content for the STOL and CTOL aircraft is concentrated at very low frequencies, namely,0.1 Hz or less, in contrast to the corresponding higher frequency of about 1.3 Hz for the train. Thus, if and when the vibration

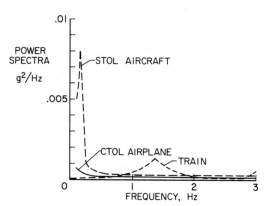

Figure 14.- Sample power spectral density plots.

levels are high, the tendency would be for one to experience motion sickness (nausea) in aircraft due to the low-frequency, high-amplitude, motions or annoyance and discomfort in the train due to the vibrations at the higher frequencies (over 1 Hz).

Concluding Remarks

An application of aerospace instrumentation and data reduction techniques is utilized in the development of a portable, low-frequency, low amplitude vibration measuring, recording, and data reduction system. The measuring/recording system consists of commercially available components including a stereo home-type tape recorder. Necessary playback and data reduction equipment are indicated. Some examples of vibration measurements and analyses of a STOL and a CTOL aircraft, a high-speed train, and an automobile are given.

References

1. Clevenson, Sherman A.; Martin, Dennis J.; and Dibble, Andrew C.: "Low-Frequency Portable Vibration Measuring and Recording System." Paper presented at the 40th Shock and Vibration Symposium, Hampton, Virginia, October 1969.

2. Catherines, John J.: "Measured Vibration Ride Environment of a STOL Aircraft and a High-Speed Train." Paper presented at the 40th Shock and Vibration Symposium, Hampton, Virginia, October 1969.

TABLE 1.- REQUIREMENTS OF A PORTABLE VIBRATION FIELD MEASURING AND RECORDING SYSTEM.

A. Must be portable

B. Must be self-contained

C. Frequency range: 0 to 30 Hz

D. Amplitude range: 0.01 to 1.0g

E. Should be lightweight

F. Should be foolproof

G. Should be inexpensive

H. Should be easy to use

I. Should be able to record subjective evaluations simultaneously with vibration measurements

TABLE 2.- TYPE VEHICLES FOR WHICH VIBRATION MEASUREMENTS HAVE BEEN MADE

A. Jet transport aircraft

B. Helicopter

C. STOL

D. High-speed trains (Metroliner and DOT test train)

E. Automobile

GENERAL ELECTRIC PHENOL ANALYSIS EQUIPMENT

Roland J. Starkey, Jr., James J. Shull, and Elaine D. Orr
Environmental Sciences Laboratory
General Electric Company
Re-entry and Environmental Systems Division
Philadelphia, Pennsylvania 19101

Abstract

During its tenure as prime contractor for the NASA-sponsored Biosatellite Program, the General Electric Company was responsible for monitoring and controlling biological and chemical contamination of the spacecraft.* NASA specifications for fuel cell-derived drinking water called for the total concentration of phenolic compounds not to exceed 1.0 part per billion and required results within an hour of sampling to delays in launching. [15] Since the Standard Methods procedure is time consuming (>1.5 hours); requires a relatively large sample (500 ml); and is known to lack precision and accuracy, an analytical procedure was developed which overcame these deficiencies. [8, 9, 19] A sample purification technique based on manual liquid–liquid extraction enhanced specificity and eliminated the time-consuming and sensitive distillation step of the Standard Method. Concurrent modification of the 4-aminoantipyrine colorimetric test for phenolic compounds reduced the color of the reagent blank and permitted analysis of 100 ml aliquots containing 1.0 ppb or less of phenols in ~20 minutes. [18]

Recognizing the usefulness of this technique for water resources management and process control, the General Electric Company designed and developed equipment which simplifies the analytical procedure. This instrumentation will be discussed in detail.

Introduction

Phenols, hydroxy derivatives of benzene and its condensed nuclei (Table 1), are variously derived as by-products of organic synthesis and includes aromatic compounds as cresols and xylenols. For this reason

TABLE 1. HYDROXY DERIVATIVES OF BENZENE AND ITS CONDENSED NUCLEI

ALDEHYDE	HALOGEN
ALKYL	HYDROXYL
ARYL	METHOXYL
BENZOYL	NITRO
CARBOXYL	NITROSO
	SULFONIC ACID

*NASA Contract NAS2-1900

the term "phenols" represents a broad class of organic compounds and not a single species. Although these are considered to be non-toxic according to USPHS standards for potable water, [15] pre-launch analysis of the Bio-satellite water supply was considered obligatory to preclude their derivation from the fuel cell per se and plastics associated with the holding tank and dispensing assembly. Furthermore, since nothing is known about the physiological effects of phenolic-type compounds during extended periods of weightlessness, a concerted effort was made to unequivocally demonstrate that the maximum allowable concentration of phenols specified by NASA, i.e., 1.0 part per billion (ppb) were met based upon phenol (hydroxybenzene) standards.

TABLE 2. TOXICOLOGICAL EFFECTS OF PHENOL (HYDROXY-BENZENE)*

Species	Mode	Concentration	Effect
Fish	Immersion	5.0 mg/liter	Incompacitating/death.
Fish	Immersion	1.0 mg/liter	Not affected in most cases.
Rats	Drinking water (chronic administration)	15–1,000 mg/liter	No observable effect for extended periods.
Rats	Drinking water (chronic administration)	5,000 mg/liter	No effect on digestion; absorption; metabolism.
Rats	Drinking water (chronic administration)	7,000 mg/liter	Arrested growth; many stillbirths.

*Public Health Service Drinking Water Standards 1962, U.S. Department of Health, Education and Welfare, Public Health Service, Washington, D. C.

It is also well known that certain halogenated phenols as ortho-chlorophenol, 2,4-dichlorophenol, and 2,6-dichlorophenol can be detected by sensory taste panels in concentrations of 2-7 ppb whereas others fail to reach threshold levels in concentrations exceeding 1000 ppb (Table 3). Since phenolic induced odors and tastes at or above the sensory threshold level are offensive, there was concern that the sub-human primates being flown might reject or reduce their water intake during extended missions. The possibility also existed that certain halogenated species could mask the natural odors and flavor of the pelletized food supply and seriously interfere with the animals' catabolism.

TABLE 3. TASTE AND ODOR THRESHOLD CONCENTRATIONS AT $25°C$ ( )

Compound	Geometric Mean Thresholds ppb	
	Taste	Odor
Phenol	1,000	1,000
2 – chlorophenol	4	2
4 – chlorophenol	1,000	250
2,4 – dichlorophenol	8	2
2,6 – dichlorophenol	2	3
2,4,6 –trichloro-phenol	1,000	1,000

Analytical Methodology

Standard Methods Procedures

During the early stages of the Biosatellite program the Standard Methods procedures for phenols analysis were the only "official" techniques available. [17] This is dependent upon the distillation of a relatively large sample (500 ml) for the purpose of concentrating the phenols in the distillate. Depending, upon how rigorously the distillation is controlled, this step may take 1.5 to 2.5 hours to complete. The distillate in turn is reacted with 4-aminoantipyrine in the presence of an oxidizing agent (potassium ferricyanide). Any phenols present "dye couple" with the 4-aminoantipyrine and can be read in a suitable UV/visible spectrophotometer or colorimeter against a suitable blank (Figure 1).

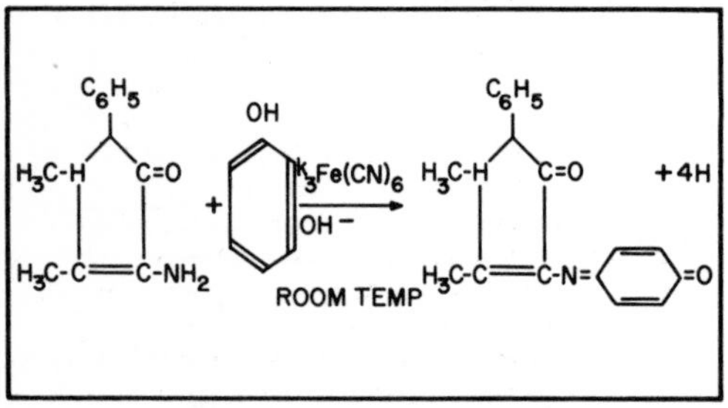

Figure 1. Phenol/4-Aminoantipyrine Dye Coupling Reaction in the Presence cf Potassium Ferricyanide

Disadvantages

It became readily apparent that the time required for this analysis seriously limited its usefulness to provide a "go" - "no go" report in the critical 30 to 60 minutes immediately prior to launch. This was

compounded by the discovery that 4-aminoantipyrine reacts with a broad spectrum of interfering substances as aryl amines or that potassium ferricyanide can be reduced by a number of inorganic compounds as $FeCl_2$ and Na_2S (Figure 2). In addition, our observation of the lack of sensitivity, accuracy, and precision of this method in concentrations of 2-3 ppb has been confirmed in a statistical analysis of the Standard Methods procedures by McFarren et al. [19]

For this reason the Standard Methods procedures were subjected to critical analysis in an effort to develop a new method of analysis which (1) could be completed in less than 30 minutes; (2) would eliminate or reduce the effect of interfering substances; and (3) provide a high degree of accuracy and precision at concentrations of 1.0 ppb or less.

Modifications of the Analytical Methodology

Since time was a critical factor, methods development dictated an approach to the problem which would simultaneously allow phenolic compounds to be removed from aqueous samples while simultaneously eliminating or minimizing the presence of interfering substances. Studies were designed to optimize the phenol/4-aminoantipyrine reaction for the purpose of extending the sensitivity of the Standard Methods [17] and ASTM [1] procedures.

Following the examination of a number of solvents it was demonstrated that phenols could be readily extracted from aqueous samples (100 ml) in a separatory funnel with 2-3 volumes of diethyl ether suitable for microchemical analysis. This was further optimized by adjusting the pH of the sample to 2.0 with HCl and significantly increasing the ionic concentration with NaCl immediately prior to the ether extraction.

Initial acidification supresses phenol ionization and decreases its water solubility. Concurrently, sodium chloride saturation forces phenols, quinone, and hydroquinone to partition favorably to the ether phase. Basic aryl amines form water soluble hydrochloride salts and remain in solution with inorganic reductants

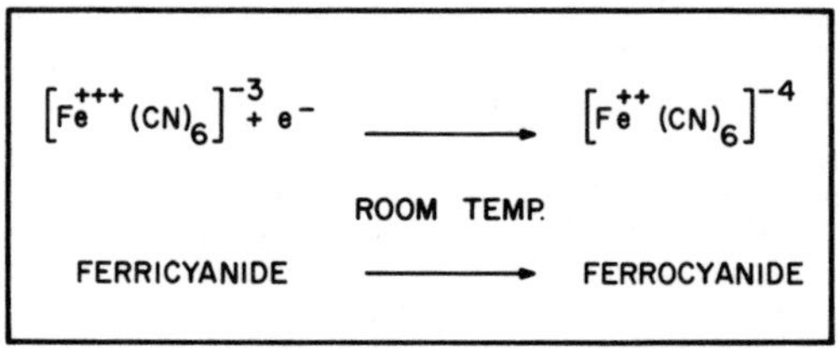

Figure 2. Oxidation-Reduction of Ferricyanide

which are capable of reducing potassium ferricyanide (Figure 2). Elimination of basic aryl amines is obligatory since they dye couple in the para position with 4-aminoantipyrine in a manner analogous to phenols and significantly interfere with the estimation of phenolics present.

Ether soluble phenols, quinone, and hydroquinone are removed from the separatory funnel and the water phase containing a variety of interfering substances is discarded. Without further delay the ether is slurried with a mixture of alumina and powdered nickle (8:1) which has been "charged" with 0.5 N LiOH. The phenols are immediately converted to lithium phenolates and become adsorbed to the alumina.

The mixture is filtered and the ether is discarded by conventional techniques. In sequence the alumina-nickel mixture is thoroughly mixed with 100 ml of deionized water for the purpose of eluting the water soluble phenolates from the adsorbent. This is filtered and the filtrate is slurried with Chromosorb P charged with 0.08 N HCl to strip off the lithium. Filtration of this mixture produces an aqueous mixture of phenols from which conventional interfering substances have been eliminated. The sample is now ready to be treated with the necessary reagents required to convert the phenols to a dye complex which can be quantitatively compared with a standard in a suitable optical readout system.

Optimization of the 4-Aminoantipyrine/Phenol Dye Coupling Reaction

The reaction pH was reduced from 10.0 to 8.7 to maximize the number of phenolic compounds that will react with 4-aminoantipyrine. A tris (hydroxy-methyl) aminomethane/HCl buffer system was substituted for the NH_4OH-NH_4Cl system and produced a sensitivity enhancement of 24%. Potassium ferricyanide and 4-aminoantipyrine formulated with this buffer have proven to be exceptionally stable and can be stored at room temperature in opaque containers for two weeks without incurring significant deterioration.

Unreacted reagent contributes significantly to absorption at 457μ in the reagent blank and sample. The quantity of 4-aminoantipyrine per phenol sample was reduced from 60μ moles to 20μ moles. This produced a 30% loss in dye production but a 40% decrease in reagent blank absorption at a phenol concentration of 400 ppb or less in 100 ml samples. At a phenol concentration of 100 ppb or less in 100 ml of water no loss of dye production is detected and the reagent blank is still diminished by 40%. The potassium ferricyanide reagent does not contribute to absorption and was therefore not reduced in concentration. Following the alkaline condensation of phenol with 4-aminoantipyrine the pH is adjusted to less than 4.0 with tartaric acid buffer to reduce reagent blank blank absorption immediately prior to extracting the dye complex with chloroform. The chloroform phase is removed with a separatory funnel and the absorbance is read at 457μ using a similarly processed sample of deionized water as a blank.

Based upon this technique phenol and a number of its derivatives can be reproducibly analyzed in concentrations of 1.0 ppb or less within 20 minutes (Table 4). Typical interfering substances that can be eliminated are summarized in Table 5.

TABLE 4. DETECTION LIMITS FOR PHENOL AND SEVERAL OF ITS DERIVATIVES BASED UPON THE MODIFIED PHENOL/4-AMINOANTIPYRINE DYE COUPLING REACTION

Compound	Concentration ppb*	Wavelength λ max
Phenol	1.0	457
2 – Chlorophenol	1.0	470
4 – Chlorophenol	2.0	457
2,4 – dichlorophenol	1.0	470
2,5 – dichlorophenol	1.0	475
Resorcinol	10.0	440

*Beckman DB-G UV/Visible Spectrophotometer 4cm cells

TABLE 5. TYPICAL INTERFERING SUBSTANCES REMOVED BY LIQUID–LIQUID EXTRACTION WITH DIETHYL ETHER

Compound	Concentration ppb
8–Hydroxyquinoline	100
Thymol	100
para–quinone	200
Hydroxyquinone	200
Phenolphthalein	400
alpha–Naphthylamine	1000
Aniline	1000

Development of Semi-automatic Instrumentation for the Analysis of Discrete Aqueous Samples for Phenolic-Type Pollutants

Derivation of Phenolic Pollutants

Phenolic pollutants derived from ground and surface water (Table 6), including phenol per se, halogenated species, cresols, xylenols etc., pose a continuous threat to the acceptability of water by the domestic consumer, including water treatment plants, beverage producers, and food processors. In many instances municipal treatment plants, due to inadequate surveillance techniques, may unknowingly commit large volumes of phenolic-contaminated water to its mains or reservoirs before the laboratory is able to report that a serious problem exists. Concurrently, large volume industrial consumers as food processors, brewers etc., with or without secondary treatment with activated charcoal filters, may be continuously drawing on this supply. Content with the premise that the treatment plant is monitoring for phenolics on a twenty-four hour a day basis, or perhaps in their own laboratory on an infrequent basis, gross contamination may only be determined "after the fact" by sensory taste panels.

TABLE 6. SOURCES OF PHENOLIC POLLUTION
OF GROUND AND SURFACE WATERS

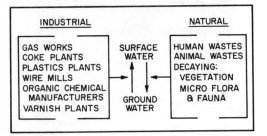

Although certain bulk products as beverages can be salvaged by diluting the phenolics below the odor and taste threshold, re-processing costs can seriously affect the margin of profit. For goods that are already packaged, the manufacturer, usually the president or chief executive officer, must make the decision as to whether the lot should be condemned or risk loss of consumer acceptance. In either case the economic consequences are grave. This can only be circumvented by positive surveillance of phenolics in process waters on a scheduled basis which will allow the quality control laboratory to provide manufacturing with advanced notice of an impending crisis.

Conventional techniques of analysis (Table 7), including the Standard Methods[17] previously described, are variously limited by lack of sensitivity[8,9,19], precision, accuracy[19], specificity[8,9], interfering substances[17], time consuming procedures, requirements for technically trained personnel and sophisticated instrumentation, and generally unsuitable for "on-site" field applications.

TABLE 7. OUTLINE OF METHODS AVAILABLE
FOR THE ANALYSIS OF PHENOLIC POLLUTANTS

Method	Reference
Distillation/4-aminoantipyrine	(17, 2)
UV Spectroscopy	(14)
IR Spectroscopy	(4)
Fluorescence Spectroscopy	(13, 6)
Paper Chromatography	(5)
Thin Layer Chromatography	(12)
Gas-Liquid Chromatography	(1, 3)
Diethyl Ether Extraction	(18)

Semi-Automatic Phenol Analysis Equipment*

Recognizing the usefullness of the liquid-liquid extraction technique and the increased sensitivity produced by modification of the 4-aminoantipyrine reagents, the General Electric Company designed and

---

*General Electric Company Ø-NAL Phenol Analysis Equipment

developed equipment which simplifies the analysis of aqueous samples for phenolic compounds by individuals having minimal training and experience in analytical chemistry (Figure 3).

Figure 3. General Electric Phenol Analysis Equipment

Reagent reservoirs (deionized water; diethyl ether; HC1/NaC1 slurry; 0.05 N LiOH; 0.08 N HC1; 4-amino-antipyrine; potassium ferricyanide; tartaric acid buffer; and chloroform); sample transfer system; semi-automatic volumetric pipets; extractor; reactor; converter and deionizing columns; magnetic mixers; clean out and waste collection system are self-contained in a console (37-1/2" h X 29" w X 16-1/4" d) suitable for use in the laboratory or field.

Ether tolerant vacuum (22" Hg minimum); pressurized deionized water (7-15 psig) source; and 120 vac (60 Hz/6.5 amps) are required from conventional laboratory sources. In case vacuum or pressurized deionized water are not readily available these services can be supplied by an auxiliary pump service package designed for continuous service. This is particularly recommended for use in a mobile laboratory as a station wagon or van truck equipped with a motor generator. Ether fumes are either vented into a hood or the atmosphere via a segment of conductive tubing extending from the exhaust side of the vacuum pump. Safety precautions relevant to the use of diethyl ether must be observed at all times.

Isolation Train and Reactor Assemblies

The phenol analysis equipment is basically divided into two parts: the isolation train and reactor (Figure 5).

The isolation train consists of a magnetically stirred extractor (Figure 6) which is connected with polypropylene tubing to Pyrex[R] reservoirs for the

Figure 4. Mobile Laboratory Operation of the General Electric Phenol Analysis Equipment

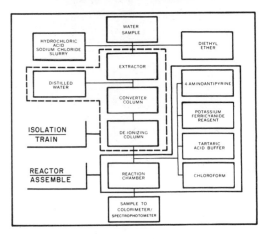

Figure 5. Schematic of Isolation Train and Reactor Assembly

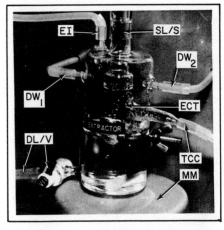

Figure 6. Magnetically Stirred Phenol Extractor — Legend: EI (Ether Input); SL/S (Salt Slurry/Sample Input); DW1 and DW2 (Deionized Water Washout Input); ECT (Ether Collection Tube); DL/V (Drain Line/Valve); MM (Magnetic Mixer); TCC (Line Delivering Ether to Converter Column).

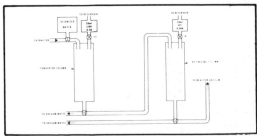

Figure 7. Converter and Deionizing Columns Prior to Regeneration

sample (100 ml); a slurry of 0.5 N HC1 and NaC1; and water saturated diethyl ether. A valved drain line connects the extractor with the vacuum waste collection system (Figure 6). In addition, the extractor is connected to the pressurized deionized water system to expedite cleaning between analyses (Figure 6 - C_1/C_2).

The ether collection tube (Figure 6 - ECT) is similarly connected by tubing and a 3-way Teflon[R] lined valve to the converter column which contains an alkali-resistant packing medium. This column in turn is connected with a second 3-way Teflon[R] lined valve and short segment of tubing to the deionizing column which is packed with an ion-exchange resin. The deionizing column discharges directly into the reactor (Figure 5). The columns can be independently isolated from the train for the purpose of charging each prior to an analysis or flushing with deionized water as required (Figure 7).

The transfer of sample and reagents to the extractor and reactor; the charging of the columns; elution of the columns; and disposal of extractor wastes is assisted by a manually controlled vacuum system.

Column Regeneration

In practice the semi-automatic volumetric pipets (20 ml) corresponding to the converter and deionizing columns are filled with 0.5 N LiOH and 0.08 N HC1, respectively (Figure 8). The columns are simultaneously charged by drawing the required reagent through each to activate the surface of the packing material (Figure 9). Column effluents of LiOH and HC1 are collected in the vacuum waste container.

Regeneration of the deionizing column displaces the lithium ions depicted in Figure 9 and restores the column to its optimum pH value. Likewise, the converter column pH has been adjusted with LiOH and is

Figure 8. Semi-Automatic Pipets and Column Charging Scheme (Legend: L (0.5 N LiOH); H (0.08 N HCl); C (Converter Column); D (Deionizing Column)

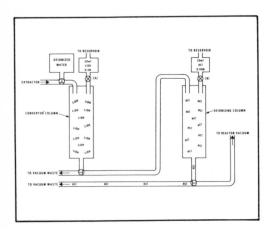

Figure 9. Converter and Deionizing Columns Following Regeneration

optimized for the formation of lithium phenolates in the ensuing analysis.

Performance of the Analysis

Valves governing the converter column, i.e., the one charged with LiOH (Figure 8-C), are adjusted to allow a vacuum of approximately 7 to 10 inches to continuously flow through the extractor and converter column into the waste container. Fifty milliliters of water saturated diethyl ether (Figure 10-A) and 10 ml of the 0.5 N HCl/NaCl slurry are pre-measured (visual sighting of meniscus) into volumetric bulbs (Figure 10-A and B) beneath their respective

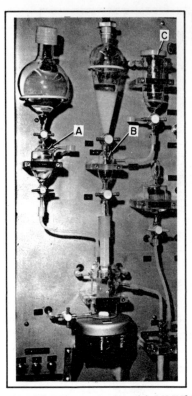

Figure 10. Ether Reservoir (A) and 0.5 N HCl/NaCl (B) Reservoir with Volumetric Measuring Bulbs; Sample Reservoir (C)

reservoirs by manual regulation of Teflon[R] stopcocks. Since these volumes are not critical minor errors introduced by careless adjustment of the menisci can be tolerated.

Immediately prior to analysis a sample is poured into the sample container and the volume is automatically adjusted to 100 ml by an overflow line which discharges directly into the ambient waste collection container located behind the console. This makes it possible to reproducibly present the same volume of sample for analysis without requiring volumetric techniques and glassware (Figure 11).

This can be visualized diagramatically in Figure 12 in which "P" represents the phenolic compounds in the sample and "I" represents organic and inorganic interfering substances. In addition, aliquots of diethyl ether and the 0.5 N HCl/NaCl have been pre-measured and are ready to be committed to the analysis.

Analysis is initiated by opening the stopcocks controlling the discharge of the sample and 0.5 N HCl/NaCl slurry into the extractor (Figure 13). As soon as this is filled the magnetic mixer is activated to expedite solubilization of the salt. With continued

Figure 11. Introduction of Sample into Reservoir
Immediately Prior to Analysis

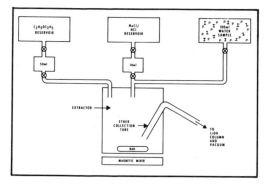

Figure 12. Extractor Prior to Adding Sample
and HC1/NaC1 Slurry

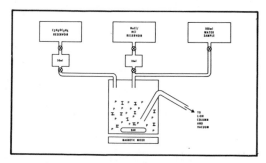

Figure 13. Extractor Following Addition of Water
Sample Containing Phenols and Interfering
Substances

mixing the stopcock controlling the discharge of diethyl ether from the volumetric bulb is opened and the addition rate is optimized by regulation of a needle valve.

As ether enters the stirred sample it is broken up into small particles and dispersed by the turbulent vortex produced by the magnetic mixing bar. Ether particles coalescing percolate through the LiOH charged converter column. Figure 14 demonstrates the progressive steps in the extraction of the phenols while the interfering substances are retained in the aqueous phase.

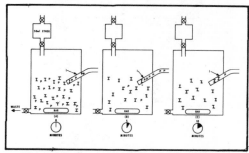

Figure 14. Successive Stages in Liquid-Liquid
Extraction of Phenol Containing Sample with
Diethyl Ether

I = Interfering Substances
P = Phenolic Compounds

Lithium phenolate reaction products (Figure 15 – LiP) are retained in the column while the ether is collected in the vacuum waste container. Complete extraction of the sample and formation of the phenolates in approximately 10 minutes is dependent upon the ether addition rate, speed of the magnetic mixer, and the vacuum level.

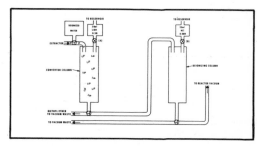

Figure 15. Conversion of Phenols to Lithium
Phenolates on LiOH Charged Converter Column

Elution of the Lithium Phenolates From the
Converter Column

As soon as the extraction process has been completed the 100 ml semi-automatic volumetric pipet is filled with deionized (ammonia and chlorine free) water stored in a one gallon reservoir mounted on the back of the console. This is used to elute the water-soluble phenolates (Figure 16) from the converter column into the HC1 charged deionizing column. This strips off the lithium and the eluate containing an aqueous mixture of phenols is collected in a magnetically stirred Pyrex[R] reactor (Figure 18).

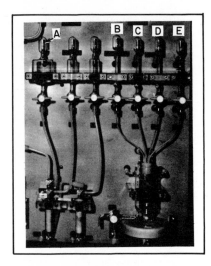

Figure 16. Semi-Automatic Pipets Required for the Elution of Lithium Phenolates Delivery of Reagents Required for the Phenol/4-aminoantipyrine Reaction: (A) 100 ml Deionized Water; (b) 1.0 ml 4-aminoantipyrine; (c) 1.0 ml Potassium Ferricyanide; (d) 1.0 ml Tartaric Acid Buffer; (E) 10.0 ml Chloroform (Spectral Grade).

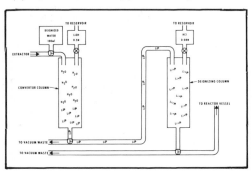

Figure 17. Elution of Lithium Phenolates from Converter Column with Deionized Water and Stripping of Lithium in HC1 Charged Deionizing Column

Phenol/4-Aminoantipyrine Reaction

One milliliter each of 4-aminoantipyrine and potassium ferricyanide (Figure 16-B and C) are added to the reactor with continuous mixing by turning each of the two-way stopcocks to the "drain" position. After

Figure 18. Reactor Assembly

timing for 1 minute, 1.0 ml of tartaric acid buffer and 10.0 ml of spectral grade chloroform (Figure 16 D and E) are added in the same manner. This is mixed an additional two minutes at high speed to concentrate the 4-aminoantipyrine/phenol dye complex in the chloroform phase. At the conclusion of this period the mixer is turned off and the aqueous phase and chloroform are allowed to separate. The chloroform phase is removed from the reactor (Figure 19) and the absorbance read at 457 μ using a similarly processed sample of deionized water as a blank. The total elapsed time for the analysis is 20 minutes.

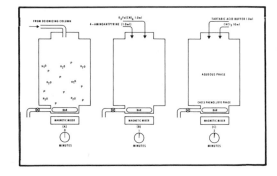

Figure 19. Sequential Operation of Reactor

Determination of Phenol(s) Concentration

The concentration of the unknown can be determined by interpolation from a standard curve or preferably by comparison with the absorbance of freshly prepared standards. It is recommended that all stock solutions and working standards should be preserved with $CuSO_4 \cdot 5H_2O$ and H_3PO_4 at pH 4.0[6]. Standards containing relatively low concentrations (1-5 ppb) should be prepared immediately before use from stock solutions to minimize chemical and/or biochemical oxidation[18].

Additional blanks of deionized water should be analyzed periodically and read against chloroform blanks as a check on the water source for the phenol analysis equipment. This technique can also be used to evaluate the thoroughness of the self-contained clean out system whenever a grossly contaminated sample has been inadvertently processed. If high blanks are reported additional cleaning of the extraction train will be required.

In the case filtered samples are analyzed a blank should be prepared by filtering an equivalent volume of deionized water through a filter of the same size. Analysis of the sample will determine if any phenolic compounds are being leached from the filter media which could produce erroneous results.

Optical Read Out System Requirements

Requirements for an optical read out system is dependent upon the specifications of an individual laboratory for sensitivity, accuracy, and precision. Phenol (hydroxybenzene) and numerous derivatives can be detected in concentrations of 1.0 ppb or less in 4 cm cells at 457 μ (Table 4) with a spectrophotometer capable of detecting 0.002 absorbance units. Typical scans of standards analyzed with the General Electric Phenol Analysis Equipment are documented in Figures 21 and 22. A standard curve is depicted in Figure 20 and can be used for the rapid interpolation of test data.

Figure 23 illustrates the capability of the isolation train to remove 1000 ppb of aniline from a sample compared to the spectral charactor practice of the aniline/4-aminoantipyrine dye complex. If conventional Standard Methods[17] or ASTM[2] techniques were being used the aniline/4-aminoantipyrine reaction product would mask any phenols present and produce highly erroneous results.

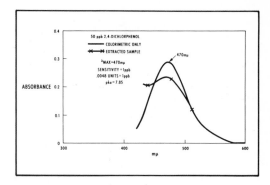

Figure 21. Scan of 50 ppb Standard of 2, 4-Dichlorophenol to Demonstrate Sensitivity and Maximum

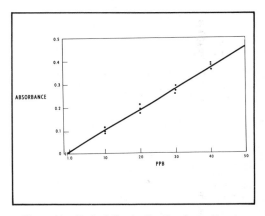

Figure 22. Typical Standardization Curve Based Upon Aqueous Phenol Samples Preserved With $CuSO_4$ and H_3PO_4 at pH 4.0

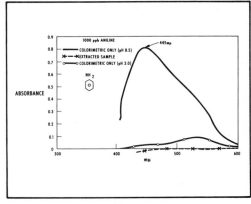

Figure 23. Scane of Aniline to Demonstrate the Capability of the Phenol Analysis Equipment to Remove Interfering Substances Capable of Reacting with 4-Aminoantipyrine

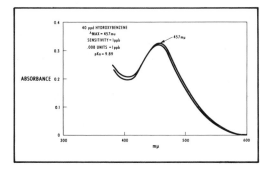

Figure 20. Scan of 40 ppb Standard of Phenol (Hydroxybenzene) to Demonstrate Sensitivity and Maximum

SUMMARY

Phenol analysis equipment with a self-contained reagent handling system has been described which can be reliably used in the laboratory or field by personnel with minimal technical training. Based upon continuous liquid-liquid extraction of discrete aqueous samples with diethyl ether, sensitivity exceeds that of existing Standard Methods[17] and ASTM procedures and features elimination of major interfering substances.

REFERENCES

(1) Arguer, R. J., Anal. Chem., 40, 122-4 (1968).

(2) ASTM Standards, Parts 23, 517 (1968).

(3) Baker, R. A., Air Water Pollution, 10, 591-602 (1966).

(4) Burtschall, R. H. et al, J. A. W. A., 51, 205-214 (1959).

(5) Chang, W. H. et al, J. Am. Chem. Soc., 74, 5766 (1952).

(6) Dwelling, R. T. Analyst Method Manual Part III, Appendix II, Guide to Laboratory Analyses and Sample Handling, FWPCA, U. S. Dept. of the Interior.

(7) Emerson, E. et al, J. Org. Chem., 8, 417 (1943).

(8) Faust, S. D., Water Research, 1, 405-18 (1967).

(9) Ibid., 509-22.

(10) Faust, S. D. and Aly, O. M., J. A. W. W. A., 54, 235 (1962).

(11) FWPCA Methods for the Chemical Analysis of Water and Wastes. Federal Water Pollution Control Administration, Division of Water Quality Research, Analytical Quality Control Laboratory, U. S. Department of the Interior (1969).

(12) Gebott, M. D., Solutions (Ann Arbor), 6, 8-10 (1967).

(13) Kullbom, S. D. et al, Paper No. 288 - Presented at the 1970 Pittsburgh Conference on Analytical Chemistry and Applied Spectroscopy.

(14) Martin, J. M. et al, J. Water Pollution Control Federation, 39, 21-32 (1967).

(15) Public Health Service Drinking Water Standards 1962, U. S. Department of Health, Education and Welfare, Public Health Service, Washington, D. C.

(16) Smith, H. F., Research/Development, July (1968).

(17) Standard Methods for the Examination of Water and Wastewater. APHA, AWWA, and WPCF, 514-523, 12th ed (1965).

(18) Starkey, R. J., Jr., and Orr, E. D., Presented at the 160th Annual Meeting of the American Chemical Society, Chicago, Illinois, September 14, 1970.

(19) Water Phenols No. 1., Study No. 28. Environmental Water Supply and Pollution Control, U.S. Department of Health, Education and Welfare, Public Health Service, Cincinnati, Ohio (1967).

RANKINE CYCLE POWER SYSTEMS FOR AUTOMOTIVE APPLICATION

Jerry A. Peoples
George C. Marshall Space Flight Center
Marshall Space Flight Center, Alabama 35812

Abstract

The importance of developing effective, efficient steam propulsion systems is recognized as a mandatory step in our country's technology applications to environmental improvements. With this in mind, several years of effort have been placed into the exploration of new concepts related to rankine cycle engine systems. From this effort, several concepts believed to be unique have emerged. These include a variable pressure boiler (VPB) passive pressure and temperature control, and hermetically-sealed engine configurations.

The entire problem of a steam automotive system is manifested in the control required to maintain boiler pressure and temperature under varying loads, throttle changes, and engine cutoff settings. The control approach taken by current steam car designs is based upon a fuel rate proportional to the pressure error between command and actual pressures. Speed and power are controlled by the throttle which can be varied manually by the operator. The VPB concept overcomes the control problems of the conventional fixed boiler pressure concepts.

A passive control concept is discussed which allows the boiler pressure to seek its own equilibrium level. The throttle is eliminated. The block diagram for conventional steam system operation is reviewed and compared with the VPB block diagram. Advantages of the VPB concept are discussed in terms of passive pressure control and system performance. Finally, a provocative idea of passive temperature control is introduced. Passive temperature control is a natural consequence of a VPB.

Symbols

P	Pressure — psia
T	Temperature — °R
M	Steam mass flow – lb/min
R	Gas constant — ft-lb/lb$_m$-°R
N	Engine speed — rpm
X	Cutoff — decimal
η	Efficiency — decimal
H	Enthalphy change as water passes through boiler — Btu/lb
E	Heat of combustion
k	Polytropic constant
V	Displacement
DN	Dour number
SN	Supple number
SR	Steam rate — lb/hp-hr
FR	Fuel rate — lb/min
A	Blower air — lb/min
Gear ratio	Differential ratio times wheel radius — ft

Subscripts

T	Throttle conditions
B	Boiler
S	Super heater
E	Engine
A	Exhaust condition
R	Reference
C	Command

Background

Steam automobiles flourished between 1900 and 1910. Although a few late comers made the scene in the 1920s, steam automotive engineering was washed up except for the lingering death of the Stanley Steamer. Most of the steam cars in the 1900-1910 era were unsatisfactory designs; however, in the twenties the Coats (Wisconsin Steamer, Inc., 1922-1923, Milwaukee, Wis.), Scott Newcome (Standard Engineering Company, 1921-1922, St. Louis, Mo.), and Doble (Doble Steam Motors Corp., 1914-1929,

San Francisco, Calif.) were master pieces of design excellence. It is somewhat ironic that this excellence put them out of business. Economically, they were noncompetitive.[1] The Doble has been described as the ultimate car (including everything that runs). However, the excellence of the Doble and the smoothness of the Delling (Delling Motor Co., 1923-1934, Philadelphia, Pa.) would be unacceptable from a modern automotive steam viewpoint. The validity of this statement is not manifested in style or comfort but rather in performance and daily care.

Performance
- High performance could not be sustained without steam venting steam.
- Under techniques of the 1920 era, speed/economy could not be optimized for both the low speed and high speed engines.
- Odor resulting from overheating (control problems).

Daily Care
- Frequent water fillings
- Bothersome dynamic seals
- Thermostat and pressure adjustments

The modern steam car must overcome all of these weaknesses. The purpose herein is to present a system approach which inherently solves all of these problems.

Between 1876 and 1940, many innovations were applied to the "steam engine." In spite of the wide variations in design, all steam had one common factor: an operation factor dominated by a fixed boiler pressure. The systems were designed and provided with the necessary controls to maintain boiler pressure at a fixed predetermined value. This philosophy was carried into the 1950's with the Paxton project, and more recently by Bill Lear's vapor dyne system. The necessary sensors, prime movers, plumbing, and force-balance devices employed over the past 70 years are epitomized by the plumber nightmare. The operation of a steam boiler-engine system at a fixed boiler pressure represents the greatest snag which has hindered modern steam car developments. The primary purpose of this discussion is to introduce an entirely new control concept, the VPB.

Engine Configuration

In recent years, steam engine configurations were as varied as there are people who dream them up. It appears that many configurations have been generated just to be different. Configuration selection for the modern steam car will demand more than a guess. There are two fundamental requirements which dictate the engine configuration:

1. The valving scheme (valve gear) must be hermetically sealed (zero leakage).

2. The nature of the configuration must complement the automotive propulsion problem.

Two configurations are suggested herein which meet these criteria. Both are reciprocating engines for the second reason. A relatively low-speed device can best meet the torque speed requirements of an automobile for the minimum engineering design problems. Two types of valve gears, one for each engine, are discussed:

1. Pneumatic valving

2. Piston occultation

The concept of pneumatic commutation is illustrated diagrammatically in Figure 1. Multicylinders are required to operate in paris with their crank throws 180 degrees apart. An engine of six cylinders would consist of three cylinder pairs operating on a common crankshaft. The crankshaft has been drawn separately for clarity. As shown, the engine would turn the crankshaft clockwise. Only one pair of cylinders is needed to illustrate this principle.

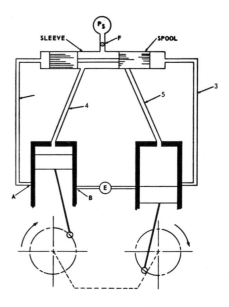

FIGURE 1. PRINCIPLE OF PNEUMATICALLY OPERATED VALVES

Commutation is provided by the movement of a cylindrical spool valve sliding in a sleeve. Left and right movement depends upon pressurization Channels 2 and 3. In the position shown, Channel 3 has just been pressurized and has forced the spool to the extreme left. Vapor enters at P_s and flows into the left cylinder by way of Channel 4.

The right cylinder has just exhausted through Port E. The left piston moves downward under the force of the supply pressure. Near the bottom of the stroke, the piston slides past Port A allowing part of the cylinder gases to escape and pressurize Channel 2. As the spool is forced to the left, Channel 4 is cut off from the supply and Channel 5 is opened. In the meantime the piston approaches bottom dead center and uncovers Port B (uniflow action) and the exhaust is ported to E. The opening at A is slightly higher up the cylinder wall than B.

The right-hand piston is now at top dead center ready for its power stroke. The same cycle is then repeated for the right piston. This simple arrangement results in a cutoff approaching 100 percent.

A throttle at F could be used to control speed and pressure; however, other control techniques will be introduced later; presently, it will be assumed that means of control exists. By proper design, this approach lends itself to zero leakage. Leakage, which occurs, is always internal. The vapor loss from the system is zero. This concept justifies speculation of long driving periods on one filling of water. The approach actually has the potential of requiring only one filling for the life of the engine.

An actual engine would require more sophistication than represented in Figure 1. A cutoff of less than 100 percent can be incorporated by providing an intermediate spool, as shown in Figure 2. The intermediate spool will be referred to as the secondary spool. The primary spool performs the same pressure polarity switching as shown in Figure 1. The location of Port C determines the cutoff valve. When Port C is uncovered by the movement of the piston, the cutoff spool is forced to the right. This movement cuts off the supply to the left cylinder and provides communication between Channels 3 and 6. However, vapor cannot flow into the right cylinder until the primary spool is displaced to the right. This occurs when the left piston is near bottom dead center and the right piston near top dead center. Movement of the secondary spool always leads the move of the primary spools by an amount indicative of the cutoff value. Inducing a second spool is essential to providing a cutoff less than 100 percent. However, the spool provides only for discrete values of cutoff. The secondary spool does not provide for variable cutoff. This would further sophistication. Two or three discrete values of cutoff could be easily accomplished by providing for multiports near Port C. These redundant channels could be switched in or out by solenoids.

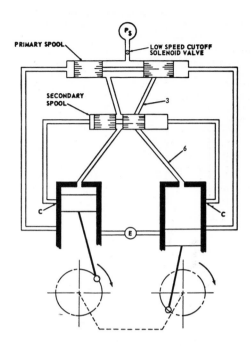

FIGURE 2. PRINCIPLE OF PNEUMATICALLY OPERATED VALVES WITH DISCRETE CUTOFF

Piston Occultation

Valving by piston occultation is illustrated in Figure 3. The pistons of each cylinder are similar to the conventional pistons in any reciprocating engine except for (1) the length, which is somewhat longer, and (2) each piston has grooves of a predetermined length, as illustrated. The supply steam is located at P_s. Although two supply sources are shown, in practice they would be common. Steam commutation is allowed under the following conditions:

- Channel 7 communicates with 16 whenever piston flow groove (A) subtends Ports 33 and 34.

- Channel 16 communicates with Channel 9 whenever piston flow groove (C) subtends Ports 35 and 36.

- Channel 11 communicates with Channel 15 whenever piston flow groove (D) subtends Ports 41 and 42.

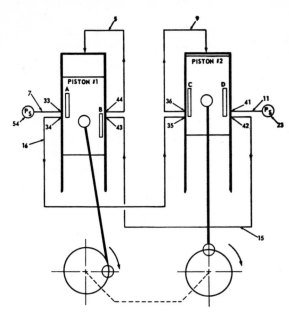

FIGURE 3. PRINCIPLE OF VALVING BY
PISTON OCCULTATION

- Channel 15 communicates with Channel 5 whenever piston flow groove (B) subtends Ports 43 and 44.

The top views of these channels are illustrated in Figure 4.

The crank throw has been drawn at 90 degrees; however, studies have shown that this occultation scheme is valid for 90 to 30 degrees between adjacent throws. Cutoff is established by the piston length of the flow grooves and

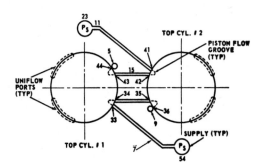

FIGURE 4. CYLINDER OCCULTATION PLUMBING

the location of the supply parts. Other discrete cutoff values can be obtained by having redundant input supply parts. Such redundant channels should be activated by solenoid. These redundant channels would effectively increase the communication time between Ports 33 and 34, 35 and 36, 41 and 42, and 43 and 44.

In the position shown, steam flows into Channel 7 through Port 33, flow groove A, and Port 34 into Channel 16. From this channel, steam is omitted to the right-hand cylinder through Port 35, flow groove C, Port 36, and Channel 9. Steam also flows through Ports 41 and 42 into Channel 15; however, the steam flow is occulted by the piston at Port 44. Cutoff to the right cylinder occurs whenever Port 33 is occulted by the piston (top of flow groove A passes Port 33). This scheme will occultate the steam to either cylinder, except at or near the top dead center position.

Analytical Approach

At first it may appear that very little could be said about analytical methods. The Mollier chart and classical thermodynamics have been used for a number of years. From the author's point of view, validity of any analytical approach can be ranked into four categories. The depth of the investigation in any category depends upon available time and accuracy allowed by the respective category. These categories are defined as follows.

First-Order Analysis

This analysis is characterized by the Mollier chart. It represents analysis of a given vapor cycle designed to operate at fixed conditions. Results are usually very optimistic. Major outputs are system thermal efficiency and work per cycle. Usually, power is obtained by assuming a flow rate.

Second-Order Analysis

The second-order analysis combines the Mollier chart and the ideal P-V diagram. This order of analysis allows for evaluation of cutoff, engine displacement, engine speed capability, and required evaporation rate, power, and the interrelationships.

Third-Order Analysis

The third-order analysis is the Mollier chart, P-V diagram with consideration for clearance volume, boiler efficiency variation with evaporation rate, friction, exhaust conditions, compression pressure, and temperature.

Fourth-Order Analysis

The fourth-order analysis is the point design and hardware tests.

Most likely, a "flavor" from each order appears in any given analytical approach. The data given herein are based on a second-order analysis. A third-order analysis has been conducted.[2] From the P-V diagram illustrated in Figure 5, the following expressions result:

$$W = \frac{P_T V_e}{12} \left[\frac{xk - x^k}{k - 1} - \frac{P_A}{P_T} \right]$$

$$M_R = \frac{P_T V_T \, xN}{12 \, RT}$$

$$hp = \frac{MRT}{33\,000} \left[\frac{xk - x^k}{k - 1} - \frac{P_A}{P_T} \right] \frac{1}{x}$$

$$S_R = \frac{1\,979\,820}{RT \left[\dfrac{xk - x^k}{k - 1} - \dfrac{P_A}{P_T} \right] \dfrac{1}{x}}$$

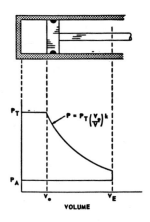

FIGURE 5. IDEAL P-V DIAGRAM

From boiler considerations and data available from the Mollier chart, the following relationship exists:

$$M_A = \eta_B \frac{E \, F_R}{H}$$

The preceding relationship completely characterizes an ideal boiler-engine system. Note that if P_T is relatively large, 600 psia or greater, P_A/P_T becomes very small. Also, observe that the quantity $(kx - x^k)/(k - 1)$ appears in the power, work, and steam rate expressions. If DN is designated as:

$$DN = \frac{kx - x^k}{k - 1} \qquad \text{(Dour Number)}$$

$$SN = \frac{DN}{x} \qquad \text{(Supple Number)}$$

The complexity of the above expressions is greatly reduced. Dour and Supple Numbers are engine parameters just as enthalphy is a parameter on the Mollier chart. Both of these numbers are dimensionless and can be tabulated as a function of cutoff and ratio of specific heat. Sample tabulations are given in Tables 1 and 2. The Dour Number varies between zero and one; the Supple Number varies between 1 and $k/(k - 1)$. These tables allow for a quick assessment of power and steam rate. Application of the Dour Number is also a great aid in development of the steam system block diagram. Other relationships involving the Dour and Supple Numbers are given in Reference 2.

TABLE 1. DOUR NUMBER

Cutoff Percent	Ratio of Specific Heat		
	1.3	1.2	1.1
6	0.1740	0.1891	0.2071
12	0.3083	0.3274	0.3493
18	0.4213	0.4413	0.4636
24	0.5186	0.5380	0.5592
30	0.6032	0.6210	0.6403
36	0.6768	0.6927	0.7096
42	0.7408	0.7545	0.7690
48	0.7962	0.8077	0.8197
54	0.8438	0.8531	0.8627
60	0.8842	0.8914	0.8988
66	0.9178	0.9232	0.9286
72	0.9452	0.9489	0.9527
78	0.9668	0.9691	0.9714
84	0.9827	0.9839	0.9852
90	0.9933	0.9938	0.9943
96	0.9990	0.9990	0.9991

TABLE 2. SUPPLE NUMBER

Cutoff Percent	Ratio of Specific Heat		
	1.3	1.2	1.1
5	2.976	3.253	3.588
10	2.662	2.845	3.056
15	2.446	2.578	2.728
25	2.134	2.210	2.294
30	2.010	2.069	2.134
40	1.801	1.837	1.875
45	1.710	1.738	1.767
55	1.547	1.563	1.580
60	1.473	1.485	1.497
70	1.338	1.344	1.350
75	1.275	1.279	1.283
85	1.158	1.159	1.161
90	1.103	1.104	1.104
100	1.000	1.000	1.000

New Approach to an Old Problem

Even though Stanley, White, and Delling performed above their gas counterparts, the performance of a modern steam automobile system must be capable of exceeding previous records. It is doubtful if even the design approach used on previous steam systems has the capability of meeting modern demands. The validity of these statements is based on total performance which includes odor, as well as speed and power. Steam enthusiasm will accept steam in any form; however, the modern steam car must be designed for the man, the girl, and the lady who doesn't give a "hoot" about steam. Many thousands of people are interested only in getting there and back safely, reliably, and at reasonable cost.

The younger generation often asks, "Why did steam automobiles fail?" There have been many complicated answers. But the simple truth is that steam technology was in a mess. It literally took both an engineer and a maintenance man to keep a vehicle going.

The antique steam systems were designed for a fixed boiler supply pressure and temperature. The systems were provided with sensors and regulators to maintain boiler conditions as near as possible. Even the most modern

developments reinforce this mode of operation. It is ironic that all of the serious steam developments over the past 20 years have not introduced any new innovations. Most efforts have been concerned with refinements of existing designs through materials or gimmicks.

A boiler provides steam at the desired pressure to the engine throttle. The throttle is essentially a variable orifice which can throttle the supply steam mass flow. The throttle was, therefore, a means of speed and power control.

It is believed that the throttle of the modern steam car must take a new form from that of its historical image. In concept, the throttle can be wide open continuously. The approach taken by current developments (and antiques) is (was) to preprogram a fuel rate, depending upon a pressure error between design and actual pressures. This fuel rate is geared to the maximum heat input for the boiler. It is the intent that the predetermined fuel rate can maintain boiler pressure under all conditions. Speed and power are controlled by the throttle which can be varied manually by the driver.

Variable Pressure Boiler

In this approach the operator controls speed and power by manually varying the fuel rate. The throttle is maintained wide open after start. This new approach will be referred to as the VPB concept. The entire problem of a steam automotive system is manifested in the controls required to maintain boiler pressure and temperature under varying loads, throttle changes, and cutoff settings. These controls and necessary plumbing is a classical example of the plumber's nightmare. The primary objective of the control system recommended herein is to solve the control problems and at the same time achieve the modern characteristics mentioned earlier. The methods to achieve these ends involve more than physical hardware. The scheme proposed here is a new concept, a new philosophy for viewing techniques for making vapor power cycles practical.

The effects of boiler pressure and temperature and engine cutoff upon system performance are the guide posts for design of the modern steam automotive system. In summary, these three parameters should be varied to obtain the desired performance. The effects of pressure and temperature are to change the specific volume and heat capacity of the water. The specific volume of the supply steam greatly affects speed and boiler size. The specific volume of the supply steam can be related through the ideal gas equation:

$$\nu = \frac{RT}{P}$$

Thus, the specific volume varies directly proportional to the thermodynamic temperature and inadversely proportional to pressure. As specific volume increases, less steam is required to fill a given volume. The mass of steam required to fill any cylinder is:

$$M = \frac{V}{\nu}$$

As the specific volume increases, mass required to fill the cylinder decreases. For a given fuel rate, which can be related to an equivalent evaporation rate, an engine will run faster as the specific volume of the steam increases. Whenever a boiler is generating a constant evaporation rate, the engine reaches a steady state speed which will just consume all of the steam. There is nothing magic about this. Something is not gained for nothing. As the specific volume increases, the torque capability and thermal efficiency decreases; however, the point is that a tradeoff between torque, efficiency, and speed is perfectly feasible by varying the specific volume of the steam. This fact strongly affects design of the modern steam automotive system. The whole philosophy of the control approach presented herein relies on this tradeoff.

Steam enthusiasts are quick to point out that evaporation of 1 in.^{3} of water under atmospheric pressure will expand to 1600 in.^{3}. This figure is indeed impressive and indicative of the compression characteristics of steam; however, at a pressure of 1000 psia, evaporation of 1 in.^{3} expands only to 22 in.^{3}. If the pressure is reduced to 400 psia, 1 in.^{3} will expand to 61 in.^{3}. The selection of an operating pressure is, therefore, not arbitrary. By having a mismatch between engine displacement and boiler pressure, it is possible that the resulting design may develop 600 horsepower and have a speed limit of 500 rpm. The motivation for a **VPB** is derived from control concepts which attempt to utilize the wide range of specific volumes available. However, speed control by cutoff is not practical since steam economy rises sharply as cutoff increases. Reference 2 reveals that almost any speed can be obtained at any desired torque by the proper combination of pressure and cutoff. This is of paramount importance. It is important to recognize that a vapor engine/boiler system, even with infinitely variable cutoff, is a difficult design to meet both turnpike and low-speed driving conditions. The control approach presented herein facilitates both ends of the driving spectrum. Two ends of the spectrum are:

1. Low speed with high torque.

2. Low torque at high speeds.

At this point, it is important to realize a more fundamental contribution of pressure and steam flow rate. Normally power is calculated from the "PLAN" equation. Thus, sometimes we say power is proportional to pressure; however, there is much more to consider. As the pressure increases, the specific volume decreases. For a given speed, more steam mass is required to maintain that speed. If the boiler is not capable to supply the additional quality, the pressure and speed cannot be maintained. The "PLAN" equation will yield false results. In using the "PLAN" equation, it must be assumed or proven that the boiler is capable of producing the steam demand. As a result of these phenomena, pressure becomes more indicative of torque or work and evaporation rate more indicative of power. Power is predetermined for a given flow rate and cutoff. More detailed study indicates that power becomes more sensitive to pressure at the higher fuel rate. For average driving speeds which require 0.5 to 1.0 pound of fuel per minute, pressure has little effect upon power for the range of pressures and temperatures applicable to the modern steam car.

What are the ideal performance characteristics of a power unit suitable for automotive application? The answer has been known for years. At low speeds, capability for large traction effort and high acceleration are most desirable. As the engine (automotive) speeds up, torque should be traded off for speed since less acceleration is needed. This tradeoff can be augmented by allowing the boiler pressure to decrease with speed. Realizing that ultimately flow rate is indicative of power, the maximum power level will not be compromised. This approach allows torque to be exchanged for speed. In conventional designs, torque was controlled primarily by the throttle cutoff. The VPB concept is a technique to change gears without a transmission.

A VPB is a new concept. Its values can be realized by considering the effect of boiler pressure upon specific volume of the steam. At low speeds, the boiler exhibits a high pressure, giving high torque capability. As the engine speed increases, the boiler pressure would be allowed to decrease to some controlled value. This essentially trades off torque for speed. The whole idea is consistent with the ideal torque-speed curve.

The VPB concept also precludes the use of a normalizer. Boiler behavior actually enhances operation of the VPB principles. Under conditions of "high fire," the boiler pressure will be relatively low in accordance with the VPB concept. Also, the engine speed and power must necessarily be at a maximum. If the load were suddenly removed and the engine speed reduced to zero, the automatic fuel control would reduce the fuel rate to zero; however, the residual heat in the boiler would continue to cause evaporation (thermal lag). Even though no fire is supplied to the boiler, the pressure will more than double. In the past this pressure rise has been controlled by use of a normalizer.

In systems which employ the VPB concept, the boiler pressure at "high fire" will be about 400 psia. Under sudden shutdown conditions, this pressure will rise to about 1000 psia, which is normal for the VPB concept under starting conditions. The normal behavior of fired pressure vessels facilitates the VPB concept. Normalizers are not required to limit the pressure since under normal operation of the VPB concept pressure rise is desirable to facilitate starting conditions. Sudden shutdown represents extreme conditions. Under less extreme conditions, the pressure rise will be less pronounced, thus being proportional to the pressure rise required in the VPB concept.

Probably the greatest advantage of the VPB concept is the way which it lends itself to electronic rather than mechanical force balance systems. Before integration schemes can be discussed, it is necessary to further define the pressure variation process. There are two basic concepts:

- First, the pressure may be controlled within a predetermined lower limit. This situation will be referred to as the "controlled" case.

- Second, the pressure variation may be uncontrolled. Resulting pressure depends upon engine load. This situation will be referred to as the "Run Wild" case.

Attention will be given here only to the second case.

It is noted that a variable pressure boiler provides a means of activating other auxiliaries. The variable pressure serves as a sensor and prime mover for performing switching functions.

The "Run Wild" approach offers a decisive advantage in the control area. The entire system is almost automatic. Speed and power are controlled entirely by the common input. At first, it may appear that the "Run Wild" approach would be completely unacceptable. Actually, for any common input, a steady state equilibrium is achieved between boiler pressure and wheel torque required to sustain the speed represented by the command.

The VPB concept is an approach to solve the problem of vapor engines. Even though at first it appears that more difficulty is introduced by the concept of a variable pressure boiler and a variable cutoff based on engine speed, actually the problems are reduced. This results from the dependency of each function on another; e.g., the feasibility of passive temperature control depends upon changes in boiler pressure and cutoff with speed, and at the same time, cutoff depends upon boiler pressure speed. The control problem has been integrated such that specific control functions have lost their identity. There is no single component which controls temperature pressure or speed. Control depends upon the "state" of all parameters. All of these parameters are so connected to complement each other. This philosophy is the backbone of the VPB concept.

Implementation of the VPB concept is a "natural." The mathematical representation of integrated controls is very complicated, but actual hardware is simple and well within the state-of-the-art. Some characteristics necessary to the operation of integrated controls are automatically introduced as results of interaction with other system parts.

The VPB concept is one of speed control rather than power control. This does not imply that an engine of small power has less speed capability. The variation of pressure and cutoff for fulfillment of passive temperature control is truly a "natural" in modern steam technology. This implies that a fuel rate alone can be mechanized to control the boiler pressure and at the same time limit supply steam temperatures. Note that this scheme is possible only if pressure is a function of speed. For design based on a fixed boiler pressure, the fire would have to burn continuously to rebuild pressure during acceleration periods. There would be no opportunity to limit the temperature by passive techniques. The VPB concept allows the boiler fire to burn less time and less vigorously since a lower pressure is to be rebuilt. The theoretical basis for passive temperature cutoff will be presented later.

A flow diagram of the hardware is shown in Figure 6. First, by a start sequence logic circuit, not shown, the boiler is brought up to its initial state. The pressure transducer and amplifier, ϕ_6, cuts out the command input amplifier. To start the engine, an electrical input is applied to the command input amplifier. However, at this time the fuel pump has been made inactive. Simultaneously with initiation of the input the throttle is opened 100 percent. The boiler pressure drops very quickly. As the pressure drops below the trip level of ϕ_7, a free flow is realized proportional to the control input. Cutoff is a function of engine speed depending upon the trip level of the amplifier; e.g., cutoff would be changed by dropping out a redundant port as suggested with the piston occultation valving engine. The car will accelerate to a speed which will balance the cylinder pressure in proportion to the power level represented by the input command.

Performance of the VPB Concept

Performance characteristics of systems employing the VPB concept will now be considered. The mathematical development of conventional systems is developed in Reference 2. Representation of the VPB concept will be developed as appropriately required. For purposes of completeness, the block diagram of conventional systems will be reviewed briefly. Figure 7 represents the block diagram form of conventional systems. Three main parts are identified:

1. Boiler
2. Engine dynamics
3. Feedback dynamics

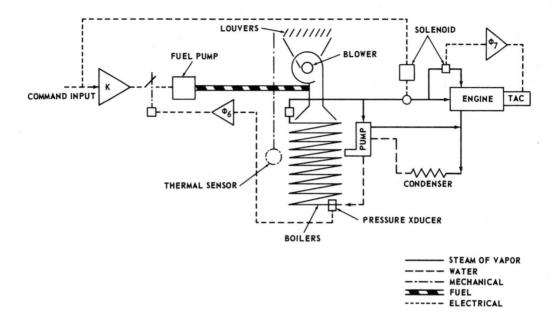

LOUVERS

FUEL PUMP

BLOWER

SOLENOID

Φ_7

COMMAND INPUT

K

Φ_6

THERMAL SENSOR

PUMP

ENGINE | TAC

CONDENSER

PRESSURE XDUCER

BOILERS

STEAM OF VAPOR
WATER
MECHANICAL
FUEL
ELECTRICAL

FIGURE 6. VPB FLOW DIAGRAM FOR "RUN WILD" CONCEPT

This diagram does not account for boiler warm up. It is assumed that the boiler is at operating pressure at start. The diagram accounts for the thermal lag after the throttle is opened. The pressure reference (PC) is preprogrammed by virtue of adjustments within the system. In the White Steam car, this reference pressure was set by the Finnigan Pin. The system reacts to maintain this pressure within the boiler. The boiler acts as a mechanical capacitor.

As energy is withdrawn through the engine a pressure drop is sensed which activates the fuel flow mechanism. The sensing signal is (P_e) which is the difference between the reference boiler pressure and actual boiler pressure. The amount of fuel flow is determined by the pressure error (P_e) and the gain (K_p). The amount of steam taken from the boiler is determined by the engine displacement, cutoff temperature, and speed. These parameters combined to subtract out the proper amount of steam. The steam consumed by the engine is designated as (M_u). If more steam is being taken out than being generated, the boiler pressure will continue to drop. In conventional systems, the design approach has been to select (K_p) such that the boiler pressure can be rebuilt under heavy demands; however, care has to be exercised to avoid unstable situations.

In the past, stability has been at the mercy of trial and error. An analysis of engine performance based upon block diagram techniques can establish the best value for (K_p). Also, the best gear ratio for a given engine displacement can be determined with authenticity. Realizing the "control system theory" was not developed until the late 40's, it is remarkable that the early steam control system operated as well as it did. Establishment of gains can only be understood through mathematics and not through the physics of the control problem. No attempt has been made in the analysis given herein to opportunize the parameters. A scan was made of sufficient depth to pick the value which gave reasonable performance.

The "Run Wild" approach to control of the modern steam automotive system is the most provocative idea in steam power since Papin (1690) discovered the power in a partial vacuum. The most unique factor is the absence of a throttle. While running, the primary valve is wide open (100-percent throttle). The steam is not throttled. Power and speed are controlled only by the fuel rate input.

The block diagram representation of the "Run Wild" approach is shown in Figure 8. This diagram appears

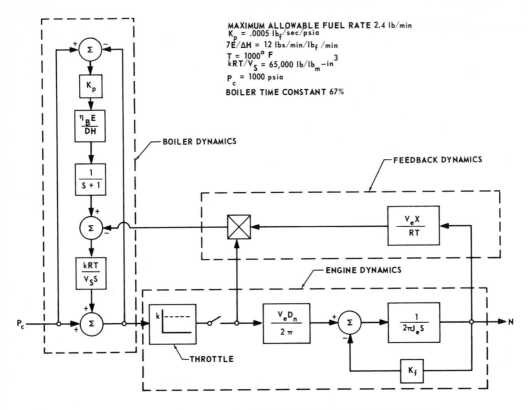

MAXIMUM ALLOWABLE FUEL RATE 2.4 lb/min
$K_p = .0005$ lb$_f$/sec/psia
$7E/\Delta H = 12$ lbs/min/lb$_f$/min
$T = 1000°$ F
$kRT/V_S = 65,000$ lb/lb$_m$ $-$in^3
$P_c = 1000$ psia
BOILER TIME CONSTANT 67%

BOILER DYNAMICS

FEEDBACK DYNAMICS

ENGINE DYNAMICS

THROTTLE

FIGURE 7. BLOCK DIAGRAM OF A CONVENTIONAL BOILER-ENGINE SYSTEM

similar to the conventional system. There are two primary differences:

1. All feedback circuits have been eliminated which controls the boiler pressure (P_B).

2. The cutoff is changed depending upon speed. For speeds less than 20 mph the cutoff is 33 percent. For any speed greater than 20 mph the cutoff is changed to 12 percent unless otherwise noted.

There is also a pressure cutoff which removes the fuel pump from the line whenever the pressure reaches a predetermined level. For our purposes here, this level has been established at 1000 psia. This pressure reference is noted at (P_R) on Figure 8. Details of the start sequence will be given later.

The selection of the speed at which the cutoff changes is arbitrary and does not represent any level of optimization. A command input is provided by the operator as shown. The command is operated on by a pure grain block which converts the command to a fuel rate. As long as a given fuel rate is imposed, the generator will provide essentially a fixed evaporation rate. This rate will not cease until the command input is changed or the boiler reaches 1000 psia. There are no feedbacks to adjust the fuel rate as in the Stanley or White vehicles. This rate represents a specific power level. As the vehicle accelerates, the pressure drops immediately to saturate the boiler at a pressure governed by the gear ratio and torque saturation characteristics. When cutoff is changed to a lower value, the boiler becomes unsaturated. Thus, the boiler pressures will rise rapidly; however, as acceleration continues, steam demand is greater and the boiler seeks a new saturation level. Experiences have

222

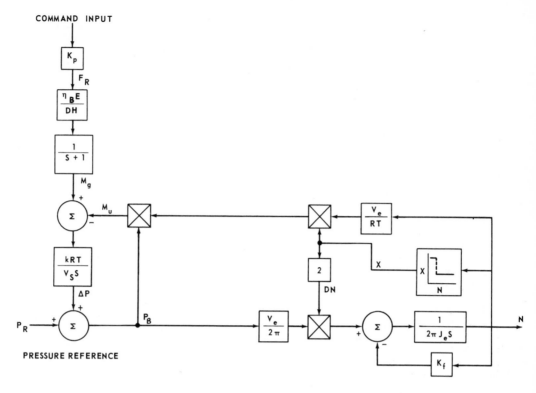

COMMAND INPUT

FIGURE 8. BLOCK DIAGRAM OF THE "RUN WILD" SYSTEM

indicated that the primary factor affecting the amount of boiler pressure drop depends upon fuel rate.

For low fuel rates the pressure will drop below 100 psia. Associated with this is a low speed (20 mph), thus a relatively high cutoff is maintained (33 percent). A 33-percent cutoff can easily sustain a 100-psia pressure without "loops" occurring in the P-V diagram. The ability to hold a long cutoff at low fuel rate is, therefore, the reason why the "Run Wild" approach works.

It would be impossible to bleed the boiler to zero pressure since the vehicle will accelerate only to the speed represented by the torque saturation as set by gear ratio, engine displacement, and cutoff.

The basic nature of boiler pressure is given in Figure 9. Two curves are shown, one for a relatively low fuel rate, the other for a relatively high fuel rate. In both cases, the pressure drops immediately from the 1000-psia reference pressures. The pressure always recovers, and a new

equilibrium pressure is established. Even though a very wide variation is experienced by the boiler pressure, the acceleration proceeds smoothly as will be shown.

As mentioned earlier, this case was set up for a maximum cutoff of 33 percent; higher maximum values may be more suitable to accommodate the low pressure occurring in the fuel range. For the top curve (0.9 lb/min), cutoff is changed to 12 percent at about 1.5 seconds from start. In the lower curve (0.09 lb/min), the cutoff change occurs at about 12.5 seconds.

The fact that pressure varies over a wide range constitutes the term "Run Wild." Actually, this name is not indicative of this approach since the pressure can be predicted for any given fuel rate, gear ratio, engine displacement, and cutoff speed-level change. The change in speed as a result of the pressure variation is shown in Figure 10. The driver would not notice the pressure change unless he watched the pressure gauge. Notice that 60 mph is obtained after an elapsed time of 12 seconds for a fuel rate of 0.9 lb/min.

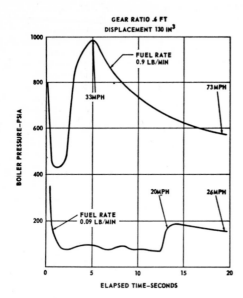

FIGURE 9. PRESSURE CHARACTERISTICS
OF THE "RUN WILD" VPB CONCEPT (Low
pressure and low speeds are characterized by
a low fuel rate. The throttle is opened to
100 percent at time-zero. Wide open
throttle is maintained throughout
the acceleration period.)

Now that the basic charter of pressure has been
revealed, it is necessary to establish the effect of other characteristics. Figure 11 illustrates the effect of gear ratios
and engine displacement. These graphs have been constructed for a fuel rate of 0.72 lb of fuel per minute. It is
interesting to observe that an 80-in.³ displacement engine
with a gear ratio of 1.0 ft performs exactly as a conventional
engine. The reference pressure is maintained throughout
the acceleration period. The lowest pressure experienced
during each period increases as displacements increase and
decreases as the gear ratio decreases.

It is noticed that the pressure tends to oscillate
slightly at its lowest and highest peaks. The reason for this
is not known; however, it is not an unstable situation. In
all cases investigated, the pressure never became uncontrollable. In an actual vehicle, this "ripple" may never
occur since it will probably be washed out by the dynamics
of the drive train and wheels. Stiffness of the drive train
was not considered in the model. Figure 11 covers gear
ratios between 1.0 and 0.4 ft. These in combination with
different engine displacements produce almost every kind

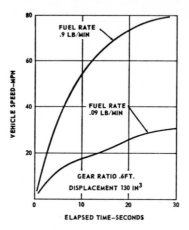

FIGURE 10. ACCELERATION CHARACTERISTICS
OF THE "RUN WILD" SYSTEM (Even though
large pressure variations are exhibited by
the "Run Wild" approach, acceleration
characteristics are normal to those of
conventional systems. A slight
sag appears in the curve for
small fuel rates.)

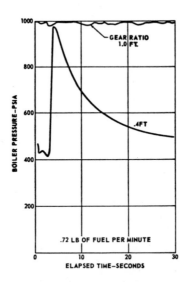

FIGURE 11. AFFECT OF GEAR RATIO UPON THE
"RUN WILD" SYSTEM FOR AN 80-IN.³
DISPLACEMENT ENGINE (A gear ratio of 1.0 ft
allows the boiler to be unsaturated.)

224

of pressure behavior. Regardless of the pressure variation, the vehicle will accelerate smoothly to any desired speed as determined by the fuel input.

At first, it may have appeared that speed control would be a near impossibility with the "Run Wild" approach. Also, one may have guessed that proper selection of gear ratio in conjunction with engine displacement would become a very difficult engineering problem. However, an analysis indicates that the "Run Wild" approach inherently provides solutions to many of the optimizing problems. Optimizing as used here is meant to imply the selection of parameters which best suit the widest speed range. Even though the pressure may be "running wild," this behavior in itself is relatively unimportant providing speed control and fuel economy exhibit normal or superior performance. In this statement lies the true value of the "Run Wild" system.

Figure 12 is the steady state speed and fuel consumption as a function of gear ratio. These data are plotted

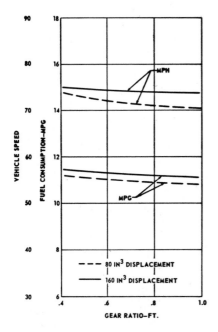

FIGURE 12. SENSITIVITY OF GEAR RATIO AND ENGINE DISPLACEMENT UPON STEADY STATE VEHICLE SPEED AND FUEL CONSUMPTION FOR A CONSTANT 0.72 POUND OF FUEL PER MINUTE INPUT (Vehicle speed is primarily a function of fuel input rather than gear ratio or engine displacement. The flatness of these curves are of primary significance.)

for two displacements; 160 and 80 in.[3]. Performance is very different from that exhibited by either the conventional or controlled approach. It is remarkable that both fuel consumption and vehicle speed are virtually insensitive to both gear ratio and displacement. This allows the gear ratio and displacement to be picked for other reasons than speed considerations. Thus, the designer has greater freedom. The flat nature of these curves is inherent and peculiar to the "Run Wild" system. The pressure variation is what makes this characteristic possible. At high gear ratios, the steady state pressure is relatively high, thus increasing the saturation torque level. But, the high gear ratio tends to lower the saturation torque level. The high gear ratio results in a relatively low engine speed. At low gear ratios, the steady state pressure is relatively lower; however, the saturation torque level is raised as a result of the low gear ratio, thus the engine tends to run faster to satisfy the saturation requirements. The saturation torque level loss caused by pressures is compensated for almost one to one by the low gear ratio. In the case of the high gear ratio, the saturation torque loss as a result of the gear ratio is compensated for by the greater pressure. This tradeoff is a "natural" and results in a relatively flat speed curve. Since the speed is nearly constant and since a constant fuel input is applied, the fuel consumption is also nearly constant.

The nature of fuel economy as a function of speed is illustrated in Figure 13. The dashed curve is applicable to the "Run Wild" system.

The "Run Wild" approach may be the answer to the control problem of the modern automotive steam vehicle. The system is easier to design, insensitive to gear ratio and engine displacement, and provides an overall superior performance.

Because of the simple nature of the "Run Wild" approach, this system would have merit even though inferior performance existed. The fact that better performance is obtained puts the "Run Wild" approach in a class all by itself. This is the "new steam."

"Run-Wild" Parametric Data

Sizing of an engine which is to operate in the "Run-Wild" mode can only be accomplished successfully through a system approach. The engine displacement and gear ratio depends upon allowable fuel rates and automobile weight. If these variables are selected at random, a combination may result which allows the boiler pressure to decay below desired levels. It is therefore desirable to have parameter data for a given engine and automobile weight which illustrates the sensitivity of boiler pressure to displacement, temperature, gear ratio, and fuel rate. Such data are presented in Figures 14 and 15.

Figure 14 illustrates a steady state boiler pressure as a function of displacement with temperature as an

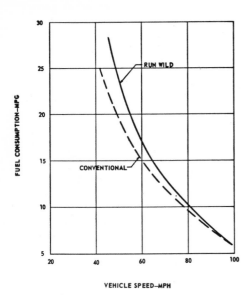

VEHICLE SPEED—MPH

FIGURE 13. RELATIONSHIP BETWEEN THE CON-
VENTIONAL AND "RUN WILD" SYSTEMS FROM A
FUEL CONSUMPTION VIEWPOINT (The "Run Wild"
system requires simpler controls and provides
superior performance.)

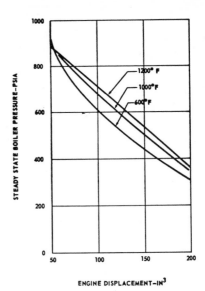

ENGINE DISPLACEMENT—IN^3

FIGURE 14. THE RELATIONSHIP BETWEEN STEADY
STATE BOILER PRESSURE AND ENGINE
DISPLACEMENT IS INDEPENDENT OF SUPPLY
PRESSURE (These curves are valid for a cutoff
of 15 percent, a fuel flow of 1.08 lb per
minute and a total gear ratio of 0.6 ft.)

argument. There are two characteristics predominant in this graph. First, at a displacement of just above 50 in.³ there appears to be a crossover point. To the left of this point, a temperature of 600°F produces a larger steady state boiler pressure than 1200°F; however, the difference is only slight. The "real" existence of these characteristics has not been confirmed and may result from over extension of the math model to predict performance over wide temperature and displacement ranges; however, the math model accounts for the variation of the gas constant with pressure and temperature. These data, therefore, represent more than a second-order evaluation.

The second unique characteristic of Figure 14 is the independency of pressure. These curves are valid for control pressure between 800 and 1200 psia. It is expected that steady state boiler pressure be completely independent of pressure. It is important to recognize that these data were obtained for a fixed fare rate of 1.08 lb/min, a 3000-pound car with a gear ratio of 0.6 ft.

To evaluate the sensitivity of steady state boiler pressure for a variety of gear ratios and fuel rates, a 100-in.³

engine was selected operating with 1000°F steam. As already mentioned, the steady state boiler pressure is not a function of the initial pressure. The results are shown in Figure 15. It was shown previously that gear ratio had little effect on speed; however, the pressure level can be controlled to any level by selection of gear ratio.

No attempt has been made to establish the characteristics of the "Run-Wild" approach for fuel rates below 0.36 lb/min. The nature of the supply temperature and boiler efficiency at the lower fuel rates was not known with sufficient confidence to warrant an extension of the math model into this region. Intuitively there must be some "cutoff fuel rate" below which boiler pressures cannot be sustained. The nature of such a "cutoff" must be known to make any confident predictions.

As a last word concerning performance of the "Run-Wild" approach, some details of the circuit for the start cycle will be covered. This circuit is illustrated in Figure 16. First, the individual compounds will be defined:

The start switch activates all portions of the control circuit from the adjoining battery. By opening the circuit, the fan, fuel pump, and spark coil are deactivated.

Thermal Relay

This is a thermal time relay activated upon closing the start switch. This relay controls a predetermined combustion rate during the start-up period. It prevents "driving off" prior to a given time after initiation of the start switch.

Accelerator

The accelerator is a potentiometer which becomes activated whenever the thermal time delay switches from position (A) to position (B). Position (B) will relinquish all fuel commands to the accelerator as long as the start switch is closed. The accelerator also incorporates a microswitch which opens the throttle (100 percent) whenever a sufficient command is given.

Pressure Transducers

Two pressure transducers are provided. One is a mechanical pressure switch, whereas the other has an output proportional to pressure. At a sufficiently high pressure, this transducer fires the limiter pressure transducer which activates relay (D). These two transducers control the upper

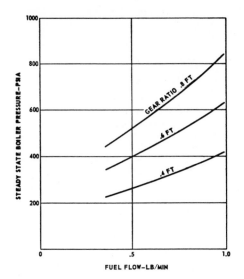

FIGURE 15. STEADY STATE BOILER PRESSURE CAN BE CONTROLLED TO ANY DESIRED LEVEL BY ADJUSTING THE TOTAL GEAR RATIO (These data are valid for a 100-in.^{3} engine, with 15-percent cutoff and supply steam at 1000°F.)

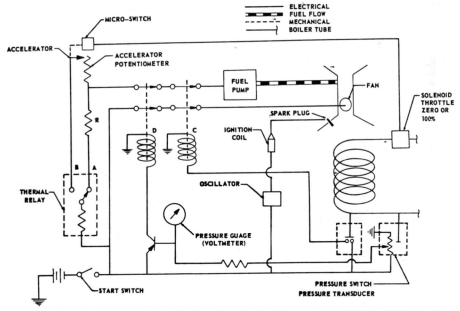

FIGURE 16. THE ROOD ELECTRICAL LOGIC SYSTEM FOR THE "RUN WILD" PRESSURE CONTROL CONCEPT

limit on boiler pressure. The only purpose for two transducers is reliability.

Spark Coil and Oscillator

The spark coil is activated upon closing the start switch and remains on until the switch is opened.

Pressure Gauge

The pressure gauge senses the voltage output from the second pressure transducer. The gauge is calibrated to read boiler pressure.

Cyclic Operation

Upon closing of the start switch, the proportional pressure transducers become activated. This also begins the elapse time required to trip the thermal time relay. Immediately upon closing the switch, a predetermined voltage is input into the fuel pump.

This voltage is controlled by the size of resistor (R). Also, the fan and spark oscillators are activated. The thermal time delay valve is selected just over the normal time for the boiler to reach about 900 psia. Afterwards, the thermal accumulator effects will drive the pressure upward to about 1000 psia. When 900 psia is obtained within the boiler, the output of the proportional transducer is sufficient to trigger the limiter pressure transistor relay (D). This relay removes voltages from the fuel pump and fan. In the event of a failure of this transducer, the pressure switch will activate relay (C), accomplishing the same results. After these events occur, the thermal relay switches to position (B). The accelerator is now the only means to control the voltage on the fuel pump. Remember that either relay (C), (D), or both is still holding the fuel pump and fan circuit in the open position.

Now, depress the accelerator, triggering the microswitch and opening the throttle to 100 percent. The steam will flow through the engine, causing a 400- to 600-psia pressure drop within the boiler. This occurs within the first second. Meanwhile, the car begins to accelerate. As the pressure drops below 900 psia, the limiter transducer will cut off and drop the fuel pump and fan back on the line. The boiler pressure will then seek a steady state pressure in the fashion described earlier. The final pressure will depend upon the actual fuel rate input, gear ratio, and engine displacement. If passive temperature control proves to be practical, only this little circuit will be required to start and control the car. Such an event would represent a step increase in modern steam system control technology.

Passive Temperature Control

The purpose here is to provide a theoretical basis to justify more comprehensive analysis and to develop the necessary mathematical requirements for passive temperature control.

Passive temperature depends upon the combined effects of fuel rate, excess air, and a variable pressure boiler. If these variables are controlled in a particular relationship it may be possible to eliminate active boiler temperature control. This is an interesting technical challenge and, indeed, offers a great advantage to the simplicity of boiler controls. On this basis alone, its study is justified.

This paper does not provide proof that passive control is possible; however, the necessary considerations are developed. For a given boiler configuration the change in temperature of the supply steam can be described completely by the total derivative of the temperature (T). The equations presented herein cannot be solved as a result of unknown boiler characteristics; however, such data can become available through development testing.

$$dT = \frac{\partial T}{\partial P}\,dP + \frac{\partial T}{\partial M}\,dM$$

Affect of steam demand

Affect of a variable pressure boiler

$$+ \frac{\partial T}{\partial F_R}\,dF_R + \frac{\partial T}{\partial A_E}\,dA_E$$

Affect of excess

Affect of energy input

The partial $\partial T/\partial P$ provides for the effect of steam density upon heat transfer. The partial $\partial T/\partial M$ is negative since an increase in mass for a given fuel rate will cause a decrease in the steam temperature. This effect results from the shorter heating period associated with higher mass flow. The partial $\partial T/\partial F_R$ is positive and accounts for the combustion effects.

Normally, for the conventional boiler operation, the partial $\partial T/\partial P$ would not be considered since the boiler is designed to operate at a fixed pressure. However, by considering variable pressure boilers, this term becomes necessary for the proper mathematical representation. It also allows for an additional parameter which can be adjusted to achieve passive temperature control. Excess air has the effect of reducing the combustion gas temperature.

It is desirable that the total derivative dT be zero. This implies that the change in the supply temperature be zero over the entire range of M, F_R, and pressure. Indeed, if passive temperature control is to be effective, the change must be zero or at least small within acceptable limits.

$$\frac{\partial T}{\partial P} \, dP + \frac{\partial T}{\partial M} \, dM + \frac{\partial T}{\partial F_R} \, dF_R$$

$$+\frac{\partial T}{\partial A_E} \, dA_E = 0$$

Dividing by dF_R and setting the equation to zero yields:

$$\frac{\partial T}{\partial A_E} \frac{dA_E}{dF_R} + \frac{\partial T}{\partial F_R} + \frac{\partial T}{\partial M} \frac{dM}{dF_R}$$

$$+ \frac{\partial T}{\partial P} \frac{dP}{dF_R} = 0$$

$$\frac{\partial T}{\partial A_E} \frac{dA_E}{dF_R} + \frac{\partial T}{\partial F_R} + \frac{\partial T}{\partial M} \frac{dM}{dF_R}$$

$$+ \frac{\partial T}{\partial P} \frac{dP}{dM} \frac{dM}{dF_R} = 0$$

But,

$$\frac{dM}{dF_R} = \eta_B \frac{E}{\Delta H} = \beta$$

$$\frac{\partial T}{\partial A_E} \frac{d A_E}{dF_R} + \frac{\partial T}{\partial F_R}$$

$$+ \beta \left[\frac{\partial T}{\partial M} + \frac{\partial T}{\partial P} \frac{dP}{dM} \right] = 0$$

It is noted that dM/dF_R has been designated as a constant. This is not entirely true since ΔH changes with pressure. However, this change is slight, even over a wide pressure range. Typically, β equals 10 lb/min/lb$_f$/min.

The partials $\partial T/\partial M$, $\partial T/\partial P$, $\partial T/\partial A_E$, and $\partial T/\partial F_R$ have to be determined by tests. The derivative dA_E/dF_R can be constant or variable depending upon the need to satisfy the equation. Its value is controlled primarily by the

fan motor and metering the ram air. For the conventional control approach, the derivative dP/dM would be zero since the system is designed to operate at a fixed pressure. However, by introducing a variable pressure boiler, another variable is obtained for controlling the nature of the passive temperature control equation.

The exact nature of dP/dM depends upon the specific control system employed. A control system which results in boiler pressure as a function of mass flow rate has already been described.

Now, assume that the combustion gas temperature can be controlled by the amount of excess air such that the effect of fuel rate has no effect on the steam outlet temperature:

$$\frac{\partial T}{\partial A_E} \frac{dA_E}{dF_R} + \frac{\partial T}{\partial F_R} = 0$$

This is a reasonable assumption since combustion gas temperature can be controlled by ± 500°F by a ± 20-percent change in excess air. At high speeds, sufficient ram air is present for 400-percent excess air. Under these conditions, the passive temperature control equation reduces to:

$$\frac{\partial P}{\partial M} = - \frac{dP}{dM}$$

This equation is satisfied whenever pressure (steady state) is a function of mass rate of flow only (for a given design). The temperature obtained by the supply steam will depend only on the design of the system.

References

1. Jerry A. Peoples; "Autoaniquarian News," AACA, Vol. 6, No. 5, North Alabama Region, December 1969.

2. Jerry A. Peoples; Steam Automotive Analysis, Carlton Press, New York, 1970

Acknowledgement

Appreciation is hereby acknowledged for the support provided by: Mr. William K. Evans of Tucker, Georgia, Mr. Orville T. Guffin of Huntsville, Alabama, and Mr. Robert W. Rood of Madison, Alabama.

UTILIZATION OF HOMOGENEOUS CHEMILUMINESCENT GAS REACTIONS IN AIR POLLUTION MONITORING AND CONTROL

Arthur Fontijn,* Alberto J. Sabadell, and Richard J. Ronco
AeroChem Research Laboratories, Inc., P.O. Box 12, Princeton, N.J. 08540
a subsidiary of Sybron Corporation

Abstract

Aerospace programs and aerospace-oriented laboratory research have provided quantitative information on a number of homogeneous chemiluminescent gas reactions of molecules which are air pollutants. Measurements of the emission intensity of such reactions can be used to determine the concentrations of the pollutants. In a detector based on this principle, ambient air and the second reactant can be continuously flowed through and mixed in a reactor under moderate vacuum (typically ≈ 1 Torr). After calibration a continuous record of pollutant concentration can be obtained. Specific sensitivity to a given pollutant is achieved by a suitable choice of the second reactant and a light filter. To demonstrate the feasibility of the method, the detection of NO using O_3 has been studied experimentally. A linear response from ≈ 4 ppb (v/v) to at least 100 ppm NO is obtained. NO_2, CO_2, CO, C_2H_4, NH_3, SO_2, and H_2O in concentrations encountered in air quality control do not interfere with NO monitoring. Calculations based on these results and published experimental data for other chemiluminescent reactions indicate strongly that homogeneous chemiluminescence monitors can probably also be developed for at least O_3, NO_x (= NO + NO_2), and CO.

I. Introduction

As a result of their multifold applications in aerospace programs, our knowledge of chemiluminescent gas reactions has increased considerably in the past twenty years. Releases of chemicals in the upper atmosphere leading to chemiluminescent reactions with ambient species have been used to characterize atmospheric mass transport processes (speed, direction, and shear of winds, turbulence, and diffusion),[1-3] composition,[1,4,5] and temperature.[6] Observations of such releases have also affected our knowledge of chemical kinetics; one interesting example of this interaction of disciplines is the observation that NO clusters are formed by the isentropic expansion following its release in the upper atmosphere and that such clusters produce chemiluminescence in their reaction with O atoms at a much faster rate than do free NO molecules.[7,8] Chemiluminescence has also been studied in connection with re-entry wakes,[9,10] rocket exhausts,[11,12] and propellant burning characteristics.[13]

Several of the species encountered or used in the above work are also formed in combustion sources and are major air pollutants, e.g., NO, NO_2, and CO. The extensive knowledge of the reactions of these species which has now become available[14-16] can be applied to the study of pollution problems. Thus, the chemiluminescent reactions of O atoms,[17,18] H atoms,[19] and O_3[20,21] with NO, and of O atoms[22] with CO can be used as diagnostic tools in a chemically reacting system. The observation of light emission does not require the use of a probe or sampling device and therefore does not interfere with the system being studied. An investigation of NO formation in internal combustion engines, based on this principle, has recently been reported.[23] The presence of "steady-state" concentrations of pollutants, e.g., in ambient air, in stack gases, or in the exhaust from an automobile tail pipe can be monitored by continuous sampling and mixing of the sample with a second reactant such as O atoms, etc., to produce chemiluminescence. In some applications the monitor may also be used as a feed-back type of control device. The present paper concerns a feasibility study for a continuous monitor based on this principle, and demonstrates the practicality of the concept.†

The use of homogeneous gas-phase chemiluminescent reactions for monitoring purposes is attractive for a number of reasons, particularly the following: (i) the emission is specific for the pollutant being monitored (suitable choice of the second reactant and a light filter allows interference-free measurements), (ii) the chemiluminescence light intensities from homogeneous gas-phase reactions in continuous flow systems are rather insensitive to changes in surface properties, and (iii) a family of chemiluminescence monitors could be constructed, each of which is specific for one pollutant, but all of which are similar in

This work was supported by the National Air Pollution Control Administration under Contracts CPA 22-69-11 and CPA 70-79. We have benefited from discussions with J. Hodgson, R.K. Stevens, and A.E. O'Keeffe of the National Air Pollution Control Administration.

*To whom all inquiries should be addressed.

†We have previously reported[24] the data given here and are currently building an instrument for field use, based on the reported findings.

operation. In the operation of monitoring stations, the convenience of families of instruments with similar manipulation and maintenance requirements would be considerable.

A schematic design of the chemiluminescence detector is shown in Figure 1. The air to be monitored and the second reactant, e.g., O_3, enter the reaction vessel through separate inlets. Rapid mixing occurs and a chemiluminescent reaction takes place. A preset flow of the gases is maintained by a mechanical vacuum pump. The pressure in the reaction vessel is typically 1 Torr and the size of the vessel 1 liter. The intensity of the light emitted is measured by a photomultiplier tube and associated read-out devices (current meter and recorder). After calibration with samples of known concentration, a continuous record of the concentration of the pollutant in air is obtained.

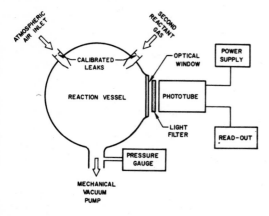

Fig. 1 Chemiluminescence Detector

To determine the feasibility of the method and its optimum operation conditions, an experimental monitoring system has been built and incorporated in an apparatus which allows for convenient changes in flow rates and pressure. Our studies with this device have concentrated on the detection of NO, using O_3 as the second reactant; the lack of interference by other common air constituents and pollutants with the response of the NO/O_3 system has been established. Based on calculations using rate constants and spectral data obtained mainly from aerospace-inspired laboratory work, the concept is shown (see Section IV) to be practical for other pollutants also.

II. Experimental

A schematic of the Pyrex/stainless steel/copper flow system is shown in Figure 2. Oxygen (Linde, Aviators Breathing Grade) and nitrogen (Matheson, Prepurified), dried near atmospheric pressure by activated alumina, pass through flow meters and needle valves into the low pressure

part of the system. On the high pressure side the O_2 is ozonated ($\approx 0.5\%$ v/v) photolytically. N_2 serves as the carrier gas for NO and the other pollutants for which possible interference with NO detection was investigated. The NO is introduced into a 3 liter spherical Pyrex exponential dilution flask, containing a completely enclosed magnetically-driven stirrer. The O_2/O_3 and N_2/pollutant streams are mixed in the 1 liter spherical Pyrex reactor. The flow is maintained with a 5 cfm Welch Duo-Seal vacuum pump.

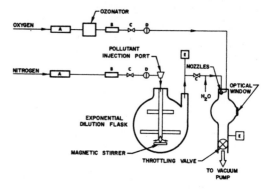

Fig. 2 Gas Flow System
A, absorbing tower; B, flowmeter; C, needle valve; D, stopcock; E, manometer

The gas streams enter the reaction flask through nozzles having small openings (1 to 2 mm diam) in the direction perpendicular to the neck of the flask. The reactor has a 7.5 cm diam flat quartz window facing the photo-cathode of the photomultiplier tube used for light intensity measurements. The reactor is coated externally with Eastman white reflectance paint ($BaSO_4$) and is packed with MgO powder inside an aluminum box. The use of this powder further increases the available light intensity and provides for a light-tight detection system.

The emission is filtered through a Corning CS 2-60 filter, cutting off radiation of $\lambda < 6100$ Å; its intensity is measured with an EMI 9558 QA trialkali photomultiplier tube. The tube is contained in a thermoelectrically-cooled housing, maintained at $\approx -20°C$, and operated at a cathode-to-anode voltage of 1400 V. The tube output is measured by an electrometer with dc zero-offset and recorded.

The experiments were performed at room temperature at the following reactant concentrations (in moles liter^{-1}): $[N_2] = 2.7 \times 10^{-5}$; $[O_2] = 2.7 \times 10^{-5}$; $[O_3] = 1.1 \times 10^{-7}$. Total reaction pressure was held at 1 Torr ($[M] = 5.4 \times 10^{-5}$ mole l^{-1}). The flow rates of O_2 and N_2 into the system were 1.25 ml (STP) sec^{-1}. The O_3 flow was measured by iodometric titration.

NO concentrations were varied over a range of 4 ppb to 100 ppm of that of N_2 (1×10^{-13} to 3×10^{-9} mole 1^{-1}). The NO was purified by passage over activated alumina (for removal of H_2O) and Ascarite (for removal of NO_2). Atmospheric pressure samples were injected with a gas-tight syringe through the rubber stopper of a 5 liter Pyrex predilution flask, containing prepurified N_2 at atmospheric pressure. After thorough mixing, samples containing NO in concentrations in the range of 10 to 10^5 ppm were taken from this flask and injected through the rubber stopper injection port of the exponential dilution flask of the main flow system (Figure 2). Under these conditions the concentration of a sample injected in the flask decreases exponentially:[25]

$$C = C_0 \exp(-Qt/V) \qquad (1)$$

where C_0 = initial concentration; Q = volume flow rate at the flask pressure; V = effective volume of the dilution flask; t = time elapsed from start of dilution. The pressure in the flask was maintained at 50 Torr, which gave a convenient time constant (V/Q on the order of 150 sec) for our measurements. The recorder gives a continuous record of the system response; the points shown on the dilution plots (see below) are from these continuous records.

In a number of experiments the effect of the presence of other air constituents and pollutants on the detector response to NO was investigated. Best regular grade gases were used. CO_2, SO_2, C_2H_4, and NH_3 were taken directly from cylinders. CO was first passed through a liquid N_2 trap for removal of carbonyl compounds. NO_2 was taken from a blackened Pyrex flask in which it had been mixed with an equal portion of atmospheric air; this procedure was followed to oxidize trace amounts of NO to NO_2 and to prevent photodissociation of NO_2. These interference gases were injected in the same exponential dilution flask as used for NO. Separate predilution flasks were used.

Water vapor could be introduced with a second N_2 flow system. Up to 75% of the total N_2 flow was diverted through this system, which was designed so that N_2 passed either through a saturator or directly to the H_2O port (Figure 2). This set-up allowed for rapid comparison between the detector response to NO with 75% saturated and dry N_2. The saturator was filled with H_2O at 45°C. Complete saturation of N_2 flowing through the H_2O port was achieved, as evidenced by the formation of droplets in a room temperature trap downstream from the saturator.

III. Results and Discussion

The Reaction Between NO and O_3

O_3 was selected as a suitable second reactant for NO monitoring on the basis of the following a priori considerations. The reaction between NO and O_3 had been investigated extensively[20, 21] and it had been established that the chemiluminescence is due to

$$NO + O_3 \rightarrow NO_2^* + O_2 \qquad (2)$$

$$NO_2^* \rightarrow NO_2 + h\nu \qquad (3)$$

The presence of NO in air is accompanied by that of NO_2,[26] which reacts only slowly with O_3, producing higher oxides.[27,28] Other reactants such as O and H atoms also produce a rather intense chemiluminescence with NO.[18,19] However, they react rapidly with NO_2, producing NO.[29,30] As a result, these atoms appear suitable for the measurement of $[NO] + [NO_2]$, but not for $[NO]$ in the presence of NO_2.

The light intensity of the NO/O_3 reaction is given by:[20]

$$I_3 = 12 \{ \exp(-4180 \pm 300)/RT \} \{[NO][O_3]/[M]\} \sec^{-1} \qquad (4)$$

for the 6000 to 8750 Å region for M = air. The [M] appears in the denominator because the emitting species, NO_2^*, is quenched by M, i.e., any gaseous species present. The units of I_3 obtained from Equation (4) are, e.g., einsteins 1^{-1} sec^{-1} or quanta ml^{-1} sec^{-1}, depending on whether moles 1^{-1} or number of particles ml^{-1} concentration units are employed. From the relative intensity distribution of the emission spectrum[21] it may be seen that no light is emitted below ≈ 6000 Å. Comparison to the EMI 9558 QA phototube spectral response characteristic shows that the tube's peak sensitivity falls at wavelengths shorter than 6000 Å. Therefore the use of the CS 2-60 filter does not appreciably interfere with the sensitivity of the monitor for NO detection by O_3, but decreases the possibility of interference by other pollutants. The phototube response cuts off near 8750 Å; therefore the I_3 value given by Equation (4) is roughly that for the useful emission region of our experiments.

The rate constant for the overall reaction, as defined by

$$-\frac{d[O_3]}{dt} = -\frac{d[NO]}{dt} = k[NO][O_3] \qquad (5)$$

is 1×10^7 1 $mole^{-1}$ sec^{-1} at room temperature.[20] This figure indicates that $\approx 40\%$ of the NO is consumed in the reaction flask (residence time $\approx$ 0.5 sec; $[O_3] = 1.1 \times 10^{-7}$ mole 1^{-1}).

Linearity of Response and Limit of Sensitivity for NO Detection

Figure 3 gives a composite plot of the detector response to NO. It may be seen (i) that the light intensity varies linearly with NO concentration over the range of concentrations investigated ($\approx$ 4 ppb to 100 ppm), and (ii) that 4 ppb represents the approximate limit of sensitivity for our operating conditions. Two types of data points may be distinguished: (i) those obtained from the initial injection of NO into the dilution flask and (ii) points taken from exponential dilution plots, cf. Figure 4, on the assumption that a decrease in intensity by a factor x corresponds to a decrease in NO concentration by a factor x. It may be seen from Figure 3 that both types of points fall along the same line, thus confirming the linearity of response with respect to NO concentration. The scatter in the data of Figure 3 increases with decreasing NO concentration. This can reasonably be attributed to a decreasing accuracy of sample preparation.

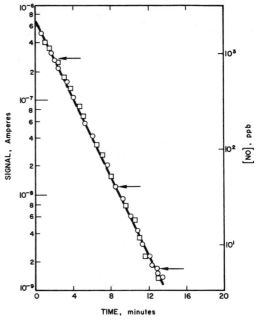

Fig. 4 Effect of NO_2 on Detector Response to NO

$\square$ = NO
$\bigcirc$ = NO + NO_2

The arrows indicate the points at which 9 ppm NO_2 was injected during the exponential dilution process.

Effect of Other Air Constituents on the Detector Response to NO

The possibility of interference by other commonly encountered air pollutants/constituents was investigated by adding them to the N_2/NO flow. A typical test run is shown in Figure 4 for the case of NO_2. This figure shows points obtained (i) in a normal NO dilution run and (ii) an NO run during which NO_2 was injected. Because the concentration of NO_2 decreased in the dilution process (presumably at the same rate as that of NO), it was desirable to repeat the NO_2 injections several times in the course of one NO run. It may be seen from this figure that the presence of 9 ppm NO_2 does not influence the detector's response to NO down to $\approx$ 6 ppb. The same procedure as for NO_2 was followed for CO_2, CO, C_2H_4, NH_3, and SO_2.

The results are summarized in Table 1 in terms of concentration of the constituent tested which was found not to interfere with the NO signal at [NO] $\leq$ 10 ppb. It may be seen that these concentrations exceed--and in most cases are considerably higher--than typical high concentrations of these compounds in polluted air. By using concentrations of NO_2, C_2H_4, and NH_3 about two times higher than given in the last column of Table 1, signals in excess of those obtained at 10 ppb of NO

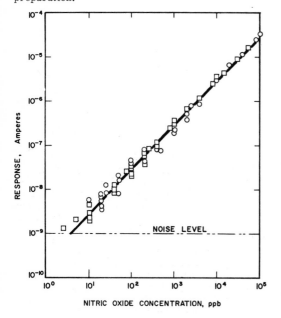

Fig. 3 Dependence of the Response of the Chemi·luminescence Detector on Nitric Oxide Concentration

$\bigcirc$ = Initial concentrations
$\square$ = Data from exponential dilution plots

The maximum concentration of NO encountered in air quality control is $\approx$ 1 ppm.[26] The present-day "natural" background level is not known, but concentrations below $\approx$ 5 - 10 ppb do not appear to be of much practical interest. The linearity of response and sensitivity of the detector are thus quite satisfactory for its use as a monitor of NO in air.

Table 1 Lack of Interference of Other Air Constituents with Nitric Oxide Monitoring by Ozone

Constituent	Maximum Concentration Encountered in Air Quality Monitoring [a] $(ppm)^b$	Concentration Used at which no Interference was Detected at $[NO] \leq 10$ ppb (ppm)
NO_2	3	9
CO_2	500	650
CO	100	300
C_2H_4	1^c	5
NH_3	3	9
SO_2	3	25
H_2O	100% saturation	75% saturation

[a] Data from Tebbens.[26]

[b] All concentrations given are on a molar (v/v) basis.

[c] Private communication from R. K. Stevens of the National Air Pollution Control Administration.

were observed. The cause of these signals was not further investigated. For the other compounds this column gives the highest concentrations tested.

The H_2O data were obtained in a different manner. They pertain to a comparison between streams of N_2/NO dried and 75% saturated with H_2O; no difference was observed in signals from these streams. With the experimental set-up employed, we could not use a 100% saturated stream (some of the NO would have been absorbed in the H_2O of the saturator). However, it appears very unlikely that any major interference could occur due to the fractional increase in $[H_2O]$ represented by the increased saturation.

IV. Monitoring of Other Gases

A major advantage accruing to the application of homogeneous chemiluminescent reactions for monitoring of air pollutants would be the use of a set of similar instruments for a number of pollutants. One can have an idea of the likelihood of obtaining such multifunctional detectors by discussing a few examples. This is done here by using the experimental data obtained in the present work and published spectral distributions and rate constants for light emission of a number of chemiluminescent reactions.

O_3

The NO/O_3 reaction could also be used to monitor O_3. In this case one would merely replace the O_2/O_3 flow line (Figure 2) with a carrier gas/ NO flow line. The sensitivity of the method at $[NO] = 1.1 \times 10^{-7}$ mole l^{-1} (equal to the O_3 concentration used above) would be the same as that found above for NO, i.e., 4 ppb, and interference effects would also be the same as for NO detection by O_3. The sensitivity could be increased by using higher

NO concentrations.

NO_x (= NO + NO_2)

O atoms react with NO to produce light emission via

$$O + NO \rightarrow NO_2 + h\nu \qquad (6)$$

NO_2 is rapidly converted to NO on a 1:1 basis[29] via

$$O + NO_2 \rightarrow NO + O_2 \qquad (7)$$

while the oxidation of NO by O atoms and O_2 are comparatively slow processes.[16,29] Hence, O atoms could be used to determine the sum of the concentrations of NO and NO_2 as NO via Reaction (6). The rate constant and spectral distribution of this reaction have been determined by Fontijn, Meyer, and Schiff.[18] The light is emitted in a continuum, stretching from 3875 Å well into the infrared. Over the wavelength region for which the 9558 QA tube is sensitive, the rate constant, k_6, is $\approx 2.5 \times 10^4$ 1 mole^{-1} sec^{-1}. O atoms can be generated at the same pressure and flow conditions as used in our NO/O_3 experiments, by replacing the ozonator with a microwave discharge on the downstream side of the stopcock D in the O_2 line, Figure 2. Previous work, e.g., Reference 18, indicates that under these conditions [O] in the reactor would be $\approx 1 \times 10^{-6}$ mole l^{-1}. Thus, the light intensity $I_6 = k_6[O][NO] \approx 2.5 \times 10^{-2} [NO]$ sec^{-1}. Using Equation (4), we obtain $I_3 = 1.7 \times 10^{-5} [NO]$ sec^{-1}, for our NO/O_3 experiments. Hence the sensitivity of the detector as an NO_x detector using O atoms would be some 3 orders of magnitude higher than it is as an NO detector using O_3. It would actually be somewhat higher yet, since the phototube sensitivity decreases with increasing wavelength for the spectral region of interest in comparisons of NO/O to NO/O_3 emissions.

235

It must be recognized that because of the possibility of interference by emissions from reactions of O atoms with other air pollutants, the full spectrum of the NO/O reaction may not be available. However, it appears that even if a relatively narrow wavelength region is selected by the use of an appropriate filter, the sensitivity of the detector for NO_x by O would still exceed that of the NO/O_3 detector.

CO

CO could be monitored by using its reaction with O atoms:

$$CO + O \rightarrow CO_2 + h\nu \qquad (8)$$

which results in emission of the carbon monoxide flame bands. This banded emission spectrum falls in the 3000 - 5000 Å region, cf. Dixon[31] and Pearse and Gaydon.[32] The rate constant for light emission, k_8, has been determined by Clyne and Thrush[22] as 1.2×10^1 1 mole^{-1} sec^{-1}. Hence at $[O] = 1 \times 10^{-6}$ mole 1^{-1}, $I_8 = k_8 [O] [CO] = 1.2 \times 10^{-5} [CO] sec^{-1}$. Comparison to our NO/O_3 results gives 6 ppb as the approximate limit of sensitivity. However, the phototube response curve shows that in the wavelength region of the CO/O emission, the tube sensitivity is some 5 times higher than in the region of the NO/O_3 emission. This then places the limit of sensitivity at $\approx$ 1 ppb. Again, interference by other pollutants could in practice result in a higher useful limit.

It must be noted that the rate constants for light emission of the NO/O_3 and CO/O reactions, quoted in this paper, were measured by comparison to the NO/O reaction in the same apparatus. The absolute values were then obtained[20,22] by using the directly measured absolute value for the NO/O reaction.[18] The fact that the intensity ratios used here depend on relative measurements made in one apparatus enhances their accuracy.

SO₂

This major air pollutant is also known to participate in chemiluminescent reactions, e.g., with O atoms.[33] However, no rate constants for light emission of SO_2 reactions are available; hence the limit of sensitivity cannot presently be estimated.

Applications

The natural atmospheric background levels of O_3, NO_x, and CO are, according to Tebbens,[26] approximately 10, 20, and 100 ppb, respectively. Because the light-emitting reactions are of first order in the pollutant concentrations, linear responses can be predicted. It thus appears highly likely that the homogeneous chemiluminescent detector can be used for the monitoring of these pollutants over the full range of their concentrations in polluted air. Of course, experimental confirmation remains desirable. Such confirmation and the building of prototype monitors are being pursued by us and at several other places (see, e.g., Refs. 34 - 36).

It is known[14] that many chemiluminescent gas reactions occur. Therefore, it is likely that the method described can be extended to other gases and to other environments, e.g., engine emission and stack gas monitoring. The application to these environments, where higher concentrations of pollutants are of interest,[37,38] would reduce the demands on the system somewhat, e.g., less sensitive photomultiplier tubes could be used.

References

[1] Rosenberg, N. W., "Chemical Releases at High Altitudes," Science, Vol. 152, 1966, pp. 1017-1027.

[2] Rosenberg, N. W., Golomb, D., and Allen, E. F., "Chemiluminescent Techniques for Studying Nighttime Winds in the Upper Atmosphere," Journal of Geophysical Research, Vol. 68, 1963, pp. 3328-3330.

[3] Golomb, D. and MacLeod, M. A., "Diffusion Coefficients in the Upper Atmosphere from Chemiluminous Trails," Journal of Geophysical Research, Vol. 71, 1966, pp. 2299-2305.

[4] Golomb, D., Rosenberg, N. W., Aharonian, C., Hill, J. A. F., and Alden, H. L., "Oxygen Atom Determination in the Upper Atmosphere by Chemiluminescence of Nitric Oxide," Journal of Geophysical Research, Vol. 70, 1965, pp. 1155-1173.

[5] Golomb, D. and Good, R. E., "Upper Atmosphere O-Atom Densities by Wind Tunnel Simulation of Nitric Oxide Releases," Journal of Geophysical Research, Vol. 71, 1966, pp. 5753-5756.

[6] Rosenberg, N. W., "Ionospheric Temperatures Obtained from Photography of Shock Waves," Journal of Geophysical Research, Vol. 69, 1964, pp. 2323-2328.

[7] Fontijn, A. and Rosner, D. E., "NO + O Chemiluminescent Reaction Using Adiabatically Expanded Nitric Oxide," The Journal of Chemical Physics, Vol. 46, 1967, pp. 3275-3276.

[8] Golomb, D. and Good, R. E., "Clusters in Isentropically Expanding Nitric Oxide and Their Effect on the Chemiluminous NO - O Reaction," The Journal of Chemical Physics, Vol. 49, 1968, pp. 4176-4180.

[9] Schapker, R. L. and Camac, M., "NO₂ Chemiluminescent Wake Radiation," AIAA Journal, Vol. 7, 1969, pp. 2254-2261.

[10] Reis, V., "Chemiluminescent Radiation from the Far Wake of Hypersonic Spheres," AIAA Journal, Vol. 5, 1967, pp. 1928-1933.

[11] Wolfhard, H. G. and Hinck, E., "Elementary Processes in Low-Pressure Flames and Their Relation to Rocket-Exhaust Radiation," Eleventh Symposium (International) on Combustion, The Combustion Institute, Pittsburgh, 1967, pp. 589-595.

[12] Zirkind, R., "Radiation from Rocket-Exhaust Plumes," Eleventh Symposium (International) on Combustion, The Combustion Institute, Pittsburgh, 1967, pp. 613-620.

[13] Gordon, A.S., Drew, C.M., Prentice, J.L., and Knipe, R.H., "Techniques for the Study of the Combustion of Metals," AIAA Journal, Vol. 6, 1968, pp. 577-583.

[14] Carrington, T. and Garvin, D., "The Chemical Production of Excited States," in Comprehensive Chemical Kinetics, Vol. 3: The Formation and Decay of Excited Species, C.H. Bamford and C.F.H. Tipper, eds., Elsevier, Amsterdam, 1969, Chap. 3.

[15] Cohen, N. and Heicklen, J., "The Oxidation of Inorganic Non-Metallic Compounds," in Comprehensive Chemical Kinetics, C.H. Bamford and C.F.H. Tipper, eds., Elsevier, Amsterdam, in preparation.

[16] Heicklen, J. and Cohen, N., "The Role of Nitric Oxide in Photochemistry," Advances in Photochemistry, Vol. 5, Wiley, New York, 1968, pp. 157-328.

[17] Kaufman, F., "The Air Afterglow and Its Use in the Study of Some Reactions of Atomic Oxygen," Proceedings of the Royal Society of London, Vol. A247, 1958, pp. 123-139.

[18] Fontijn, A., Meyer, C.B., and Schiff, H.I., "Absolute Quantum Yield Measurements of the NO-O Reaction and Its Use as a Standard for Chemiluminescent Reactions," The Journal of Chemical Physics, Vol. 40, 1964, pp. 64-70.

[19] Clyne, M.A.A. and Thrush, B.A., "Mechanism of Chemiluminescent Reactions Involving Nitric Oxide - the H + NO Reaction," Discussions of the Faraday Society, Vol. 33, 1962, pp. 139-148.

[20] Clyne, M.A.A., Thrush, B.A., and Wayne, R.P., "Kinetics of the Chemiluminescent Reaction between Nitric Oxide and Ozone," Transactions of the Faraday Society, Vol. 60, 1964, pp. 359-370.

[21] Clough, P.N. and Thrush, B.A., "Mechanism of Chemiluminescent Reaction between Nitric Oxide and Ozone," Transactions of the Faraday Society, Vol. 63, 1967, pp. 915-925.

[22] Clyne, M.A.A. and Thrush, B.A., "The Kinetics of the Carbon Monoxide Flame Bands," Ninth Symposium (International) on Combustion, Academic Press, 1963, New York, pp. 177-183.

[23] Lavoie, G.A., Heywood, J.B., and Keck, J.C., "Experimental and Theoretical Study of Nitric Oxide Formation in Internal Combustion Engines," Combustion Science and Technology, Vol. 1, 1970, pp. 313-326.

[24] Fontijn, A., Sabadell, A.J., and Ronco, R.J., "Homogeneous Chemiluminescent Measurement of Nitric Oxide with Ozone. Implications for Continuous Selective Monitoring of Gaseous Air Pollutants," Analytical Chemistry, Vol. 42, 1970, pp. 575-579; see also "Feasibility Study for the Development of a Multifunctional Emission Detector for Air Pollutants Based on Homogeneous Chemiluminescent Gas Phase Reactions," Final Report, Clearinghouse PB 188 104, Sept. 1969.

[25] Lovelock, J.E., discussion following paper, "Argon Detectors," in Gas Chromatography 1960, R.P.W. Scott, ed., Butterworths, London, 1960, pp. 26-27.

[26] Tebbens, B.D., "Gaseous Pollutants in the Air," in Air Pollution, 2nd ed., Vol. I, A.C. Stern, ed., Academic Press, New York, 1968, Chap. 2.

[27] Johnston, H.S. and Crosby, H.J., "Kinetics of the Fast Gas Phase Reaction between Ozone and Nitric Oxide," Journal of Chemical Physics, Vol. 22, 1954, pp. 689-692.

[28] Ford, H.W., Doyle, G.J., and Endow, N., "Rate Constants at Low Concentrations. I. Rate of Reaction of Ozone with Nitrogen Dioxide," Journal of Chemical Physics, Vol. 26, 1957, p. 1336.

[29] Kaufman, F., "Reactions of Oxygen Atoms," Progress in Reaction Kinetics, Vol. 1, Pergamon Press, New York, 1961, Chap. 1.

[30] Kaufman, F., "Aeronomic Reactions Involving Hydrogen. A Review of Recent Laboratory Studies," Annales de Géophysique, Vol. 20, 1964, pp. 106-114.

[31] Dixon, R.N., "The Carbon Monoxide Flame Bands," Proceedings of the Royal Society of London, Vol. A275, 1963, pp. 431-446.

[32] Pearse, R.W.B. and Gaydon, A.G., The Identification of Molecular Spectra, 3rd ed., Wiley, New York, 1963, pp. 123-124.

[33] Mulcahy, M.F.R., Steven, J.R., Ward, J.C., and Williams, D.J., "Kinetics of Interaction of Oxygen Atoms with Sulfur Oxides," Twelfth Symposium (International) on Combustion, The Combustion Institute, Pittsburgh, 1969, pp. 323-329.

[34] Stuhl, F. and Niki, H., "An Optical Detection Method for NO in the Range 10^{-2} to 10^3 ppm by the Chemiluminescent Reaction of NO with O_3," SR 70-42, March 1970, Ford Motor Co., Dearborn, Mich.

[35] Snyder, A.D. and Wooten, G.W., "Feasibility Study for the Development of a Multifunctional Emission Detector for NO, CO, and SO_2," Monsanto Research Corp. final report for National Air Pollution Control Administration, Contract CPA 22-69-8, October 1969.

[36] Stevens, R.K., O'Keeffe, A.E., and Ortman, G.C., "Current Trends in Continuous Air Pollution Monitoring Systems," ISA Transactions, Vol. 9, 1970, pp. 1-8.

[37] Hurn, R.W., "Mobile Combustion Sources," in Air Pollution, 2nd ed., Vol. III, A.C. Stern, ed., Academic Press, New York, 1968, Chap. 33.

[38] Engdahl, R.B., "Stationary Combustion Sources," ibid., Chap. 32.

MANUAL AND AUTOMATED-COMPUTERIZED SYSTEM IN
SIDE-LOOKING RADAR APPLICATIONS FOR LAND USE SURVEY

Dr. Ervin Y. Kedar
Department of Geography
State University of New York
at Binghamton
Binghamton, New York 13901

Abstract

In a study of side-looking radar microtexture, small sections of
the image were analyzed. The process included   photographic enlargement,   isodensitracer scanning,   false color enhancement, and
computer graphic mapping.

It was found that it was possible to enhance the individual resolution cells, which were the "return" and "no-return" of the radar signals.
The individual resolution cells consist of a core and a periphery. The
core is the representation of the reflecting terrain feature, and the
periphery is the corona-like reflection of the target. The individual
resolution cells are the composition of density values, contrast values,
and contrast frequency values. The parameter values display certain
textural characteristics that are unique to different targets. Thus, a
geometric-statistic study of the signatures of the various terrain
features make it possible to discriminate among the various cultural and
physical terrain elements. The same parameters have been used to generate patterns representing different kind of land use, and geological
structures by computer graphics. A pattern recognition system, by
computer graphics, is presently under study, which will eventually permit automated handling of the side-looking radar imagery.

Introduction

Possible application of side-looking radar (SLR) imagery in earth
sciences investigations have been suggested since SLR imagery became available over 10 years ago.   The SLR is of special interest because it can
provide earth scientists with imagery obtained through clouds and haze,
in day or night, independent of solar illumination and with broad area
coverage in continuous strip formats.

Other characteristics of SLR imagery that contribute to the excite-
ment of earth scientists are the imagery obtained from the SLR in the
electromagnetic band far from the visible band (like infrared), with a

lookangle much closer to horizontal, with a different perspective from the vertical aerial photographs, but still in the control of the SLR operation. Polarization capability, which is both horizontal and vertical at the same operational flight, is comparable to multiband photography and has been proven to be an effective element for better discrimination of terrain features.

Thus, the application of SLR to earth sciences are numerous, such as geology, geomorphology, hydrography, land use, urban investigation, et cetera. The only limitation of these applications are the facts that the traditional identification and interpretation techniques applied for aerial photography cannot be used and adapted for SLR image analysis; the enormous inflow data from SLR require an automate computerized system for future handling of the data.

Consequently, new data processing techniques have to be developed prior to the sound application of SLR imagery. An investigation in appropriate techniques for manual and automated data processing for land use survey has been carried out by the author, while he was a senior resident research associate of the National Research Council assigned to Earth Observation Division, at the Manned Spacecraft Center, NASA, Houston, Texas**. New techniques are suggested in this study both for manual data analysis, and automated computerized, both of which are based on the microtexture of the SLR imagery.

The SLR Characteristics

The characteristics, advantages, and disadvantages of SLR imagery have been discussed widely by many investigators (1). The basic elements of SLR imagery are known (2). The purpose of this study is to investigate a new dimension of the SLR imagery, namely, the SLR microsections of the original SLR film.

A few concepts should be stated previous to the discussion:
1. The SLR image is a two-dimensional patchwork of radar reflectivity from enormous individual resolusion cells (IRC), which constitute the macro- and micro-texture in the image of the SLR. The association of the cells represent the gross terrain features (3).
2. The size, shape, and tonal grades of the patches that represent the reradiation of the IRC are affected by the specific reflectivity properties of the individual terrain elements (4).
3. The IRC is possibly the imagery representation of the radar cross section, which is the product of the effective area of the target, and the gain of the target as a radiator in the direction of the receiving antenna (5).
4. Each patch may be made of many small patches reradiating from different terrain features in a diversified amplitude and phase (6).
5. All terrain features have one distinctive spectral signature which is determined by the atomic and molecular structure of the object and other radar reflectivity components (7).

**It is a great pleasure to acknowledge the help of Mapping and Sciences Division, Computation and Analysis Division, and Earth Observation Division, MSC, NASA, without which this study could not be carried out.

6. The photographic elements of the SLR imagery, like tone, texture, shape, size, pattern, and spatial geometry, are different from those of metric camera imagery, and may be applied for identification of the IRC.

7. As a consequence, interpretation of SLR imagery is difficult prior to the understanding of the basic elements of the microtexture image and the IRC constitution (8).

8. The microtexture is a function of the lookangle, altitude of the SLR above the terrain, the azimuth and will change respectively with changes in these parameters.

The object of this study, therefore, is the microtexture of the SLR imagery and its application for terrain environmental studies.

Manual Operation

Microtexture Image Analysis by Photographic Enlargement

The SLR image is essentially a representation of terrain features responding to radar beams. The texture of the image is the result of the distribution and density of the reradiation of the IRC which is commonly known as the scintillation phenomena, or "Rayleigh fading". The tone and texture of the SLR image are also modified by radar echoes, which are reflected from side lobe and recorded by the radar. The echoes possibly have a different diffraction pattern, which is represented by different shades of the gray tone in the IRC patch.

The IRC can be classified into "return" resolution cells and "no return" resolution cells. The combination of these cells produce an overall texture which looks like the "salt-and-pepper" image of the SLR. These categories in turn can be subdivided into many more groups, according to the nature of the rereflective characteristics.

Smaller but stronger reradiators will result in more enhanced returns. In a microtexture image analysis, the IRC is the subject of the investigation. In a macrotexture image analysis, the association of the IRC is the major concern. To be capable to perceive the IRC with naked eye, it is required that the original SLR image should be enlarged. In this study, microsections of the SLR image were enlarged 80 to 100 times. By the enlargement, the IRC were big enough and clearly defined and isolated from each other (fig. 1 and 3). Also, the photographic enlargement permits orientation and general interpretation of the image. The IRC were compared with comparable terrain features seen on the aerial photograph (Fig. 2 and 4). In the process of the analysis, the two major categories of IRC "return" and "no return" were delineated by proper isolines. Eventually, each cell was identified and the whole microtexture image identified. An urban area San Francisco, California, was the sample study. It appears that the "return" IRC represents facades of buildings and the "no return" IRC indicates the radar shadow of the buildings. Though many other terrain features interfere in the patchwork of the imagery, the imagery as a whole is a representation of the multistory houses complex. Some patches of no return indicate parks and vacant land. The IRC are distributed in a random pattern, and

Figure 1(a)

SLR image of San Francisco, California. Flown and scanned by
Westinghouse, flight No. 101, AN/APQ(XE-1), during NASA program,
July - August 1966.

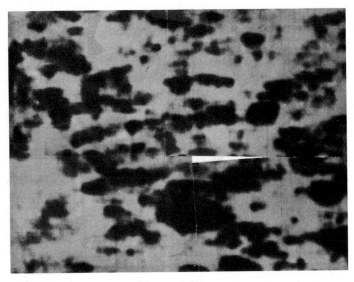

Figure 1(b)

Section 1 enlarged. Microtexture image of the core of the
downtown, San Francisco. The diagonal line is Market Street and the
rest of the street pattern is readily seen in the image (compare with
Fig. 2).

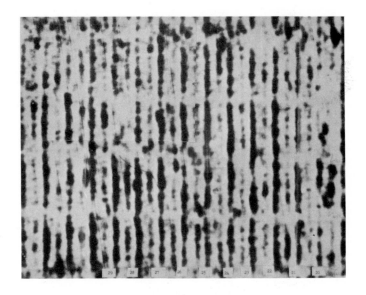

Figure 3

Section 2 enlarged. Microtexture image of the residential
section south of the Golden Gate Park, San Francisco, California.
Block pattern readily seen in this image. Also, the row of buildings is recognizable (compare with fig. 4). The specific block is
enclosed by 24th and 25th Avenues, and Kirkham and Lawton Streets.

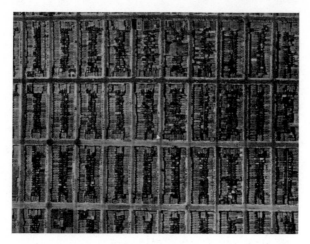

Figure 4

Aerial photograph comparable to the area shown in Figure 3.

Figure 5

IDT of the microtexture of the residential area section of
San Francisco (0.25 break). The scanning strongly enhanced the
street and block pattern, and permits identification of individual
terrain features which either have a strong return or an extremely
weak return. Interpretation of the terrain is facilitated by IDT
scanning.

apparently interfere with each other.   Therefore, they are classified
into two groups:
        1. combined IRC, when the return cells of two or more IRC are com-
bined together in such a way that the visual separation of the component
of the IRC are impossible; and 2. interrupted IRC, when a no return
cell is dissected by patches of return cells or by peripherial corona
of adjacent return cell patches, or vice versa (9). In a similar way,
the average areal tone(s) might interfere with the IRC; also, the topog-
raphy of the terrain might heavily distort the shape and size of the
IRC (10).

Application

        Photographic enlargements of small sections of the SLR image by
50 to 100 power permit:
        1.   The refined orientation of the SLR interpreter in the area of
the SLR imagery
        2.   The comparison of the microtexture imagery of the SLR with the
comparable conventional aerial photographic information
        3.   The isolation of the IRC and the identification of the outstand-
ing cells with terrain features.

Isodensitracer Scanning of SLR Image

        To overcome geometric infidelity of the microtexture in the SLR
image and to separate the IRC when more than one object exists in the
field of view, the isodensitracer scanning (IDT) was applied (11).   The
IDT automatically scans and measures the optical density of all points
in a film transparency and plots the measured density values in a
quantitative two-dimensional isodensity tracing of the scanned area.
New records and significant information may be recognized from the image
which previously could not be seen with the naked eye. This information
was discovered from the very small tonal differences in the image related
to the IRC. By scanning these tonal differences which were below the
threshold of visual recognition, it was possible to separate the IRC
from average areal tone and other background noise. Also, if the terrain
is a composite feature, which is usually the case in any area scanned, the
radar cross section will be an average over the recorded area. It is
hypothesized here that the IDT permits the separation of the image of
the reradiators from each other in a composite target.

        The selected San Francisco residential area scanned was 4.8- by
4.8-mm on the original film. The scanning aperture at the film plane was
11.5 microns and a density data point was read every 12 microns along
the scan. The scan lines were 12 microns apart (stepping increment).
This resulted in a 400-density data points per scan and 400 scans. The
final IDT plot of the residential area represented a magnification of
approximately 62 times (fig. 5).

        The selected downtown area scanned was 4.5- by 4.5-mm on the film.
The scanning aperture at the film plane was 11.5 microns and a density
data point was read every 9 microns along the scan. The scan lines were
9 microns apart (stepping increment). This resulted in 500-density data
points per scan and 5000 scans. The final IDT plots of the downtown area

represented a magnification of approximately 83 times (fig. 6). Three
different density intervals were used to produce three different representations of the selected downtown area (12) (fig. 7).

Application

Isodensitracer scanning of SLR film permitted the interpreter to
obtain the following:
1. Additional information on the patches that represent the reradiators on the terrain. This information was beyond the visible band.
2. The isolation of the core of the IRC, and the separation of the
core from their periopheries. It is possible to identify the reradiating
target features and the corona of their reflection.
3. The enhancement of IRC geometric lines, the identification of
the radar noise, and the separation of pertinent reradiation cells from
electronic noise.

False Color Enhancement

It was felt that the relative density scanning and plotting performed by the IDT was not fully a satisfactory solution for the enhancement of the extremely subtle variations on tone in the microtexture of
the SLR image. It seems important to detect and delineate the heart of
the cells since the patches are representations of the return echoes
that may be produced by composite targets. A search for an absolute
density representation of the potential information enveloped by the
subtle gray tones which fade below the threshold of detectability was
required. Also, a manually operated electro-mechanical instrument was
needed to allow the SLR image analyst to select the most preferred
enhanced image. These objectives were achieved by the color video-
enhancement viewer manufactured by Philco-Ford (13).

This electronic equipment is capable of performing the required
separation necessary for discrimination, combination and enhancement of
the subtle gray tone densities. By using the viewer, in different combinations,   it was possible to enhance the geometric fidelity of the
microtexture images. The specific false color viewer has two channel
input, which permitted the comparison between the two polarizations
(vertical and horizontal), and facilitated the detection of the cores
of the IRC, which represented the terrain reradiators. The images were
displayed in different false colors, at various degree of enhancement,
which was helpful for the identification of target features and their
geometric shapes.

The major disadvantage of the viewer is the fact that the images
were arbitrary, related merely to the relative densities on the original
film. The colors, by no means, represented any specific homogeneous
categories of terrain elements. It was left to the interpreter to tell
what the false colored image represents.

The following steps in the experimentation were taken:
1. Single channel(vertical or horizontal polarization), single
color enhancement

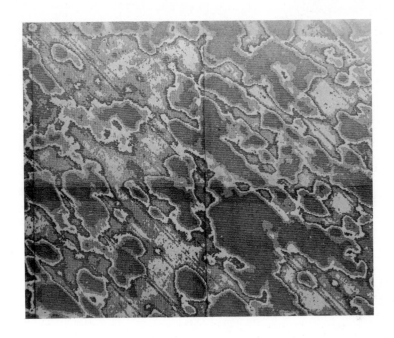

Figure 6

IDT of the microtexture of the core of the downtown San
Francisco, California (break 0.3). The scanned image can be
applied for : (1) a refined delineation of the core of the IRC;
(2) sharpening geometric lines and edges (see. a); and (3) enhancement of the radar noise for discrimination between noise and terrain
features return. Also, the radar shadow is highly enhanced by the
IDT scanning.   On the other hand, this break grade is still
too coarse to pinpoint the core of the cells of the strongest
return or no return.

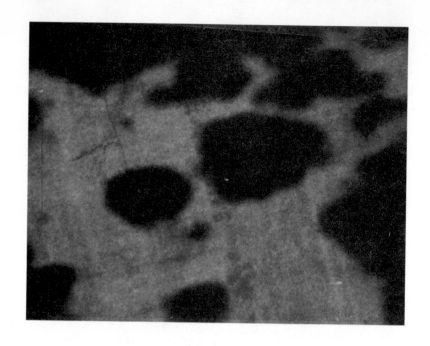

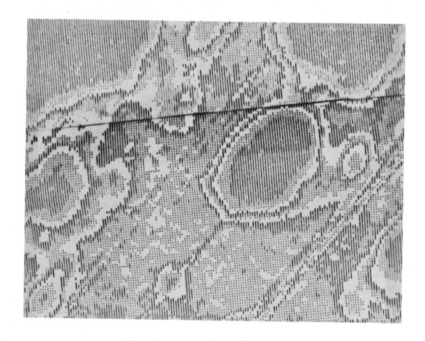

Figure 7

A multistory building represented by the SLR image photographically enlarged (a); the image scanned by the IDT (b).

2. Single channel, multicolor enhancement
3. Single channel, single color digitized
4. Single channel, multicolor digitized
5. Inverted the same as 1 to 4
6. Two channels (14) the same as 1 to 4 (in Channel 1, vertical polarization; Channel 2, horizontal polarization)
7. Double channel with one positive against the other inverted image, as 1 to 4

The result of this experimentation is represented in figures 8 to 11.

Application

The color video enhancement viewer suggested to be used by the SLR microtexture image interpreter to study:
1. The IRC and their effective reradiation cores, their peripheries and geometric shapes
2. The association of the IRC and their cores with each other for a shape and pattern analysis
3. The macrotexture and microtexture SLR image in a more sophisticated, educated, and intelligent way

Manual Operation Conclusions

SLR image texture enlarged photographically, scanned by IDT, and enhanced by false color resulted in the portrayal of an enormous amount of information. These systems permitted the isolation, delineation, and discrimination of the IRC.

Photographic enlargement proved to be helpful for refined identification and orientation in the study of the IRC and in the general image texture. Also, it facilitated the secondary and tertiary SLR texture analysis.

The IDT facilitated the delineation of the IRC reflection core of the rereflection of IRC and the separation between interfering adjacent cells. By the use of the IDT, multiple reflecting surfaces can be separated into its integrating factors. An isopleth map can be produced by the IDT to plot the spatial distribution of the cells and their cores, peripheries and boundary lines of the core, and the territories of each individual reflecting cell.

Flexible experimentation with the false color enhancement permitted a refined detection of the IRC core size and the pinpointing of the heart of the core of the IRC. The false color enhancement proved to be desirable for the identification and interpretation of SLR microtexture. The limiting factor is the interpreter's capability to correlate the imagery with the terrain features. The image reader must continuously place terrain features in proper perspective with the respective distorted tone values so that he can conceive the unseeable information and enhance the geometric fidelity of the terrain features. Once the operator can adjust the readout in these three systems with his mental picture, the microtexture of the SLR might be highly useful for earth resources research (15).

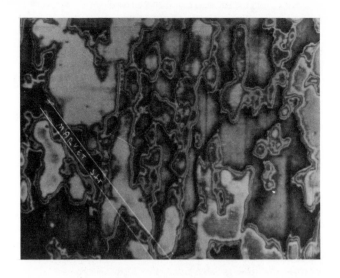

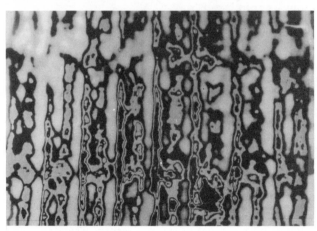

Figure 8 and Figure 9

    False color enhancement of   the down-town area and   the
residential area. There are different degrees of enhanced contrast-
ing colors, which were performed to separate slight tonal variations and display them. These tonal variations are not perceptible
to human eyeballs. Thus, the SLAR microtexture has been refined
by false color enhancement and another dimension has been added
to it. The refined texture might be called: the secondary and
tertiary microtexture. A careful interpretation, with a precise
comparison with the comparable aerial photograph, would help to
locate the individual resolution cells, and explain their associ-
tion. It could help in the inferences of the gross SLAR texture image
and in the spatial arrangement of the tonework. Also, it is possible
to lift out of the image any tone-color level which has a specific
terrain representation, such as the radar shadow. The contour like
lines are devices to define the resolution cells, which otherwise
could not be delineated.

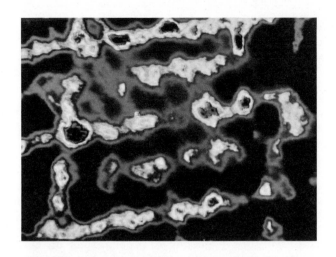

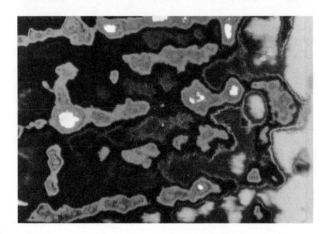

Figure 10 and Figure 11

    Two stages in the color enhancement of the residential sec-
tion of San Francisco. In these enhancements, the macrotexture has
been subdivided into defined patterns which represent urban block
structure. Also, by the enhancement a higher degree of geometric
fidelity has been achieved. All of this information was suppressed
on the original film and was beyond the threshold of visual detecti-
vity. These series of color enhancement prove that the degree of
enhancement is limited by the grain and film-fog elements. The
enhanced image though adds a new dimension to the microtexture.
The "core-of the-individual-resolution-cell" which has been represented by peaks of tonal densities in these images is defined.
The exact meaning of these peaks has not yet been explained, but
it was suspected that they are the most efficient reradiators, with
the highest dielectric properties and other radar reflectivity
components.

Automated and Computerized Operation

With the overwhelming increase of SLR data gathered over broad areas and the future expected inflow of SLR data possibly from space platforms, the manual operation becomes obsolete. New data processing techniques have to be developed. This paper essentially discusses experiments toward the realization of this requirement.

It has been realized that SLR microtexture can be analyzed and computed by certain quantitative parameters (16). The parameters obtained from isodensitracer are the density value, contrast value, and contrast frequency value (fig. 12).

The process of determining which parameters are pertinent for a certain application to discriminate between various terrain features must be accomplished by experiments. The investigator needs to have at his disposal the ability to compute the variety of parameter combinations and has to perform a number of operations on the SLR date prior to the determination of the specific adopted parameters.

Once the parameters have been determined, the data analysis procedures can be followed along computational modules which currently are available; that is, such operation as pattern recognition by transform procedures (Walsh, Hadamard and Fourier) and/or statistical analysis procedures, i.e., correlation function, spectral densities and convariance measurements, and ultimately multivariate discriminatory analysis.

It is that the investigator needs the ability to perform these operations to determine which specific operation shows promise as applicable to his specific need, such as agricultural land use classification, various timber stand location, or soil classification, et cetera.

Proceeding further with this concept, it seems reasonable to provide the investigator with an interactive facility that allows him to work with his data and process it both as a visual-graphic display and numberical-analog form. In the final stage of this evolutionary process, graphic display could overtake the system, and provide complete presentation of the data, which can be generated both in real time and nonreal time enviornments.

Accordingly, in the initial step of the investigation, a software (17) was applied which permitted the computed and stored SLR parameter data to display in block diagram shape, along x,y, and z axes (fig. 13).

The diagram was very useful in representing visually the roughness of the surface of the specific terrain under study (fig. 14). A more advanced approach is the computation of the isodensitracer scanning data, along axes (x and y and oblique angles) into many analog curve lines, by means of the least square method, which represents the best of all the

b

Figure 12
An agricultural land use area was chosen for this part of
the study.   (a) SLR gross image west of Houston, Texas (Flown and
scanned by Westinghouse Electric Co., Se. No. 61-15-N100 RI-R4,
cross polarized image, 12   foot altitude, on July 31, 1969).
(b) is a comparable aerial photograph (photograph by NASA, MSC,
EOD from RB57F aircraft).
(The SLR image is reversed). (Cont.)

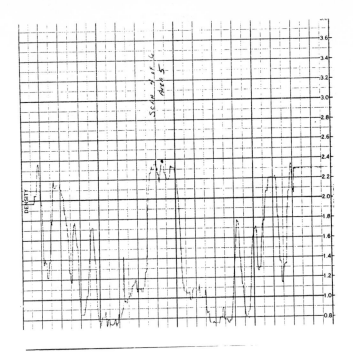

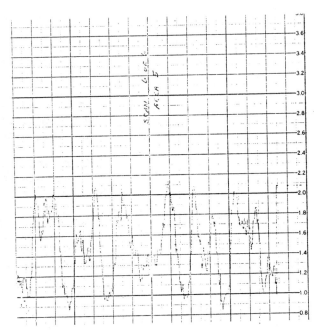

Figure 12 (cont.)

IDT sample scanned lines, showing the three parameters; also, the microtexture is represented by the pattern of the scanned lines.

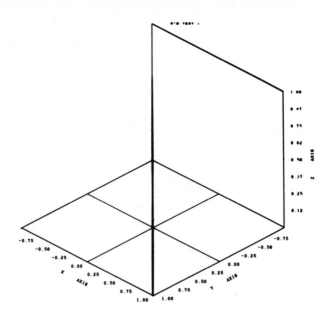

Figure 13

X and Y axes represent scanning axes and Z axis the density values.

many numerous scanned lines (fig. 15). These fitted curve lines can be
considered as "keys" for a certain terrain features, thus, it is possible
to adopt a set of curve lines for a certain crop which represent that
crop "microtexture roughness" of the SLR reradiation surface. Similarly,
it is possible to compute sets of keys for other crops, from IDT scanned
curve lines of those specific crops microtexture roughness.

As soon as this operation has been specified, selected, and completed,
routine operation can be started, and SLR data analysis in an automated-
computerized way can be applied (see flow chart).

The final stage leads to the discrimination of the computerized
data which has been achieved by pattern recognition. This has been
done by constructing a classification decision rule, and employing this
rule in order to identify set of measurements (18). More precisely, it has
been achieved by recognizing at one time one of the patterns of the key
curve lines with sets of curve lines of unknown features (fig. 16).

If these parameters fail to achieve the power of discrimination,
any of the convenient transform procedures, can be performed leading to
natural grouping into similarity sets. In addition, SLR imagery obtained
from different altitudes and polarization can be used to obtain additional
parameters so as to increase discriminatory power. These procedures can
be   followed, in which SLR data can be handled, analyzed and classified
by automated-computerized technique.

255

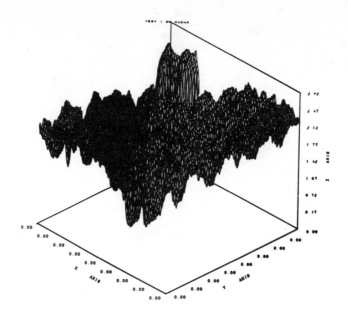

a

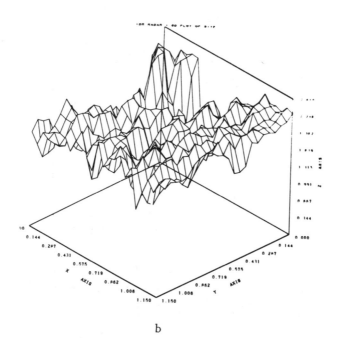

b

Figure 14

a. Computer display of all 200 scanned lines

b. Computer display of every fifth scanned line

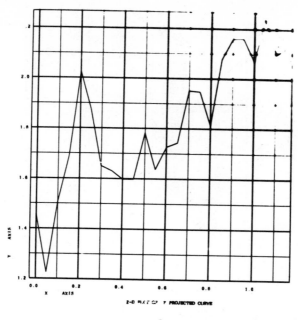

2-D PLOT OF Y PROJECTED CURVE

a

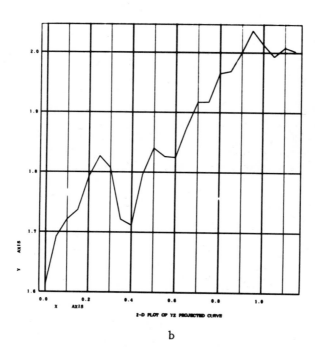

2-D PLOT OF YZ PROJECTED CURVE

b

Figure 15

The mean average line of all 200 scan lines

(a) along the X axis, (b) along the Y axis

257

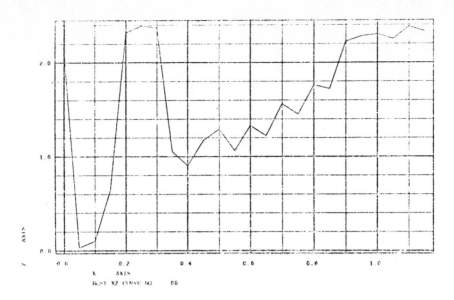

Figure 16

The best XZ curve line, picked out by pattern recognition, it fits best the
X axis mean average curve line (compare with Figure 15a).

Application

     Automated computerized technique of the microtexture image of the
SLR will permit the following:
     1. Continuous screening of the inflow of data from aerospace plat-
forms into certain and definite categories
     2. Classification of the data according to certain keys in concord-
ance with a predetermined complex of parameters
     3. Display, both numerically and graphically, the inflow SLR data
information.

Conclusions

     The practical problem of this study was how to understand more
intelligently SLR imagery, which are different from photographic imagery
and how to handle the mass of inflow information from SLR scanning
earth from aerospace platforms.

     The technique presented in this paper
which can be applied both in science and industry, is based on the statistical analysis of the microtexture of the SLR imagery. It has been
ignored so far, however.

     The microtexture of the SLR image is the only representation of the
specific nature of the terrain feature, because it is the strength of the
radar reradiation (19). Therefore, it is the most reliable information
for recognizing the nature of the target.

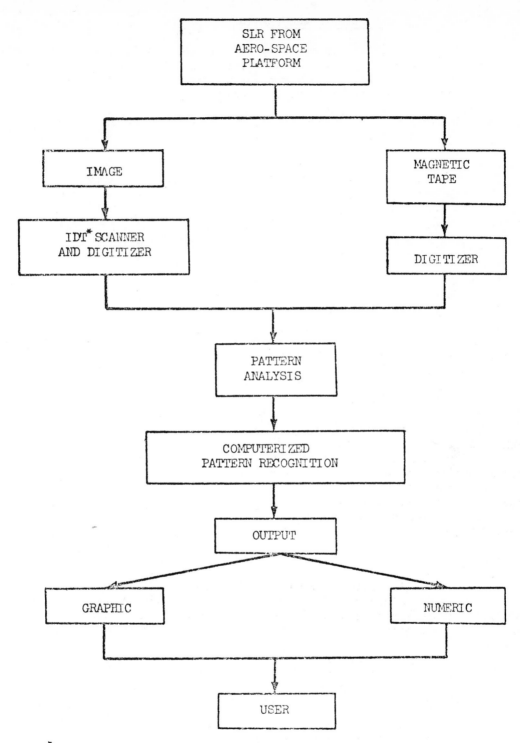

```
            ┌─────────────────┐
            │   SLR FROM      │
            │   AERO-SPACE    │
            │   PLATFORM      │
            └─────────────────┘
```

SLR FROM AERO-SPACE PLATFORM

IMAGE   MAGNETIC TAPE

IDT* SCANNER AND DIGITIZER   DIGITIZER

PATTERN ANALYSIS

COMPUTERIZED PATTERN RECOGNITION

OUTPUT

GRAPHIC   NUMERIC

USER

*IDT = isodensitracer

FLOW CHART

Footnotes and Bibliography

1. D. J. Barr, Annotated Bibliography of the Use of Side-Looking Air-borne Radar (SLAR) Imagery for Engineering Soil Studies, U.S. Army Engineering Topographic Laboratories, Fort Belvoir, Virginia, June 1968, Part 1 - Unclassified Literature.

2. See Accession List for the Earth Resources Data Research Facility, MSC-NASA, Houston, Texas, items under Sections 5, 6, 7, 8, 9, 10, and 33.

3. P. R. Hoffman, Progress and Problems in Radar Photo Interpretation, Photogrammetric Engineerings, 1960, 26, 1, 612-637.

4. H. C. Mackdonald et al Geologic Evaluation by Radar of NASA Sedi-mentary Test Site, Inst. Elec. Electro. Engin. Inc., GE-5, 3, 1967, 72-78.

5. The University of Michigan Notes for a Program of Study in Remote Sensing of Earth Resources, Feb. 14 - May 3, 1968, MSO/NASA, Houston, Texas, Cont. NAS 9-7676.

6. L. Stafford, MSC/NASA, personal communication. It is suggested that in a multiple terrain target the core and periphery phenomena occurs primarily where several large reflectors are within a very small area, so their returns merge. In this case, the periphery is actually the return from the first reflector, and the return gets stronger and it creates a core. When the return from several other reflectors begin to arrive at the time the core is enhanced. This could be checked by determining that the width of this periphery did or did not correspond to the radar resolution dimension in that direction at that range and depression angle.

7. Bill Streams, A New Picture of the World, Engin. Bull. 16, 3, 1968, 4-11.

8. Y. Kedar, A Geographic Approach to the Study of Photo Interpretation, Photogrammetric Engineering, 1958, 584-587.

9. The Average Areal Tone indicates the general reflecting characteristic of a regional terrain surface, see D. J. Barr, Use of Side-Looking Airborne Radar Imagery for Engineering Soils Studies, Geo. Scien. Div., U. S. Army Eng. Topog. Lab., Fort Belvoir, Virginia, June 1968, p. 81-2.

10. C. Fiore, Side-Looking Radar Restitution, Photogrammetric Engineer-ing 33, 2, 1967, 215-220.

11. Isodensitracer and IDT are trademarks for Isophotometer equipment developed by Technical Operation, Inc., Burlington, Massachusetts.

12. This information was supplied by J. H. Salinas, Lockheed Electronics, MSC/NASA. It is a pleasure to thank Mr. Salinas for his technical support in scanning the SLAR image with the IDT and supplying the information.

13. Image Enhancement for Photographic Analysis, Philco-Ford Co.,
     Space @ Reentry System Division, Palo-Alto @ New Port Beach,
     Cal. See Also D. S. Ross, Image-Tone Enhancement, 1969 Annual
     Meetings of the Am. Soc. Photogrammetric and Am. Cong. of Surv,
     and Mapping, Washington, D. C.

     The image discrimination enhancement combination and sampling
     (IDECS) is a similar system developed by the University of
     Kansas. See D. S. Simonett, Application of Color Combined
     Multiple Polarization Radar Image to Geoscience Problems, CRES
     Tech. Report 61-28, Dec. 1966.

14. Differences between horizontal and vertical polarization have
     indicated the possibility of obtaining more information from the
     study of both types than from the study of one type only. The
     values of the Aij represent the action of the type of material
     and its geometry upon the amplitude of the reflected wave (5).

15. R. D. Leighty, Terrain Information from High Altitude Side Looking
     Radar Imagery of an Arctic Area, Proceedings of the Fourth
     Symposium on Remote Sensing of Environment, June 1966, p.575.

16. D. H. Berger, Texture as a discriminant of Crops on Radar Imagery,
     Dept. of Geog. Univ. of Kansas, Lawrence, Kansas. 1969 FSC69-5009

17. Crop growth parameters have been recorded by airborne radar. The
     resulting analog tapes were digitized and converted to engineering
     units. The purpose of this program is to read the digitized tapes
     and produce plots the recorded data. The plots are (1) a surface
     representing crop density over an area; (2) the average crop density
     when looking along the y-axis; (3) the average crop density when
     looking along the x-axis. The SC-4060 microfilm recorder and the
     Integrated Graphics System (IGS) software are used for plotting.
     The program which reads the tapes and controls the plotting was
     written in Fortran V for use on the Univac 1108 computer.

     The input to the program is simple. The first three cards are
     titles to be written on the suface plot, the xz (y-axis average)
     plane plot, and the yz (x-axis average) plane plot, respectively.
     A maximum of 72 characters is allowed for each title. The fourth
     card contains numeric control information as follows:

Card Cols.	Variable	Description
1-10 11-20	DELX	These two variable represent the incre- ments along the x- and y-axes. A decimal must be punched.
21-30 31-40	XINIT	The two variables represent the origin of the x- and y-axes. A decimal must be punched.

41-50	PCASE	Character case to be used on the plots. This value is usually input as 2.0. A decimal must be punched.

51-60	PT	X- and y-axis scale factors. The x and y arrays are generated by

$$X_i = X_{i-1} + PT*DELX$$

$$Y_i = Y_{i-1} + PT*DELY$$

A decimal must be punched.

61-65	NPT	The sample rate to be used in plotting. This value is the integer value of PT described above. The value must be in the rightmost part of the field and a decimal must not be punched.

66-70	LINE	This integer variable controls the connection of plotted points with straight lines. If entered as a zero, the points are not connected. If entered as a one (1), the points are connected. The value must be placed in the rightmost part of the field and a decimal must not be punched.

The tape containing the raw data must be mounted on logical unit A (Fortran Unit 1). A tape must be mounted on logical unit H (FORTRAN Unit 10) for the plot output. If the user wishes to save the y axis averages, a tape must be mounted on logical Unit E (FORTRAN Unit 7). If a tape is not mounted on Unit E, the averages are written on the drum. The IGS plot package is available from permanent files on the drum. To gain access to the IGS package, assign logical unit B (FORTRAN Unit 2) to$IGS. Then execute the complex utility routine and perform an "IN B" operation.

The program executes rapidly considering the number of data points it must read and plot. The program handled 55 records of 600 points each in 75 seconds. 153 pages were output on the printer.

18.   R. M. Haralick et. al., Pattern Recog. etc. Proce. IEEE, 57, 4, April 1969, p. 654-665.

19.   Imaging Radar for Earth Resources, Technical Report, LEC/HASD no. 649D-21-006 Cont. NASA-5191, Houston, Texas, 1969.

POWER FROM SPACE - TECHNOLOGY TRANSFER FOR HUMAN SURVIVAL

Peter E. Glaser
Head, Engineering Sciences Section
Arthur D. Little, Inc.
Cambridge, Massachusetts

Abstract

A concept for a satellite solar power station is described to meet future large-scale electrical power requirements without producing undesirable pollution of the environment. Considerations are given to satellite orbit, solar energy conversion, microwave generation and transmission, and conversion of microwave energy to electrical power on earth. The design considerations and the development tasks for a large satellite solar power station are reviewed and the potential technological needs are identified.

INTRODUCTION

It is an axiom that technology unless used has no intrinsic value. Historically, technology transfer has occurred whether fostered or inhibited. Today, however, the urgency of problems faced by society has increased and to the extent that space technology can provide a solution, the time span between development and application of that technology needs to be shortened. Well-developed plans and directed efforts are required to obtain maximum benefits from existing space technology. It is most productive when the technology can be applied to the solution of a recognized problem. Such a problem now confronts our society and it appears that we have a potential solution on hand.

The problem is to generate power to meet ever-increasing requirements without further deteriorating the environment. The solution is the extension of space technology to the development of satellite solar power stations to provide power without pollution.

For the first time in history, man is conscious of the possibility of the inadvertent extermination of his species through his own actions. Science and technology have provided the systems and processes to attain a high standard of living but without a rational assessment of the consequences--one of the most signifi-

cant being pollution which is so nondiscriminatory and all-embracing
that it represents a systematic trespass against all persons and
property.

Since James Watts' steam engine helped start the first industrial revolution, progress has been equated to the number of smoke-
stacks. Today the usage of electrical power is looked upon as a
weather vane of technical sophistication. As a consequence, the
present sources of energy for producing power and their undesirable effects on the environment represent the most important
problem facing technologically advanced nations. A new approach
will be to tap the energy source basic to the creation and sus-
taining of life on earth--the sun.

SOLAR ENERGY UTILIZATION

Utilization of the sun's energy is an old dream.[1] Solar
energy has long invited collection and conversion into other useful
forms, such as mechanical and electrical power. While past attempts
at such conversion have succeeded on a small scale, they have not
yet shown enough economic promise to find widespread application.

With collectors located on Earth the large-scale generation
of power from solar energy appears to be impractical because even
areas where solar energy is received throughout most of the year
would require energy storage systems more effective by orders of
magnitude than batteries, spinning turbine standby power generators,
fuel cells, or pumped storage to fill in for interruptions
of solar energy by weather and by nightfall. To supply a
significant fraction of the U.S. power demands would require
a fuel cell technology beyond the state-of-the-art or extensive water storage areas which even now are difficult to
locate.

Conversion of solar energy into other useful forms has
traditionally been dismissed as a less feasible means of
generating power compared to fission or fusion processes.
This rationale was understandable when considered in the
light of the technology available for the conversion of solar
energy before the 1960's. But this was before man enlarged his
boundaries to include successful entry for extended periods into
space. Now, space as a source of energy should be considered in
the same sense--and with the same inherent challenge--that the
inner space of the atomic nucleus has been considered as a source
of energy over the past few decades.

CONCEPT OF A SATELLITE SOLAR POWER STATION

Figure 1 shows the concept of a satellite solar power station
to provide large-scale power to the Earth. The satellite consists
of a solar collector to convert solar energy to electricity, a
transmission cable to supply the electricity to microwave generators,

264

and an antenna to beam the microwaves from the satellite, in a synchronous Earth orbit, to an Earth-receiving station where they are converted to electricity.

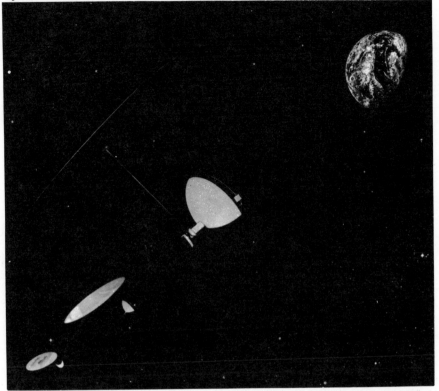

FIGURE 1   ARTIST'S CONCEPT OF A SATELLITE SOLAR POWER STATION

In the following sections, the state-of-the-art of the system and its components are described and projected to indicate their future development potential.

1.   Systems Technology

Systems engineering and management techniques prepared to direct and control massive engineering undertakings have heavily contributed to the success of our national space program. The development of a satellite solar power station would require that these techniques be used to determine the size and capacity of each component of the system and to predict the performance of the assembled systems for the various anticipated operating conditions, and to plan the mission.

First, the major components of the system: the solar collector, transmission line, microwave generator, antennas, guidance and control, and cooling equipment (Figure 2) will have to be well-defined. The components' characteristics will have to be identified.

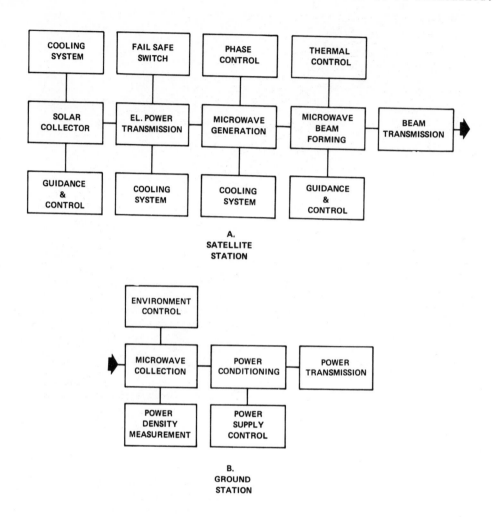

FIGURE 2   MAJOR COMPONENTS OF A SATELLITE SOLAR POWER STATION SYSTEM

Finally the sequence in which they are to be connected will have to be established, their functions analyzed, and the differences between various approaches reconciled. Although candidates for most of the components now exist, at least in the form of laboratory models, new and quite different components can be expected to be developed. How each will perform if fully developed is uncertain, but systems engineering techniques can be used to approximate and compare the performance and costs of the various system configurations, to estimate the dependency of the performance on the component characteristics, and to set quantitative targets for component development based on forecasts of component technology and performance.

2.   Solar Energy Conversion

Silicon solar cells have been the primary source of electric power for almost all unmanned spacecraft, both for space exploration programs and the application of space technology to communications, navigation, and meteorology.[2] Improvement of the technology of silicon solar cells has been accelerated by the increased requirements of large spacecraft for missions in earth orbit, for exploration of the moon, and for exploration of the planets. The size of solar cell arrays has increased tremendously: cumbersome arrays covering a few square feet have been succeeded by large lightweight deployable solar cell arrays covering several thousand square feet and with power levels of tens of kilowatts.[3]

The N/P silicon solar cells with superior radiation resistance and good control over mechanical and electrical tolerances have been the mainstay for space missions. New processes such as the manufacture of solar cells from webbed dendrite silicon[4] or from extrusion of a ribbon of silicon single crystals are expected to increase the cell size, resulting in cost reduction, especially for the large solar cell arrays. Lithium-doped silicon solar cells have the potential of providing a fifty-fold improvement in radiation resistance over the conventional N/P silicon cell.[5] Optical concentrators to focus solar radiation on an individual solar cell have also been investigated to reduce the number of cells required.[6] Roll-out solar cell arrays with specific powers of 30 watts per pound are within the state-of-the-art and further improvements can be envisaged.[7]

The cadmium sulfide thin-film cell should prove useful if two major limitations--instability and low efficiency--can be overcome. The development of such thin-film cells points the way towards lower weight and lower cost solar cell arrays.[8]

The most significant long-term opportunity is for a major advance in photovoltaic efficiency. While the single-transition silicon solar cell is theoretically limited to efficiencies of 20-25%, solar cells with higher efficiencies are theoretically possible. For example, a multicellular device consisting of two or more photovoltaic layers in a sandwich configuration could use wavelength bands where the materials have high quantum efficiencies and thereby considerably increase overall efficiency.

Organic compounds which show characteristic semi-conductor properties, including the photovoltaic effect,[9] have only recently been considered as possible energy-conversion devices.

At present, their efficiencies are only a fraction of a percent, but efforts are underway to synthesize polymers with good photovoltaic characteristics and to study the behavior of other organic compounds.[10]

3. Transmission of Electrical Power

Electric power produced through photovoltaic conversion will have to be gathered at the solar collector and transmitted to the microwave generators. The high power levels will require that the transmission line be superconducting to reduce weight and power losses. For example, transmission of 10^7 kilowatts (20 kv at 5 x 10^5 amp) would require two conductors of two-inch diameter cooled to about 15°K, each suitably insulated. The state-of-the-art of the thermal insulations required for this purpose is well-advanced and the design would reduce heat losses to a minimum.[11] Multiple-staged refrigerators would provide the desired temperatures over the length of the transmission line. At the superconducting temperature, 1000 watts of refrigeration capacity would be sufficient to cool the line and to absorb heat leaks at the cable ends. Such refrigerators have already entered an advanced development stage and would be adaptable for this purpose.

The transmission line itself would have to be articulated to provide relative movement between the solar collector and the microwave generators. Because the solar collector has to be pointed approximately at the sun while the microwave radiating antenna is beamed to a receiving antenna on earth, relative motion between the solar collector and the antenna will have to be provided. Rotary joints at the warm end of the transmission line with low friction and capability to carry the power would have to be developed. Experience with movable joints, their lubrication requirements, and the influence of the space environment on frictional characteristics would provide a bench mark for this development.[12]

4. Generation of Microwaves

Microwave tubes are now capable of generating hundreds of kilowatts of continous power for the DC-to-microwave conversion. Laboratory models have achieved 425-kilowatt outputs in the 10-centimeter band at 75 percent operating efficiency. Further improvements in operating efficiency of up to 90 percent are projected. The principle behind these tubes is the use of a continuous crossed-field interaction such as in a conventional magnetron oscillator.[13] In addition to the magnetron's high efficiency and simple construction, the newer microwave tubes (amplitrons) can operate over a broad frequency band. One of the amplitron's outstanding characteristics is the relative insensitivity of the phase shift through the device to changes in operating parameters so that accurate phasing of the output energy can be achieved.

268

The transmission and conversion of microwave to DC electric power has been demonstrated by tests in which a microwave beam was used to power a helicopter a short distance away.[14] Work is now underway to test similar transmissions of power to determine the feasibility of using them over greater distances, not only to power a helicopter but to guide and control it as well. The feasibility of microwave power transmission between a space station and a satellite space station[15] is now being investigated. This means of power transmission is particularly significant when a close approach to zero-G conditions is desired in a satellite space station.

Heat is generated at the cathode and the anode of each generator; therefore, the microwave generators will have to be cooled. On Earth the heat, directly a function of the efficiency of the generator system, can be removed by circulating water. In the satellite the heat could be removed by a closed system using a circulating fluid and then radiated into space by means of heat pipes or space radiators distributed over the structure of the microwave antenna. If this heat is removed at a high enough temperature, it may be possible to use it--prior to radiating it into space--to run auxiliary power systems[16] for space processing and manufacturing purposes.[17] The waste heat radiator could be combined with the antenna in the form of a composite structure. Since the antenna will always face the earth the radiator would view space, and the solar collector could be arranged to maintain it in its shadow during orbit.

If 10% of the microwave power generated has to be rejected in the form of heat, perhaps as much as 10^6 kilowatts of residual heat would have to be removed. Thus, the efficiency of heat pipes and space radiators would significantly affect the overall weight of the satellite structure. The technology of heat pipes has been advancing rapidly and projected weights of 1/10 per pound per kilowatt appear to be feasible.[18] The art of coatings and thermal insulations to attenuate and control the flow of heat has advanced to the state that thermal control of surfaces which are required to be kept at predetermined temperatures can be accomplished.

5. Transmission of Microwave Beams

To produce the microwave beam, the microwave generators will have to be assembled and the microwave power fed to an antenna. The beam should be narrow so that the Earth-receiving antenna can intercept most of the beam. The efficiency of power transmissions is largely a function of the area of the aperture of the transmitting antenna, the receiving array, and the wavelength of the radiation. The satellite antenna should be of as small an aperture as feasible while the power density of the beam reaching the earth should be as low as possible to limit harmful effects.

The specific arrangement of microwave generators will depend
on the power output which can be obtained from each generator.
For example, to produce 10^7 kilowatts using 1000-kilowatt amplitrons
would require that 10,000 amplitrons be assembled into a 200 x 200
foot array feeding into one large antenna. More likely, array
antennas such as dipole or slot arrays assembled into array panels
each fed by one microwave generator would be utilized. To produce
the required power density profiles the panels would be of different
sizes, depending on their position. Phasing of the microwave
generators could be accomplished with a system which locks the
phase of the field of the respective array panel to a reference
signal. This reference signal could be transmitted to the panel
by a centrally located laser beam phase-locked to a subharmonic
of the transmitted microwave frequency.[19] Larger microwave
generators would require fewer generators, and the panels of the
slot array antenna could be increased in size. For example,
Electromagnetic Amplifying Lenses may possibly reach outputs of
500 mw.[20]

6. Microwave Beam Antennas

The antenna required to transmit microwaves from geosynchronous
orbits to an Earth-receiving station will have to form a beam of
approximately uniform illumination to minimize side lobe losses in
the far field regions. Sparked by the recommendation of the National
Academy of Sciences that radio telescopes with apertures of about
20 kilometers be studied for possible application to long-wave radio
astronomy,[21] investigations of large space-erectable communication
antennas and radio telescopes have been carried out. For example,
to meet the limited payload volume obtainable during one mission a
rotationally deployed and stiffened paraboloidal dish 1500 meters
in diameter was analyzed.[22] Although such a dish has no bending
stiffness of its own, its centrifugal forces would enable it to
withstand perturbation loads and to maintain its shape.

Communication antennas are usually petal-type or folding-type
thin-shell erectable-paraboloid or erectable-truss structures.[23]
A paraboloidal expandable truss antenna with an 80% open metallized
knit precoated weave material for the reflector would weigh about
0.1 pound per square foot of antenna aperture. Its thermal dis-
tortion in orbit would be low and its natural frequencies would be
compatible with an attitude control system. Pressurized inflatable
structures consisting of toroidal rings and stiffening members
have been investigated to produce a 2000-foot-diameter aluminized
plastic reflector to be deployed in a synchronous orbit.[24] Antenna surface tolerances of a few millimeters to limit scattering
losses when coupled with the desire to achieve a low mass for the
structure and to reduce distortions due to forces acting upon it,
indicate that development of an efficient antenna requires an extension of the present state of the art; particularly as existing

antennas are limited to apertures of about 500 wavelengths.

7.   Guidance and Control

The large size of structures which have to be guided and controlled to achieve a significant microwave power output from a
satellite solar power station will require that the state-of-the-
art of guidance and control systems also be further extended. Thus,
the solar collector would have to face the sun at all times. Combinations of sun sensors, star trackers, or horizon seekers could
provide the desired accuracy of at least one degree. Except for the
size of the structure which has to be controlled, the types of devices required are within the state-of-the-art.

The microwave beam will have to lock onto the Earth-receiving
antenna and it would be highly desirable to prevent its straying
more than 500 feet in any direction, not only to maintain a high
efficiency for transferring microwave power but also to assure
environmental safety during operation. To achieve this the pointing
accuracy would have to be less than one-half second of arc. This
requirement stretches the present limits of attitude control techniques and pointing accuracies.[25] It may be easier to achieve
the desired pointing accuracy by developing electrical steering
systems utilizing phased-array feeds. The significant advance
achieved in guidance and control over the last decade would indicate that a further extension of this technology could be expected
to meet the requirements of a satellite solar power station.

A guidance and control system will have to deal with the forces
acting on the satellite to maintain a circular orbit. Among these
is the radiation pressure acting on the solar collector and to a
lesser extent on the antenna. The force in a direction opposite
to the sun on the solar collector will be about 300 newtons; this
force will be partially averaged out during an orbit. The force
in a radial direction away from the earth on the antenna will be
about 200 newtons; this force would have to be counteracted with
thrusters. Gravity gradients will introduce a torque about an axis
perpendicular to the equatorial plane as long as a circular equatorial
orbit is maintained. To counteract continuous angular displacement,
thrusters would also be required. Electrical propulsion for the
thrusters would be available and high specific impulse could be
achieved using ion engines; an outgrowth of present technology.[26]

8.   Conversion of Microwave Power to DC Power

Microwave energy can be converted into DC power at acceptable
efficiencies by semi-conductor diodes.[27] These devices can operate
continuously, provide an output impedance compatible with that of
electric motors, and handle high power inputs. Although a single
diode has a limited power output, four diodes can be combined into

a bridge rectifier assembly. For example, Gallium-arsenide Schottky barrier diodes which operate with tested efficiencies of 75% can handle a 6-watt output and be cooled by natural convection. Theoretically, diode efficiencies greater than 90% could be achieved.[28]

The diodes can be assembled to collect and rectify the microwave energy into a receiving antenna (rectenna).[29] Rectennas have large, comparatively non-directive apertures that do not have to be pointed accurately in the direction of the transmitter. For example, the rectenna could be arranged in saw-toothed fashion so that it is always normal to the microwave beam. In the rectenna, the smallest aperture size corresponds to that of the half-wave dipole. (See Figure 3.)

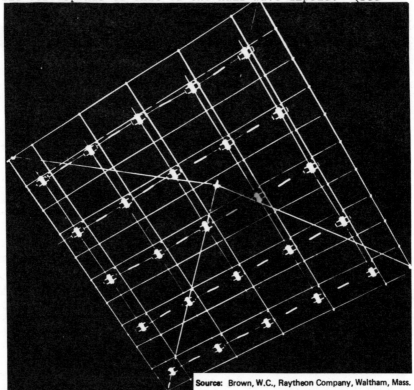

Source: Brown, W.C., Raytheon Company, Waltham, Mass.

FIGURE 3   SECTION OF SILICON RECTIFIER DIODE ANTENNA

Because the diodes are distributed over a large area, natural convection can be used to dissipate heat from the antenna. The heat released on an area basis would be comparable to the heat released in an urban area. Collection efficiencies approaching 90% can be obtained by the use of a reflecting plane one-quarter wavelength behind the rectenna face, careful design of the rectenna face, and best choice of DC load. The most difficult task in designing the rectenna structure is to prevent the generation of harmonics.

SYSTEM CONSIDERATIONS

1.   Payload

A reusable space shuttle is expected to result in significantly reduced costs of orbiting payloads in the 1975-1985 time
period.[30] As envisaged, the space shuttle will be capable of
carrying payloads of at least 50,000 pounds with a cost of about
$50 per pound when placed in a low earth orbit. A space tug
powered by ion engines could transport the satellite station
which was assembled in a low earth orbit to synchronous orbit
over a period of several months. Alternatively, a reusable
nuclear stage could be used to transport manned spacecraft and
supplies between low earth orbit and synchronous orbit. The concept of a satellite solar power station rests on the availability
of an efficient and economical space transportation system. Its
successful development over the next few decades coupled with
experience gained in placing large manned space stations in orbit
indicates that many common technical problems will be addressed.
Thus, the capability to produce large structures in space which
will be essential for the assembly of modular space stations envisioned for future missions should be available during the next
decade.[31,32] The experience gained in the assembly of such
large structures by human operators--subsequently with the help of
automated tele-operators--will be a necessary first step for a
satellite solar power station to become a reality.

2.   Orbit Location

A geosynchronous orbit at the distance of 22,300 nautical
miles parallel to the earth or equatorial plane would make the
satellite stationary with respect to any point on earth. At this
distance the earth subtends a 17-degree angle at the satellite.
Near the equinoxes, the satellite would pass through the earth's
shadow for about one hour each day for 25 days preceding and
following equinox.

The use of at least two satellites will avoid interruption of
service when each is positioned; at least one would be illuminated
by the sun at all times. A network of satellites spaced so that
no more than one was eclipsed at one time could simultaneously serve
a number of ground stations only one less than the total number of
satellites. The possibility also exists of having one satellite
serve several ground stations through time sharing with a repetition
rate of a fraction of a second, perhaps synchronously at a rate of
60 cycles per second, requiring rapid and accurate switching of the
transmitting beam. At more modest power levels such technology is
already well-developed for an electronically steered radar.

3.   Microwave Beam Interactions

The microwave beam wavelength and frequency can be selected
to minimize, if not totally eliminate, atmospheric absorption.
Attenuation and absorption of millimeter waves propagating through
the atmosphere is caused primarily by gas molecules with electric
or magnetic dipole moments and by water formation such as clouds,
fog, and rain.[33]   For example, for a model atmosphere at a nadir
angle of 0°, 1% of the microwave power transmitted would be lost;
whereas at a nadir angle of 60°, up to 2-1/2% would be lost.   Since
the nadir angle will be less than 10°, the losses at a wavelength
of 10 centimeters will be less than 2%.   For a complete cloud cover,
which is assumed to occur about 10% of the time, attenuation in the
10-centimeter region is less than 2%.   For a moderate rainfall,
assumed to occur less than 4% of the time, the attenuation will be
less than 3%.[34]

The microwave beam power density would be reduced to as low
a level as possible consistent with the desire to limit possible
radiological health hazards.   At levels such as 0.01 watt per square
centimeter, the microwave beam would not have destructive effects on
either objects or living tissues exposed to it for a short period.
Exposure at a level of 0.01 watt per square centimeter would only
occur in the beam proper, but with suitable safety devices and
regulations, entry of living beings or objects into the beam could
be avoided to minimize any possible long-term biological effects.
This level is considered an allowable radiation energy absorption
limit in this country; although in Russia, permissible levels
have been set at 0.001 watt per square centimeter for prolonged
periods.[35]

At levels such a 0.01 watt per square centimeter, the microwaves passing through the upper atmosphere will cause a voltage
gradient of less than 2 volts per centimeter, at which gradient
ionization of the atmosphere would be very unlikely.   The specific
levels to be set for permissible voltage gradients will depend on
an increased understanding of nonlinear effects in the ionosphere,
such as electromagnetic drift caused by activity of the sun and
thermal and gravitational atmospheric tides.

WEIGHT AND COST PROJECTIONS

Detailed design concepts for a satellite solar power station
have not yet evolved to the point that cost and weight trade-offs
among components can be made.   However, the first step towards this
goal can be taken by projecting from the present state-of-the-art
the direction that future developments may have to take.   Table 1
shows the projected weights for the major components for the
satellite portions of a system designed to provide about 10^7
kilowatts of power based on the approximate dimensions shown
in Figure 4.

TABLE 1
WEIGHT PROJECTIONS FOR SATELLITE SOLAR POWER STATION

COMPONENT	WEIGHT IN MILLIONS OF LBS.
SOLAR COLLECTOR[1]	2.50
MICROWAVE ANTENNA[2]	1.00
MICROWAVE GENERATORS	0.50
GENERATOR COOLING EQUIPMENT	0.50
ELECTRICAL TRANSMISSION LINE	0.20
WASTE HEAT RADIATORS	0.10
CREW QUARTERS	0.05
CONTROL THRUSTERS AND CONSUMABLES	0.05
	4.90

NOTES:

(1)   THE SOLAR COLLECTOR WEIGHT INDICATED IS ABOUT AN ORDER OF MAGNITUDE DECREASE IN THE WEIGHT OF STATE-OF-THE-ART COMPONENTS. THE BASIS FOR THE PROJECTION IS A SOLAR CELL WEIGHT OF 10^5 POUNDS PER SQUARE MILE.

(2)   THE MICROWAVE ANTENNA WEIGHT IS BASED ON A WEIGHT REDUCTION OF ABOUT AN ORDER OF MAGNITUDE FROM PRESENT DESIGNS SUCH AS THE EXPANDABLE TRUSS.

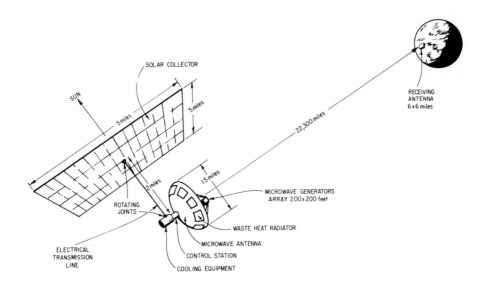

FIGURE 4   DIAGRAM OF SATELLITE SOLAR POWER STATION TO PRODUCE 10^7 KW

Table 2 shows the projected costs for the satellite and Earth-station system.

TABLE 2
COST PROJECTIONS FOR SATELLITE SOLAR POWER STATION

INSERTION INTO SYNCHRONOUS ORBIT	$ 50/kw [1]
SOLAR COLLECTOR	$300/kw [2]
MICROWAVE GENERATOR	$ 50/kw [3]
MICROWAVE ANTENNA	$ 50/kw [4]
EARTH RECEIVING ANTENNA	$ 50/kw [5]
	$500/kw

NOTES:

(1)   PAYLOAD INSERTIONS COSTS WILL BE ABOUT $100 PER POUND.

(2)   NEAR-TERM PROJECTIONS INDICATE THAT LARGE SILICON SOLAR CELLS WOULD COST ABOUT $1000 PER KILOWATT WHEN A MARKET WOULD JUSTIFY CONSIDERABLE DEVELOPMENT COSTS FOR MANUFACTURING IMPROVEMENTS. THIN FILM CELLS COULD BE PRODUCED AT SOMEWHAT LOWER COSTS THAN SINGLE-CRYSTAL CELLS.

(3)   NEAR-TERM COST PROJECTIONS FOR MICROWAVE GENERATORS ARE ABOUT $10 PER KILOWATT; $40 PER KILOWATT IS ALLOCATED FOR THE COOLING SYSTEM, AND WASTE HEAT RADIATORS.

(4)   BASED ON PROJECTED MANUFACTURING COSTS.

(5)   BASED ON THE ALREADY ACHIEVED RECTIFICATION OF MICROWAVES WITH THREE POUNDS OF SOLID-STATE RECTIFIERS PER KILOWATT AND THE EXPECTATION THAT THE COST OF MATERIALS REQUIRED WILL BE REDUCED SEVERALFOLD.

CONCLUSION

The preceding discussion indicates the extent to which space technology could be utilized to exploit the potential of solar energy as an alternative to other energy sources. The large-scale use of solar energy to provide power directly to the Earth, and as an energy source to produce other materials in space for use on earth, could sustain a highly-energy-dependent world culture for a period much longer than the few centuries associated with fossil fuel or even nuclear power. Solar energy can be counted upon to continue to provide energy at present rates for millions of years and the least that should be done is to examine the feasibility of the potential of the large-scale use of solar energy.

Progress in space technology should be continued even in the face of the many nontechnical problems that society now faces. Exclusive concern with contemporary problems without regard to the future runs the danger that the intellectual reservoir will rapidly be depleted. We will fail in our duty to society if we focus exclusively on the immediate social concerns of our own time. Such a society would not deserve a future and most likely would not have one.

REFERENCES

[1]   Daniels, F.: Direct Use of the Sun's Energy. Yale Univ. Press,
       New Haven, Conn., 1964.

[2]   Smith, A.: Status of Photovoltaic Power Technology. ASME Winter
       Annual Meeting, New York, Dec. 1, 1968. Paper no. 68-WA/sol-1.

[3]   Boretz, J.E.: Large Solar Arrays--The Emerging Space Power
       Workhorse. 6th Space Conference Proceedings, Vol. II, Cocoa
       Beach, Florida, March 1969.

[4]   Wise, Jr.: Dendritic Silicon Solar Cells and Utilization Ex-
       perience. Supplement to IEEE Trans. on Aerospace and Elec-
       tronic Systems, Vol. AES-2, No. 4, July 1966.

[5]   Wysocki, J.J.: The Effect of Lithium on Radiation Damage in
       Silicon Solar Cell Devices. Proc. Fifth Photovoltaic Specialists
       Conference, Vol. 2, Section D-G, October 1965.

[6]   Beckman, W.A., Schoffer, P., Hartman, W.R., Jr. and Lof, G.O.G.:
       Design Considerations for a 50-watt Photovoltaic Power System
       Using Concentrated Solar Energy. J. Solar Energy, Vol. 10,
       No. 3, 1966, pp. 132-136.

[7]   Shepard, N.F. and Hanson, K.L.: A Design Concept for a 30 watt
       per pound Roll-up Solar Array. Proc. Intersociety Energy Con-
       version Engineering Conference. IEE Publication 68C21-Energy,
       1968, pp. 549-559.

[8]   Shirland, F.A., Forestieri, A.F., and Spakowski, A.E.: Status
       of the Cadmium Sulfide Thin Film Solar Cell. ibid, pp. 112-115.

[9]   Golubovic, A.: Organic Photovoltaic Devices. Proc., Dept.
       of Air Force, OAR Research Applications Conf., March 1967, pp.
       211-225.

[10]   Air Force Cambridge Research Laboratory, Bedford, Mass., Ener-
       getic Processes Research Project 8659, Commerce Business Daily,
       No. PAS-5083, June 9, 1970, p. 6.

[11]   National Aeronautics and Space Administration, Office of
       Technology Utilization, Thermal Insulation Systems - A
       Survey. Arthur D. Little, Inc., NASA SP-5027, 1967.

[12]   Bisson, E.E. and Anderson, W.J.: Advanced Bearing Technology.
       NASA SP-38, 1964.

[13] Skowron, J.F., Brown, W.C., and MacMaster, G.H.: The Super Power
      CW Amplitron. *Microwave J.*, October 1964.

[14] Brown, W.C.: Experimental Airborne Microwave - Supported Plat-
      form. Technical Report No. RADC-TR-65-188.

[15] Robinson, W.J., Jr.: The Feasibility of Wireless Power Trans-
      mission for an Orbiting Astronomical Station. NASA TM No. 53806,
      May 27, 1969.

[16] Boretz, J.E.: Large Space Station Power Systems. *J. Spacecraft &*
      Rockets, Vol. 6, No. 8, August 1969, pp. 929-936.

[17] vonBraun, W.: Opening Remarks. Space Processing and Manufacturing.
      Proc. of Conference at NASA, MSFC, October 21, 1969, NASA Report
      ME-69-1.

[18] Turner, R.C. and Harbaugh, W.E.: Design of a 50,000-Watt Heat-
      Pipe Space Radiator. ASME Aviation and Space Progress and
      Prospects, Annual Aviation and Space Conference, June 16-19,
      1968, pp. 639-643.

[19] Goubau, G.: Microwave Power Transmission from An Orbiting Solar
      Power Station. Presented at 5th International Symposium, Inter-
      national Microwave Power Institute, Scheveningen, The Netherlands,
      October 7-9, 1970.

[20] Investigation of MHD Power Generation, Vol. II, Integration with
      Crossed-Field Microwave Devices. Contract No. AF30(602)-2487,
      Report No. RADC-TDR-62-444. Raytheon Company, Waltham, Mass.

[21] National Academy of Sciences, Space Science Board, July 1965.

[22] Hedgepeth, J.M.: Low Frequency Telescope. Astro Research
      Corp., Final Report, Contract NAS7-426, Vol. I, ARC-R-300,
      September 27, 1968.

[23] Fager, J.A.: Large Space Erectable Communication Antennas.
      IAF Paper SD9, 19th Congress of the Int. Astr. Fed., New York,
      October 13, 1968.

[24] Reflecting Satellite. *Science*, 155:304, January 20, 1967.

[25] Chubb, W.B. Attitude Control and Precision Pointing of the
      Apollo Telescope Mount. *J. Spacecraft & Rockets*, Vol. 5,
      August 1968.

[26] AIAA 8th Electric Propulsion Conference, Stanford University,
      Stanford, Calif., August 31-September 2, 1970.

[27] George, R.H.: Solid State Microwave Power Rectifiers. Tech-
      nical Report No. RADC-TR-65-224, August 1965, p. 24. Clearing-
      house for Federal Scientific and Technical Information, Spring-
      field, Va. 22151.

[28] Brown, W.C.: Private Communication. June 30, 1970.

[29] Brown, W.C.: Progress in the Design of Rectennas. J. Micro-
      wave Power, Vol. IV, No. 3, pp. 168-175, October 1969.

[30] Reusable Space Shuttle Effort Gains Momentum. Aviation Week &
      Tech., October 27, 1969, p. 22.

[31] Experiment Program for Extended Earth Orbital Missions. NASA,
      September 1, 1969.

[32] America's Next Decades in Space. A report for the Space Task
      Group. NASA, September 1969.

[33] Symposium on the Application of Atmospheric Studies to Satellite
      Transmissions. Air Force Cambridge Research Labs., Boston, Mass.,
      September 3, 1969.

[34] Falcone, V.J., Jr.: Atmospheric Attenuation of Microwave
      Power. Presented at 5th International Symposium, Inter-
      national Microwave Power Institute, Scheveningen, The
      Netherlands, October 7-9, 1970.

[35] Symposium on the Biological Effects and Health Implications
      of Microwave Radiation. Richmond, Virginia, September 1969.

MOLECULAR-BEAM SAMPLING OF GASES IN ENGINE CYLINDERS[+]

W.S. Young, Y.G. Wang, W.E. Rodgers, and E.L. Knuth [*]
Energy and Kinetics Department
School of Engineering and Applied Science
University of California
Los Angeles, California 90024

Abstract

A supersonic molecular-beam system developed initially for aerospace-oriented research is being used presently for air-pollution-control research. The gas mixture in the combustion chamber of an internal-combustion engine is expanded via a small orifice as a free jet into a vacuum chamber. The core of the free jet is skimmed and collimated to form a molecular beam. The densities of the several species in the beam are measured, as a function of time during the engine cycle, by a quadrupole mass spectrometer. Qualitative beam densities of N_2, O_2, C_3H_8, H_2O, CO_2, NO, and CO, and quantitative pressure and bulk temperature of the gas mixture in the combustion chamber have been determined. Hence the feasibility of using molecular-beam techniques and mass spectroscopy for sampling the instantaneous compositions in the combustion chamber of an internal-combustion engine has been demonstrated.

Introduction

In October 1957, the advent of the space age intensified motivations for studies of molecule-molecule and molecule-surface collisions, particularly at energies of the order of magnitude encountered at satellite speeds. A month later, the publication in Jet Propulsion of Estermann's review of Ramsey's book[1] on Molecular Beams called the attention of Aerospace Engineers and Scientists to this valuable aid to the entry of additional laboratories into molecular-beam research[*]. Partly as a result of this favorable timing, molecular-beam technology (including the technology of high-intensity intermediate-energy beams) advanced rapidly during the past decade, and numerous aerospace-oriented molecular-beam researches were initiated.

The initial motivation for the Molecular-Beam Laboratory at UCLA, established in 1959, was aerospace-oriented studies of molecule-surface collisions. Beam energies up to about 2 eV were realized using arc heating of single-species gases[2] and up to about 20 eV using arc heating of a binary mixture[3]. Aerospace-oriented studies subsequently completed include studies of gas-surface interactions[4-6] and free-jet expansions[7].

When the need arose for studies of air-pollution control, the Laboratory experience with high-temperature, binary-mixture, high-intensity beams appeared to be relevant to sampling studies of internal-combustion engines. Since the internal-combustion engine appears to be a serious candidate for the automobile power plant for at least the near future, searches for new engine designs and for modifications of existing engines to minimize the emissions of air pollutants are worthwhile. Such searches would be aided by more detailed information on the chemical processes in the combustion chamber. Hence a study of the feasibility of using molecular-beam techniques and a mass spectrometer for sampling the instantaneous composition in an internal-combustion engine was initiated in early 1969.

Direct molecular-beam sampling from an internal-combustion engine is considered to be a challenging task. Complications might be introduced by the nonsteady nature of the beam source, the high peak pressure of the source, the nonsteady time of flight, the nonuniformity of the gas in the source, chemical relaxations in the free jet, and mass separations in the sampling process. The relatively complicated problem of direct sampling from automobile engines is being approached via a series of increasingly complex studies.

In the first phase of these studies, the characteristics of a single-species inert supersonic molecular beam with cycling-pressure source was studied numerically and experimentally. Computer programs were written and used to predict the cyclic variations of (a) the mass and the thermodynamic state of the gas in the engine cylinder, (b) the mass flow through the sampling orifice, and (c) the beam density. The sampling process was studied experimentally as a function of sampling orifice-skimmer distance, gas-flow rate, and engine speed using a modified single-cylinder 2-stroke model-airplane engine. Measured cyclic variations in beam densities agree qualitatively with predictions for most of the cases studied. Skimmer interference was noted only at high gas-flow rates and small orifice-skimmer distances. Scattering by background gases was significant only near the end of the cycle and for large orifice-skimmer distances[8].

In the second phase of these studies, several binary mixtures of known compositions were sampled

---

[+]Supported by National Air Pollution Control Administration, Consumer Protection and Environmental Health Service, Public Health Service, Grant No. 5 R01 AP00834-02 APC.

[*]Some investigators form a molecular beam from a source with known properties in order to have a beam of known properties as a tool for studies of molecular processes. Other investigators form a molecular beam from a source with unknown properties in order to study, via measurements of beam properties, states and processes within the source. The molecular-beam application described in the present paper falls into the latter category.

using the same motored engine used in the first phase. Possible mass separations (due to pressure diffusion, size diffusion, skimmer-induced separation, background scattering, etc.) were studied by varying (a) the pressure level in the engine cylinder, (b) the nozzle-skimmer distance, and (c) the engine cycle frequency[9].

For the preliminary studies of sampling of combustion gases, the motored model-airplane engine was replaced by a 2-HP, 4-stroke single-cylinder engine. A typical test is with a compression ratio of 7.5, a fuel of propane, an air/fuel ratio of 14.3, an engine speed of 1575 rpm, and negligible load. Qualitative beam densities of N_2, O_2, C_3H_8, H_2O, and CO_2, and quantitative pressure and bulk temperature of the gas mixture in the combustion chamber were reported[10].

Extensions of these forementioned studies are reported here. The measurements were made under conditions differing from the conditions of Reference 10 only in that a light load was imposed on the engine. As a result of refinements in measuring techniques, the list of detected species has been extended to include the pollutants NO and CO.

Engine Combustion Processes and Air Pollutant Formations

Studies of internal-combustion engines date back to 1927[11]. Early studies emphasized chemical-equilibrium properties of combustion gases[12-14] and engine design parameters[15]. The primary goal was higher engine thermal efficiency.

It is now recognized that the automobile engine is the main source of three atmospheric pollutants--carbon monoxide, nitric oxide, and unburned hydrocarbons. It has been found that, whereas a high combustion temperature favors a high thermal efficiency, the two major pollutants (CO and NO) are formed at the peak-temperature part of the cycle. This unfortunate situation was clarified in recent studies[16,17] which consider effects of chemical kinetics and predict that the near-equilibrium compositions realized near the peak temperature will lag changes in temperature and pressure during the expansion process. Hence the primary goal (high thermal efficiency) must now be supplemented by considerations of air pollutant control. Brief descriptions of the origins of pollutants emitted by engines are given in the following paragraphs.

Unburned Hydrocarbons

It has been estimated that, of the unburned hydrocarbons which enter the atmosphere, 55 percent come from the engine exhaust, 25 percent from the crankcase, and 20 percent from evaporation. Studies of unburned hydrocarbons in engine exhaust indicate[18-20] that they originate mainly in unburned gases adjacent to the chamber walls and in crevices. Miss-fire cycles also emit significant quantities of unburned hydrocarbons. For example, if an engine miss-fires one out of 100 cycles, then the unburned hydrocarbon emission is approximately 600 ppm.

Carbon Monoxide

The formation of carbon monoxide in a combustion process is frequently termed "incomplete combustion." Incomplete combustion arises from several causes including incomplete mixing and quenching by the cylinder wall. In all cases, it is aggravated by a high fuel/air ratio, i.e., by insufficient oxygen for complete conversion of CO to CO_2. Hence, for a given engine, the fuel/air ratio is the dominant parameter for correlating CO emissions[18,21].

The elementary reactions involving conversion of CO to CO_2 are

$$CO + H_2O \rightleftharpoons CO_2 + H_2 \qquad (1)$$

$$CO + O_2 + H_2 \rightleftharpoons CO_2 + H_2O \qquad (2)$$

Using these equations, Starkman and Newhall[17] found that, for lean and chemically correct mixtures, the predicted equilibrium CO exhaust concentrations were higher than those measured by Hagen and Holiday[18]. In the case of fuel-rich mixtures, reaction (1) dominates the process and the equilibrium composition is found to be a weak function of temperature; therefore the equilibrium composition does not vary much throughout the expansion process. The measured exhaust CO concentration agreed with the predicted equilibrium value.

In more recent studies, Newhall[22] considered the following bimolecular reaction:

$$CO + OH \rightleftharpoons CO_2 + H \qquad (3)$$

The equilibrium value of the ratio n_{CO}/n_{CO_2} in the reaction is expressed by

$$\frac{n_{CO}}{n_{CO_2}} = K_3 \frac{n_H}{n_{OH}} \qquad (4)$$

where K_3 is the equilibrium constant of reaction (3). During the expansion process, the ratio n_{CO}/n_{CO_2} is determined by the ratio n_H/n_{OH} which is controlled by the partial equilibrium described by the following bimolecular reactions

$$OH + H \rightleftharpoons H_2 + O \qquad (5)$$

$$OH + O \rightleftharpoons O_2 + H \qquad (6)$$

$$OH + H_2 \rightleftharpoons H_2O + H \qquad (7)$$

$$OH + OH \rightleftharpoons H_2O + O \qquad (8)$$

Newhall calculated and found that when the temperature decreases during the expansion, these reactions tend to produce values of n_H/n_{OH} much greater than would be the case for total equilibrium. Accordingly, at the end of expansion, the concentrations of CO will exceed the equilibrium value.

Nitric Oxide

The formation of NO in combustion processes has been studied by several investigators[16,23,24]. As for carbon monoxide, it is generally recognized that the air/fuel ratio plays a major role in engine NO emission. Furthermore, measurements indicate that NO concentrations in engine exhausts are frequently close to the equilibrium values calculated for the peak gas temperatures. Newhall[22] studied numerically the kinetics of NO formation in an engine, and predicted that the NO concentration will freeze during the expansion process.

Many elementary reactions of the nitrogen oxide system have been suggested. Among them, the mechanism suggested by Zeldovich[25] is generally considered sufficient to account for NO formation in an internal combustion engine:

$$N + O_2 \rightleftharpoons NO + O \tag{9}$$

$$O + N_2 \rightleftharpoons NO + N \tag{10}$$

It is seen that the presence of O atoms in the combustion process plays an important role in the kinetics of NO formation. In case of low temperature and excess air, such as in the combustion in a furnace, the following reaction will become important in the NO formation:

$$N_2O + O \rightleftharpoons NO + NO \tag{11}$$

Early in 1935, Rassweiler and Withrow[26] measured a substantial temperature difference (several hundred degrees Kelvin) across the engine chamber. This difference is due to different combustion times for different parts of the gas mixture; the early burned gas compresses the unburned gas, while the late burned gas recompresses the early burned gas. The net effect is a higher temperature for the early burned gas. References 27 and 28 calculated the temperature histories for different parts of the gas inside an engine. Based on the calculated temperature, they predicted nonuniform concentrations of NO across the engine cylinder; the early burned gas would have a higher NO concentration. Using optical spectroscopy, they measured the NO concentrations along different optical paths through the engine cylinders and indeed observed the nonuniform NO distributions predicted by the theoretical calculations. Their results have shown that it is necessary to consider the effect of location on samplings, especially when the mixing of gas inside the engine is incomplete.

Experimental System

With the exception of the molecular-beam source, the molecular beam system in the study reported here was essentially the same as those described in References 2 and 3. The apparatus is shown schematically in Fig. 1. This system, downstream from the sampling orifice, is a typical supersonic molecular-beam system. The efflux from the sampling orifice forms a free-jet, the core of which is isolated by a skimmer. The molecular beam is subsequently collimated and detected. The vacuum system is a three-stage system with individually pumped source, collimating, and detection chambers. The pressures in these three chambers are respectively from 1×10^{-3} to 7×10^{-3} torr, about 5×10^{-6} torr, and about 5×10^{-7} torr.

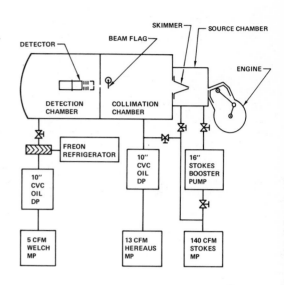

FIG. 1 ENGINE SAMPLING SYSTEM

In References 8 and 9, a modified model airplane engine (ENYA Model 09-III) with a 1.04-cm bore, a 1.22-cm stroke, and a volume compression ratio of approximately 8 was used as the beam source. Since the purpose of those studies was to investigate the general characteristics of beams with cycling pressure sources, the engine was driven by a variable speed synchronous motor. The engine source used in Reference 10 and this study is a modified Briggs and Stratton Model 60152 4-stroke 2 HP engine (see Fig. 2). The cylinder head (originally flat) was redesigned in order to accommodate the sampling orifice and a pressure transducer (Dynasciences Model 755-2560). As shown in Fig. 3, the combustion chamber has been extended into the cylinder head; in order to preserve the original compression ratio of $\gamma = 7.5$, the piston also has been extended. Both the cylinder head and the extension of the piston are made of aluminum. The grooves shown on the cylinder head increase the cooling surface. A small air blower has been used to augment the cooling. The inlet valve of the engine is closed at nearly 43° after bottom dead center (ABDC), while the exhaust valve is opened at nearly 140° after top dead center (ATDC). Spark ignition occurs at nearly 35° before top dead center (BTDC). A tachometer generator driven by the engine supplies a DC output to an AC-to-DC converter for engine speed indication. The tachometer output also feeds back to a servo load system for engine speed control. A photo-cell triggering system connected to the tachometer shaft supplies the triggering signal for the electronic devices. The photocell is presently triggered at 20° ABDC. The air flow to the engine is monitored by a Fischer and Porter (Model 10A1700) flow meter. The air/fuel ratio is monitored by a Doyle air-fuel analyzer. The fuel is propane.

A slightly modified commercial EAI QUAD 250

FIG. 2 ENGINE SOURCE USED IN PRESENT STUDY

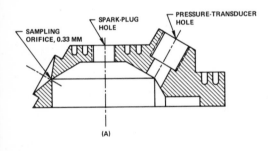

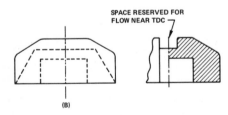

FIG. 3 MODIFIED CYLINDER HEAD (A) AND CORRES-
PONDING ADDITION TO PISTON (B)

mass-spectrometer beam detector is located in the
detection chamber. It consists of a through-flow
(density sensitive) ionizer, a quadrupole mass filter, and a Beryllium-Copper electron multiplier.
This quadrupole detector can be operated either as
a residue gas analyzer or to monitor the beam composition. While the engine is running, a small

percentage of the beam molecules is ionized by
electron bombardment. These ions are then accelerated and focused into the quadrupole section.
Adjustment of the mass selector facilitates selection of ions of interest (based on mass-to-charge
ratio) for transmission through the quadrupole.
Signals of those ions which do pass through the
quadrupole section are then amplified by the electron multiplier. The current output from the
electron multiplier is further amplified by a
laboratory-made DC amplifier. The amplified signal is then stored in a Fabri-Tek Model 1062 signal averager. A typical beam signal is digitized
into 256 channels. Each beam signal is added over
either 512 or 1024 (depending on the signal-to-
noise ratio) repetitive sampling cycles. Then the
beam is blocked by a beam flag located upstream
from the collimating orifice and the signal averager is operated in the subtraction mode for the
same number of repetitive cycles. This procedure
eliminates the background signal so that the signal baseline can be established. The output data
of the signal averager were then recorded by an IBM
024 card punch. (The interface between the averager and the card punch is a laboratory-made
analog-to-digital converter.) The punched cards
are then available for computerized data processing.

Data Processing

Since the signal averager is triggered by the
photocell output generated at nearly 20° ABDC, this
crank position corresponds to the zero time of the
signal-averager sweep. Since the pressure-trans-
ducer response time is about 15 μsec while the typical engine cycle time is about 60 msec, the output
signal of the pressure transducer follows closely
the engine cycle. The time of flight (TOF)
required for the molecules to travel from the beam
source to the detector, of the order of 1 msec, is
not negligible compared with the engine cycle time.
Therefore, corrections of TOF must be made in
order to correlate the beam signals with the engine
cycle. Procedures for reducing the pressure, temperature, and beam-signal data are given here.

Pressure

As mentioned above, the pressure signal follows closely the engine cycle. The pressure vs.
crank angle is then obtained from the relations

$$p(\theta) = S_p(I) \tag{12}$$

$$\theta = \theta_o + I \cdot t_r \cdot \omega \tag{13}$$

where θ is the crank angle, θ_o (20° ABDC) is the
crank angle at which the averager is triggered, ω
is the crank-shaft angular speed, t_r is the time
resolution of the signal averager, and I is the
channel number of the averager.

Bulk Temperature

The bulk temperature of the gas in the engine
is calculated using the measured instantaneous
pressure. Assuming the gas mixture is a thermally
perfect gas, one has

$$T_o(\theta) = \frac{p(\theta)V(\theta)}{M(R/\bar{m})} \tag{14}$$

284

where $V(\theta)$ is the chamber volume at crank angle θ, M is the total mass of the gas, R is the universal gas constant, $\bar{m}$ is the mean molecular weight of the gas mixture, and $T_o(\theta)$ is the bulk temperature of the gas at crank angle θ.

Two significant uncertainties are encountered upon use of the above equation. First, since the gas mixture composition is not known, an accurate calculation of $\bar{m}$ is prohibited. However, an estimate can be made using the main combustion equation

$$C_3H_8 + 5O_2 + 5x\frac{79}{21}xN_2 \rightarrow 3CO_2 + 4H_2O + 5x\frac{79}{21}xN_2 \quad (15)$$

One finds that the total number of moles varies only about 4% throughout the combustion process. It therefore seems reasonable to use the mean molecular weight of the air-fuel mixture prior to combustion. Second, the total mass inside the cylinder, M, varies due to two leaks: the flow through the beam orifice and the leaks through the piston rings. Based on the measured chamber pressure, one estimates that, during the engine cycle, about 5% of the total molecules escape through the beam orifice. The magnitude of the leakage through the piston rings is not known. Due to the leakage, the instantaneous total mass will be less than the initial total mass of the cycle, which is calculated from

$$M \approx \dot{M}/(2N)$$

where $\dot{M}$ is the measured total mass flow rate per minute, and N is the engine RPM. The factor 2 takes into account that only half of the engine revolutions are used for cycle charge. Since $T_o(\theta)$ is calculated using the initial total mass, the calculated values will be lower limits.

Determinations of Gas Species from the Measured Beam Signals

Molecule fragmentation and mass resolution are the two main difficulties encountered in applications of a mass spectrometer. The former complicates the identification of the parent species; the latter makes the separation of two adjacent masses difficult if the difference in their masses is small. The handling of these problems is described here.

(a). N_2 spectrum. The N_2 spectrum contains two peaks: (1) m/e = 28, and (2) m/e = 14. The ratio of these two peaks was constant within the experimental range. In the engine samplings, the m/e = 14 peak was used for N_2 detection. The other peak was disregarded due to the fact that the combustion product CO and the CO fragment of CO_2 also contribute to the m/e = 28 peak.

(b). O_2 spectrum. The oxygen spectrum contains two peaks: (1) m/e = 32, and (2) m/e = 16. The m/e = 32 peak is used for O_2 signal detection because (1) the signal intensity at m/e = 32 is much stronger than at m/e = 16 and (2) the O fragment of the combustion product H_2O also appears at m/e = 16.

(c). C_3H_8 spectrum. Due to its complex structure, C_3H_8 produces the most complicated fragment pattern among the species involved in engine samplings. Relatively strong fragment peaks appear

at m/e = 27, 28, and 29. The m/e = 29 peak is found to be produced only by C_3H_8. Hence, the m/e = 29 peak is used for C_3H_8 detection.

(d). CO_2 spectrum. The CO_2 spectrum contains peaks at m/e = 12, 16, 28, and 44. In this sampling study, CO_2 data were obtained from the m/e = 44 peak according to

$$S_{CO_2} = S_{44} - R_{44/29}S_{29} \quad (16)$$

where S_{CO_2} is the CO_2 signal, S_{44} is the measured beam signal at m/e = 44, S_{29} is the measured beam signal at m/e = 29, and $R_{44/29}$ is the ratio of the m/e = 44 and m/e = 29 peaks for C_3H_8.

(e). H_2O spectrum. The water vapor peaks are found at m/e = 16, 17, and 18. The m/e = 18 peak is used for water vapor identification.

(f). NO spectrum. Detection of NO is difficult in the present study due to two reasons: (1) the NO production is low under present engine operation conditions (low air/fuel ratio and light engine load), and (2) the spectrum of NO at m/e = 30 appears to be one of the (weak) fragments of C_3H_8. The NO content was determined according to

$$S_{NO} = S_{30} - R_{30/29}S_{29} \quad (17)$$

where S_{NO} is the NO signal, S_{30} is the beam signal measured at m/e = 30, and $R_{30/29}$ is the ratio of the m/e = 30 and m/e = 29 peaks for C_3H_8.

(g). CO spectrum. The CO spectrum contains the peaks at m/e = 12, 16 and 28. The strongest peak occurs at m/e = 28. The CO signal is determined from

$$S_{CO} = S_{28} - S_{14} R_{28/14} - S_{CO_2} R_{28/CO_2} \quad (18)$$

where S_{CO} is the CO signal, S_{28} and S_{14} are the beam signals detected respectively at m/e = 28 and m/e = 14, S_{CO_2} is the CO_2 signal found in step (d), and $R_{28/14}$ and R_{28/CO_2} are the calibration factors for N_2 and CO_2 respectively.

TOF Correction

As mentioned above, changes in detected beam signals lag (due to nonzero TOF) changes in realized combustion-chamber gas states. In order to make the required TOF correction, one needs the molecular speeds. It has been found[3,29,30], that for a mixture expanding from a source with Reynolds number greater than 1000, the slip velocity between molecules with different molecular weights is negligible, i.e., all species will travel with nearly the same stream velocity $\bar{U}$. This velocity can be calculated from[3]

$$\bar{U} \approx \sqrt{\frac{2\bar{\gamma}}{\bar{\gamma}-1} \frac{k}{\bar{m}} T_o} \quad (19)$$

where $\bar{\gamma}$ and $\bar{m}$ are respectively the average specific heat ratio and the average molecular weight of the gas mixture, T_o is the stagnation temperature, and k is Boltzmann's constant. Once $\bar{U}$ is calculated, the signal of species i at crank angle θ, $S_i(\theta)$, is found from

$$S_i(\theta) = S_i(I) \qquad (20)$$

$$\theta = \theta_o + (I \cdot t_r - L/\bar{U}) \cdot \omega \qquad (21)$$

where L(= 135 cm) is the distance between the beam source and the detector.

Results and Discussions

The measurements were made while the engine was operated with an air/fuel ratio of 14.25 and at a speed of 1760 rpm. A slight engine load was imposed. Data were reduced using an IBM Model 360/91 digital computer provided by the UCLA Campus Computing Network.

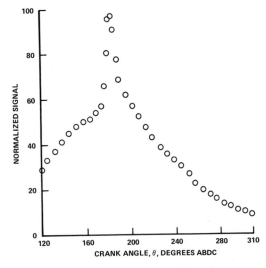

FIG. 5 NORMALIZED SIGNAL FOR NITROGEN

tion in beam density is due to compression and expansion of the combustion gas; the N_2 mole fraction in the bulk mixture varies only slightly throughout the engine cycle.

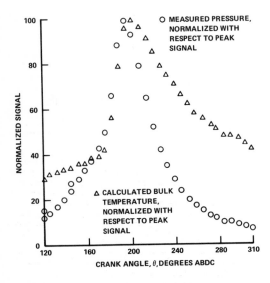

FIG. 4 PRESSURE AND TEMPERATURE IN ENGINE CYCLE

The measured pressure and the calculated temperature are plotted in Fig. 4. Both curves have been normalized with respect to their peak values. The peak pressure of 323 psia occurred at nearly 197° ABDC, while the calculated peak temperature of 2410°R occurred at nearly 201° ABDC. This peak temperature is considerably higher than the one observed in Reference 10, probably due to the slight load imposed on the engine.

The normalized nitrogen signal is plotted as a function of crank angle in Fig. 5. The strong spike near the TDC was due to high-energy molecules from after combustion catching up with the slower particles from before combustion[10]. This catching-up phenomenon would be reduced by shortening the distance of flight. It is noted that the varia-

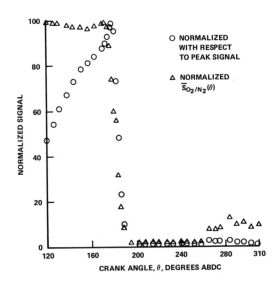

FIG. 6 NORMALIZED SIGNALS FOR OXYGEN

Two oxygen signals (the beam density normalized by its peak value, and the quantity $\bar{S}_{O_2/N_2}(\theta)$ defined by the ratio of the non-calibrated oxygen-beam density divided by the nitrogen-beam density, $\bar{S}_{O_2/N_2}(\theta) \equiv S_{O_2}/S_{N_2}$) are plotted as functions of the crank angle in Fig. 6. Since the N_2 mole fraction in the bulk mixture varies only slightly throughout the engine cycle, the quantity $\bar{S}_{O_2/N_2}(\theta)$ represents the non-calibrated O_2 mole fraction in the engine cycle. It is seen that the O_2 mole fraction remains nearly constant before top dead center. The rapid drop of O_2 mole fraction which occurs between 170° and 195° ABDC indicates that the combustion process occurred during that period. The weak O_2 intensity and the low O_2 mole fraction after combustion indicate almost complete consumption of the oxygen. The reason for the increase in O_2 content starting at nearly 260° ABDC is not clear. In view of the increase in C_3H_8 and decrease in the combustion products during nearly the same part of the cycle, it is possible that some unburned air/fuel mixture is being sampled. Perhaps some unburned gas mixture was sampled from the quenched-reaction zone near the combustion-chamber wall.

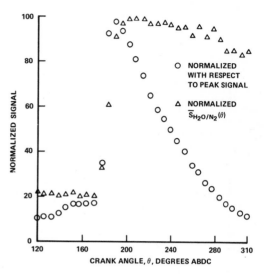

FIG. 8   NORMALIZED SIGNALS FOR WATER VAPOR

8, 9, 10, and 11 respectively. The relative concentration of water vapor indicates that H_2O production took place from 170° to 195° ABDC, in agreement with the consumption of oxygen and fuel during the same part of the cycle. The formation of NO shown in Fig. 9 is quite different from those reported in References 27 and 28; a peak is found at nearly 200° ABDC, followed by a relative concentration decrease at a significant rate until 240° ABDC where the relative concentration begins to freeze. The NO decrease after 260° ABDC is due possibly to the sampling of some unburned gas mixture. Also shown in Fig. 9 is the predicted "first-burned" NO concentration given in Fig. 3 of Reference 28. Since the concentration of NO obtained in this study is not calibrated, the qualitative comparison is made by normalizing the predicted value with respect to its peak value.

The carbon dioxide signals are shown in Fig. 10. The production of CO_2 follows closely the production of H_2O except that the slow increase in CO_2 relative concentration between 200° and 230° ABDC is rather unexpected. Since the relative concentration of CO does not decrease during this part of the engine cycle (see Fig. 11), no conversion of CO to CO_2 is expected. This question will be investigated in future work.

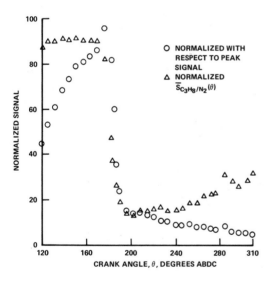

FIG. 7   NORMALIZED SIGNALS FOR PROPANE

Similar to the oxygen signals, two propane signals are shown in Fig. 7. The rapid drops in the C_3H_8 signals between 170° and 195° ABDC (as for oxygen) confirm that the combustion process indeed took place during this part of the engine cycle. The excess propane for the air/fuel ratio of 14.25 (i.e., for the equivalence ratio ϕ of 1.1) might account for the unburned fuel after combustion. Also, the increase in the fuel mole fraction after 260° ABDC supports the hypothesis that some unburned gas mixture was sampled during the later part of the engine cycle.

The CO signals shown in Fig. 11 indicate a constant relative concentration of CO after 200° ABDC. The data between 180° and 190° are not shown due to some uncertainties in data reduction; a strong spike in the m/e = 28 signal overloads the signal-averager memory. This difficulty will be reduced in the future measurements by reducing the flight-path length.

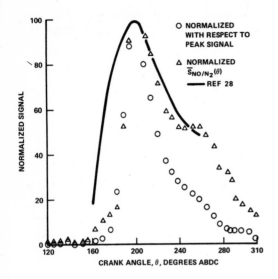

FIG. 9 NORMALIZED SIGNALS FOR NITRIC OXIDE

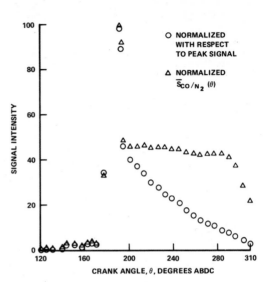

FIG. 11 NORMALIZED SIGNALS FOR
CARBON MONOXIDE

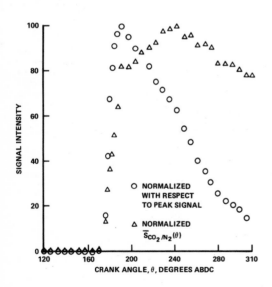

FIG. 10 NORMALIZED SIGNALS FOR
CARBON DIOXIDE

References

1. Ramsey, N. F., _Molecular Beams_. Oxford: Oxford University Press, 1956.

2. Knuth, E. L., N. M. Kuluva, and J. P. Callinan, "Densities and Speeds in an Arc-Heated Supersonic Argon Beam," _Entropie_ No. 18, pp. 38-46, Nov.-Dec. 1967.

3. Young, W. S., and E. L. Knuth, "A Binary-Mixture Arc-Heated Supersonic Molecular Beam," _Entropie_ No. 30, pp. 25-29, Nov.-Dec. 1969.

4. Alcalay, J. A., and E. L. Knuth, "Experimental Study of Scattering in Particle-Surface Collisions with Particle Energies of the Order of 1 eV," _Rarefied Gas Dynamics_ (C. L. Brundin, ed.)1:253-268. New York: Academic Press, 1967.

5. Callinan, J. P., and E. L. Knuth, "An Experimental Study of the Particle, Momentum, and Energy Flux Distributions of Products of Collisions of 1 eV Argon Atoms and Surfaces," _Rarefied Gas Dynamics_ (L. Trilling and H. Y. Wachman, eds.)2:1247-1255. New York: Academic Press, 1969.

6. Hays, W. J., "Scattering of Argon Beams with Incident Energies up to 20 eV from a (111) Silver Surface," _Report No. UCLA-ENG-7061._ Los Angeles: UCLA School of Engineering and Applied Science, July 1970.

7. Fisher, S. S., and E. L. Knuth, "Properties of Low-Density Freejets Measured Using Molecular-Beam Techniques," _AIAA Journal_ 7:1174-1177, June 1969.

8. Young, W. S., W. E. Rodgers, C. A. Cullian, and E. L. Knuth, "Supersonic Molecular Beams with Cycling-Pressure Sources," submitted for publication.

9. Young, W. S., W. E. Rodgers, C. A. Cullian, and E. L. Knuth, "Molecular Beam Sampling of Gas Mixtures in Cycling-Pressure Sources," Presented at the Seventh International Symposium on Rarefied Gas Dynamics, Pisa, Italy, 29 June-3 July 1970.

10. Young, W. S., R. E. Rodgers, C. A. Cullian, Y. G. Wang, and E. L. Knuth, "A Method for Sampling the Instantaneous Chemical Compositions in an Internal-Combustion Engine," to be published in Proceedings of the Second International Air Pollution Conference, held at Washington, D. C. 6-11 December 1970.

11. Goodenough, G. A. and J. B. Baker, Univ. of Illinois Expt. Station Bul. 160. Urbana: Univ. of Illinois, 1927.

12. Hershey, R. L., J. E. Eberhardt and H. C. Hottel, "Thermodynamic Properties of the Working Fluid in Internal Combustion Engine," SAE Journal 39:409-424, October 1936.

13. Vickland, C. W., F. M. Strange, R. A. Bell and E. S. Starkman, "A Consideration of the High Temperature Thermodynamics of I.C. Engines," SAE Transactions 70:785-794, 1962.

14. Newhall, H. K. and E. S. Starkman, "Thermodynamic Properties of Octane and Air for Engine Performance Calculations," SAE Technical Progress Series 7:38-48, 1964.

15. Caris, D. F. and E. E. Nelson, "A New Look at High Compression Ratio Engines," SAE Transactions 67:112-124, 1959.

16. Wimmer, D. B. and L. A. McReynolds, "Nitrogen Oxides and Engine Combustion," SAE Transactions 70:733-744, 1962.

17. Starkman, E. S. and H. K. Newhall, "Characteristics of the Expansion of Reactive Gas Mixtures as Occurring in Internal Combustion Engine Cycles," SAE Transactions 74:826-838, 1966.

18. Hagen, D. F. and G. W. Holiday, "The Effect of Engine Operating and Design Variables on Exhaust Emissions," SAE TPS 6:206-223, 1964.

19. Daniel, W. A., "Flame Quenching at the Wall of an Internal Combustion Engine," Sixth Symposium (International) on Combustion, 886-894. New York: Reinhold Publishing Co., 1957.

20. Daniel, W. A., "Why Engine Variables Effect Exhaust Hydrocarbon Emissions," Paper 700108. SAE Automotive Engineering Congress, Detroit, 1970.

21. D'Alleva, B. A. and W. G. Lovell, "Relation of Exhaust Gas Composition to Air-Fuel Ratio," SAE Transactions 31:90-98, 116, 1936.

22. Newhall, H. K., "Kinetics of Engine-Generated Nitrogen Oxides and Carbon Monoxide," Twelfth Symposium (International) on Combustion, 603-613. Pittsburgh: The Combustion Institute, 1969.

23. Hanson, T. K. and A. C. Egerton, "Nitrogen Oxides in Internal Combustion Engine Gases," Proc. Roy. Soc. A163:93-100, Nov. 1937.

24. Spindt, R. S., C. F. Wolfe and D. K. Stevens, "Nitrogen Oxides, Combustion, and Engine Deposits," SAE Transactions 64:797-811, 1956.

25. Zeldovich, Ya. B., "The Oxidation of Nitrogen in Combustion Explosions," Acta Physiochimica U.S.S.R. 21:577-628, 1946.

26. Rassweiler, G. M. and L. Withrow, "Flame Temperatures Vary with Knock and Combustion-Chamber Position," SAE Transactions 30:125-136, 1935.

27. Lavoie, G. A., J. B. Heywood and J. C. Keck, "Experimental and Theoretical Study of Nitric Oxide Formation in Internal Combustion Engines," Combustion Science and Technology 1:313-326, 1970.

28. Caretto, L. S., L. J. Nuzio, R. F. Sawyer and E. S. Starkman, "The Role of Kinetics in Engine Emission of Nitric Oxides," presented at the Third Joint Meeting, The American Institute of Chemical Engineers and Instituto Mexicano de Ingenieros Quimicos, Aug. 30-Sept. 2, 1970, Denver, Colo.

29. Becker, E. W. and W. Henkes, "Geschwindigkeitsanalyse von Laval-Strahlen," Z. Physik 146: 320-332, 1956.

30. Abuaf, N., J. B. Anderson, R. P. Andres, J. B. Fenn, and D. G. H. Marsden, "Molecular Beam with Energies above One Electron Volt," Science 155:997-999, Feb. 1967.

UTILIZATION OF AEROSPACE TECHNOLOGY IN THE STABILITY OF MOTOR VEHICLES

James D. Iversen
Professor of Aerospace Engineering
Engineering Research Institute
Iowa State University, Ames, Iowa 50010

Abstract

Aerospace technology is, by necessity, much further advanced than automotive technology, especially in the areas of experimental and theoretical aerodynamics and in the analysis and determination of desirable stability, control, and handling characteristics. A research program is proposed in which existing knowledge in the aerospace field would be extended to improve the state of automotive technology. Such a program would include wind tunnel testing of motor vehicles (including dynamic experiments), automobile stability analysis, and the development of stability and handling criteria for motor vehicles. Existing techniques would also be extended to provide analytic determination of aerodynamic forces on automobile shapes by means of surface singularity methods and/or time-dependent finite-difference methods. New concepts in motor vehicle shapes and control systems could be provided by experienced aerospace engineers.

Nomenclature

a   longitudinal distance, center of gravity to front wheel axis

ATC   tire aligning torque coefficient

b   longitudinal distance, center of gravity to rear wheel axis

C   tire cornering force coefficient

C_D drag coefficient, D/qS

C_L lift coefficient, L/qS

C_m pitching moment coefficient, $M/qS\ell$

C_N yawing moment coefficient, $N/qS\ell$

C_Y side force coefficient, Y/qS

D   drag force

d_F lateral distance between stabilizing fins

I_z mass moment of inertia about lateral axis through center of gravity

ℓ wheelbase distance

f   longitudinal distance, fin aerodynamic center or hinge line to center of gravity

L   lift force

M   pitching moment about lateral axis through center of gravity

m   mass

N   yawing moment about vertical axis through center of gravity

q   dynamic pressure, $\frac{1}{2} \rho u_o^2 (1 + \tan^2 \beta_W)$

r   yawing angular velocity

s   Laplace transform variable

S   frontal area

S_F fin area, per fin

u_o forward speed

W   weight

Y   side force

β sideslip angle

δ steering angle

ρ air density

Subscripts

A   aerodynamic

F   front

R   rear

r   derivative with respect to r

W   wind

β derivative with respect to β

δ derivative with respect to δ

I. Introduction

The automobile is the most popular form of transportation in the United States. It offers convenience, comfort, privacy, and accessibility to almost anyplace on the continent. It is also the major source of air pollution and by far the major cause of accidental deaths and injuries among our various forms of transportation.

There are, of course, several contributing factors to the high automobile accident rate. Among these are poor highways, overcrowded highways, drunk driving, lack of proper training, injudicious driver licensing, and poor handling qualities and instability of the automobiles themselves. The stability and handling quality of the automobile is the subject of this paper.

A great variety of motor vehicles use our highways. Among these are cars with front-wheel drive, cars with rear-wheel drive, and cars with and without power steering and/or power brakes. There are different kinds of transmissions, different power-to-weight ratios, and a multitude of body shapes. There are different suspension systems and different kinds of tires. Some automobiles have most weight on the front tires while some have it on the rear tires. As a result of these differences, automobiles show widely varying, even unsafe, directional stability and handling characteristics. These variations, as indicated by automotive design engineers, point to the fact that a set of realistic stability criteria and better methods of stability analysis are badly needed[1].

Although there are many differences among motor vehicles, there are several common characteristics. One of these is that they are all affected by aerodynamic forces, much more so than most people realize. For example, for a typical American sedan traveling at 70 mph with a 30 mph crosswind, the aerodynamic forces and moments have been measured as follows[2] (the aerodynamic sideslip angle is 23.2 degrees):

Lift — 384 lb

Drag — 128 lb (compared to rolling friction retarding force of 55 lb)

Side force — 300 lb

Pitching moment — 362 ft-lb

Yawing moment — 489 ft-lb

Rolling moment — 453 ft-lb

It is interesting to note that most wind tunnel tests of automobiles to date have measured only aerodynamic drag, since that is the main force component affecting automobile performance — i.e., speed, power required, and fuel consumption[3]. However, for the example cited[2], the magnitude of the drag, even with rolling friction added, is considerably less than the lift and side force component magnitudes. The lift and side force components and the three moment components, their variations with sideslip and pitch angles, and their effects on tire and suspension system forces are intricately involved in determination of the handling and stability characteristics of motor vehicles.

Although interest in automobile aerodynamics dates back almost to the invention of the motor vehicle, only recently have major manufacturers begun to move automobile aerodynamics from the analysis of a design presented by the stylists to incorporation of aerodynamic consideration in the styling departments themselves[4,5].

Aerospace technology is, by necessity, much further advanced than automotive technology, especially in the areas of experimental and theoretical aerodynamics and in the analysis and determination of desirable stability, control, and handling characteristics. Much use can be made of these achievements to advance the state of automotive technology[6]. A research program is thus suggested in which existing knowledge in the aerospace field is extended to improve the state of automotive technology in the following areas:

- Wind tunnel testing of motor vehicles

- Stability analysis of motor vehicles

- Stability and handling criteria

- New concepts in motor vehicle shapes

- Analytical determination of aerodynamic forces

- Other contributions to safety such as energy-absorbing devices and man-machine integration.

II. Wind Tunnel Testing of Motor Vehicles

Many wind tunnel tests, a few of which have been fairly comprehensive, have been used to determine the aerodynamic characteristics of automobiles[7-13]. Those which have concerned determination of stability derivatives, i.e., the variation of forces and moments as functions of the variables describing vehicle motion, have measured lift, drag, and side force components and pitching, yawing, and rolling moment components as a function of the aerodynamic sideslip angle, β.

To the author's knowledge, the force and moment components as functions of the vehicle angular rates have not been previously measured for the motor vehicle, at least not in this country. One related wind tunnel experiment has been performed in which the forces on an automobile model were measured while the model was traversing the wind tunnel test section[14]. Unsteady aerodynamic forces were thus measured on the model from which it would be possible to make crude estimates of some of the aerodynamic damping terms. However, considerably better and more complete results can be obtained from the types of free and forced oscillation experiments performed regularly with aerospace vehicle models[15]. A major portion of the suggested experimental effort would thus consist of measuring pitch and yaw rate aerodynamic derivatives for a variety of vehicle shapes. These data, plus the measurement of static force and moment components as functions of pitch, yaw, and roll angles, would be used to obtain more information with which to perform more realistic stability analyses.

Preliminary wind tunnel tests have been performed on a one-eighth scale model of a typical sports coupe (Jaguar XK-E) in the Iowa State University Wind Tunnel[16]. The variations of aerodynamic yawing moment and side force coefficients with sideslip angle resulting from these tests are shown in Figs. 1 and 2. These curves are typical of similar curves plotted for other automobile shapes. The yawing moment coefficient curves, however, are usually nonlinear for sideslip angles greater than 20 degrees. Most of the remaining moment and force coefficients are extremely nonlinear[8]. An example of pitching moment data taken with the Jaguar model is shown in Fig. 3. Pitching moment coefficient curves for most automobile shapes are more nonlinear than for the Jaguar, even for the small sideslip angle range depicted. The Jaguar model was supported in the wind tunnel just above a ground plane simulator by a sting projecting through the rear of the model. A dynamic sting balance was used to measure model damping by measuring the model motion after an initial deflection. Damping coefficients (i.e., the portion of the moment coefficients proportional to angular velocity) can be measured for both pitch and yaw angular motion. For example, the damping coefficient in yaw, $C_{n_{\dot{\beta}}} - C_{N_r}$, for the Jaguar model had values of about 2.8. This damping coefficient is usually small compared to the damping contribution of the tires, but would be significant for the stability of vehicles under icy or slick road conditions.

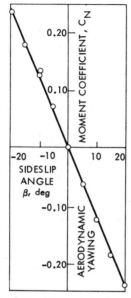

Fig. 1. Variation of aerodynamic yawing moment coefficient with sideslip angle.

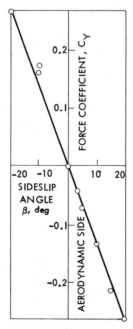

Fig. 2. Variation of aerodynamic sideforce coefficient with sideslip angle.

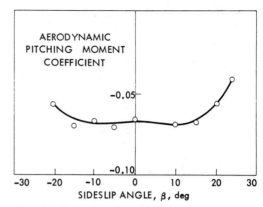

Fig. 3. Variation of aerodynamic pitching moment coefficient with sideslip angle.

III. Stability Analyses of Motor Vehicles

Current stability analyses[17-25] either do not include aerodynamic forces at all, involve the assumption of linear variations for the aerodynamic coefficients (an assumption which is often inaccurate), or consider the effects of crosswind as a constant force irrespective of aerodynamic sideslip angle, which is incorrect.

The motion equations for an automobile, considering two-degree-of-freedom motion (lateral motion and yaw) with a constant forward speed u_o can be written as

$$mu_o(\dot{\beta} + r) = Y_\beta \beta + Y_{\dot{\beta}} \dot{\beta} + Y_r r + Y_\delta \delta + Y_{\beta_A} \beta_W \qquad (1)$$

and

$$I_z(\dot{r}) = N_\beta \beta + N_{\dot{\beta}} \dot{\beta} + N_r r + N_\delta \delta + N_{\beta_A} \beta_W. \qquad (2)$$

Inherent in these equations is the assumption of linear terms with the stability derivatives[26-28], Y_β etc., held constant for each solution of the equations. Also inherent in the two-degree-of-freedom model is the assumption that the vehicle is rigid and the tires and suspension system do not deflect linearly or angularly under load.

The Laplace transform of the equations is

$$(Y_\beta - mu_o s + Y_{\dot{\beta}} s)\bar{\beta} + (Y_r - mu_o)\bar{r} = - Y_\delta \bar{\delta} - Y_{\beta_A} \bar{\beta}_W$$

and

$$(N_\beta + N_{\dot{\beta}} s)\bar{\beta} + (N_r - I_z s)\bar{r} = - N_\delta \bar{\delta} - N_{\beta A} \bar{\beta}_W. \qquad (4)$$

The forcing terms on the right side of the equations are those due to steering deflection, δ, and crosswind angle, $\bar{\beta}_W$.

The characteristic stability equation is found by equating the determinant of the coefficients of the equations' left side to zero:

$$(mu_o I_z - Y_{\dot{\beta}} I_z) s^2 + [Y_{\dot{\beta}} N_r - N_{\dot{\beta}} Y_r + mu_o(N_{\dot{\beta}} - N_r)$$
$$- I_z Y_\beta] s + (Y_\beta N_r - N_\beta Y_r + N_\beta mu_o) = 0. \qquad (5)$$

Thus the two-degree-of-freedom rigid vehicle linear model is a second-order system.

The stability derivatives due to tire and aerodynamic forces are

$$Y_\beta = C_F + C_R + C_{Y_{\beta A}} qS,\tag{6}$$

$$Y_r = (C_F a - C_R b) \frac{1}{u_o} + C_{Y_r} \frac{qS\ell}{u_o},\tag{7}$$

$$Y_\delta = -C_F,\tag{8}$$

$$N_\beta = aC_F - bC_R + C_{N_{\beta A}} qS\ell$$

$$+ \text{ATC}_F \left[\frac{b(W - C_L qS) - C_M qS\ell}{\ell} \right]$$

$$+ \text{ATC}_R \left[\frac{a(W - C_L qS) + C_M qS\ell}{\ell} \right],\tag{9}$$

$$N_r = (a^2 C_F + b^2 C_R) \frac{1}{u_o} + C_{N_r} \frac{qS\ell^2}{u_o}$$

$$+ \text{ATC}_F \frac{(a)}{\ell u_o} [b(W - C_L qS) - (C_m qS\ell)]$$

$$- \text{ATC}_R \frac{(b)}{\ell u_o} [a(W - C_L qS) + C_M qS\ell],\tag{10}$$

$$N_{\dot\beta} = C_{N_{\dot\beta}} \frac{qS\ell^2}{u_o},\tag{11}$$

$$Y_{\dot\beta} = C_{Y_{\dot\beta}} \frac{qS\ell}{u_o},\tag{12}$$

$$N_\delta = -aC_F - \text{ATC}_F \left[\frac{b(W - C_L qS) - C_M qS\ell}{\ell} \right],\tag{13}$$

$$Y_{\beta A} = C_{Y_{\beta A}} qS,\tag{14}$$

$$N_{\beta A} = C_{N_{\beta A}} qS\ell.\tag{15}$$

The damping of the two-degree-of-freedom system, represented by the coefficient of s in Eq. (5) is usually positive and therefore stable for typical value ranges for the stability derivatives. The static stability, represented by the constant term, can be positive or negative depending upon the values of center of gravity location and speed. The condition of neutral stability is found by setting the constant term equal to zero:

$$Y_\beta N_r - N_\beta Y_r + N_\beta m u_o = 0.\tag{16}$$

Substituting the stability derivatives into Eq. (16) gives

$$Ju_o^3 + (K + H)u_o + \frac{G}{u_o} = 0,\tag{17}$$

where

$$J = \left(\frac{\rho S\ell}{2}\right)^2 \left[C_{Y\beta} C_{N_r} - C_{N_\beta} C_{Yr} + (C_M C_{Y\beta} + C_L C_{Yr}) \frac{\text{ATC}}{\ell} \right.$$

$$\left. - 2m(\text{ATC}) \frac{C_L}{\rho S\ell^2} \right],$$

$$K = \frac{\rho SC}{2} \left\{ 2\ell [C_{N_r} \ell + (\text{ATC}) C_M] + (a^2 + b^2) C_{Y\beta} \right.$$

$$+ (b - a)\ell \left[C_{Yr} + C_{N_\beta} - \frac{(\text{ATC}) C_L}{\ell} \right]$$

$$\left. - 2(\text{ATC}) \frac{C_{Yr} \ell W}{\rho SC} \right\},$$

$$H = m[C(a - b) + \text{ATC}(W)],$$

$$G = C^2 [\ell^2 \frac{(\text{ATC})}{C} W(a - b)].$$

It is assumed for simplicity in the above expressions that $C_F = C_R = C$ and $\text{ATC}_F = \text{ATC}_R = \text{ATC}$. Notice that the J and K terms contain the aerodynamic parameters and that H and G contain only terms due to the tires.

In general the tire terms are dominant, and the aerodynamic terms will destabilize the vehicle by a small amount. There are situations, however, when the aerodynamic terms are very important. One such situation is the large disturbance maneuver. If the driver turns the wheel sharply to avoid hitting an obstacle or for some other reason, he often "loses control" and is often cited for "failure to have his vehicle under control." The reason for losing control is that the tires are very nonlinear[29,30] as shown in Figs. 4 and 5, and their contribution to stability decreases at higher values of sideslip angle. The cornering coefficient, C (proportional to the slope of the curves in Fig. 4), decreases with increasing sideslip angle, β, until it reaches zero. The aligning torque coefficient, ATC (proportional to the slope of the curves in Fig. 5), changes sign at a relatively small angle of sideslip and becomes destabilizing at higher values of sideslip.

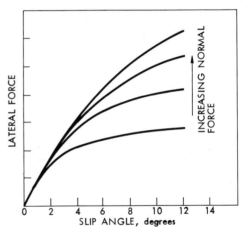

Fig. 4. Tire cornering force as a function of slip angle and normal force.

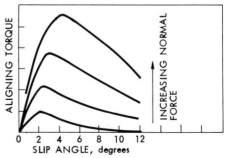

Fig. 5. Tire aligning torque as a function of slip angle and normal force.

Braking causes the aligning torque coefficient to change sign and become destabilizing. If the aerodynamic properties of the vehicle are destabilizing, which is almost always true, and the skidding tires lose their effectiveness, there is no stabilizing influence left and divergence results.

A second situation when aerodynamics becomes important is slippery condition of the road surface due to rain, ice or snow, or loose gravel. In such situations the friction between the rolling tire and the road surface can be greatly decreased, causing aerodynamic terms to be equal or greater in importance than the tire contributions. Again, instability can result, and control can be lost much more easily than with dry pavement.

A strong crosswind can also make aerodynamics a more critical factor. For aerodynamically unstable vehicles (which includes nearly all, if not all), the driver must turn his steering control into the direction from which the wind is blowing in order to maintain direction parallel to the road. The front wheel suspension on cars is designed so that there is a tendency for the wheels to return to zero steering angle when the steering control is deflected. This is achieved by cambering the wheels so that the plane of symmetry of the wheel is offset from the vertical, and by providing a trailing or castoring action. There is also a small deadband so the wheel can be turned a small amount to the right or left without the wheels turning. It has been found that this deadband or backlash is necessary to eliminate anxiety on the part of the driver[31]. Both the symmetry of the zero-steering-angle returning tendency and the deadband, however, are lost to the driver when a strong crosswind is present and the straight-path steering angle is no longer zero. The driver will continue to turn the steering wheel back and forth, as in driving without crosswind, but because of the lack of backlash, the car will respond to the steering motion; the driver is uncomfortable, and feels he cannot fully control the vehicle. The lack of symmetric returning tendency for the non-zero steering angle adds to the problem.

The amount of steering angle (tire angle) needed to establish equilibrium in a crosswind can be obtained from Eqs. (1) and (2) by letting β, $\dot{r}$ and r be zero, giving

$$\delta_o = \left(\frac{N_\beta Y_{\beta A} - N_{\beta A} Y_\beta}{N_\delta Y_\beta - N_\beta Y_\delta}\right) \beta_W. \quad (18)$$

A small amount of sideslip is also necessary:

$$\beta_o = \left(\frac{Y_\delta N_{\beta A} - Y_{\beta A} N_\delta}{N_\delta Y_\beta - N_\beta Y_\delta}\right) \beta_W. \quad (19)$$

The magnitude of δ_o is approximately proportional to the product of vehicle speed and crosswind velocity and can easily exceed one degree in a strong crosswind for some cars. Although this magnitude of tire steering angle is still within the linear range of the rolling tire for contact with dry pavement, a sudden maneuver in this situation can be dangerous since the additional sideslip angle necessary to reach negligible cornering stiffness is decreased. Hazardous road conditions such as ice, snow, and loose gravel in the presence of a strong crosswind greatly increases the likelihood of unstable motion.

A simplified example of the effect of aerodynamics on the stability of a motor vehicle is shown by the curves in Fig. 6. The static margin

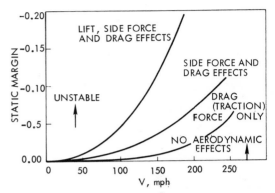

Fig. 6. The effects of aerodynamic forces on the static margin of a rear-drive automobile.

of a hypothetical vehicle is shown having neutral static margin if aerodynamic effects are not considered. The static margin in this case is defined as $- N_\beta/(Y_\beta \ell)$. The effect of adding the drag term is due to decreased cornering stiffness of the rear wheels because of the traction force.

To do a complete study of automobile stability, of course, requires that all degrees of freedom be included in the analysis, including the capability of the sprung mass of the vehicle to pitch, roll, and translate with respect to tires. The motion of the sprung mass, of course, causes changes in the vertical forces supported by the tires[32] and therefore changes in the tire contribution to stability. Aerodynamic forces affect the way the sprung mass moves with respect to the tires and should be included in a complete analysis. All the nonlinearities of the tires and aerodynamic effects should be included. One of the best ways to handle nonlinear multiple degrees-of-freedom problems of this sort is to employ the analog computer to obtain solution of the motion equations. Analytic techniques[33] are also available for studying system stability of nonlinear systems without having to obtain solutions.

IV. Stability and Handling Criteria

In the development of the airplane in the last 50 years, great progress has been made in analysis of the stability and control of aircraft[26], and in the development of realistic criteria for determining proper handling qualities[34]. No large-scale effort has been made in the development of stability and control analysis and handling quality requirements for the automobile, although sporadic and partial efforts have been undertaken.

Ultimately, of course, the stability of motor vehicles is dependent not only upon vehicle dynamics, but also upon the dynamic response of the driver who closes the feedback path in order to make the vehicle controllable. A great deal of effort within aerospace technology has been expended to determine approximate mathematical models for the transfer function of the human in a control situation[35]. The results of such studies have been quite successful in aiding the determination of appropriate control and handling qualities for aircraft and are just beginning to be applied to the automobile-driver combination [36,37]. Such studies should be incorporated into motor vehicle stability analyses in an effort to come closer to the goal of a proper set of automobile handling quality criteria.

The difficulties involved in developing such a set of criteria are partially illustrated by considering the rear-engined automobile. From the equations of motion and from the definition of the directional stability derivative N_β in Eq. (9) it is seen that moving the center of gravity rearward is destabilizing. This is apparent from the term $a C_F - b C_R$, where a is the longitudinal distance from the center of gravity to the front wheel axis, and b the distance to the rear wheel axis. For the rear engine car, a is greater than b and since C_F and C_R are negative quantities, the contribution of that term would be negative (destabilizing). C_F and C_R are somewhat dependent upon weight distribution, but not enough to negate the negative contribution of the front cornering force term. The instability of the rear-engined vehicle can be overcome, however, by reducing the front tire pressure, thus reducing C_F, and by wheel camber and suspension system design. However, the rear engine vehicle is also normally more unstable aerodynamically because of the rearward location of the center of gravity, and thus more affected by high crosswinds.

It would appear from the previous discussion that the rear-engine car is undesirable from a stability standpoint, but in the author's opinion this is not necessarily so. Under very slick roadway conditions, the greater traction on rear wheels provided by the greater vertical force on the rear wheels can be used to create a stabilizing moment by decelerating the vehicle while it is in gear. The automatic transmission is not as desirable as the conventional geared transmission from that standpoint.

The preceding example should serve to emphasize the need for more complete stability analysis of a great variety of configurations. The analog computer and nonlinear methods of analysis should be employed to obtain answers to the question of stability. All kinds of configurations should be studied with all degrees of freedom involved under a large variety of standard and emergency situations, and with simulation of the driver included. The human driver, himself, in the case of the analog computer and appropriate additional hardware, can be included in the simulation as is done regularly in the aerospace industry. It is not presumed that answers to the complex question of developing a set of automobile handling quality criteria would be forthcoming either quickly or easily, but rather it is hoped that the experience obtained in aerospace technology can be utilized to gain insight into the automobile problem and to come closer to that ultimate goal.

V. New Concepts in Motor Vehicle Shapes

A number of physical alterations, mostly to racing cars, have been made in the past to try to improve drag, stability, and/or handling characteristics[38]. Such alterations have included the

use of devices such as spoilers, fins, wings, and reshaping of various parts of the automobile body[39]. These alterations have been implemented largely from an empirical standpoint, rather than from the results of a systematic study of the aerodynamic effects of the various types of alterations.

Experienced aerodynamicists, with their knowledge of how changes in body shape affect aerodynamic properties, should be employed by the automobile manufacturers. Completely new innovative shapes should be studied. A simple example, although not very innovative to the aircraft designer and perhaps not salable from an esthetic point of view in the present context of automobile design, is the inclusion of stabilizing fins.

The addition of fins for stabilization is represented in Fig. 7. The moment tending to turn

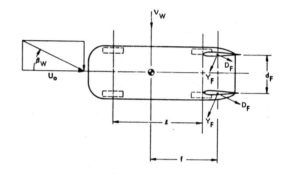

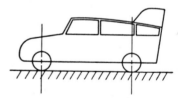

Fig. 7. Fixed-fin stabilizers.

the vehicle into the direction from which the wind is blowing is

$$N = 2Lf \cos \beta_w + 2Df \sin \beta_w \qquad (20)$$

and the side force is

$$Y = - 2L \cos \beta_w - 2D \sin \beta_w. \qquad (21)$$

The dimensionless stability derivatives (portion due to fins), found by dividing Eqs. (20) and (21) by qS and qSℓ respectively, by differentiating with respect to β_w, and by evaluating the derivatives at $\beta_w = 0$ are

$$C_{N\beta} = 2(C_{L\alpha} + C_D) \frac{S_F}{S} \frac{f}{\ell} \qquad (22)$$

and

$$C_{y\beta} = - 2(C_{L\alpha} + C_D) \frac{S_F}{S} . \qquad (23)$$

296

For purposes of example, let $C_{L_\alpha} = 5$, $C_D = 0.05$, $f/\ell = 1$, and $d_f/\ell = 0.5$. The values of the stability derivatives C_{N_β} and C_{y_β} are then 3 and - 3, respectively. A value of the stability derivative C_{N_β} of 3 represents a strong contribution to stability. However, the large value of C_{y_β} of - 3 could be detrimental to stability in providing a strong side force and rolling moment. The question of whether the vehicle should have a slightly positive or a zero value of C_{N_β} is not yet answered and will have to await further analysis.

To obtain a large ratio of directional stability, C_{N_β}, to side force, C_{y_β}, floating fins could be used[15]. Cambered fins oriented oppositely are depicted in Fig. 8. Each fin is allowed to rotate freely about a hinge line located

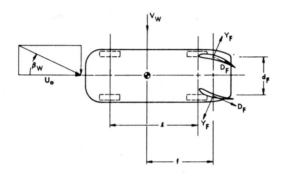

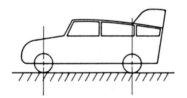

Fig. 8. Floating-fin stabilizers.

between the fin aerodynamic center and the mid-chord and has a specific equilibrium angle of attack as shown in Fig. 9. The net yawing moment is

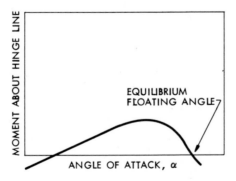

Fig. 9. Hinge moment vs angle of attack.

$$N = 2Df \sin \beta_W + Ld_F \sin \beta_W \tag{24}$$

and the side force is

$$Y = - 2D \sin \beta_W. \tag{25}$$

The floating fin stability derivative contributions are

$$C_{N_\beta} = \frac{S_F}{S} \left(2C_D \frac{\ell_F}{\ell} + C_L \frac{d_F}{\ell} \right) \tag{26}$$

and

$$C_{y_\beta} = - 2C_D \frac{S_F}{S}. \tag{27}$$

Assuming a lift coefficient of two and otherwise the same numerical values as the fixed fin example results in values of the stability derivatives C_{N_β} and C_{y_β} of 0.33 and - 0.03 respectively. The contribution to stability is much lower than for the fixed fin example but the ratio of C_{N_β} to C_{y_β} is 11 instead of 1. The high side force and rolling moment are thus greatly reduced. The value of C_{N_β} for the same size fin could be increased by adding a geared flap[15].

Such sets of stabilizing fins would represent revolutionary and probably unsatisfactory changes to existing automobile designs. More innovation in body shape by the aerodynamicist working with the industrial designer is probably necessary to enable incorporation of stabilizing devices.

Another type of alteration is needed for those vehicles which, because of their shape, affect the aerodynamic forces on oncoming or trailing vehicles. The large semi-trailer truck, with its very unstreamlined bluff rear end, creates a large strength Karman vortex trail[40] in its wake. The high speeds in the centers of these wake vortices can cause very large aerodynamic forces on other vehicles, perhaps causing unstable motion to occur. This effect can be enhanced by high crosswinds. Wind tunnel studies should be initiated to determine these effects more precisely and to determine practical methods of eliminating the high-strength vortex trails. Other peculiar shapes, such as pickup campers, should be investigated to determine the effect of their aerodynamic characteristics on vehicle stability.

VI. Analytical Determination of Aerodynamic Forces

One of the needs enunciated by engineers in the automotive industry is the capability to determine the surface pressure distribution on an automobile shape analytically[1]. Although problems exist because of the automobile's peculiar aerodynamic shape and because of its close proximity to the ground, techniques evolved for predicting pressure distribution on the surfaces of flight vehicles should be capable of extension to the automobile[41-44]

The most recent and currently best procedures for predicting pressure distributions analytically involve the technique of placing surface singularity distributions analytically on the surface of the aerodynamic body. These singularity distributions may include source, sink, vortex, and doublet distributions either singly or in combination. A variety of methods have been used to distribute these singularities such as patches of surface area of constant singularity strength, linearly varying strength, and discrete points or lines. Some computational experimentation would be necessary to determine the most satisfactory way of representing the automobile shape.

The singularity methods do involve the assumption of potential flow, and the method would have to be modified to account for viscous separation effects. An alternative to the potential flow methods would be a numerical flow-field calculation using the viscous Navier-Stokes equations. Such a flow-field calculation could be done using either relaxation techniques[45] or the currently popular time-dependent techniques[46]. Such techniques do have problems such as numerical instability, difficulty in satisfaction of boundary conditions, and necessity for very large computer storage capability and calculation times. Eventually, however, such techniques should be applicable to the problem of predicting pressure distributions on automobile shapes.

VII. Additional Applications of Aerospace Technology

There are additional ways in which experience in the aerospace industry could be used to improve motor vehicle design. Not very much has been said about the psychological aspects of the driver's environment. The American automobile, in particular, with its smooth ride, low plush seat, broad expanse of hood and rear deck, and high horsepower engine, seems to be designed to give the driver a false sense of security. The driver cannot get the feel of the road because of the soft ride and cannot tell where his car is on the road because of the broad expanse of metal surrounding him. Indeed, the environment of the driver seems to be intended to lull him to sleep rather than to be sensitive to the ever present dangers on the highway.

The concept of man-machine integration, which has been used extensively in the design of cockpits and instrument panels in aircraft and even on a much more intensive scale in manned spacecraft[47], could be used in automobile design to a much greater degree than before. The driver's seat should be designed on a different basis than the passenger's chair[31]. The instrument panel and the controls should be standardized as much as possible, and their design should be studied on the same thorough basis as in the design of the Apollo space capsule.

Another area in which aerospace experience could be utilized is crashworthiness. The aerospace structural engineer, by necessity, is the leader in designing strong, yet lightweight structures, and has also considered the energy-absorption and passenger-protection problems involved in the design of aerospace vehicles. Energy absorption devices have also been designed for lunar and planetary landing vehicles. Some of the principles learned in the structural and energy absorption areas certainly could be transferred to automobile design.

VIII. Conclusions

The design of automobiles has been greatly influenced by what automobile manufacturers think people wish to have in their personal vehicles such as speed, power, beauty, and comfort. Having decided what people want, the automobile manufacturers proceed to advertise heavily to convince people that those desired qualities the manufacturers have selected are indeed what the public wants to buy. The advertising media could be used just as well to sell safety based on new concepts and techniques learned in the aerospace industry. Apparently, additional federal legislation is needed to convince the manufacturers that safety is the best route. Automobile stability, a very important factor in the consideration of automobile safety, needs fresh thinking and experience from other technical areas. Aerospace technology can supply a great deal of the technical ability needed to make the automobile a much safer device.

References

1. Anon., "Auto Aerodynamics," Industrial Research, p. 33, July 1968.

2. Bundorf, R. T., and F. N. Beauvais, "Aerodynamic Characteristics of a Car-Trailer Combination," SAE Journal, 76: 7, 64, 1968.

3. White, R. G. S., "Rating Scale Estimates Automobile Drag Coefficient," SAE Journal, 77: 6, 52, 1969.

4. Korff, W. H., "The Body Engineer's Role in Automotive Aerodynamics," Paper No. 649B, SAE Trans., 1964.

5. Kelly, K. B., and H. J. Holcombe, "Aerodynamics for Body Engineers," Paper No. 649A, SAE Trans., 1964.

6. Legg, Keith, "The Influence of Aerospace on Future Transport Systems," Aeronautical Journal, 72, 771, 1968.

7. Barth, R., "Effect of Unsymmetrical Wind Incidence on Aerodynamic Forces Acting on Vehicle Models and Similar Bodies," SAE Trans., 74: 650136, 557, 1966.

8. Bowman, W. D., "Generalizations on the Aerodynamic Characteristics of Sedan Type Automobile Bodies," SAE Trans., 75: 660389, 608, 1967.

9. Toti, G., "Aerodynamic Effects of Vehicles Moving in Stationary Air and Their Influence on Stability and Steering Control," International Automotive Engineering Congress, SAE No. 948D, 1965.

10. Gross, D. S., and W. S. Sekscienski, "Some Problems Concerning Wind Tunnel Testing of Automobile Vehicles," SAE Trans., 75: 660385, 593, 1967.

11. Fosberry, R. A. C., R. G. S. White, and G. W. Carr, "A British Automotive Wind Tunnel Installation and Its Application," SAE Trans., No. 65001, 1966.

12. Beauvais, F. N., S. C. Tignor, and T. R. Turner, "Problems of Ground Simulation in Automotive Aerodynamics," SAE Trans., No. 680121, 1968.

13. Grunwald, K. J., "Aerodynamic Characteristics of Vehicle Bodies at Crosswind Conditions in Ground Proximity," National Aeronautics and Space Administration Technical Note TN D-5935, 1970.

14. Beauvais, F. N., "Transient Nature of Wind Gust Effects on an Automobile," SAE Trans., No. 670608, 1967.

15. Iversen, J. D., "Longitudinal Stability of a Body of Revolution with Floating Fins and Tabs," Sandia Corporation TM 428-58(51), 1959.

16. Myers, T., "The Aerodynamic Aspects of Automobile Stability," Iowa State University Aerospace Engineering Department Report, 1969.

17. Bundorf, R. T., D. E. Pollack, and M. C. Hardin, "Vehicle Handling Response to Aerodynamic Inputs," SAE Trans., 72, 1964.

18. Milliken, W. F., "Research in Automobile Stability and Control and in Tire Performance," Proc. Institution of Mechanical Engineers, p. 287, 1956.

19. Chiesa, A., and L. Rinonapoli, "Vehicle Stability Studies with a Non-Linear Seven Degree Model," SAE Trans., No. 670476, 1967.

20. Segel, L., "Theoretical Prediction and Experimental Substantiation of the Response of the Automobile to Steering Control," Institute of Mechanical Engineers, Automobile Div., Proc., p. 310, 1956-7.

21. Bundorf, R. T., "A Primer on Vehicle Directional Control," General Motors Engineering Publication A-2730, 1968.

22. Bergman, Walter, "The Basic Nature of Vehicle Understeer-Oversteer," SAE Trans., No. 650085, 1965.

23. Milliken, W. F., and D. W. Whitcomb, "General Introduction to a Program of Dynamic Research," Proc. Institution of Mechanical Engineers, p. 3, 1956.

24. Whitcomb, D. W., and W. F. Milliken, "Design Implications of a General Theory of Automobile Stability and Control," Proc. Institution of Mechanical Engineers, p. 83, 1956.

25. Rocard, Y., Dynamic Instability, Chap. 5, Frederick Ungar Publishing Co., New York, 1957.

26. Etkin, B., Dynamics of Flight, John Wiley and Sons, Inc., New York, 1959.

27. Rasmussen, R. E., F. W. Hill, and P. M. Riede, "Typical Vehicle Parameters for Dynamics Studies," General Motors Proving Ground Engineering Publication A-2542, 1970.

28. Anon., "Vehicle Dynamics Terminology," Society of Automotive Engineers, SAE J670b revised, May 1970.

29. Nordeen, D. L., and A. D. Cortese, "Force and Moment Characteristics of Rolling Tires," General Motors Research Laboratories, GMR-404, 1963.

30. Fonda, A. G., "Tyre Tests and Interpretation of Experimental Data," Proc. Institution of Mechanical Engineers, p. 64, 1956.

31. Black, Stephen, Man and Motor Cars, W. W. Norton and Co., New York, 1966.

32. Hales, F. D., "A Theoretical Analysis of the Lateral Properties of Suspension Systems," Institute of Mechanical Engineers, Automobile Div., Proc., p. 179, 1964-65.

33. LaSalle, Joseph, and Solomon Lefschetz, Stability by Liapunov's Direct Method, Academic Press, New York, 1961.

34. Kolk, W. R., Modern Flight Dynamics, Prentice-Hall, Inc., Englewood Cliffs, New Jersey, 1961.

35. McRuer, D. T., "New Approaches to Human Pilot/Vehicle Dynamic Analysis," Air Force Flight Dynamics Laboratory, AFFDL-TR-67-150, 1967.

36. Iacovoni, D. H., "Vehicle-Driver Simulation for a Cross-Wind Disturbance Condition," SAE Trans., No. 670609, 1967.

37. Weir, D. A., and D. T. McRuer, "Dynamics of Driver Vehicle Steering Control," Automatica, 6, 87, 1970.

38. Korff, W., "Aerodynamic Design of the Goldenrod — To Increase Stability, Traction, and Speed," SAE Paper 66039, 1966.

39. Pershing, B., ed., "The Aerodynamics of Sports and Competition Automobiles," AIAA Los Angeles Section Monographs, 7, Western Periodicals Co., North Hollywood, Calif., 1969.

40. Lamb, Horace, Hydrodynamics, Dover Press, New York, 1945.

41. Ashley, H., and M. Landahl, Aerodynamics of Wings and Bodies, Addison Wesley, Reading, Mass., 1965.

42. Hess, John L., "Calculation of Potential Flow about Arbitrary Three-Dimensional Lifting Bodies," Douglas Aircraft Company, McDonnell-Douglas Corp., Report No. MDC-J0545, Dec. 1969.

43. Krzywoblocki, M. Z. V., and G. Salyer, "Analytical Simulation of the Three-Dimensional Flow-Field about a Ship," Final Report, Project K6 (N00178-68-C-0192), US Naval Weapons Laboratory, Dahlgren, Va., 1969.

44. Trulin, D. T., and J. D. Iversen, "Pressure Distribution about a Finite Axisymmetric Nacelle," Journal of Aircraft, 7, 85, 1970.

45. Steger, J. L., "Application of Cyclic Relaxation Procedures to Transonic Flow Fields," PhD Thesis, Iowa State University, 1969.

46. Bailey, F. R., "A Study of Finite Amplitude Disturbances in Plane Poiseuille Flow by Finite Difference Methods," PhD Thesis, Iowa State University, 1970.

47. North, W. J., and C. H. Woodling, "Apollo Crew Procedures, Simulation, and Flight Planning," Astronautics and Aeronautics, $\underline{8}$: 3, 56, Mar. 1970.

A STRATEGY FOR REMOTE SENSOR USE

IN MINING, HYDROLOGY, AND POLLUTION CONTROL

Ethel I. Curtis, Consultant
R. Collmer Associates
Tucson, Arizona 85701

ABSTRACT

The thesis is a simple one. A remote sensor and survey technology already exists ... rich, complex and potentially highly useful to the resource manager. A logical breakdown is possible in survey sponsorship--from the versatile, general records of orbital missions, to the special-purpose findings of local, low-level flights.

In order to fulfill this potential, there is a need for systematic communications between all levels. At the national-international survey levels, the specialized, local-area needs must be known. Similarly, the regional and local users must have some familiarity with the survey technology available from above, as well as ready access to the records.

This paper attempts a brief review of relevant sensors and their capabilities in the context of three specific resource-management uses. A logical hierarchy of survey sponsorship is advanced. Sample guidelines are provided to the tradeoffs of survey planning. Also outlined is a suggested two-way communications network -- simplistically, with questions going up the channel and answers coming down.

Rationale

There are 50 million square miles of land surface on earth for potential resource use, management, and control. To accomplish his work, the resource manager needs a variety of specific information -- both surface and subsurface,both static and timely -- over a domain ranging from a few hundred to possibly a million square miles. Many regions of interest are currently inaccessible by land. In any case, ground surveys are costly, and their areas must be pinpointed with care.

Over the past 10 years, the aerospace industry has developed a variety of multispectral imagers (cameras, radars, and infrared scanners), as well as radiometers, variously suited for high-aircraft and orbital use. Far below, close to the ground, fly a group of non-imaging sensors -- specialized probers and sniffers developed for geology and pollution monitoring. Below them lies the hard, overland trek after ground truth.

The imagers in particular have a basic support potential as yet scarcely tapped. For mineral exploration, hydrology, pollution control, and related applications, they are the logical preliminary search tools. Their versatility is important to the case. So is their high-flying, wide-ranging coverage capability. A single flight record may serve many agencies with data. The overview provided may save many hours of abortive, low-level search.

To date, this remote sensing potential has been under-used. The limitations are two-fold -- knowledge and cost.

Within the broad spectrum of sensors, there is a vast spread both in equipment and flight cost, and in the know-how required to apply the sensors effectively and to reduce the resulting floods of data to useful information. This leaves many of the devices in a never-neverland beyond the reach of the individual research team and planning agency.

However, there is a fortunate correlation between survey altitude, flight cost, data volume, and versatility -- leading to a logical breakdown in survey sponsoring agencies from the national to the regional and local level.

Figure 1 relates these factors in simplified fashion. The inverted central triangle represents flight altitude and sensor class versus breadth of ground coverage. To the left are general functions and likely sponsors. To the right are weather limitations.

Survey altitudes range from orbit to ground. Sensors vary from the most sophisticated radars and cameras to special-purpose spectrometers and sniffers. And sponsors, as appropriate to initial investment, range from NASA to your local research team.

For such a model to function effectively naturally requires a positive, operating communications network joining the various levels.

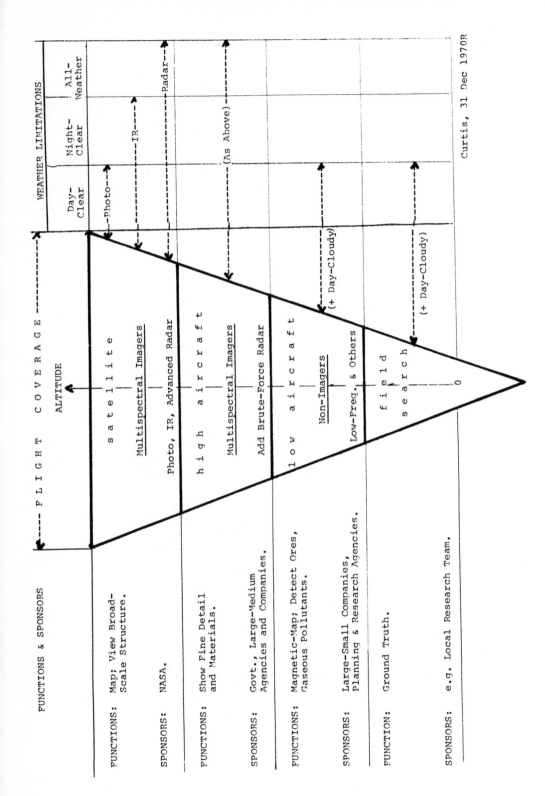

FIGURE 1. SURVEY-FLIGHT TRIANGLE.

Sensors and Capabilities

Table 1 presents a panoramic view of remote sensors potentially useful in mapping, mineral exploration, hydrology and pollution monitoring. These are classed as imaging and non-imaging sets.

The imagers include varied cameras and films, infrared scanners and radars - plus the developing laser radar in the visual frequency range.

The non-imagers are an assorted group, ranging from radiometers through low-frequency detectors, to magnetometers, spectrometers, sniffers, and particle collectors. (The term "sniffer" is adopted here to describe the varied family of vapor detectors, including surface-effects detectors and others(1)).

In resource application, the sensors run the gamut from crude mapping to refined detection of specific gas traces. Their altitude limits range from satellite to ground. The table gives value judgments on ease of equipment acquisition, field use, and data interpretation, rated on a 1 to 3 (best to worst) scale. Definition of mining functions generally follows Barringer (2); of hydrology functions, Curtis (3).

The Uses of Diversity

A more graphic presentation of the sensor categories is provided by Figure 2. Here, four classes are loosely distinguished:- A) imaging, B) spectral, C) other physical, and D) physicochemical devices.

Properly used, the sensors are not truly competitive, but complementary. The total information to be gained from a well-planned survey package is equal to far more than the sum of the parts. And the integrated records from diversified surveys raise our information by orders of magnitude.

For example, the familiar, readable pictorial image helps us interpret the more esoteric data forms of the other sensors. Multispectral imagery itself provides the key to distinguishing terrain materials. Among the non-imagers, a similar case may be made for multispectral radiometry.

All known materials, both natural and man-made, vary in their reflectance (and emittance) to differing wavelengths in the electromagnetic spectrum. It takes several spectral bands to establish the positive signatures necessary for materials distinction. Hence the advantage of pictures of the same terrain taken at visual, infrared, and microwave frequencies.

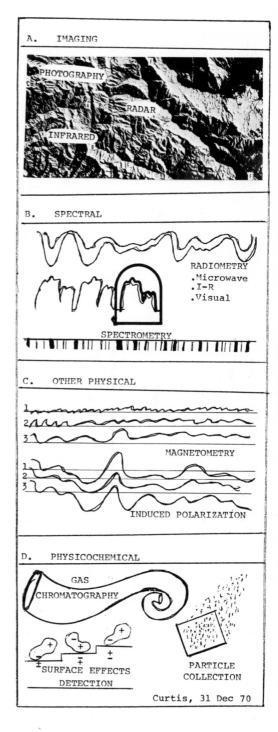

A. IMAGING

PHOTOGRAPHY

RADAR

INFRARED

B. SPECTRAL

RADIOMETRY
.Microwave
.I-R
.Visual

SPECTROMETRY

C. OTHER PHYSICAL

MAGNETOMETRY

INDUCED POLARIZATION

D. PHYSICOCHEMICAL

GAS CHROMATOGRAPHY

SURFACE EFFECTS DETECTION

PARTICLE COLLECTION

Curtis, 31 Dec 70

FIGURE 2. SENSOR CATEGORIES

TABLE 1. REMOTE SENSOR POTENTIAL UTILITY IN EARTH-RESOURCE APPLICATIONS.

Curtis, 31 Dec 1970 R

KEY to STATUS (Lower Box)

ALTITUDE LIMITS (Potential)

S = Satellite potential
A = High-aircraft 1K-50K ft
L = Low-aircraft, as 400 ft
G = Near-ground, e.g. 40 ft

EASE (1 = Best, 3 = Worst)

e.g. Equipment Acquisition:
1 = Commercially available.
2 = Available at a price.
3 = Relatively unattainable

** NOTE: In unmanned satellite, TV usually replaces photography, with degraded capability, although package delivery of photographs is possible from orbit.

** See KEY Above.

	IMAGERS — PHOTOGRAPHY**								IMAGERS — IRscan		IMAGERS — FADAR				NON-IMAGERS — RADIOM.			NON-IMAGERS — LOW-F			NON-IMAGERS — OTHER PHYSICAL					
	Black & White Frame	B&W + IR and UV	Stereo	Panoramic	Multiband	False Color	Color	Color IR	3 – 5 Micron	8 – 14 Micron	Classical	Brute-Force Side-Lk	Syn. Aperture "	Laser	Visual	Infrared	Microwave	VLF	Induced Field	Natural Field	Magnetometer	Gravity Meter	γ-Ray Spectrometer	Far IR Spectrometer	Sniffer	Particle Collector
MAPPING Horizontal: Crude	X										X	X	X	X												
Fine	X	X	X	X								X	X	X												
Contour: Crude			X																							
Fine			X																							
GEOLOGY Identify Major Structure	X	X		X	X		X		X		X	X	X		X		X	X	X	X	X	X	X	X	X	
Classify Rocks, Alterations	X	X		X	X	X	X	X	X	X									X		X		X	X	X	
ID Plants = Rocks/Anomalies		X			X	X	X	X	X	X		X			X		X	X	X	X	X	X	X	X	X	
Detect Ore, Mantle, Ducts																										
HYDROLOGY View Overall Watershed	X	X		X	X		X	X	X	X		X	X				X	X	X	X	X					
Delineate System Elements	X	X		X	X	X	X	X	X	X		X	X	X			X									
ID Materials, Water Depth	X						X		X	X					X	X	X									
Find Subsurface Ducts																	X	X								
Trace Shoreline, Currents																										
POLLUTION MONITOR Thermal																										
Gas, Particle					X		X		X																X	X
STATUS Altitude Limits	S	S/L	S	S	S	S	S	S	A	S	L	L	A	S	S	S	S	L	L	L	L	L	L	L	L	A
Ease — Equipment Acquisition	1–2 (LO-HI Resolution ——→)		1	1	1	2	1	1	2	2	1	3	2	3	2	2	2	1	2	2	1	1	2	2	2	1
of: Field (Flight) Use	1–2		2	2	3	+	2	1	2	2	2	3	2	3	2	2	3	2	2	2	2	1	2	2	2	1
Data Interpretation	2	2	2	2	3	2	1	1	2	2	1	2	3	2	3	3	3	2	2	2	2	1	2	2	1/3	3

304

Imagers

The imagers, in general, capture surface phenomena only. (An exception is ultraviolet film, which sees through clear water.) Thus, the three major imaging techniques - cameras, I-R scanners, and radar - perform as broad-area search tools and as a first step in detailed inspection. Their records serve to reveal:-

a. Worldwide maps.
b. Broad-scale mountain systems and watersheds.
c. Major structures within them.
d. Detail patterns of exposed strata, contours, faults, and streams.
e. Exposed rock shapes, colors, and some materials distinctions.
f. Vegetation, or ground cover -- extent, type, and vigor.
g. Thermal pollution.

Examples of recent survey shots by camera, side-looking radar, and infrared scanner are shown in Figures 3A-C.

Photography is by far the best and cheapest day-fair-weather performer for mapping, broad-area search, and detail-pattern distinction. It provides superior resolution and dynamic range with economy in dollars, weight, and power expended.

This is particularly true of the conventional silver-halide-film camera. Substitution of television severely degrades performance, as noted by Katz (4) for the currently planned ERTS satellite.

Black-and-white photography lends itself to precision mapping and to edge enhancement processing techniques, which are highly effective in revealing structure. Overlapping shots from single or multiple camera assemblies provide for stereo contouring (Figure 3A).

Materials distinction is added by the several film variations - ultraviolet, near-infrared (to about 1-micron wavelength), multiband, and color - as well as by I-R scanners and radars.

The multiband cameras provide for synchronous, identically placed shots of the scene. This is done by use of light-splitting optics and selected film-filter combinations within the visual spectrum. The technique has been of value in surveying the type and vigor of farm and forest crops, as demonstrated by Colwell over a period of years (5) to (6).

Of special interest here is the multispectral potential for distinguishing rock types and ground cover. The nature and state of the vegetation may provide insight into 1) the organic and mineral content of the soil, and 2) local air and soil pollution. Also, water pollution may be monitored directly.

To exploit multispectral techniques successfully -- to interpret the survey data -- we need good signature libraries on the spectral reflectance of materials of interest over the relevant band of frequencies. Equally important is the systematic correlation of survey shots with ground truth, as performed in a recent U.S. Geological Survey program (7).

Color photography emerges from Table 1 as probably the most versatile and readable of the sensors. The color shots from Apollo flights 4 through 12 provide a remarkable example of the descriptive capability of satellite surveys in delineating worldwide geological structure (8).

Both the panoramic camera and the infrared scanner employ scanning mirrors or prisms to sweep out a wide arc transverse to the flight path. Scan speed is synchronized with survey velocity-to-height ratio. The similarity of their optical systems leads to ready integration of the two techniques and their results.

In the pan camera, the instantaneous return from a small field is then passed through a narrow slit to a continuous-strip film. Since the device makes use of the distortion-free center of the optics, it lends itself to high-resolution systems.

In the infrared scanner, the received energy is focused on a mosaic of sensitive cells, typically of semiconductor material. Suitable detectors have been developed in two principal wavelength ranges - 3 to 5 microns and 8 to 14 microns. These coincide with so-called windows in the atmosphere where infrared transmission is possible.

The longer wavelength region correlates with the peak energy emission from cool surfaces like the earth, with an average temperature of about 293 degrees Kelvin. Thus, detection at 8 to 14 microns probably holds more promise for high-altitude survey development.

Spatial resolution for infrared sets is in the order of a fraction of a degree of arc. Temperature resolution is generally a fraction of a degree Kelvin. To date, this capability has worked well for moderate-altitude surveys of terrain structure and materials. It has served to detect thermal pollution, as well as the presence and source of organic pollutants in coastal waters (9). An automated, multichannel scanner for crop survey has been designed at Purdue University (10), (11) with detector cells in both the visual and infrared ranges.

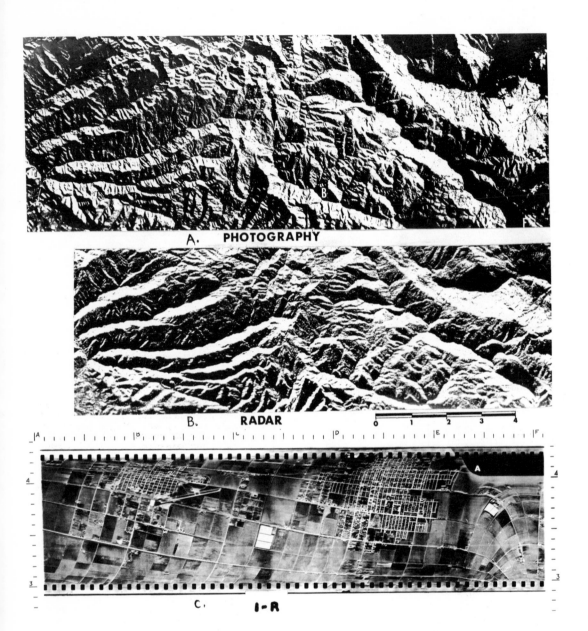

FIGURE 3. TRI-SENSOR IMAGERY -- A) Low-sun-angle photography (27° sun) simulates radar shadowing effect to reveal structure. Made with K17B camera, 6-inch lens, 60% overlap, minus-blue filter, Plus-X Aerographic film. B) Radar shot of same Central California Coast Range Region by Westinghouse brute-force, K-band, side-looking radar. (Both records from Lyon and Lee (12)). C) Infrared imagery of Imperial Valley, California by 8-13-micron scanning system, from HRB-Singer, Inc.

Infrared, like light energy, suffers weather effects and is severely attenuated by atmospheric water vapor. However, unlike the day-limited camera, the infrared set works well at night, capturing emitted as well as reflected energy. Day and night shots of the same scene differ radically - almost like a matched pair of positive and negative prints. Even pre-noon and post-noon shots exhibit this reversal of tone. Hence, identifying flight data and some sophistication are necessary in the interpretation of shots.

Radar is unique among the imagers in several respects. It is an active sensor recording the echoes of its own transmitted energy. It functions day and night in all weather, at least at wavelengths down to X-band (3 centimeters).

Of primary interest for surface imagery is the side-looking radar. Advanced forms provide survey records of superior pictorial quality. The side-looker casts a thin, fan-shaped beam perpendicular to the flight path. In its brute-force version, the device depends on a long antenna and relatively short wavelength (e.g. millimetric) for good azimuth resolution - along the flight line. It depends on short pulse length for good range resolution - in the transverse direction.

The synthetic-aperture radars are a further refinement. These employ antennas of moderate length. However, they simulate long antennas by tagging output pulses and storing and integrating echo returns as the aircraft flies along, thus providing extremely fine azimuth resolution. Pulse compression techniques yield correspondingly good range resolution.

The most sophisticated version is the focused synthetic-aperture radar - the only sensor which gives a distortion-free image of terrain, the scale unvarying with range. In short, it eliminates perspective.

The side-looking radars require processing and correlation of the raw data return in order to produce the finished picture. Generally, this is a post-mission operation.

The phenomenon of radar shadow serves as a positive aid to the geologist in identifying major structures. Because radar imagery depends on active transmission, the only portion of the terrain imaged is that floodlighted obliquely from above by transmitted energy from the survey craft. Hence, any irregularity or protruberance in the scene casts a definite, dark shadow which serves to outline the major features of the landscape (Figure 3B). Predictably, the shadow effect is best when the structure parallels the flight path.

The developing laser radar offers a remarkable potential for precision height measurement. Operating in the visual frequency range, it is weather-limited like photography.

Spectral Sensors

Classed here as spectral sensors are the radiometers and spectrometers, symbolically represented by Figure 2B.

Radiometers operate at visual, infrared, or microwave frequencies to measure energy levels. Generally non-imaging devices, they are useful for periodic, dynamic surveys of temperature, currents, and pollution status. The shorter wavelength devices have been effective in atmospheric soundings and sea-state readings (13), (14).

Microwave radiometers, at X-band and longer wavelengths, hold promise for these and more general geophysical application (15). There is some evidence that they may aid in subsurface probing for underground ducts or streams.

Spectrometers are highly refined optical devices for the positive identification of trace elements. Classically, they employ diffraction gratings to spread the wavelengths of received light, and they record the spectral positions of either bright-line emissions from burning solids or dark-line absorption patterns of gases.

In general, survey spectrometers are specialized designs for the location of particular rock types. Using preset energy windows or correlation masks, they admit and measure specific, naturally occurring radioactive or fluorescent emissions characteristic of the materials sought, or - similarly - the absorption spectra of out-gassed vapors.

Barringer (2) describes a 4-channel gamma-ray spectrometer for detection of potassium-40, thorium, and uranium. Three discriminating windows are set for the peak gamma radiations of the three elements. The fourth channel registers total gamma-ray count of the surface under survey.

Similar techniques are in development (2) for sensing the characteristic infrared emissions of various silicates. Also under study are the absorption spectra of iodine and mercury vapors - the first as a possible clue to oil fields, the second, to gold and porphyry copper deposits.

The air pollutant, sulfur dioxide, may also be monitored by spectrometric methods.

Other Physical Devices

As reported in the referenced Barringer papers (16), (17), an assortment of low-flying, deep-probing survey devices are operationally associated in mining exploration (Ref. Figure 2C). Probably the best known is the airborne magnetometer, widely used in mapping magnetic anomalies, and valuable in tracing ferrous, sulfide, magnetite, and sedimentary oil deposits.

For ordinary usage, the original fluxgate magnetometer is now being supplanted by the proton magnetometer. The latter is a lightweight instrument with about 1-gamma sensitivity, and with direct digital output to computer processing. Sedimentary-rock surveys are currently conducted with the highly sensitive, optically-pumped magnetometer. Presently, the proton device is expected to develop the 1/10-gamma refinement minimal for this purpose.

Also important here are a number of low-frequency, long-wavelength, electromagnetic systems, since depth-penetration is a function of wavelength. VLF, at frequencies in the order of 20 kilohertz and wavelengths of about 10 miles, penetrates 50 to 1000 feet into the earth, depending on ground resistivity. ELF, with wavelengths two orders greater, penetrates ten times as far.

While the propogated electrical field is virtually unaffected by ground characteristics, the magnetic components of the field are substantially phase-shifted as a function of earth conductivity. And conductivity proves an important clue to the composition of the subterranean mass.

Instruments have been developed for the simultaneous measurement of induced electrical and magnetic fields. Alternatively, the sets depend on one of three propogation sources:-
1) Operational VLF radio signals, independently beamed thousands of miles around the world;
2) Natural lightning discharges; or
3) Electromagnetic transmission from the survey craft, pulsed or continuous wave, at one or two frequencies, for example 900 hertz.

Copper-zinc-silver deposits have been among the valuable findings of these low-frequency, induced-field systems. As a class, they are inherently heavy and cumbersome, and employ large detection coils. For the self-contained-transmitter system, the flight problem has been solved by placing the equipment in a separate "bird," towed by the aircraft.

Physicochemical Devices

Diverse pollution-monitoring instruments may be grouped together here, as represented symbolically in Figure 2D.

High-altitude, aerosol-particle collectors fly commercial aircraft worldwide. In ground-scraping flight, sensitive vapor detectors monitor gas traces – potentially in parts per billion - with the aid of supporting laboratory techniques. References (18), (19), and (20) provide general background.

A three-phase process may be involved --sampling, concentration, and detection. In the case of the particle collectors, an adhesive surface serves the first function, followed by spectrometric analysis.

Far more sensitive than spectrometry in vapor analysis is the combination of gas chromatography and surface-effects detection.

The chromatograph is a device for separating and concentrating effluent components such as polyhalogens and some aromatics. Typically, it is a curved glass tube lined with absorbent material. As air samples passing through are alternately cooled and heated, their components are absorbed and re-vaporized. Based on adsorptivity and volatility, like molecules travel at the same rate -- leading or lagging the others. Thus. each effluent arrives at the output on schedule, in concentrated form, for detection.

An effective detector class employs a pair of conductor plates, one coated with highly specific sensor molecules. As the contaminant sought is adsorbed, it changes the electrical characteristics of the sensor, producing a measurable voltage.

A variety of sensing compounds and molecular forces are being explored:-

Dispersion
Dipole interaction
Hydrogen bonding
Charge-transfer complexes,
    involving donor and acceptor
    molecules
Electron capture

The electron-capture technique is potentially capable of detecting an adsorbed effluent only a trillionth of a monolayer in thickness.

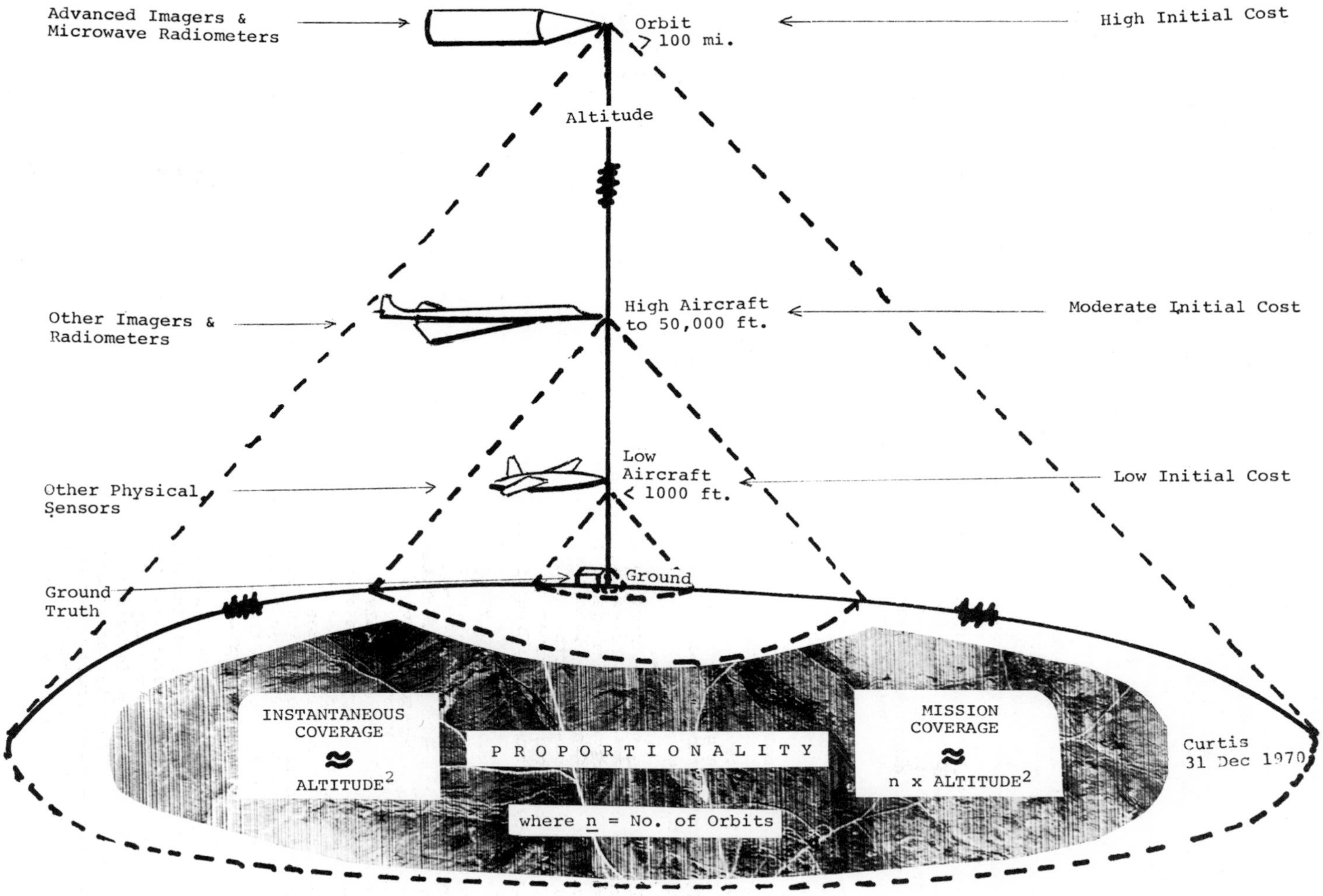

FIGURE 4. ALTITUDE AND COVERAGE.

Advanced Imagers & Microwave Radiometers

Other Imagers & Radiometers

Other Physical Sensors

Ground Truth

High Initial Cost

Moderate Initial Cost

Low Initial Cost

Orbit > 100 mi.

Altitude

High Aircraft to 50,000 ft.

Low Aircraft < 1000 ft.

Ground

Curtis 31 Dec 1970

MISSION COVERAGE $\approx$ n x ALTITUDE^2

P R O P O R T I O N A L I T Y

where n = No. of Orbits

INSTANTANEOUS COVERAGE $\approx$ ALTITUDE^2

Sensor Hierarchy

In operational altitude capability, sensors range from orbit to treetop. Figure 4 records this sensor hierarchy, along with the gain in instantaneous coverage area as a function of altitude-squared. In orbital missions, the total area surveyed may also multiply enormously by <u>n</u>, the number of orbits.

With advanced flight levels, come advantages as well as problems.

While gross continental outlines are revealed from orbit even by an ordinary, handheld camera, detailed inspection requires sophisticated imagers (long-focal-length cameras, synthetic-aperture radar) and possibly microwave radiometers.

Lesser imagers and radiometers, as well as pollution-particle collectors, serve well at high aircraft altitudes--5000 to 50,000 feet--flight level dropping as finer ground detail is sought.

The other physical sensors, in general, are restricted to low aircraft flights, for example at 400 feet.

Major orbital advantages are pictured in Figures 5 and 6, for both static and dynamic information needs.

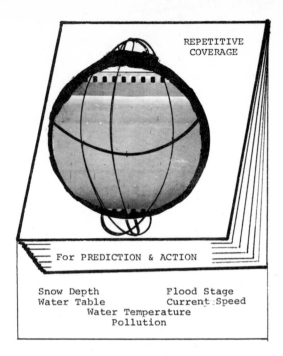

For PREDICTION & ACTION

Snow Depth	Flood Stage
Water Table	Current Speed
Water Temperature	
Pollution	

FIGURE 6.   ORBITAL ADVANTAGES: DYNAMIC.

A single pass may reveal the broad-scale view pf a mountain system or watershed. Such records may serve in the design of dam and irrigation projects, or in tracing geological structure and water sources for mining, transport, agriculture and fisheries.

For low-cost, repetitive survey of dynamic factors, the unmanned satellite has unique capability. Potentially, it may be used to monitor snow depth, flood stage, current speed, water temperature and pollution.

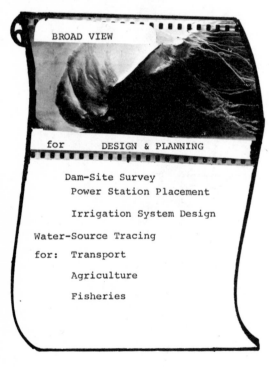

FIGURE 5.   ORBITAL ADVANTAGES:STATIC DATA.

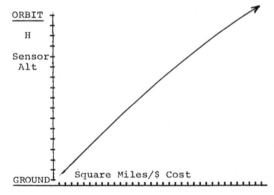

FIGURE 7. COVERAGE COST VS ALTITUDE

The orbital imagery package is versatile in application and global in range. Shared mission uses on a cooperative, multi-nation basis should logically follow. One satellite system may serve to map, survey earth resources, monitor weather and thermal pollution.

However, the initial cost of both sensors and flight vehicles rises with altitude, leaping astronomically in the transition from aircraft to orbit.

Orbital problems are outlined in Table 2. With increased altitude come demands for extreme sensitivity, resolution, and locational accuracy. Data interpretation is hampered by the sheer volume of input data. Better signature libraries are needed correlating recorded indicators with ground truth.

The correlation between altitude and the initial-cost/versatility/coverage trio continues generally from orbit down to low aircraft flight levels. Thus a logical hierarchy is formed of flight functions, survey sponsors, and sensor complements, as pictured in the earlier Figure 1 inverted survey triangle.

At the top is NASA's versatile, broad-ranging orbital imagery, carefully planned, costly to initiate, picturing surface phenomena for thousands of users. Below in regular sequence are successively more specialized, more restricted, deeper-probing surveys by area and local sponsoring agencies--launched at need at lower initial cost, but at far higher cost per square mile surveyed.

Weather limitations are shown at the righthand side of Figure 1.

PROBLEM	PARAMETRIC RELATIONSHIP	
INITIAL COST:	$\dfrac{\text{Orbital Cost}}{\text{Low-Alt Cost}} \geqq 10^4$	
SENSI-TIVITY:	Energy Received	$\approx 1/\text{Altitude}^2$
RESOLU-TION:	Resolvable Ground Size	$\approx$ Altitude
DATA RATE:	$\dfrac{\text{Data In}}{\text{Unit Time}}$	$\sim \left\{ \begin{array}{l} \text{Alt}^2 \times \text{Speed} \\ \times \text{ Sensor No.} \\ \times \text{ Dynamic Range} \\ \times \text{ Coverage} \\ \times \text{ Resolution} \end{array} \right.$
($\sim$ = Proportionality)		
NAVIGA-TION:	Angular Accuracy	$\approx 1/\text{Altitude}^2$
OTHER:	Privacy Indicator Needs	Qualitative

TABLE 2.   ORBITAL PROBLEMS

Guidelines

The message of the sensor hierarchy is that some survey tasks are better done higher, some lower, in both altitude and sponsorship level. Figure 8 shows the simple logic of decision/information needs for cooperative implementation of such a scheme.

As noted, the hierarchy of sensors implies a division of labor in sponsors, in turn implying decision needs at each agency level. Systematic communication is necessary between the decision-makers at all levels from the orbital to the most local. Simplistically, questions go up the channel. Answers come down.

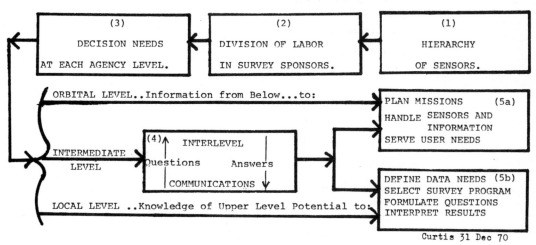

FIGURE 8.   DECISON/INFORMATION LOGIC DIAGRAM

311

To serve user needs well, the orbital decision-makers require a discrete set of information goals from below as a guide to mission planning, sensor choice, survey locales, and data-handling.

Local planners require a knowledge of upper-level potential in order to define their own data needs in proper terms, select an optimum survey program, formulate upward-bound questions, and interpret the results returned.

Intermediate state and regional agencies function both as users and servers.

Hopefully, the future strategy of planning a remote-sensing program will consist of formulating the pertinent questions--what?..where?..when?..how?.. how much?--using low-cost answers available from above, and filling in the gaps with special surveys, as needed.

Table 3 provides a checklist of sample questions useful to survey planning. The indicators of Item A are the key to translating the sensed record into reality. Here, a library of material signatures from prior surveys is helpful. Much information is already on file with U.S. Government agencies (21)-(24).

As suggested by Figure 9, useful flight altitude increases with our knowledge of surface indicators.

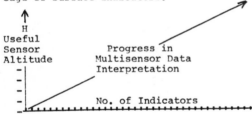

FIGURE 9. USEFUL ALTITUDE VS INDICATORS.

Item B gauges the scope of the survey, as well as weather conditions. C proceeds to the problem of matching information needs with sensors; scope and sensors with altitude; and the resultant with cost. (Ref. Figure 4 and Table 2.)

Item D summarizes cost factors to be considered--initial, flight, and ground costs. Field marking and data interpretation are important budgetary factors.

E notes the data-handling problem, the need for a correlation file of survey records, crossfiled by location and specific material. Beyond the skill of the individual record interpreter, the ability to correlate multisensor data from many flights is the key to survey value.

A. INDICATORS

What specific materials are sought?

What are the surface indicators? (21-24)

In major structure?	Temperature?
In fine contour?	Outgassed vapors?
In color?	Radioactivity?
In vegetation?	Fluorescence?
Multiband response?	

What are the subsurface indicators?

| Magnetic anomalies? | Conductance? |
| Discontinuities? | Ducts? |

B. GEOGRAPHY

Where is the area of interest?

| How wide? | What is the weather? |
| How long? | Is field marking needed? |

C. SENSOR CAPABILITY

What sensors apply?..based on:
Specific data needed?
Precision sought?

At what altitude? .. based on: (Table 2)
Sensor sensitivity?
Angular resolution?
Multisensor correlation?
Swath width and cost?

Sensor special requirements?
Refined mounting?
Weather?..Day/night use?   (Figure 1)
Automatic readout?
Sensor cost vs budget?   (Item D)

D. COSTS

What are initial costs..Sensors/Vehicles?

What are flight costs?

Cost   = Survey Miles x $/Mile.

$$\text{Survey Mi.} = \frac{\text{Survey Area } (1 + \text{Overlap})}{\text{Coverage per Pass} - \text{Overlap}}$$

Overlap: Stereo = 60%;   Other = 10%

What are ground costs?
For field marking? Data interpretation?

E. DATA-HANDLING

How is the record interpreted?
For imagers?   Use correlation file
Stereo?
Multiband?   } Automatic readout
Non-imagers?   } may be available.

How will data be filed?
By geographical location? } Both are
By materials of interest? } needed.

TABLE 3.   SAMPLE QUESTIONS FOR SURVEY PROGRAM PLANNING.

Correlation & Communications

What is suggested here is the possibility of a continuous, long-term control and communications system for earth-resource survey -- cooperative in its nature, probably independently funded at each level of operation, but responsive to the needs of the ultimate user -- the state and area resource planning commission, the research institution, the private development company.

The problems are manifold in performing such a marriage between great server capability and great user need. Problem areas are at least three -- political, organizational, and technical.

There are questions of privacy to be resolved and budgetary questions. Even the basic clearinghouse mechanism is not immediately obvious.

The mere magnitude of information to be transmitted and stored requires careful appraisal. Big computers and specialized automatic aids must be applied to the chores of cataloguing, correlation, and control.

Two basic system elements--the nerve center and the communications access net

-- are briefly sketched here.

At the core of each information-serving and using agency, a nerve center is needed where correlation and decision functions are performed. Figure 10 provides a functional diagram of a postulated upper-level, server-only center.

Here questions and information goals are collected and pre-correlated with survey records already on file. Available answers are returned, and other questions delegated to question store. Based on this backlog of information needs, future survey missions are planned and flown.

Output information must be correlated in several ways to bring together all the information on a single scene ...

. By coincident shots of many sensors.
. By successive orbits of one mission.
. From new and past missions.

New survey records may be compared with shots of known terrain for purposes of materials recognition. Thus two files are needed: geographical and materials.

New answers result for the users.

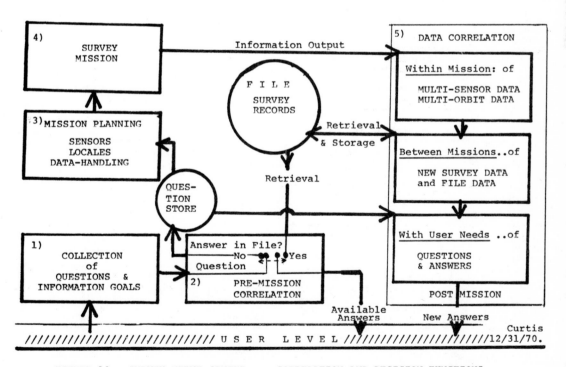

FIGURE 10. SURVEY NERVE CENTER ... CORRELATION AND DECISION FUNCTIONS.

Figure 11 shows a simplified schematic of a postulated U.S. communications access network serving such survey information centers at three levels--national, regional, and local. Two-way communications are indicated between all levels. A central file of survey data is an important element of each block. An international connection is suggested at the top of the diagram.

The figure simply serves as a logical response to the information exchange requirements already outlined.

Access is the important factor to be stressed -- the need for informed, cooperative action in the efficient use of our remote-sensing capability.

It is fairly obvious that emphasis is not required on new communications techniques, but rather on a new, cooperative, organizational mechanism. Existing phone, cable, and mail routes, in general, will serve. Even emergency information, as of an impending flood, may traverse normal communications channels with sufficient speed.

For low-density information, such as radiometry and magnetometry, present digital-data transmission techniques may be exploited. Small-area, high-contrast

imagery - in special cases - might be sent by facsimile transmission for purposes of preliminary examination -- or perhaps by closed-circuit television.

However, general imagery, particularly in color, requires high-quality reproduction for physical delivery.

Analysis of the detail survey records is best left to the ultimate using agency --with the higher center serving the data gathering and preliminary correlation functions. A feedback on the specific utility of the delivered information is desirable.

Thus the format of the lower-echelon information request again emerges as a key factor in good, cooperative action. Prepared questionnaires may be indicated along the lines of those NASA has developed for space-research scientists. For the earth-resource-user requests, variety and flexibility must be envisioned, to fit the varied information goals.

This paper has served to record the obvious advantages of an integrated, user-oriented, remote-sensing survey system. The problems remain to be solved.

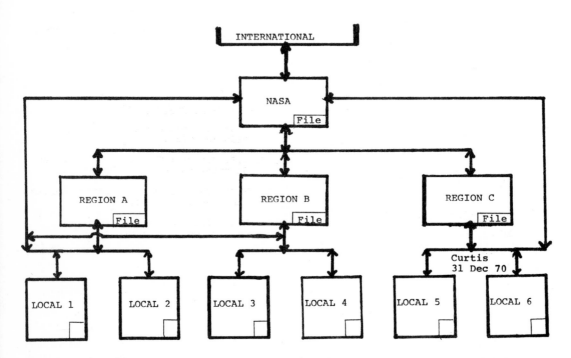

FIGURE 11. SCHEMATIC: TWO-WAY COMMUNICATIONS ACCESS NET FOR SURVEY INFORMATION.

Acknowledgements

The writer is indebted to Dr. Willard
C. Lacy, Head of the Department of Geological Engineering of the University of
Arizona, for his skilled insights into
the information needs of the working
geologist; and to Mr. Jan Cannon, on
leave from the U.S. Geological Survey,
Denver, for his informed analysis of his
experimental comparison of survey records with ground truth.

For the conclusions drawn in this
paper, the writer takes full responsibility.

References

1. Andrew Dravnieks, Physicochemical
   Basis of Olfaction, Ann. N.Y. Acad.
   of Sci., 116(2), 429-39, Jul. 1964.

2. A.R. Barringer, Remote Sensing
   Techniques for Mineral Discovery,
   1st Ann.IRSI Symp.Proc.1,39,1969.

3. E.I.Curtis, Survey of Water Resources from Orbit, Prepoposal,
   No.Amer-Rockwell Space Div, 1965.

4. Amrom Katz, ERS Resolutions, Astronautics & Aeronaut. 8,53,1970.

5. R.N. Colwell, Some Practical Appli-
   cations of Multiband Spectral
   Reconnaissance, Amer. Scientist,
   Mar. 1961.

6. R.N. Colwell, Multispectral Remote
   Sensing, 1stAnn.IRSI Symp.Proc,
   1, 1, 1969.

7. U.S. Geol. Survey for NASA, 2nd Ann.
   Earth Resources Aircraft Program
   Status Review, 3v., Sept. 1969.

8. NASA, Color Slides, Apollo Flights
   4 thru 12, Technology Distribution
   Center, Albuquerque, New Mexico.

9. Woods Hole Oceanog. Institute,
   Oceanography from Space, No.65-10,
   Woods Hole, Mass., Apr. 1965.

10. R.A.Holmes, R.B.MacDonald, System
    Design for Remote Sensing in Agri-
    culture, Proc.IEEE, 57(4),629,1969,

11. K.S. Fu, D.A. Landgrebe, T.L.Phil-
    lips, Information Processing of
    Remotely Sensed Agricultural Data,
    Proc.IEEE,57(4), 639, 1969.

12. R.J.P. Lyon, Keenan Lee, Remote Sens-
    ing in Exploration for Mineral Depos-
    its, Economic Geol. 65, 785, 1970.

13. R.W. Austin, Techniques of Measure-
    ment, Applied Optics, 3,584, 1964.

14. E.D.McAlister, Two-Wavelength Radi-
    ometer for..Total Heat Exchange,Air-
    Sea Interface, Appl.Op.4.145,1965.

15. D.H.Staelin, Passive Remote Sensing
    at Microwave Wavelengths, Proc.IEEE,
    57(4), 427, 1969.

16. A.R. Barringer, Deep-Probing Methods
    of Remote Sensing, 1st Ann. IRSI
    Symp. Proc. 1, 39, 1969.

17. D.W. Holdsworth, A.R. Barringer,
    Studies of Radar Properties of
    Rocks, Proc 4th Symp, Remote Sensing
    of Environment, 475, U. Michigan,
    Ann Arbor, Mich. Dec. 1966.

18. B. Kaye, Sizing Solid Particles,
    Int. Sci.&Technology, Mar 1964.

19. J.I.Bregman, A. Dravnieks (Ed),
    Surface Effects in Detection,
    Spartan-MacMillan Ltd., 1965.

20. A.B.Littlewood, Gas Chromatography,
    Academic Press, 1962.

General U.S. Documentation Sources:

21. Supt. of Documents, U.S. Govt.
    Printing Ofc., Washington, D.C.

22. U.S. National Technical Information
    Service, Springfield, Va. 22151.

23. NASA, Technology Distribution Center,
    Albuquerque, New Mexico.

24. U.S. Geological Survey, Federal
    Center, Denver, Colorado 80225.